# COMMENTARY TO THE
# GERMANIC LAWS AND
# MEDIAEVAL DOCUMENTS

By LEO WIENER

PROFESSOR OF SLAVIC LANGUAGES AND LITERATURES
AT HARVARD UNIVERSITY

THE LAWBOOK EXCHANGE, LTD.
Clark, New Jersey

ISBN 978-1-58477-005-3

Lawbook Exchange edition 2000, 2024

*The quality of this reprint is equivalent to the quality of the original work.*

## The Lawbook Exchange, Ltd.
33 Terminal Avenue
Clark, New Jersey 07066-1321

*Please see our website for a selection of our other publications
and fine facsimile reprints of classic works of legal history:*
www.lawbookexchange.com

**Library of Congress Cataloging-in-Publication Data**

Wiener, Leo, 1862-1939.
    Commentary to the Germanic laws and  mediaeval documents  / by Leo
Wiener.
         p. cm.
    Originally  published:  Cambridge:   Harvard University Press, 1915.
    Includes bibliographical references and index.
    ISBN 1-58477-005-8   (cloth  :  acid-free paper)
    1. Law, Germanic—Sources.   2. Law, Medieval Sources.   3. Germany
History Sources.   I. Title.
    KJ195.W54   1999
    340.5'5—dc21                                 99-23969
                                                     CIP

*Printed in the United States of America on acid-free paper*

# COMMENTARY TO THE
# GERMANIC LAWS AND
# MEDIAEVAL DOCUMENTS

By LEO WIENER

PROFESSOR OF SLAVIC LANGUAGES AND LITERATURES
AT HARVARD UNIVERSITY

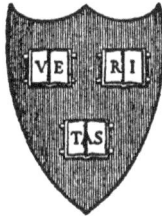

CAMBRIDGE
HARVARD UNIVERSITY PRESS
LONDON: HUMPHREY MILFORD
OXFORD UNIVERSITY PRESS
1915

TO

ABBOTT LAWRENCE LOWELL
PRESIDENT OF HARVARD UNIVERSITY

WHO HAS ENCOURAGED ME IN
MY LABOR OF RESEARCH

THIS VOLUME IS GRATEFULLY
DEDICATED

# PREFACE

SEVERAL years ago the study of the private and public documents of the Middle Ages, which I consulted for the etymology of difficult words, revealed to me a strange fact: the vast majority of words treated by the Germanic, Romance, and Slavic philologists had been studied with an utter disregard of documentary evidence. At every turn the facts belied the scientific deductions. Neither chronology nor phonetics were approximately correct in any given case. The starred forms never corresponded to the real variants in the earliest recorded documents. The semantic history of the words was not even attempted, or, if it was, it rarely hit upon the attested evolution of the meaning.

Puzzled by this obvious discrepancy, I passed more than five years in analyzing and excerpting all the accessible documents, to the number of 250,000 or more, from the earliest times of the Roman Empire to the year 1300. When I finally arranged my material, and, in the light of the facts thus discovered studied the Germanic laws and everything that had been written on the subject, I was shocked to find that hardly a historical fact, hardly a law, had been ascertained in connection with the morphological and semantic development of intrinsic words. If the historian had to deal with a difficult word, he consulted the etymological dictionaries, and if the etymologist needed a historic fact in order to explain the meaning of a word, he consulted a historian. Thus there was created a vicious circle which produced Germanic, Romance, and Slavic philology.

It was clear that the whole science of modern philology needed revision. I published a few of my discoveries in the

*Zeitschrift für romanische Philologie,* but I held back an enormous number of far more important results, because I was at every turn non-plussed by the fact that words which from the study of the documents could not possibly have existed before the sixth or seventh century, invariably turned up in the Gothic vocabulary. I was chagrined, because the facts were obviously contradictory. It never occurred to me that the Gibraltar of Germanic philology, the Gothic language, stood on a foundation of sand.

After writing and rewriting some of my articles half a dozen times, in order to harmonise the contradictions, I finally turned in despair to a microscopic study of the Gothic language. To my great surprise I found that there was not a single fact which could be construed as a proof that the Gothic documents, as we possess them, were written in the fourth century by Ulfilas. It soon turned out that the palaeographic proof was flimsy and that the subject matter of the Skeireins could not have been composed before the ninth century. What had been assumed to be an Arian tract was nothing more than an anti-Adoptionist pamphlet, identical in every particular, in some cases even with the very phrasing, of Alcuin's writings.

With this difficulty removed, my studies assumed an entirely new aspect. Every evidence, every document, every law had to be subjected to a new investigation. In the present volume I give but a very small part of my material. The second volume will discuss the more than two hundred words of Arabic origin in the Gothic Bible and in all the Germanic languages. I will also show that the Naples and Arezzo Gothic documents are late eighth century forgeries, that Jordanes has come down to us in manuscripts interpolated about the same time, that Germanic mythology is of a literary Gothic origin, based on Arabic sources, and that no literary documents in Anglo-Saxon, Norse, and Old High German exist which do not show the influence of the Arabicised Gothic language.

Before closing, I must publicly give my thanks to all those in the Harvard Library who have for years patiently aided me in getting and collating books, a task which was particularly irksome on account of the dispersion of the books in various buildings. The work which I have done would have been an utter impossibility in any other library in the world. The enormous mass of books consulted, sometimes in one day, could not have been brought together elsewhere in years. It would have taken the lifetime of more than one man merely to discover the books which the access to the marvelously arranged shelves in the Harvard Library has disclosed to me day after day. My deepest thanks are due to my colleague, Professor A. C. Coolidge, who as director of the Library has assisted my labors in a most substantial manner. I needed only to complain of the absence of a certain category of books, and they were procured through his more than official interest. Complete sets of Statuti, Fueros, Coutumiers, the Codex Diplomaticus Hungariae, and other extremely rare and expensive works were supplied to me as if by magic. My thanks are also due to Dr. F. W. C. Lieder, who has patiently read the proof, and to Mr. Phillips Barry, who has worked out the Index to this volume.

# SOURCES OF DOCUMENTARY EVIDENCE QUOTED

Achery, Luc d'  Spicilegium sive collectio veterum aliquot scriptorum, 3 vols., Paris 1723.
Acta Sanctorum quotquot toto orbe coluntur, Antverpiae 1643–1910.
Alcimi Ecdicii Aviti Epistulae, in Migne, vol. LIX.
Alianelli, N.  Delle antiche consuetudini e leggi maritime delle provincie napolitane, Napoli 1871.
Archiv für Urkundenforschung, edited by K. Brandi, etc., Leipzig 1907–
Archives de Bretagne, Nantes 1883–
Archives historiques du Poiton, Poitiers 1872–
Archivio della r. Società romana di storia patria, Roma 1878–
Archivio storico italiano, Roma, 1842–
Arnold, W.  Ansiedlungen und Wanderungen deutscher Stämme, Marburg 1875.
Atti del Reale istituto veneto, Venezia 1865–

Balari y Jovany, J.  Orígenes historicas de Cataluña, Barcelona 1899.
Baluze, E.  Miscellanea, 7 vols., Paris 1678–1715.
Basilica.  See Heimbach.
Baudouin, E.  Les grands domaines dans l'empire romain, Paris 1899.
Berganza, F. de.  Antiguedades de España, 2 vols., Madrid 1719–21.
Berger, A.  Die Strafklauseln in den Papyrusurkunden, Leipzig und Berlin 1911.
Bernard, A.  Cartulaire de l'abbaye de Savigny, Paris 1853.
Bernard, A., and Bruel, A. Recueil des chartes de l'abbaye de Cluny, Paris 1876–
Bibliothèque de l'Ecole des chartes, 1839–
Blume, Lachmann and  Die Schriften der römischen Feldmesser, Berlin 1852.
Rudorff.
Böcking, E.  Notitia dignitatum, Bonnae 1839–1853.
Bonaini, F.  Statuti inediti della città di Pisa dal XII al XIV secolo, 3 vols., Firenze 1854–70.
Bonazzi, G.  Il Condaghe di San Pietro di Silki, testo logudorese inedito dei secoli XI–XIII, Sassari-Cagliari 1900.
Bouquet, M.  Recueil des historiens des Gaules et de la France, 1869–80.
Bourrienne, V.  Antiquus cartularius ecclesiao Baiocensis, 2 vols., Rouen, Paris 1902–3.
Brisson, B.  De formulis et solennibus populi romani verbis libri VIII, Halae et Lipsiae 1731.
De verborum quae ad jus pertinent significatione libre XIX, Lipsiae 1721.

xii    SOURCES OF DOCUMENTARY EVIDENCE

| | |
|---|---|
| Brunetti, F. | Codice ' diplomatico toscano, 2 vols., Firenze 1806–33. |
| Bruns, K. G. | Fontes iuris romani antiqui, 7th ed., 2 vols., Tubingae 1909. |
| Brutails, J. A. | Etude sur la condition des populations rurales du Roussilon au moyen âge, Paris 1891. |
| Bry, M. J. | Essai sur la vente dans le papyrus gréco-egyptiens, Paris 1909. |
| Budmani, P. | Rječnik hrvatskoga jezika, Zagrab 1880–1910. |

Bullettino dell' istituto storico italiano, Roma 1886–

| | |
|---|---|
| Camera, M. | Memorie storico-diplomatiche dell' antica città e ducato d'Amalfi, 2 vols., Salerno 1876–81. |
| Capasso, B. | Monumenta ad neapolitani ducatus historiam pertinentia, 2 vols., Napoli 1881–92. |
| Capmany y de Montpalau, A. de | Memorias historicas sobre la marina, comercio y artes de la antigua ciudad de Barcelona, 4 vols., Madrid 1779–92. · |
| Cassiodorus. | Variae, see MGH., Auctores antiquiores. |
| Cazauran, J. M. | Cartulaire de Berdoues, La Haye 1905. |
| Ceruti, A. | Statuta communitatis Novariae anno 1277 lata, Novariae 1879. |
| Chambure, E. de. | Glossaire du Morvan, Paris, Autun 1878. |

Chartes de l'église de Valpuesta, in Revue hispanique, vol. VII.

| | |
|---|---|
| Chevalier, C. U. J. · | Cartulaire de l'abbaye de Saint-André-le-Bas de Vienne, Lyon 1869. |
| | Chartularium Ecclesiae Petri de Burgo Valentiae, 1869. |
| Chevin. | Dictionnaire latin-français des noms propres des lieux, Paris 1897. |
| Cipolla, C. | Monumenta novaliciensia vetustiora, 2 vols., Roma 1898–1901. |
| Clergeac, L'abbé. | Cartulaire de l'abbaye de Gimont, Paris, Auch 1905. |

Close Rolls, Henry III, vol. 3.
Codex diplomaticus cavensis, ed. by M. Morcaldi etc., 8 vols., Neapoli 1873–93.
Codex diplomaticus Cremonae, in HPM.
Codex diplomaticus Majoris Poloniae, Poznaniae, 1877–1908.
Codex diplomaticus Sardiniae, in HPM.
Codex Justinianus.
Codex Theodosianus cum perpetuis commentariis Jacobi Gothofredi, ed. J. D. Ritter, 6 vols., Lipsiae 1736–45.
Codice diplomatico barese, 8 vols., Bari 1897–
Codice diplomatico padovano dal secolo sesto a tutto l'undecimo, ed. by A. Gloria, Venezia 1877.
Collección de documentos para el estudio de la historia de Aragon, Zaragoza 1904–
Constitutiones Regni Siciliae, ed. by Todaro della Galia, Palermo 1887.
Corpus glossariorum latinorum, ed. by G. Goetz, Lipsiae 1888–
Cortes de los antiguos reinos de Aragon y de Valencia, Madrid 1896.

Cortes de los antiguos reinos de Leon y de Castilla, Madrid 1861–

Crum, W. E.      Catalogue of Coptic Manuscripts in the Collection of the John Rylands Library, Manchester 1909.

Cusa, S.      I diplomi greci ed arabi di Sicilia, Palermo 1868–81.

Dahn, F.      Die Könige der Germanen, 12 vols., München 1861–1909.

Daremberg, Ch. and Saglio, E.      Dictionnaire des antiquités grecques et romaines, Paris 1873–

Dareste, Haussoulier, Reinach. ·'      Recueil des inscriptions juridiques grecques, Paris 1895.

Davidsohn, R.      Forschungen zur älteren Geschichte von Florenz, Berlin 1896.

Deloche, M.      Cartulaire de l'abbaye de Beaulieu, Paris 1859.

Desimoni, C.      Statuto dei padri del comune della repubblica genovese, Genova 1885.

Devic, C., and Vaissete, J.      Histoire générale de Languedoc, vols. II and V, Toulouse 1872–1893.

Digby, K. E.      Introduction to the History of Real Property, Oxford 1884.

Douais, C.      Cartulaire de l'abbaye Saint-Sernin de Toulouse 1887.

Ducange.      Glossarium ad scriptores mediae et infimae graecitatis, 2 vols., Lugduni 1688.
Glossarium mediae et infimae latinitatis, ed. Léopold Favre, Niort 1883–87.

Earle, J.      A Handbook to the Land-charters and other Saxonic Documents, Oxford 1888.

Engelbrecht, A.      Claudiani Mamerti Opera, Vindobonae 1885.

Erman, H.      Conceptio formularum in factum, in Zeitschrift für Savignystiftung, Romanistische Abth., vol. XIX.

Ernault, E.      Glossaire moyen-breton, Paris 1895.

Escalona, R.      Historia del real monasterio de Sahagun, Madrid 1782.

España sagrada.      Theatro geographico-historico de la iglesia de España, ed. by H. Florez, etc., 51 vols., Madrid 1747–1879.

Fantuzzi, M.      Monumenti ravennati de' secoli di mezzo, 6 vols., Venezia 1801–04.

Férotin, M.      Recueil des chartes de l'abbaye de Silos, Paris 1897.

Ficker, J.      Urkunden zur Reichs- und Rechtsgeschichte Italiens, Innsbruck 1874.

Förstemann, E.      Altdeutsches Namenbuch, 2nd ed., 2 vols., Bonn 1900.

Frati, L.      Statuti di Bologna dall' anno 1245–1267, 3 vols., Bologna 1869–77.

Friedländer, L.      Darstellungen aus der Sittengeschichte Roms, 8th ed., Leipzig 1910.

Fueros y observancias del Reyno de Aragon, Zaragoza 1667.

Gallia christiana in provincias ecclesiasticas distributa, ed. by Denis de Sainte
    Marthe, etc.
Gattola, E.     Historia abbatiae cassinensis per saeculorum seriem
    distributa, 2 vols., Venetiis 1733.
Girard, H.     Textes de droit romain, 4. ed., Paris 1913.
Giry, A.     Les établissements de Rouen, Paris 1885.
Giulini, G.     Memorie spettanti al governo ed alla descrizione
    della città e campagna di Milano ne' secoli bassi,
    vol. vii, Milano 1854–57.
Godefroy.     Dictionnaire de l'ancienne langue française, Paris
    1881–1902.
Graff, E. G.     Althochdeutscher Sprachschatz, 6 vols., Berlin
    1834–42.
Gregorius I.     Registri, in MGH., Epistolae.
Gregorius Turonensis.     Historia Francorum, in MGH., Scrip. rer. merov.
Gromatici veteres, see Lachmann.
Guérard, B.     Cartulaire de l'abbaye de Saint-Victor de Mar-
    seille, 2 vols., Paris 1857.
Guilhiermoz, P.     Essai sur l'origine de la noblesse en France au moyen
    âge, Paris 1902.

Haignéré, D.     Les Chartes de Saint-Bertin, Saint Omer 1886.
Haillant, H.     Dictionnaire phonétique et étymologique, Epinal
    1885.
Hänel, J. J.     Monumenta historico-juridica Slavorum meridiona-
    lium, Zagrebiae 1877.
Heimbach, K. W. E.     Basilicorum libri lx, vols. 6, Lipsiae 1833–70.
Hessels, J. H. and     Lex Salica, the ten texts with the glosses and the lex
Kern, H.     emendata, London 1880.
Horn, P.     Grundriss der neupersischen Etymologie, Strassburg
    1893.
HPM.     Historiae patriae monumenta, Augustae Taurinorum,
    vols. i and vi, Chartae, 1836–53.
    vols. ii and xvi, Leges municipales, 1838–76.
    vols. iii, v, and xi, Scriptores, 1834–63.
    vols. vii and ix, Liber jurium reipublicae genu-
    ensis, 1854–57.
    vol. viii, Edictum regum langobardorum, 1855.
    vols. x and xii, Codex diplomaticus Sardiniae,
    1861–68.
    vol. xiii, Codex diplomaticus Langobardiae, 1873.
    vol. xvii, Codex diplomaticus Ecclesiensis, 1877.
    vols. xxi and xxii, Codex diplomaticus Cremo-
    nae, 1909.

Ilarregui y Lapuerta, P. Fuero general de Navarra, Pamplona 1869.
Indice de los documentos del monasterio de Sahagun, de la orden de San
    Benito, Madrid 1874.

Jal, A.    Glossaire nautique, Paris 1848.

Jokl, N.    Studien zur albanesischen Etymologie und Wörter-
bildung, in Sitzb. d. k. Akad. d. Wiss. in Wien,
1911.

Jones, W., and Ma-   Charters and Documents illustrating the History
cray, D.    of the Cathedral, City, and Diocese of Salisbury,
London 1891.

Kenyon, F. G.    Greek Papyri in the British Museum, London 1898.

Krammer, M.    Kritische Untersuchungen zur Lex Salica, in Neues
Archiv, vol. xxx.

Lachmann, C., and    Gromatici veteres, Berolini 1848.
Rudorff.

Lalore, CH.    Cartulaire de l'abbaye de Montiéramey, Paris,
Troyes 1890.

Lami, G.    Lezioni di antichità toscane, Firenze 1766.
Sanctae ecclesiae florentinae monumenta, Florentia
1758.

Lasteyrie, R. de.    Cartulaire général de Paris, 2 vols., Paris 1887.

Lauer, Ph., and Sa-   Les diplômes originaux des mérovingiens, Paris 1908.
maran, Ch.

Laurent, J.    Cartulaire de l'abbaye de Molesme, 2 vols., Paris
1907–11.

Lecrivain, G.    Les soldats privés aus Bas Empire, in Mélange d'archéologie et d'Histoire, vol. x.

Leicht, P. S.    Studi sulla proprietà fondiaria nel medio evo, Verona-
Padova 1903.

Lelong, E.    Cartulaire de Saint-Aubin d'Angers, Paris 1903.

Les Olim ou régistres des arrêts, ed. by A. A. Beugnot, 4 vols., Paris 1839–48.

Levy, E.    Provenzalisches Supplements-Wörterbuch, Leipzig
1892–

Lex ....    See under MGH.

Lex salica.    See Hessels.

Liebermann, F.    Die Gesetze der Angelsachsen, Halle a. S. 1898.

Lupi, C.    Sull' origine e significato della voce Parlascio, in
Archivio storico italiano, ser. 4, vol. vi.

Lupi, M.    Codex diplomaticus civitatis et ecclesiae Bergomatis,
Bergomi 1784.

Luschin von Eben    Der Denar der Lex Salica, in Sitzb. d. k. Akad. d.
greuth.    Wiss. in Wien 1911.

Mansi, G. D.    Sanctorum conciliorum et decretorum collectio nova.

Marca, P. de.    Marca hispanica sive Limes hispanicus, Paris 1688.

Mariano, Arigita y    Coleccion de documentos ineditos para la historia
Lasa.    de Navarra, Pamplona 1900.

Marini, G.    I papiri diplomatici, Roma 1805.

Martène and Durand.    Veterum scriptorum et monumentorum collectio, 9
vols., Paris 1724–33.

|  |  |
|---|---|
|  | Thesaurus novus anecdotorum, Lutetiae Parisiorum 1717. |
| Mayer, E. | Italienische Verfassungsgeschichte von der Gothenzeit bis zur Zunftherrschaft, 2 vols., Leipzig 1909. |
| Mayer, G. | Etymologisches Wörterbuch der albanischen Sprache, Strassburg 1891. |
| Memorie e documenti per servire alla storia di Lucca, 16 vols., Lucca 1813–1881. | |
| Méry, L. and Guin- ·don, F. | Histoire analytique et chronologique des actes et des délibérations du corps et du conseil de la municipalité de Marseille depuis le X<sup>me</sup> siècle jusqu'à nos jours, Marseille 1842. |
| Métais, Ch. | Cartulaire de l'abbaye cardinale de la Trinité de Vendôme, Paris 1893. |
| MGH. | Monumenta Germania e historica. |
|  | Auctores antiquissimi 1879–1913. |
|  | Diplomata Imperii, 1872. |
|  | Diplomata Karolinorum, 1906. |
|  | Formulae, in Leges sec. v. |
|  | Epistolare, 1887–1912. |
|  | Leges, 1835–89. |
|  | Legum sec. i, etc., 1883–1913. |
|  | Scriptores rerum langobardicarum et italicarum, 1878. |
|  | Scriptores, 1826–1913. |
|  | Scriptores rerum merovingicarum, 1884–1913. |
| Migliore, F. L. del. | Firenze città nobilissima illustrata, 3 parts, Firenze 1684. |
| Miklosich, F. | Etymologisches Wörterbuch der slavischen Sprachen, Wien 1886. |
| Miklosich, F., and Müller, | Acta et diplomata graeca, 6 vols., Vindbonae 1860– |
| G. | 1890. |
| Minieri Riccio, C. | Saggio di codice diplomatico formato sulle antiche scritture dell' archivio di stato di Napoli, Napoli 1878.' |
| Miscellanea di storia italiana, Torino 1862– | |
| Mittarelli, J. B. | Annales camadulenses Ordinis Sancti Benedictini, 9 vols., Venetiis 1755–73. |
| Mitteis, L. | Griechische Urkunden der Papyrus-Sammlung zu Leipzig, Lepzig 1906. |
| Moisy, H. | Dictionnaire de patois normand, Caen 1887. |
| Mommsen, Th. | Ostgothische Studien, in Hermes, vol. xxiv. |
| Monti, P. | Vocabolario dei dialetti della città e diocesi di Como, Milano 1845. |
| Monumenta Boica, Monachii 1763– | |
| Monumenta medii aevi historica res gestas Poloniae illustrantia, Cracoviae 1874– | |
| Monumenta spectantia historiam Slavorum meridionalium, Listine, Zagrabiae 1868– | |
| Monumenti di storia delle provincie modenesi, Parma, etc., 1861. | |

Morice, P. H.            Memoires pour servir de preuves à l'histoire ecclé-
                         siastique et civile de Bretagne, 3 vols., Paris
                         1742–61.
Müller, G.               Documenti sulle relazioni delle città toscane coll'
                         oriente fino all' anno MDXXXI, Firenze, 1879.
Muñoz y Romero, T.       Coleccion de fueros municipales y cartas de las
                         reinos de Castilla, Madrid 1847.
Muratori, L. A.          Antiquitates italicae medii aevi, 6 vols., Mediolani
                         1738–42.
                         Rerum italicarum scriptores, Mediolani 1723–51.
Musset, G.               Cartulaire de Saint-Jean d'Angély, in Archives de
                         la Saintonge et de l'Aunis, vol. xxx.

Odorici, F.              Storie bresciane dai primi tempi sino all' età nos-
                         tra, 11 vols., Brescia 1853–65.
Osio, L.                 Documenti diplomatici tratti degli archivij milanesi,
                         Milano 1864.

Pansa, E.                Istoria dell' antica repubblica d'Amalfi, Napoli
                         1724.
Pardessus, J. M.         Diplomata, chartae, epistolae, 2 vols., Lutetiae Pari-
                         siorum 1843–49.
Pasqui, U.               Documenti per la storia della città di Arezzo, Firenze
                         1899.
Piot, Ch.                Cartulaire de l'abbaye de Saint Trond, Bruxelles
                         1870.
PMH.                     Portugalae monumenta historica.
                         Diplomata et chartae, 1867–
                         Leges et consuetudines, 1856–73.
Preisigke, F.            Die ptolemäische Staatspost, in Klio, vol. VII.
                         Griechische Papyrus zu Strassburg, Leipzig 1912.
Puitspelu, N. du.        Dictionnaire étymologique du patois lyonnais, Lyon
                         1890.

Quantin, M.              Cartulaire général de l'Yonne, Auxerre 1854.

Ragut, C.                Cartulaire de Saint-Vincent de Mâcon, Mâcon 1864.
Recueil des anciennes coutumes de la Belgique, Coutumes du Pays et Comté
                         de Hainaut, ed. C. Faidor, 1883.
Regesto di Farfa.        Gregorius Catinensis, Il Regesto di Farfa, ed. by L.
                         Giorgi and U. Balzini, 3 vols., Roma 1879–88.
Regii neapolitani archivi monumenta, 6 vols., Neapoli 1845–61.
Rezasco, G.              Dizionario del linguaggio italiano storico et ammi-
                         nistrativo, Firenze 1881.
Ritz, W.                 Urkunden und Abhandlungen zur Geschichte des
                         Niederrheins und der Niedermaas, Aachen 1824.
Robolini, G.             Notizie tenenti alla storia della patria, Pavia 1826.
Romanin, S.              Storia documentata di Venezia, Venezia 1853.
Roncioni, R.             Delle istorie pisane libri XVI, Firenze 1844.

Rostowzow, M. — Angariae, in Klio vol. vi.
Studien zur Geschichte des römischen Kolonats, in 1. Beiheft zum Archiv für Papyrusforschung.

Rozière, E. de — Recueil général des formules dans l'empire des Francs du Vᵉ au Xᵉ siècle, Paris 1859–71

Sacy, S. de. — Chrestomathie arabe, Paris 1826.

Salmon, A. M. — Philippe de Beaumanoir, Coutumes de Beauvaisis, Paris 1899.

Santa Rosa de Viterbo, J. — Elucidario, Lisboa 1865.

Schiaparelli, L. — I diplomi di Berengario I, Roma 1903.
I diplomi di Guido e di Lamberto, Roma 1906.
I diplomi di Lodovico III e di Rodolfo II, Roma 1910.

Schmeller, J. A. — Bayerisches Wörterbuch, München 1878.

Schweizerisches Idiotikon, Frauenfeld 1905–.

Sella, P. — Statuta comunis Bugelle, Biella 1904.

Sota, F. — Chronica de principes de Asturias y Cantabria, Madrid 1681.

Statuta civitatis Mutinae ad iudices Aquarum pertinentia, Mutinae 1575.

Statuta civitatis Pisauri, Pisauri 1531.

Statuta Lucensis civitatis 1539.

Statuta magnificae communitatis Regii, Regii 1582.

Statuti del comune di Vicenza, mcclxiv, Venezia 1886.

Steinmeyer and Sievers. — Althochdeutsche Glossen.

Tafel, G. L. F. and Thomas, G. M. — Urkunden zur ältern Handels- und Staatsgeschichte der Republik Venedig, 3 vols., Wien 1856–7.

Tardif, E. J. — Coutumiers de Normandie, Rouen, Paris 1896.

Tardif, J. — Monuments historiques, 2 vols., Paris 1866.

Tarlazzi, A. — Appendice ai monumenti ravennati, Ravenna 1869.

Teulet, A., etc. — Layettes du Trésor des chartes, 5 vols., Paris 1863–1909.

Thesaurus linguae latinae.

Thierry, A. — Recueil de monuments inédits de l'histoire du tiers état, 4 vols., Paris 1850–70.

Tiraboschi, G. — Stoira dell' augusta badia di S. Silvestro di Nonantola, Modena 1785.

Trémault, Ch. A. — Cartulaire de Marmoutier pour le Vendômois, Paris, Vendôme 1892.

Trinchera, F. — Syllabus graecarum membranarum, Neapoli 1865.

Troya, C. — Codice diplomatico langobardo dal dlxviii al dcclxxiv, 5 vols., Napoli 1852–56.

Ughelli, F. — Italia sacra, 3. ed., Ron ae 1644–62, 2. ed., 10 vols., Venetiis 1717–1722.

Uhlenbeck, C. C. — Kurzgefasstes etymologisches Wörterbuch, Amsterdam 1900.

| | |
|---|---|
| Valsecchi, A. | Gli statuti di Albenga, Albenga 1885. |
| Van Drival, E. | Cartulaire de l'abbaye de Saint-Vaast d'Arras, Arras 1875. |
| Vari, R. | Incerti scriptoris byzantini saeculi x liber de re militari, Lipsiae 1901. |
| Vignati, C. | Codice diplomatico laudense, Milano 1879. |
| Villanueva, J. | Viage literario á las iglesias de España, 22 vols., Madrid 1806–52, 1902. |
| Waitz, G. | Deutsche Verfassungsgeschichte, 2nd ed. |
| Warnkoenig L. A. (Gheldolf). | Histoire de la Flandre, Paris 1835–64. |
| Wartmann, H. | Urkundenbuch der Abtei Sanct Gallen, 5 vols., Zürich 1863–1913. |
| Wilcken, U. | Griechische Ostraka aus Aegypten und Nubien, Leipzig, Berlin 1899. |
| Winnefeld, H. | Sortes sangallenses, Bonnae 1889. |
| Wright, Th. | Anglo-Saxon and Old English Vocabularies. |
| Yepes, A. de. | Coronica general de la orden de San Benito, Patriarca de Religiosos, 1609–1621. |
| Zdekauer, L. | Statutum potestatis comunis Pistorii, Mediolani 1888. |
| Zeumer, K. | Über zwei neuentdeckte westgothische Gesetze, in Neues Archiv, vol. xxiii. |

# CONTENTS

# INTRODUCTION

## I

### INDIAN PARALLELS

PROBABLY no fallacy has done more harm to historical and linguistical science than the assumption that biological evolution is physically operative in the field of human actions, that mental processes and moral changes are subject to gradual and imperceptible transformations, that no amount of external influence can more than bend the original type of a civilisation, and so forth. Without denying the interaction of physical laws in the realm of reason, every student of history must realise that human society has frequently progressed by sudden and utterly unforeseeable jumps. The Hungarians passed from a Nomadic to an agricultural life, with a stable and permanent government, in an incredibly short time. The Mandingo and Woloff Negroes have in Anglo-Saxon countries become thoroughly Anglo-Saxon linguistically, with hardly a trace of their native dialects, still spoken by the slaves a century or two ago. The amalgamation of heterogeneous peoples in the United States is not only complete intellectually, but late investigations go to show that even the cranial structure of the second generation is in America violently changed in the direction of an American type.

Regardless of such obvious phenomena, the number of which may be indefinitely increased, Germanic scholars have proceeded from the theory that the sudden appearance of the Teutons on the political scene in the fifth century, their activity in establishing law and order, which followed their settlement in the conquered territories, their agricultural habits, which they evinced from the start, were all indicative of a long, fairly uniform civil existence of those nations which Caesar and Tacitus knew only as German barbarians. On this theory a proto-Germanic civilisation has been postulated, and its continuance has been proved from documents following the migration of the nations down to Carolingian times and even later, although all these documents are compiled in the Latin language and betray the Roman notarial attitude towards legal and social institutions.

In the following pages I shall study these documents in the light of the Roman law, here I will analyse only the analogous case of the American Indians, where deductions from documents and conditions are controllable by contemporary evidence from other sources, in order to test the reliability of the method pursued by scholars in the case of the early history of the Germanic nations.

The description which Caesar and Tacitus give of the semi-nomadic Germans almost fits that which one might have given of the Indians of North America, when the White settlers first set foot there. Like the Germans, they lived on the produce of the chase, occasionally cultivating corn fields with no determined boundaries, knew no landed property, were constantly engaged in warfare, carrying their families with them in their raiding expeditions, lived in flimsy structures, covered their bodies with animal skins. Some of the Indians, the Five Nations, had formed an alliance similar to the Ingvaeonian union of the northern Germans, and, as the bravery, simplicity, hospitality of the Germans has been praised by Tacitus, so the Indians have had their panegyrists. Like the comitatus of the Teutonic princeps were the companies of the Indian braves about their chiefs, with whom they took counsel; and, though possessing no definite organisations, the various tribes of the Indians had their separate "spheres of influence" in their hunting grounds, not unlike the territorial divisions ascribed to the early Germans. But it is the Cherokees, relatives of the Iroquois Nations, and the Chickasaws and Choctaws, of the Muskohegan family, that bear the most striking resemblance to the Teutons of the period of accomplished migrations. I shall confine myself chiefly to the history of the Cherokees.

When the White man set foot in North America, the Cherokees dwelt in the region of the Blue Ridge, but at an earlier time they are supposed to have lived as Mound Builders in the Ohio Valley. "His blood of his ancestors, as well as his enemies, could be trailed from the Hiwassee to the Ohio. The trophies of his skill and valor adorned the sides of his wigwam and furnished the theme for his boastful oratory and song around the council fire and at the dance. His wants were few and purely of a physical nature. His life was devoted to the work of securing a sufficiency of food and the punishment of his enemies. His reputation among his fellow men was proportioned to the skill with which he could draw his bow, his cleverness and agility in their simple athletic sports, or the keen and tireless manner that characterized his pursuit of an enemy's trail. His life was simple, his wants were easily supplied and, in consequence, the largest measure of his existence was spent in indolence and frivolous amusements. Such proportion of the family food as the chase did not supply was found in the cultivation of Indian corn." [1]

At the period of the English settlement of the Carolinas, the Cherokees occupied parts of these regions and also of what now are West Virginia and Kentucky. From 1721 on, there were frequently made between them and the English government treaties, by which their boundaries were shifted and generally contracted. Similar treaties were made with

[1] Chas. C. Royce, *The Cherokee Nation of Indians*, in *Annual Report of Bureau of American Ethnology*, 1883–4, p. 371 f.

the government of the United States, resulting in similar diminutions of their territory. In 1816 it was proposed to make a tender of their whole territory to the United States in exchange for lands on the Arkansas River, whither a portion of the Cherokees moved in 1818. In 1825 a report was submitted to the War Department of the United States, showing that "numberless herds of cattle grazed upon their extensive plains; horses were numerous; many and extensive flocks of sheep, goats, and swine covered the hills and the valleys . . . the soil of the valleys and plains was rich, and was utilized in the production of corn, tobacco, cotton, wheat, oats, indigo, and potatoes; considerable trade was carried on with the neighboring States, much cotton being exported in boats of their own to New Orleans; apple and peach orchards were quite common, much attention was paid to the cultivation of gardens; butter and cheese of their own manufacture were seen upon many of their tables; public roads were numerous in the Nation and supplied at convenient distances with houses of entertainment kept by the Nation; many and flourishing villages dotted the country; cotton and woolen cloths were manufactured by the women and home-made blankets were very common; almost every family grew sufficient cotton for its own consumption; industry and commercial enterprise were extending themselves throughout the Nation, nearly all the merchants were native Cherokees." [1] By the treaty of 1828 their territory on the Arkansas River was determined to be seven million acres in extent, various grants of money were given them, one of $500 to George Guess, the discoverer of the Cherokee alphabet, and the "United States agreed to furnish the Cherokees, when they desired it, a system of plain laws and to survey their lands for individual allotment." [2]

[1] Chas. C. Royce, *The Cherokee Nation of Indians*, in *Annual Report of Bureau of American Ethnology*, 1883-4, p. 240.     [2] *Ibid.*, p. 230.

The Cherokees had as early as 1810 abolished clans and "in 1820 the Nation was reorganized, and by a resolve of its National Council, divided into eight districts, each of which had the privilege of sending four members to the legislature. The pay of the members was established at one dollar per day, that of the speaker being fixed at one and a half dollars, and the principal chiefs were to receive $150 a year. Some of their principal laws and regulations were: a prohibition of spirituous liquor being brought into the nation by white men. If a white man took a Cherokee wife, he must marry her according to their laws; but her property was not affected by such union. No man was allowed but one wife. A judge, marshal, sheriff and deputy, and two constables were commissioned in each district. Embezzlement, intercepting and opening sealed letters was punished by a fine of $100 and 100 lashes on the bare back. No business was allowed on Sunday; and the fences were regulated by statute. They also had a statute of limitations, which, however, did not affect notes or settled accounts. A will was valid, if found on the decease of its maker to have been written by him, and witnessed by two creditable persons. A man leaving no will, all his children shared equal, and his wife as one of them; if he left no children, then the widow to have a fourth part of all the property; the other three fourths to go to his nearest relatives. And so if the wife died, leaving property. Before the division of the nation into districts, and the appointment of the above-named civil officers, there was an organized company of light-horse, which executed the orders of the chiefs, searched out offenders, and brought them to justice. It was a fundamental law, that no land should be sold to the white people without the authority of a majority of the nation. Transgressors of this law were punished with death." [1]

It is obvious that the ideas expressed by the words "mar-

[1] G. E. Foster, *Literature of the Cherokees*, Ithaca, N.Y., 1889, p. 36 *f*.

shal, sheriff, deputy, constable, letters, pecuniary fine, Sunday, fences, statute, limitation, will, light-horse" were first obtained from the White man and that all these laws were fashioned after those of their civilised neighbors, but some of them are so transformed as to appear at first sight to represent an Indian tradition. Thus the formation of an organised company of horse to execute the orders of the chiefs, which is amazingly like the organisation of the Burgundian wittiscalci, the Salic trustis dominica, is in reality nothing more than an attempt at carrying out the laws of the Whites among lawless Indians. In fact, it can be shown that the organisation of this light-horse emanated from the government of the United States, for in a treaty between the Choctaws and the United States of 1820 we read, "To enable the Mingoes, Chiefs, and head men, of the Choctaw Nation, to raise and organize a corps of light horse, consisting of ten in each district, so that good order may be maintained, and that all men, both White and Red, may be compelled to pay their debts, it is stipulated and agreed, that the sum of two hundred dollars shall be appropriated by the United States, for each district, annually, and placed in the hands of the agent, to pay the expenses incurred in raising and establishing said corps; which is to act as executive officers, in maintaining good order, and compelling bad men to remove from the Nation, who are not authorized to live in it by a regular permit from the agent." [1]

As soon as proper officers were substituted, the institution fell into desuetude, and there is no further mention of this in the laws. The establishment of the principal chief, which at first thought would appear as a continuation or development of the Indian sachem and might lead to a comparison with the evolution of royalty from the German chiefs, a fact

[1] H. B. Cushman, *History of the Choctaw, Chickasaw and Natchez Indians,* Greenville, Texas, 1889, p. 117.

which is actually assumed by German scholars, has nothing whatsoever to do with the Indian dignity but the name. In the Chickasaw laws [1] the chief magistrate is styled "the Governor of the Chickasaw Nation," and the yearly salary paid to the Cherokee Principal Chief and his tenure of office by popular election show conclusively that we are dealing here with an institution of the Whites. So, too, the name of Principal Chief is due to the conceit of the White Americans, who have as lavishly conferred this appellation on the Red man's leaders, as Tacitus has that of princeps on the more prominent Germans.

In the Constitution of the Cherokee Nation [2] passed in 1839 there are still more startling resemblances to "proto-Germanic" conditions. "The lands of the Cherokee Nation shall remain common property, but the improvements made thereon, and in the possession of the citizens of the Nation, are the exclusive and indefeasible property of the citizens respectively who made, or may rightfully be in possession of them: Provided, that the citizens of the Nation possessing exclusive and indefeasible right to their improvements, as expressed in this article, shall possess no right or power to dispose of their improvements, in any manner whatever, to the United States, individual States, or to individual citizens thereof." [3] This is precisely like the Burgundian law according to which no property could be sold to a foreigner. [4] In either case the weakly developed sense of individual ownership and the strong desire to preserve nationality intact led

---

[1] *Constitution, Treaties and Laws of the Chickasaw Nation*, Atoka, I.T., 1890, p. 11.

[2] *Constitution and Laws of the Cherokee Nation*, St. Louis, 1875.

[3] *Ibid.*, p. 9.

[4] "Hoc etiam interdictum, ut quisque, habens alibi terram, vendendi necessitatem habet, in comparandum, quod Burgundio venale habet, nullus extraneus Romano hospiti praeponatur, nec extraneo per quodlibet argumentum terram liceat comparare," *Monumenta Germaniae historica, Leg.* sec. I, vol. II [1], p. 107.

to the enactment of laws of self-preservation, which in a very few generations became inoperative through adaptation to surroundings. In neither case can we predicate a continuance of a communistic system previous to a contact with a new civilisation. ·The Indians and the proto-Germans had no conception of and no need for "common property," for the reason that land did not present to them the idea of possession, but merely acted as a background on which to exert their activities. We have no evidence that they actually worked the land in common, in some such way as did the Peruvians. We only know that they had no idea of distinct divisions of land, even as Tacitus spoke of such absence of boundaries among the Germans. The attempt occasionally made by scholars to accuse Tacitus of a mistake of judgment in this and to postulate a communistic state seems futile in connection with what we actually know of the Indians previous to their enactment of the above apparently communistic law.

"In all elections by the people, the electors shall vote viva voce. All free male citizens, who shall have attained to the age of eighteen years, shall be equally entitled to vote at all public elections."[1] The same law holds among the Chickasaws,[2] except that majority is reached at nineteen years. The Indian, like all primitive races, considers the young man to be mature at an earlier age than among civilised people, and a viva voce election is imperative among a tribe consisting chiefly of illiterates. Neither fact entitles one to the conclusion that it is based on a popular method of election, for the reason that no elections existed among the Indians, even though they possessed a National Council and deliberated matters in common. The viva voce vote is of the same kind as the verbal wills which, by an act of 1876 of the Chickasaw Nation, were valid, if made in presence of two witnesses.[3] The late date alone of this enactment shows that we have

, [1] *Cherokee Constitution*, p. 12.   [2] *Chickasaw Constitution*, p. 6.   [3] *Ibid*, p. 57.

here no continuance of an old custom of Indians, who had no use for wills.

It is also interesting to note that, like the Germans, the Cherokees and Chickasaws passed stringent laws against the cutting down of fruit-bearing trees. "Every person who shall wilfully cut down, kill or destroy any pecan, walnut, hickory or other fruit or nut-bearing tree, standing and growing upon the public domain of the Cherokee Nation, or shall cut down for the nuts or fruit thereof, shall be deemed guilty of a misdemeanor."[1] Here, again, there is no reference to an Indian custom, but merely the result of a new source of income from the abundant nut-bearing trees of the lately acquired domain. This law was incorporated in 1874 in the Cherokee New Code of Laws and only two years later passed as an Act of the Chickasaw Nation. This Act is as modern and as unrelated to the past as another Act of the Chickasaws of the same year establishing a Female Seminary into which no students shall enter "until they can read well in McGuffey's Fifth Reader,"[2] a statement which a millennium hence will give the historian food for reflection and theorising.

I have carefully selected all the laws which distinctly differ from those of the United States and which to the uninitiated would seem as an inheritance from the Indian past, and have shown that in no way do they permit of such interpretation. There is but one single statement in the Chickasaw laws which seems to give an indication of a previous custom, and that is the one which refers to polygamy. "Neither polygamy nor concubinage shall be tolerated in this Nation, from and after the adoption of this Constitution,"[3] but as this Act of 1867 is repeated in 1876 as an Act to prohibit polygamy "from and after the passage of this Act," there arises a doubt as to whether we really have here an Indian

[1] *Cherokee Constitution*, p. 143; *Chickasaw Constitution*, p. 91.
[2] *Chickasaw Constitution*, p. 99.   [3] *Ibid.*, p. 6.

survival. It is more likely that the reference is merely to a looseness of manners, common in any new society, and this is made certain by the Act of 1876, which shows that chiefly the Whites, and not the Reds, are meant by it, for we are told that "no right of citizenship whatever shall be acquired by such unlawful marriages," that is, that White men, who by their marriage to Chickasaw women could be adopted into the Nation, were to be deprived of this advantage, if they lived in polygamy, whether by not being divorced from their White wives, or otherwise.

Thus it appears that, while in character and daily habits Cherokees and Chickasaws may have preserved many ancient traits, they have, since the establishment of the United States and until their complete amalgamation with the Whites in 1906, when they were made citizens of the new state of Oklahoma, changed from the hunting to the agricultural and industrial state, have acquired the Anglo-Saxon ideas of property, individualism, education, politics, and have become as thoroughly American as the Franks of Carolingian times were Roman. Previous to 1906 a stranger resident among the Indians could live by the laws of the United States, even as in the Frankish Empire one could live by Roman or Salic or Lombard law. The Indians constantly opposed their far more simple and less intricate laws to those of the White man, utterly unconscious of the fact that these simple laws were one and all deduced from those of their neighbors, nay, that the United States, through its agents, really had framed the laws for them, either directly or by advising the Indian legislators. Even so the Franks were utterly unaware of the fact that their simple Salic and Ribuarian laws were derived from the Roman laws just as much, though not so directly, as were the Burgundian and Visigothic laws, and were based on the Theodosian Code and local Roman enactments.

## II

### THE GOTHIC BIBLE

THERE does not exist the slightest proof that the fragments of the Gothic Bible, as we now possess it, were part of a translation made by Ulfilas in the fourth century. The tradition which has grown up in regard to the whole Gothic question is based on a vicious circle of which the authorship of the Bible is the initial step. Upon close inspection the whole structure of Germanic philology, in so far as it rests upon the assumption of a fourth century Gothic literature, collapses from its own weight, and a new building has to be reared after the débris have been cleared away.

All that we know of the relation of Ulfilas to the Gothic Bible is based on the statements made by Auxentius, Philostorgius, Socrates, Sozomenus, Jordanes, Isidor of Seville, and Walafrid Strabo.[1] Auxentius had been a pupil and close friend of the Gothic bishop Ulfilas, yet all he had to say about his teacher's Gothic activity was that he had preached in Gothic and had left behind many tracts and interpretations in Greek, Latin, and Gothic.[2] No amount of theorising can explain Auxentius' silence in regard to a translation of the Bible, if it existed. The only inference we can draw from this statement is this that the Goths may have possessed in Ulfilas' time brief extracts or discussions on the Bible, such as were later known under the name of *catena* or *speculum* and as may readily be summed up as "tracts and interpretations."

---

[1] W. Streitberg, *Die gotische Bibel*, Heidelberg, 1908, p. xiii *ff*.

[2] "Haec et his similia exsequente quadraginta annis in episcopatu gloriose florens apostolica gratia grecam et latinam et goticam linguam sine intermissione in una et sola ecclesia Cristi predicauit ... et haec omnia de diuinis scribturis eum dixisse et nos describsisse, qui legit, intelligat; qui et ipsis tribus linguis plures tractatus et multas interpretationes uolentibus ad utilitatem et aedificationem sibi ad aeternam memoriam et mercedem post se dereliquid," *ibid.*, p. xvi.

Philostorgius, who died after 425 and therefore wrote fifty or more years after the probable translation by Ulfilas, informs us that Ulfilas was the inventor of the Gothic alphabet and that he translated all the Holy Writ into his native tongue, with the exception of the Books of the Kings, which he left out because the Goths were warlike and needed a check rather than encouragement in their martial spirit.[1] But Ulfilas did not invent a Gothic alphabet, having at best added a few additional signs to the Greek letters then in use, and the reference to the omission of the Book of Kings is apocryphal, totally devoid of probability.[2] We have, therefore, no reason to assume that the statement regarding the translation of the Bible is more correct. Apparently the unusual activity of the Gothic bishop had led to exaggerated accounts of his literary accomplishments among his warlike countrymen, and this legendary lore was seized upon by all the later writers. Sozomenus quoted Philostorgius almost verbatim[3] and Socrates merely paraphrased him.[4] The most amazing thing is the ignorance of the Gothic writers in the sixth and seventh centuries of any extant translation of the Bible, although it is assumed by all modern authors that the surviving fragments were written in the sixth century.

Jordanes, from whom we get the fullest account of the Goths in the sixth century, has nothing to tell us beyond the

[1] "Γραμμάτων αὐτοῖς οἰκείων εὑρετὴς καταστὰς, μετέφρασεν εἰς τὴν αὐτῶν φωνὴν τὰς γραφὰς ἁπάσας, πλήν γε δὴ τῶν βασιλείων, ἅτε τῶν μὲν πολέμων ἱστορίαν ἐχουσῶν, τοῦ δὲ ἔθνους ὄντος φιλοπολέμου, καὶ δεομένου μᾶλλον χαλινοῦ τῆς ἐπὶ τὰς μάχας ὁρμῆς, ἀλλ᾿ οὐχὶ τοῦ πρὸς ταῦτα παροξύνοντος," *ibid.*, p. xx.

[2] "Ea Philostorgii sententia a viris doctis tamquam ridicula improbata atque explosa est," H. C. de Gabelentz et J. Loebe, *Ulfilas*, Lipsiae 1843, vol. I, p. x.

[3] "Πρῶτος δὲ γραμμάτων εὑρετὴς αὐτοῖς ἐγένετο καὶ εἰς τὴν οἰκείαν φωνὴν μετέφρασε τὰς ἱερὰς βίβλους," Streitberg, *l. c.*

[4] "Τότε δὲ καὶ Οὐλφίλας ὁ τῶν Γότθων ἐπίσκοπος γράμματα ἐφεῦρε Γοτθικά· καὶ τὰς θείας γραφὰς εἰς τὴν Γότθων μεταβαλὼν, τοὺς βαρβάρους μανθάνειν τὰ θεῖα λόγια παρασκεύασεν," *ibid.*, p. xxi.

fact that Ulfilas gave the Minor Goths an alphabet, and that
these were in his day reduced to poverty in Moesia.[1] It does
not occur to him in any way to connect these Minor Goths
with the Ostrogoths or Visigoths, but if, as is assumed, the
Bible was written out in the sixth century in Italy, the
Ostrogoths at least must have possessed Ulfilas' Bible. Jordanes' silence on this matter is ominous. The same uncon-
nectedness of Ulfilas' Gothic with that of the Visigoths of
Spain is assumed by Isidor of Seville,[2] who certainly would
not have missed referring to it, if he had suspected it. More
curious still are the remarks of Walafrid Strabo in the ninth
century, who asserted that Gothic was a Germanic language
and that learned Goths had translated the Bible of which
monuments were still extant. At first it would seem that he
was aware of the existence of the Gothic Bible in his time, but
that is at once negatived by his quoting merely from book accounts (ut historiae testantur) and immediately adding that
he had it from the tales of monks that in Scythia, among the
Thomitani, services were still held in that language.[3] It may
be possible that his reference to extant monuments of the
Bible is to be taken as different from those found among the
Thomitani, but then it becomes significant that he does not
speak of a translation by Ulfilas, but by several learned men.
If we accept his statement as correct in so far as it speaks of
monuments still in use in the ninth century, we cannot reject

[1] "Erant si quidem et alii Gothi, qui dicuntur minores, populus immensus,
cum suo pontifice ipsoque primate Vulfila, qui eis dicitur et litteras instituisse.
hodieque sunt in Moesia regionem incolentes Nicopolitanam ad pedes Emi-
monti gens multa, sed paupera et inbellis," *ibid.*, p. xxiv.

[2] "Tunc Gulfilas eorum episcopus Gothicas litteras condidit et scripturas
novi et veteris testamenti in eandem linguam convertit," *ibid.*, p. xxiv.

[3] "In Grecorum provinciis commorantes nostrum i.e. theotiscum sermonem
postmodum studiosi illius gentis divinos libros in suae locutionis proprietatem
transtulerint quorum adhuc monimenta apud nonullos habentur; et fidelium
fratrum relatione didicimus apud quasdam Scytharum gentes, maxime Thomi-
tanos, eadem locutione divina hactenus celebrari officia," *MGH., Capitularia,*
vol. II, p. 481.

his assertion that the translation was made by several men, and thus the ascription of the Gothic Bible to Ulfilas is once more made impossible.

With rare exceptions all the modern writers who, since the seventeenth century, have written on the Gothic Bible have accepted the dictum of those older authorities as final and have proceeded on the assumption that we have before us genuine documents of the time of Ulfilas or, at best, of redactions not more recent than the middle of the sixth century. But a number of important facts have been overlooked by them or have been so interpreted as to fit in with the a priori assumption. It, therefore, becomes necessary to reinvestigate all the Gothic manuscripts, both textually and palaeographically, before any theory independent of the statement by Philostorgius and the other ancient writers may be propounded.

In a Salzburg-Vienna MS. of an Alcuin text, obviously of the ninth or tenth century, two Gothic alphabets and a few Gothic sentences with transliteration and phonetic commentary are recorded.[1] The alphabets, given approximately in the Latin order, do not materially differ from those of the codices and the Neapolitan documents respectively, although a few peculiarities occur. Grimm [2] sees in the attached names of the letters Anglo-Saxon forms, but the resemblance is only remote, and such names as *pertra, quertra* for AS. *peord, cweorn* makes an Anglo-Saxon influence untenable. Whatever the case may be, the writer of the alphabet either knew or copied an alphabet, the pronunciation of whose letters was still known in the ninth or tenth century. This becomes even more certain from the appended passage:

---

[1] *Jahrbücher der Literatur*, vol. xliii (Wien, 1828), pp. 1–41; F. Dietrich, *Ueber die Aussprache des Gothischen*, Marburg, 1862, p. 23 *ff.*; Streitberg, *Gotisches Elementarbuch*, Heidelberg, 1910, p. 36, *Die gotische Bibel*, pp. xxx and 475 *ff.*; H. F. Massmann, *Gotthica minora*, in Haupt's *Zeitschrift*, vol. I, p. 296 *ff.*
[2] *Jahrbücher, l. c.*

1. ˉuuortun otan auar
2. waurþunuþþan. afar
3. euang-eliū. ther Lucan
4. aiwaggeljo þairh Lokan
5. uuorthun auar thuo
6. waurþun afar þo
7. ia chuedant ia chᵘatun
8. jah qeþun.
9. ubi dicit /. genuit. j. ponitur
10. ubi gabriel .g. ponunt & alia sīm.
11. ubi aspiratioē. ut dicitur
12. gah libeda. jah libaida
13. diptongon .ai. pro e longa
14. pro ch .q. ponunt.

The writer comments upon the phonetic values of the letters in the present tense (dicit, dicitur, ponitur, ponunt) and compares them with the current Old High German sounds. It is obvious from this comparison that no period previous to the eighth century can possibly be assigned to these comments. Indeed, Grienberger [1] has shown conclusively that the writing gaar for jēr in the alphabet points to the composition of the whole passage in Burgundy by a Frankish German familiar with the Gothic of southern France, and that the information or, at least, the writing of this information cannot be placed before 910, while Massmann had long ago assumed that Gothic was still understood in the ninth century.[2] In Spain the Gothic language existed as late as the year 1091, for it was in that year prohibited by a decree of the Synod of Leon.[3]

[1] Die germanischen Runennamen, in Paul and Braune's Beiträge, vol. xxi, p. 199.
[2] "Wir entnehmen, dass im neunten jahrhunderte wohl noch handschriften der gothischen bibel vorhanden, wie noch ziemlich verstanden waren," Haupt's Zeitschrift, vol. i, p. 306.
[3] "Et interfuit etiam Renerius legatus, et Romanae ecclesiae Cardinalis,

In the sixteenth century the fragments of the Bible, later known as *Codex Argenteus*, had been described by several men who had seen it in the monastery at Werden,[1] and in 1665 they were published in full by Francis Junius at Dortrecht. The best description of the external appearance of the Codex was given by Ihre and Zahn.[2] It was executed in silver letters, the first lines sometimes in gold. The script is uncial neatly written between two guiding lines on polished purple vellum, but the color of the vellum varies to violet. The text is included in a rectangle containing twenty lines. At the inner edge of the page the number of the chapter is given according to the Eusebian canon, and occasionally notes are added, such as parallel passages from the Old Testament. The words in the text to which the notes or variants refer have a line with hooks at the end over them, as have also the nomina sacra. Zahn thinks [3] that the MS. closely resembles the *Codex Brixianus*, hence, that it cannot be a copy of Ulfilas' time, but must have been written at a later time in Italy. Gabelentz and Loebe [4] say that it was written at the end of the fifth century, or in the beginning of the sixth, when the Goths lived in Italy. "The Codex Argenteus," says Bosworth,[5] "is supposed to be the work of Italians in their own country at the close of the fifth century, or the beginning of the sixth. The only MS. in exactly the same style of writing, is the celebrated Gallican Psalter now in the

ibidemque celebrato concilio cum Bernardo Toletano primate, multa de offi: cijs ecclesiae statuerunt, et etiam de caetero omnes scriptores omissa litera Toletana, quam Gulfilas Gothorum Episcopus adinuenit, Gallicis literis vterentur," Roderici Toletani (Rodrigo Ximenes) *Chronicon*, lib. vi, cap. xxx. See Hefele, *Conciliengeschichte*, 2nd ed., vol. v, p. 201. The assertion made somewhere that the reference is to a calligraphy and not to the Gothic language is without any foundation, for the Gothic alphabet was never used for anything but Gothic.

[1] Streitberg, *Elementarbuch*, p. 24.
[2] See Zahn, *Ulfilas*, Weissenfels 1805, p. 46 *ff*.
[3] *Op. cit.*, p. 50.  [4] *Op. cit.*, vol. i, p. xxxi.
[5] *The Gothic and Anglo-Saxon Gospels*, London 1874, p. vii.

Abbey of St. Germain-de-Prés. It is of the sixth century and is said to have belonged to St. Germain, Bishop of Paris, who died May 28, 576. The vellum is stained of a purple-violet colour, and the writing is in silver letters, and a few particular words in gold. This description would serve for the Codex Argenteus, the vellum of which, however, is purple, of a reddish rather than a violet tint." Streitberg, too, knows [1] that the MS. resembles the Codex Brixianus and was written in the 5./6. century.

The date of the writing of the Codex Argenteus has been established by false presumptions and insufficient information. The fact that some fragments were found at Bobbio does not in the least entitle us to draw the conclusion that all Gothic documents originated in Italy. The ninth or tenth century sentences in the Alcuin text were written in France; there are other fragments, which were found in Egypt and whose origin in Italy is highly improbable; and the Codex Argenteus, so far as we can trace it, has never been connected with Bobbio or Brescia. Then, the date and provenience is based on the resemblance of the Gothic MS. to the Codex Brixianus. But that is a gratuitous assumption. There is absolutely nothing in the Gothic text or script that gives the slightest clue to its palaeographic dating. The only thing we see is that the letters are made with extraordinary precision and are solid in body, not as was the writing in the fifth century in the Codex Brixianus, but of precisely the same quality as in the imitative art of the Carolingians, who reproduced the fifth century writing in all its details.[2] It is true that the Codex Brixianus had gold and silver letters on purple vellum, but Berger knows of a very large number of

[1] *Die gotische Bibel*, p. xxv.
[2] "Die karolingischen Abschriften, die so oft das antike Vorbild auch in allen Aeusserlichkeiten festhalten," L. Traube, *Palæographische Forschungen*, München 1904, p. 20 (*Abh. d. k. Bayer. Akad. d. Wiss.* III Kl., vol. XXIV, part I).

MSS. of the chrysographic art in Carolingian times,[1] and the Bible of Theodulphus, the Visigoth, of the ninth century, bears as striking a resemblance to the Codex Argenteus, for it, too, has gold and silver letters on purple vellum, and the exquisite regularity of the script is the same.[2] Indeed, it was through the efforts of the Visigoth Theodulphus that such calligraphy was practiced at Fleury.[3] Hence the identification of the calligraphy of the Gothic Bible with that of the Codex Brixianus is without any foundation whatsoever. But we have a more positive proof that the Gothic Bible could not have been written before the eighth century.

The Eusebian canon is marked on the inside of the page, the number of each verse being enclosed in a calligraphic conventional ornamentation of this type ≣. At the foot of each page the parallel passages of the Eusebian canon are given within four Roman arches. Now, the very use of the Eusebian canon precludes the writing of the Bible in Ulfilas' time, because it was adopted after his death. The Roman arches, in which the canon is included, are recorded for the

[1] S. Berger, *Histoire de la Vulgate*, Paris 1893, p. 259 *ff.*

[2] "On citerait difficilement un plus magnifique monument de la calligraphie du temps de Charlemagne. Nulle part ailleurs je n'ai vu de plus remarquables exemples de régularité et de finesse d'écriture. Il n'y a point, à proprement parler, de peintures; mais l'emploi qu'on y a fait de l'or et de l'argent sur des fonds pourprés, l'élégance des inscriptions en grandes lettres enclavées, la pureté et la variété des encadrements de plusieurs pages et des médaillons réservés aux souscriptions finales, suffisent pour constituer une très belle décoration et pour augmenter encore la valeur de la bible, qui forme le plus précieux joyau du trésor de la cathédrale de Puy," L. Delisle, *Les Bibles de Théodulphe*, in *Bibliothèque de l'Ecole des chartes*, vol. XL, p. 8.

[3] "On voit que les artistes employés par Théodulphe ont modifié les formes raides des miniaturistes primitifs, et, en employant l'or et l'argent, ils donnèrent plus de richesses et de reliefs à leurs lettres, qu'entouraient d'abord de simples traits rouges. Est-il étonnant que de tels maîtres aient laissé des préceptes, et que les moines de Fleury, qui ont executé de semblables beautés, aient voulu enseigner aux générations futures le secret de leur art?" Ch. Cuissard, *Théodulphe, évêque d'Orléans*, in *Mémoires de la Société archéologique et historique de l'Orléanais*, vol. XXIV, p. 179.

first time in late sixth century Syriac and Greek Gospels.[1] In the occidental Gospels the first recorded use is of the year 716, while in Carolingian times[2] these arches are of exceedingly common occurrence. While a Syriac or Greek influence upon the ornamentation of the Gothic Bible is not excluded, it is, in this particular case, impossible. If the Bible was written in Italy, we have not a single link to connect the two, and the conventionalised use of the arches unmistakeably points to a late time. In all the extant calligraphic MSS. the four arches are surmounted by a larger arch, all of them elaborately decorated, containing the complete canon. In the Gothic Bible each page has its own part of the parallel passages, in four separate conventionalised arches. The calligraphic precision of these arches is the same as that of

the ornamentation $\overset{c}{\underline{\overline{\equiv}}}_{\scriptscriptstyle 3}$, and this latter is one of the com-

monest conventional designs in Carolingian Gospels.[3] The coincidence of calligraphy, the silver and gold lettering, the employment of the Eusebian canon, the conventional ornament, the tinting of the vellum make the dating of the Gothic Bible in Carolingian times a certainty, even if we did not have overwhelming proofs from the vocabulary of the Gothic text.

Heretofore the dating of the Gothic Bible has been determined by a vicious circle. They reasoned as follows: Several fragments of Gospels have been found at Bobbio and Milan, ergo they were written in Italy. If they were written in Italy, they must have been written before the year 552, when the Goths were driven out of the country. Now, the Codex Argenteus has external resemblances with the Codex Brixianus, hence it, too, must have been written in Italy before

[1] *Die Trierer Ada-Handschrift*, Leipzig 1889, p. 69 *f.*
[2] See the illustrations in the *Trierer Ada-Handschrift*.
[3] See, for example, plate 11 in *Trierer Ada-Handschrift*, also plates 6, 7, 9, etc.

the year 552. Hence all Gothic documents were written in Italy, and all Gothic literary activity originated among the Ostrogoths. By such reasoning one could prove that all the Carolingian illuminated MSS. were written in Germany, or Italy, or elsewhere in the sixth century. But the Codex Argenteus was not found in Italy; of the learned Ostrogoth activity we know absolutely nothing, while Ulfilas was a Visigoth; we know positively that Gothic was understood in southern France in Carolingian times, and the Gothic calligraphy bears far more striking resemblances to that of the school of Tours. I have not yet a right to claim that I have proved the latter, but the theory of the Gothic scholars is irrevocably exploded, for it rests on the flimsiest of assumptions.

From Weissenburg comes the *Codex Carolinus*. It contains on four sheets the Epistle to the Romans in Gothic and Latin. Both are written στιχηδόν, i.e., in lines representing clauses, without a separation between the words. The text is superscribed by passages from Isidor of Seville's *Liber etymologiarum*. Fortunately we possess a reproduction of one page.[1] The editor says that it seems to have been written in Spain. Schöne and Niebuhr [2] had assumed, without good reason, that the Codex Carolinus was in Bobbio calligraphy. However it may be, the dating of the Gothic text is gratuitous. It is quite true that, at first glance, one would identify the Latin column as of the fifth century, but one must again remember Traube's own statement that the Carolingian writers imitated fifth century books down to minute details. The στιχηδόν writing was by tradition used for the Epistles of St. Paul and did not die until the ninth century, and the writing of στιχηδόν in a bilingual text is attested for

[1] O. von Heinemann, *Die Handschriften der herzoglichen Bibliothek zu Wolfenbüttel*, Zweite Abth. v, p. 296.

[2] *Sitzungsberichte der Berliner Akademie der Wissenschaften* 1902, p. 446 *f.*

the seventh century in the Codex Laudianus. Hence we must have another criterion for the establishment of the date of our MS. Fortunately the page reproduced tells its own story. The palimpsest contains a text from Isidor of Seville, hence it cannot be of a date earlier than the seventh century, and the use of *thymologiae* for "etymologiae" in the colon shows that it belongs to a much later date. Heinemann thinks that the writing is Visigothic of the eighth century, but there is no reason why it may not be of the ninth. The writing is cursive, but the title of a chapter *"depurpureis"* is in precisely the same handwriting as the underlying Latin text. If one compares the rounded *d, s,* and *e,* the open *p* and *r* with the original writing, the identity is immediately obvious. There is but one possible conclusion from this striking resemblance, — the underlying text is not much older than that of the palimpsest, nay, it may have been written by the same hand, and, as the superscribed text is not earlier than of the eighth century, the Gothic is not older than of the same period.

We have a number of *Ambrosian Fragments* of the Bible with Latin writing over them. One set of such fragments is contained in a quarto Codex of 214 pages, having for its superscription some homilies of Gregory the Great on Ezekiel which Castiglione estimated as of the eighth century.[1] Another Codex, of 156 pages, contains as a superscription St. Jerome's commentary on Isaiah, of the eighth or ninth century.[2] Here, again, there is nothing in the Gothic text to warrant any dating, hence it may be as late as of the ninth century. The remaining five pages of the Ambrosian fragments are apparently of the same date.

I have not touched upon the critical apparatus in all these

[1] *Ulphilae partium ineditarum in ambrosianis palimpsestis ab Angelo Maio repertarum specimen* coniunctis curis eiusdem Maii et Caroli Octavi Castillionaei editum, Mediolani 1819, p. xv.     [2] *Ibid.,* p. xvi.

fragments, because the fact that the Gothic is said to be based chiefly on early Greek sources, instead of the Vulgate, would equally apply to Carolingian times, when Joannes Scottus preferably quoted from the older Greek fathers,[1] and the Visigoth Theodulphus, whose Bibles bear a striking resemblance to the Codex Toletanus,[2] corrected the text in conformity with Hebrew, Greek, and Latin sources.[3] When Ximenes in the eleventh century introduced the Mozarabic Liturgy, he apparently carried out the decree of the Synod of Leon, by abandoning an older, freer Gothic tradition for one more in conformity with the Gallican custom, but that freer Gothic tradition was a survival of an older past which ultimately may go back to Ulfilas, but in the form in which it is preserved to us can represent only the influence of the Gothic writings, and for these we have not been able as yet to find a date previous to Carolingian times.

We now turn to the *Skeireins*, which will definitely settle the period of the Gothic writings.[4] It is assumed that the Skeireins, a polemical commentary on St. John, is based on that of Cyril of Alexandria (about 400) and that it was, therefore, written not earlier than in the middle of the fifth century,[5] while Dietrich insists that the Skeireins may have quoted from the same source as did Cyril, that, therefore, it may still be the work of Ulfilas.[6] Were we to apply this rea-

---

[1] "Sicut in Graeco legitur," Migne, vol. cxxii, col. 298; "nam quod in Graeco scriptum est," 299; "sed si quis intentus Graecum sermonem inspexerit," *ibid.*; "quod enim in Graeco scriptum est," *ibid.*; "vel ut in Graeco scribitur," 302; "in quibusdam codicibus Graecorum singulariter sinus patris dicitur, in quibusdam pluraliter," *ibid.*; "ut in Graeco significantius scribitur," 309; "in codicibus Graecorum ἄνωθεν legitur," 315; "sed in Graeco non est ambiguum," 319; and similarly cols. 283, 285, 287, 292, 295. .

[2] Cuissard, *op. cit.*, p. 194 *f.*

[3] "Quidquid ab haebreo stylus atticus atque latinus
Sumpsit, in hoc totum codice, lector, habes," *Carmina* ii. 1.

[4] For the history of the text see Streitberg, *Elementarbuch*, p. 33 *f.*

[5] E. Bernhardt, *Vulfila oder die gotische Bibel*, Halle 1875, p. 617.

[6] Streitberg, *Die gotische Bibel*, p. xxx.

soning to the Carolingian commentaries on St. John, we could prove, either that they appeared in the fifth century, or that they were composed by Ulfilas, for Cyril of Alexandria is one of the most frequently and most earnestly quoted authors in the ninth century. Alcuin quotes long passages from him; [1] Agobard refers to him as to a good Catholic; [2] Hincmar cites him.[3] Much is made of the fact by Böhmer [4] that, since the Skeireins is a polemic against Sabellius, who died in 260, and Marcellus of Ancyra, who died in 373, it must represent "an older stadium of the Arian controversy" than offered by these Bobbio fragments. We have already seen that Cyril was considered a good Catholic and that, therefore, his being quoted in the Skeireins precludes its being an Arian polemic. But let us waive this argument for a while, and let us see at what conclusions we shall arrive if the fact that Sabellius is quoted represents an older stadium of the Arian controversy. Alcuin quotes him by the side of Arius as a bad heretic; [5] Hincmar couples him with Arius as one of the two extreme heretics; [6] Joannes Scottus refers

[1] "Videamus quid beatus Cyrillus Alexandrinus episcopus . . . de hac inquisitione senserit," Migne, vol. CI, col. 92 f.; "item beatus Cyrillus . . . sic ait," 123; "item Cyrillus . . . inquit," 175; "tamen S. Cyrillus dicit in illo libello quem contra Theodoretum scripsit," 208 f.; "quidquid beatus Cyrillus Alexandrinae Ecclesiae pontifex synodali autoritate respondit Nestorio, vobis responsum esse absque dubio sciatis," 289.

[2] "Inter Nestorium haereticum et Cyrillum catholicum," ibid., vol. CIV, col. 36; "ad quod beatus Cyrillus ita respondit," 40; "ait namque praecipuus ille expugnator Nestorianae impietatis doctissimus et beatissimus Cyrillus," 43, et passim.

[3] Ibid., vol. CXXV, cols. 493, 588.

[4] Streitberg, Elementarbuch, p. 35.

[5] "Conticescat Sabellius audiens: 'Ego et Pater,' qui unam personam Patris et Filii prava doctrina disseruit; nam 'ego et Pater,' duae sunt personae. Item erubescat Arius audiens 'Unum sumus,' qui duas naturas in Patre et Filio astruit, dum 'unum' unam naturam significat, sicut 'sumus,' duas personas," Comment. in Joan. x. 29, in Migne, vol. C, col. 894, also col. 883.

[6] "Quam multi de Trinitate contra Sabellium? quam multi de unitate Trinitatis adversus Arianos, Eunomianos, Macedonianos?" ibid., vol. CXXV, col. 482; "inter insidias horum latronum, Arianorum scilicet et Sabellianorum," 520; "ut beatus Augustinus in supradicto sermone de fide contra Sabellianos

to the Sabellian error of confounding the natures of the Trinity.[1] If all that refers to an older stadium of the Arian controversy, then Alcuin, Hincmar, and Joannes Scottus were Arians, and their works must have appeared in the fifth century. It is obvious that the method pursued by those who made out the Skeireins to be an Arian controversy and placed it in the fifth century must be abandoned by a reductio ad absurdum.

It can be shown that the palaeographic proof of the antiquity of the text is based on no firmer foundation. The MSS. of the Skeireins fragments were found in Rome and in Milan and, like all the other fragments of the Ambrosian Library at Milan, came from the monastery of Bobbio, which was founded about 614. Much weight is put on the fact, to prove the Italian origin of the Gothic MSS., but the assumption is at once negatived from the fact that Bobbio and Milan possessed a large number of Spanish MSS. from Septimania, that is, Gothia, of the tenth century.[2] We are, therefore, prepared to find at Bobbio palaeographic documents of the Carolingian type, written by Visigoths. It can easily be shown that at least the parts of the Skeireins contained in the Vatican Codex 5750 were erased by a Visigoth to make place for a Latin text in the ninth century,[3] that, conse-

et Arianos," 551; "sicuti somnitant Sabelliani . . . ceu latrant Ariani," 589; "sicut impius Sabellius asseruit," 594; also cols. 567 and 598.

[1] "Sabelliani quasi multivocum dicebant patrem et filium et spiritum sanctum. . . . Hic videtur quasi tenebras incurrere et labi in errorem Sabellianorum," E. K. Rand, *Johannes Scottus*, München 1906, p. 39.

[2] "Or nous avons quelque lieu de penser qu'il y a eu, d'autre part, entre la province ecclésiastique de Milan et la côte orientale de l'Espagne, quelque échange de textes bibliques. Des textes qui paraissent espagnols par leur origines ont été en usage, non seulement dans la Septimanie, mais dans la vallée du Rhône jusqu' à Vienne, et cela jusqu' au Xe siècle: il est fort possible que ces textes aient, eux aussi, franchi les Alpes et se soient mêlés à ceux qui, depuis les temps anciens, étaient en possession de l'autorité religieuse dans ce grand et riche pays," S. Berger, *Histoire de la Vulgate*, p. 410.

[3] Thus determined by Massmann (*Skeireins aiwaggeljons þairh Johannen*, München 1834, p. 55). Reifferscheid (*Die römischen Bibliotheken*, in *Sit-*

quently, these parts of the Skeireins are not necessarily older than of the ninth century.

We fortunately possess an excellent reproduction of the whole Codex Vaticanus 5750,[1] which enables us accurately to locate the superscribed text. The Gothic text is contained on pp. 57–62, but it is necessary to discuss the condition of the whole Codex before ascertaining the age of the Gothic script. There are three distinct groups of handwritings to be discerned in the superscribed text, which in the Milan reproduction are given respectively as I, II, III.[2] I, a semi-uncial of the seventh or eighth century,[3] runs pp. 1–4, 13–56, 79–190, 211–274. III, a semi-cursive, of possibly the same date, runs from p. 5 to the middle of p. 11. II occupies half of p. 12, pp. 57–77, 191–210, 275–286. Here majuscule and minuscule letters are mixed. The open *a* is occasionally found (p. 77), but far more generally it is closed; both the straight and round *d* are used; *e* is round, with a horizontal line across; *g* has both arches open; *i* does not run under the line, but *i*-longa is common; *m* is rounded, occasionally turning the last stroke inwardly; *n* is sometimes rounded, but far more commonly the majuscule *n* is used, always in the ligature *nt*; both the long and the rounded *s* are used; *t* sometimes turns the vertical stroke to the right, but far more commonly it has the characteristic Carolingian abruptness; of ligatures we get *nt, st, li; f* and *l* are precisely of the form found in Spanish texts. The palaeographer can-

zungsberichte der *Wiener Akad. d. Wiss.*, vol. LXIII, p. 618), without entering into a discussion of the problem, proclaimed it to be of the seventh or eighth century.

[1] *M. Cornelii Frontonis aliorumque reliquiae quae codice Vaticano 5750 rescripto continentur*, Mediolani 1906.

[2] The editor of the reproduction (p. 19 f.) makes two important mistakes in crediting p. 12 to III, though it is distinctly in the handwriting of II, and in crediting 77–195 to I, although 77, 191–195 are distinctly of the hand II, while 78 is not superscribed.

[3] Thus determined by the editor (p. 21). As I am not studying this text, I do not vouch for the date.

not help but recognise at a glance that the writing is of the end of the eighth century or of the ninth, and the use of *i*-longa proves conclusively that the writing could not be older than the eighth century [1] and is of the Visigothic or Beneventan school. In our text the following words, among others, are written with *i*-longa: *In* (p. 12), *Ipsique* (57), *Iusserat* (195), *Interrogari, Iam* (197), *Incusatus* (198), *Iuxta* (199), *Ita* (201). Unless the work of Loew can be overthrown, our text represents a Carolingian writing of a Visigothic type.

If we now turn to the underlying writing of the II palimpsest, we get some startling results. Page 12 is written over a fragment of Symmachus, the rest of Symmachus being superscribed entirely by hand III. Pages 63 and 64, containing a letter of Gallia Placidia to Pulcheria, and of Valentinianus and Marcianus, are written over a fragment from Juvenal, while the verso of page 78 is not superscribed. Pages 57–62 contain various similar letters over the Gothic Skeireins. All the remaining pages of II are written over Arian fragments. Thus we find that, with the exception of two and a half sheets, all the writings of II are of Gothic origin, the superscription being by a hand trained in the Carolingian school. If we look at the structure of the parchment, we find that the Skeireins and the Arian sheets are of a decidedly different grain from the rest of the parchments. They have coarse markings, like finger prints, running through them, while the fragments of Juvenal, Persius, and Symmachus are of the same structure as the rest of the Codex.

It thus appears that a Spanish Goth, finding many pages of the Codex missing, rewrote the wanting pages over sheets brought with him, which had lost the particular interest they

---

[1] "If we consider on the one hand the utter absence of *i*-longa in the oldest Latin MSS. in uncial and semi-uncial, and its gradual and tentative entrance only into uncial and semi-uncial MSS. of the recent type, i.e., of the 8th and 9th centuries," E. A. Loew, *Studia palaeographica*, in *Sitzungsberichte d. k. Bayerischen Akad. d. Wiss.*, München 1910, p. 4.

may have had in Gothia or Spain, for they contained writings in which only Goths could have been interested. Two sheets, where his writing material gave out, he supplied by writing over fragments of Juvenal and Persius, apparently of Italian origin, while he utilised the unused verso of hand III to fill in a brief letter. As many of the Arian fragments have records of the Council of Chalcedon written over them, the *Ambrosian Codex E. Sig. E. 147*, which contains the remaining fragments of the Skeireins, under the records of the Council of Chalcedon, belongs to the same text and was obviously made by the same writer, and the reproduction of a few lines from this Codex by Castiglione [1] shows that the writing is identical with that of the Codex Vaticanus. We are entitled to but one conclusion as to the age of the Gothic text of the Skeireins, namely, that it was written before the superscribed Latin and may be of as late a date as the ninth century. We are palaeographically entitled to no other assumption.

· Massmann [2] comes to the conclusion that the Skeireins is a polemic writing of semi-Arian character, because of the use of the homoousian by the side of the homoiousian formula, that is, because of the use of *ibns* and *galeiks* in the same passage. Krafft [3] is equally sure that the Skeireins is pure Arian in doctrine. But it is not difficult to show that the use of the two terms has nothing whatsoever to do with the homoousian and homoiousian formulae, and that these terms refer to the honor due Christ, in the sense in which they were taken by the Carolingian writers in the attack upon the Adoptionist heresy of the Goths, in order to establish an Orthodox, and not an Arian, doctrine.

The passage in question (page v), according to Dietrich's

[1] *Op. cit.*, p. 36.   [2] *Op. cit.*, p. 75 *f.*
[3] *Die Anfänge der christlichen Kirche bei den germanischen Völkern*, Berlin 1854, vol. I, p. 357.

translation,[1] runs as follows: "But since he (specified) one
as loving, the other as loved, the one as showing, the other as
imitating his work — he so specified it, since he knew of the
heresy of these future men, in order that one might learn
from it to recognize two persons, that of the Father and of
the Son, and did not repeat (what the others say). In this
respect he used a clear word and said: 'Even as the Father
raises the dead and brings them to life,' in order that He,
who by His own will and His own power imitating the One
who before had commanded to raise the dead, should con-
demn and overthrow the disputation of the unbelievers (with
these words): 'The Father in no way judges, but has given
all the judgment over to His Son.' If he were one and the
same according to the teaching of Sabellius, (only designated by different names), how could He both judge and not
judge? Does not the mere change of the names indicate the
difference of the two persons, especially the action of one
who does not judge a single man, but transfers the judgment
to the Son? And Jesus, who receives the honor from His
Father and executes all judgment according to God's will,
said : 'That all may honor the Son as they honor the Father.'
Hence, in the presence of so clear a statement, we must
honor the unborn God, and recognize that the one-born Son
is God, so that we may honor each according to His worth;
for the statement, 'That all may honor the Son as they
honor the Father,' teaches us to give, not equal, but similar
honor. The Saviour Himself interceded for His disciples
before His Father 'That Thou mayest love them as Thou
lovest me.' Not equal, but similar, love He designated in
this way."

Charlemagne called Alcuin to France to fight the Adoptionist heresy among the Spanish Goths in his possessions.
The Orthodox Alcuin felt that, in fighting Elipandus and

[1] *Die Skeireins Bruchstücke*, Strassburg 1900, p. 11.

Felix of Urgel, and in attacking their dogma that Christ was an adopted son, he ran great danger of falling into the other extreme of the Eutychian heresy. Hence he tried to steer a middle course and dwelt upon the fact that Christ was in substance both the same and not the same with God, hence should have equal glory with him. The ecclesiastic writers of the ninth century had great trouble in drawing a distinction between the terms "similar" and "equal." Joannes Scottus, commenting on Boethius' *De Trinitate*, points out that equality exists where there are two persons, and that their relation is similar.[1] The difficulty with the Adoptionists was that they maintained that Christ's nature was dissimilar to that of God, while the Orthodox Agobard insisted that it was similar,[2] even as Hincmar distinguished between the two persons whose glory, however, was equal.[3] Similarly Alcuin pointed out to the Adoptionists that the Son was equal to God.[4]

We see from these passages that "similar" and "equal" interchange, and refer, now to the person of Christ, now to his glory. In the passage in the Skeireins the duality of the persons is proved from the fact that God is represented as loving, Christ as beloved. This is taken from Alcuin who uses the Biblical passage "Hic est Filius meus dilectus, in quo mihi bene complacui" over and over again in his Adoptionist controversy, in order to prove that the two persons are

[1] "*Aequale* ut binarius. *Similis* est relatio quia *aequales* sunt," E. K. Rand, *Johannes Scottus*, p. 46.

[2] "Iterum post aliqua interrogando Felix quaerit: 'Utrum Christus Dominus in utraque natura similiter sit Filius Dei an dissimiliter,' et subjungit respondendo, 'non similiter, sed dissimiliter,'" *Liber adversum dogma Felicis Urgellensis*, in Migne, vol. civ, col. 44.

[3] "Alia est persona Patris, alia Filii, alia Spiritus Sancti: sed in deitate unitas creditur et predicatur, quia Patris et Filii et Spiritus Sancti una est divinitas, aequalis gloria, coaeternia majestas," Migne, vol. cxxv, col. 525.

[4] "Et multa talia, ubi se in divina substantia omnino Patri aequalem et Patris esse Filium non tacuit," *Adversus Felicem Urgellitanum libri septem*, in Migne, vol. ci, col. 143.

separate yet similar.[1] The words in the Skeireins, "he so specified it, since he knew of the heresy of these future men, in order that one might learn from it to recognize two persons, that of the Father and of the Son, and did not repeat (what others say)," are taken bodily from Alcuin's Commentary on St. John x. 29, of which they are an abbreviated statement.[2] Similarly the rest of the Skeireins passage is based on Alcuin's Commentary on St. John v. 21, 22, 23, where it says that God and Christ do not judge in separate capacities, but as one. The Father does not judge, but Christ, in His second nature, in which He is consubstantial with the Mother. Only the Son is seen to sit in judgment. And yet, the Father is not to be judged as greater, the Son as smaller, but both by one honor. "Honor the Son as you honor the Father."[3] The point is not clearly stated by Alcuin, for it

[1] Migne, vol. CI, cols. 143, 144, 145, 146, 157, 162, 255, 256.

[2] "Quibus profecto verbis non praesentem solummodo Judaeorum quaestionem, qua an ipse esset Christus interrogabant, explicavit, *sed etiam haereticorum perfidiam quam futuram praevidit,* quantum sit execranda monstravit. 'Conticescat Sabellius audiens Ego et Pater, qui unam personam Patris et Filii prava doctrina disseruit, nam ego et Pater, duae sunt personae. Item erubescat Arius audiens: Unum sumus, qui duas naturas in Patre et Filio astruit, dum unum unam naturam significat, sicut sumus, duas personas. Sequamur apostolicam fidem, quam beatus Petrus princeps apostolorum confessus est," Migne, vol. C, col. 893 *f.*

[3] "Sicut enim Pater suscitat mortuos et vivificat, sic et Filius quos vult vivificat. Non enim alios Pater, alios Filius vivificat; sed una potestas unam vivificationem facit; quae etiam potestas uno honore honoranda est . . . Pater enim non judicat quemquam, sed omne judicium dedit Filio, ut omnes honorificent Filium, sicut honorificant Patrem. Qui non honorificat Patrem, non honorificat Filium. Pater non judicat quemquam, quia Patris persona hominem non suscepit, nec in judicio videbitur: sed sola Filii persona, in ea forma quae judicata est injuste, et juste judicabit vivos ac mortuos. Nec enim Filius videbitur in judicio in ea natura qua consubstantialis est Deo Patri, sed in ea qua consubstantialis est matri, et homo factus est. . . . Sed ne forte Patrem quidem honorifices tanquam majorem, Filium vero tanquam minorem, ut dicas mihi: Honorifico Patrem; scio enim quod habeat Filium, et non erro in Patris nomine, non enim Patrem intelligo sine Filio, honorifico tamen et Filium tanquam minorem: corrigit te ipse Filius, et revocat dicens: Ut omnes honorificent Filium, non inferius sed sicud honorificant Patrem. Qui ergo non honorificat Filium, nec Patrem honorificat, qui misit illum. Ego, inquis, ma-

may appear, at first sight, that he wants Christ to be honored exactly as God (uno honore honoranda est), but this is merely due to an over-emphasis against the Adoptionist view that the honor should be different. Agobard, in his controversy with the Adoptionists, tried to avoid the difficulty of the emphasis, which would have taken him from Nestorianism to the opposite heresy of Eutychianism, by adhering for the orthodox dogma to Cyril, who took a middle course.[1] Hence Cyril is one of the authors most quoted by the theologians of the ninth century, even as he forms the basis of certain ideas and expressions in the Skeireins. But Cyril in this particular case distinctly says that "sicut, καθώς" shows that Christ is to be honored, not equally, but similarly, even as the statement "let the silver shine like (καθώς) the sun" shows that

jorem honorem volo dare Patri, minorem Filio. Ibi tollis honorem Patri, ubi minorem das Filio. Quid enim tibi aliud videtur ista sententia, nisi quia Pater aequalem sibi Filium generare aut noluit aut non potuit? Si noluit, invidit; si non potuit, defecit. Non ergo vides, quia ita est sentiendum: Ubi majorem honorem vis dare Patri, ibi es contumeliosus in Patrem. Proinde sic honorifica Filium, quomodo honorificas Patrem, si vis honorificare et Filium et Patrem," *ibid.*, col. 810 *f*.

[1] "Nestorius haereticus sic duas naturas in unico Filio Dei Domino nostro Jesu Christo dividit ac separat, ut in disputatione dogmatis sui sic de uno quasi de duobus loquatur, quasi alium suspicans Deum Verbum, alium Emmanuel, licet plerumque unam horum fateatur personam. E contrario autem Eutyches in dogmate suo sic de unici Filii Dei loquitur singulari persona quasi de una substantia. Et quanquam sempiternam divinitatis ejus nativitatem confiteatur, temporalem quoque humanitatis non neget; ita tamen utramque substantiam permiscet atque confundit, et una tantummodo praedicare intelligatur. Cum ergo utrumque, id est, Nestorium, et Eutychem, veritus fidei abjiciat, quae medium inter eos tenet locum; beatus Cyrillus, Alexandrinus antistes, dum vellet corrigere pravitatem Nestorii, propter obscuritatem verborum, ut pote subtilissimae rei, offendit beatum Joannem praesulem Antiochenae Ecclesiae, et eos qui cum illo erant; factaque est divisio inter Antiochenam et Alexandrinam Ecclesiam. Rogatus est autem ab Antiochenis Theodoretus Cyri episcopus, ut ageret adversum beatum Cyrillum. Et mirum in modum, dum utrique essent catholici, id est, et Antiocheni, et Alexandrini, beatus Cyrillus dum putatur esse haereticus, quod non erat, inventus est a Theodoreto inter Nestorium haereticum et Cyrillum catholicum medius locus, unde idem Theodoretus pugnans pro veritate, ageret contra veritatem; qui dum istis catholicis placeret, illis displiceret; quod tamen Deo auxiliante Joannis et Cyrilli industria correctum est," Migne, vol. civ, col. 35 *f*.

the silver has not an equal, but a similar splendor to that of the sun.[1]

While the manner of the treatment of the Skeireins passage is very much like that of Alcuin's corresponding verses, the fine distinction between *aequalis* and *similis*, which is dogmatically identical with Cyril's ideas, smacks of Johannes Scottus' "similis est relatio quia aequales sunt"; but unfortunately the fifth chapter of his Commentary on St. John is not extant, and so this identity in the same passage cannot be verified. It is significant that the Skeireins, which is an anti-Adoptionist pamphlet, is at the same time based on the Gospel of St. John. The latter was frequently commented upon by Carolingian writers, because it was theologically well adapted for the Adoptionist controversy, and Schönbach[2] has shown that the great bulk of Gospel commentaries of the Middle Ages, especially the Commentary on St. John, were based on those of Alcuin.

The passage under discussion has been used by Gothic

---

[1] "Εἰ διὰ τὸ λέγεσθαι, φησίν· 'Ίνα πάντα τιμῶσι τὸν Υἱὸν, καθὰ τιμῶσι τὸν Πατέρα', νομίζετε χρῆναι τὸν Υἱὸν ἰσομέτροις τῷ Πατρὶ καταθεμνύνειν τιμαῖς, ἀγνοεῖτε τῆς ἀληθείας μακράν που βαδίζοντες. Οὐ γὰρ πάντως τὸ 'καθὼς' ἰσότητα πραγμάτων εἰσφέρει, καθ' ὧν ἄν φαίνοιτο τεθέν, ὁμοίωσιν δέ τινα χαρακτηρίζει πολλάκις, οἷον, φησὶν, ὁ Σωτήρ που συμβουλεύει, λέγων Γίνεσθε οἰκτίρμονες, καθὼς καὶ ὁ Πατὴρ ὑμῶν ὁ οὐράνιος οἰκτίρμων ἐστίν.' Οὐκοῦν ἐπὶ μὲν τῶν ἀνομοίων κατὰ τὴν φύσιν ὅτε τάττεται τὸ 'καθὼς', οὐ πάντως ἀπαράλλακτον ἡμῖν εἰσφέρει τὴν ἰσότητα, ὁμοιότητα δὲ μᾶλλον καὶ εἰκονισμὸν, ὡς καὶ αὐτοὶ προλαβόντες ὡμολογήκατε. Ἐπὶ δὲ τῶν ἀλλήλοις κατὰ πάντα προσεικότων εἴπερ ὅρῷτο τεθέν, καὶ ἰσότητα τὴν ἐν πᾶσι καὶ ὁμοιότητα δηλοῖ, καὶ εἴ τι τούτοις ἕτερον ἰσοδυναμοῦν εὑρίσκεται. Οἷόν τί φημι. Λαμπρὸς μὲν ὁ κατ' οὐρανόν ἐστιν ἥλιος, λαμπρὸς δὲ ὁμοίως καὶ ὁ γῆθεν ἄργυρος, ἀλλ' ἡ μὲν φύσις τῶν εἰρημένων διάφορος. Νοείσθω δέ τις τυχὸν τῶν ἐπὶ γῆς πλουσίων, τοῖς κατ' οἶκον οἰκέταις, Λαμπέτω, λέγων, ὁ ἄργυρος, καθὼς καὶ ὁ ἥλιος· ἐν τούτῳ δὴ μάλα δικαίως οὐκ εἰς τὴν ἴσην ἀναβαίνειν λαμπρότητα τῷ ἡλίῳ τὴν ἐκ γῆς ὕλην φαμέν, ἀλλ' εἰς ὁμοίωσίν τινα καὶ ἐμφέρειαν, καὶ εἰ φέροιτο κατ' αὐτοῦ τὸ 'καθὼς'," Ἑρμηνεία εἰς τὸ κατὰ Ἰωάννην Εὐαγγέλιον, V. 22, in Migne, vol. LXXIII, col. 366.

[2] A. E. Schönbach, *Über einige Evangelienkommentare des Mittelalters*, in *Sitzungsberichte d. k. Akad., d. Wiss.*, Wien 1903, vol. CXLVI, part IV.

scholars to prove its relation to Ulfilas' Arianism, of which
as we have seen, not a distant trace is to be found, unless
Alcuin, Agobard, and Scot were Arians. There is not a
shadow of homoousianism or homoiousianism in the use of
the words *ibns* and *galeiks*, because the Latin equivalents
*aequalis* and *similis* have nothing whatsoever to do with the
nature of Christ, but refer only to the honor due him. What
the Skeireins and the Carolingian theologians were discussing is all a question of ὁμοιοτιμία, not of ὁμοιουσία.

There is another passage in the Skeireins, on page i, which
has been adduced by Gothic scholars as a proof that the
polemic was written at an early time. The dogmatic purpose
of this part is summarised as follows by Dietrich:[1] "To
judge from the discussion on page i in regard to salvation and
atonement, which are essentially based on Irenaeus, Christ
had a double problem. In accordance with the plan of salvation, as intended by God from the start, Christ was to become man while exercising justice; for He was not to free
humanity by force from death and from the power of the
devil by means of His divine power. He was to be as just
towards the devil in the execution of His work of salvation.
As the devil had not forced anybody to commit sin, so Christ
in justice could not force men to be converted to piety, but
was by words and work to invite humanity that had turned
away from God to follow the tenets of the Gospel, so as to
please God. But men were to turn away from the devil and
accept the teachings of the Saviour by their own free will.
But this did not conclude His work of salvation. He had to
atone to God, who was offended by the sins, by an extraordinary sacrifice. Hence Christ sacrificed himself in place
of all humanity, destroyed all sin, and saved the world."
Dietrich confesses that the resemblance to Irenaeus' theology is weak, because Irenaeus considers Christ's death as a

---

[1] E. Dietrich, *Die Bruchstücke der Skeireins*, Strassburg 1908, p. lxxvii *f*.

ransom paid to the devil for enslaved humanity,[1] while Jellinek,[2] who also knows that the theology has no resemblance to any fourth or fifth century theology but that of Irenaeus, admits that the particular passage in Irenaeus could only be adduced if the construction "be understood or misunderstood" in the sense of the Skeireins. What an amazing performance! Gothic theology, according to these authors, is based, not on the theology of its age, but on a misunderstanding in Irenaeus! The idea is too ridiculous to need any refutation.

The idea that Christ is justice itself and has come to justify men by His death, is the usual theology of Alcuin. I give here in parallel columns Massmann's Latin translation of the Skeireins and the passage in Alcuin:

| *Skeireins* | *Alcuin* |
|---|---|
| Propterea venit communis omnium salvator, omnium peccata ut expurgaret; non aequalis nec similis nostrae *justitiae* sed ipse *justitia* existens, ut mactans se pro nobis victimam et sacrificium, deo mundi perficeret redemptionem . . . propterea igitur corpus hominis induit, ut praeceptor nobis fieret *justitiae* in deo. | Ecce agnus Dei, ecce innocens ab omni peccato immunis, ut pote qui os quidem de ossibus Adam et carnem de carne peccatrice traxit maculam culpae. Ecce qui tollit peccata mundi; ecce qui *justus* inter peccatores, mitis inter impios, hoc est, quasi agnus inter lupos apparens, etiam peccatores et impios *justificandi* habeat potestatem. Quomodo autem peccata mundi tollat, quo ordine *justificet* impios, apostolus Petrus ostendit, qui ait: "Non corruptilibus, argento vel auro redempti estis de vana vestra conversatione paternae traditionis, sed pretioso sanguine, quasi agni incontaminati, et immaculati Jesu Christi (I Petr. I. 18. 19), *Comm. in Joan.* I. 29, in Migne vol. c, col. 755 *f*. |

[1] E. Dietrich, *Die Bruchstücke der Skeireins*, Strassburg 1908, p. lxxviii
[2] Paul and Braune, *Beiträge*, vol. xv, p. 439 *f*.

That Christ is justice and, therefore, he who escapes sin becomes a servant of justice, is several times expressed by
Alcuin.[1] But as man became bad only by imitation,[2] so he
can become good only by receding of his own free will from
the devil, but justice demands that Christ should not take
men over from the devil by force, but that the devil should
be conquered by the truth of justice. It is significant that this
latter point is made by Alcuin in his controversial writing
against the Adoptionists. If we now compare the rest of the
Skeireins passage with the corresponding passages in Alcuin, we find a perfect agreement in doctrine:

| *Skeireins* | *Alcuin* |
|---|---|
| Quod igitur videns Johannes con-silium, quod perfici debebat a do-mino vero dixit Ecce hic' est agnus dei, qui tollit peccatum mundi. Potuisset quidem etiam sine homi-nis corpore, potestate solummodo divina' libera re omnes diaboli vi; sed sciebat, tale potestate potentiae necessitatem declaratam fore, neque amplius servatum iustitiae consil-ium, sed necessitate se operaturum fuisse hominum salutem. Quum enim diabolus ab initio non cogeret, | Omnis enim qui in Deo manet, in verita te manet, quia Deus veritas est. Si quis a vero a Deo recesserit, mendax erit, dicente Psalmographo: Omnis homo mendax (Psal. cxv). In quantum vero homo a Deo re-cedit, in tantum mendax erit, dum se a veritate declinaverit, et inde peccator erit: quia omne peccatum non est veritas, sed mendacium, quia recedendo a Deo non habet veritatem Diabolus vero bonus creatus est, sed per se ipsum malus |

[1] "Ille solus liberare potest de peccato, qui venit sine peccato, et factus est sacrificium pro peccato. Qui manet in peccato servus est peccati, qui fugit a peccato, servus est justitiae," *ibid.*, viii. 34, in Migne, col. 869; "prima libertas est non permanere in peccato, servire justitiae, dicente Apostolo: Cum servi essetis peccati, liberi eratis justitiae" (Rom. vi. 20), *ibid.*, viii. 36, in Migne, col. 869.

[2] "Quidquid a Deo creatum est, bonum est, et omnis homo, quantum crea-tura Dei est, bonus est: quantum vero se subjicit per liberum arbitrium diabolo, a patre diabolo est. Bona est enim hominis natura, sed vitiata erat per malam voluntatem, et inde a patre erat diabolo. Quod fecit Deus non potest esse malum, si ipse homo non sit sibi malus. Inde ergo Iudaei dicti sunt filii dia-boli, non nascendo, sed imitando," *Comm. in Joan.* viii. 43, in Migne, col. 872; "si veritatem locutus sum vobis, quare non creditis mihi, nisi quia filii diaboli estis, et non veritatis, filii diaboli non natura, sed imitatione," *ibid.*, viii. 46, in Migne, col. 873.

sed deciperet hominem et per mendacium illiceret ut transgrederentur legem, id fuisset contra convenientiam, ut dominus veniens vi divina et potestate eum liberaret et necessitate ad probitatem converteret. Nonne enim visus esset in justitiae coercitione impedire consilium antea iam initio paratum? Decens igitur erat potius, qui sua voluntate obediissent diabolo ad negligendam legem dei, ut ii iterum sua voluntate assentirent Salvatoris doctrinae et aspernarentur pravitatem ejus, qui prius decepisset, veritatis autem cognitio ad renovationem conversationis in deo proponeretur.

factus est, declinando se a summo bono. Ideo ex propriis locutus est mendacium, quia in seipso invenit unde esset mendax. Homo vero deceptus a diabolo, factus est a diabolo mendax. Ideoque filius diaboli, non natura, sed imitatione. Recedamus ergo a patre mendacii, curramus ad Patrem veritatis. Amplectamur veritatem ut accipiamus veram libertatem, *Comm. in Joan.* VIII. 44, in Migne, col. 873.

Ita quippe nil in eo baptismus quod ablueret, sicut mors nihil quod puniret, invenit, ut diabolus veritate justitiae vinceretur, non violentia potestatis opprimeretur, *Adv. Elipandum epistola*, in Migne, vol. CI, col. 238.

Page II of the Skeireins coincides with Alcuin completely on the dogmatic side, for both assert that the heavenly rebirth follows baptism, and both agree that water represents the carnal, the Holy Spirit the spiritual regeneration:

*Skeireins*

Propterea quoque Salvator, nunc incipiens monstravit viam sursum ducentem in regnum Dei, dicens Amen, dico tibi, nisi quis nascatur desuper non potest videre regnum dei. Desuper autem dixit sanctum et coelestem natum alterum per lavacrum patiendum. Quod autem non intellexit Nicodemus, quia tunc primum audiebat a praeceptore, quapropter dixit: Quomodo potest homo nasci, adultus existens? num potest in uterum matris suae iterum introire et nasci? imperitus enim adhuc (existens) neque sciens consuetudinem et corporalem (natu-

*Alcuin*

Respondit enim Jesus, et dixit ei: Amen amen dico vobis: Nisi quis renatus fuerit denuo, non potest videre regnum Dei. Quae sententia tanto apertius cunctis fidelibus lucet, quanto constat quia sine hujus luce fideles esse nequeunt. Quis etenim sine lavacro regenerationis, remissionem peccatorum consequi, et regnum valet introire coelorum? Sed Nicodemus, qui nocte venit ad Jesum, necdum lucis mysteria capere noverat; nam et nox, in qua venit, ipsam ejus qua premebatur ignorantiam designat. .. Respondit ergo Dominus, et

ralem) ex utero existimans ortum, in dubitationem cecidit; quapropter dixit: Quomodo potest homo adultus nasci? num potest in uterum matris suae rursus introire et nasci? Salvator autem, futuro ejus judicio cognito, et in fide progressus (eum) facturum esse, interpretatus est ei, ut adhuc imperito, dicens: Amen, amen, dico tibi, nisi quis nascatur ex aqua et Spiritu, non potest introire in regnum dei. Necessarium enim erat et conveniens naturae, ut consilium baptismi acciperet, quum quidem homo (ex) diversis naturis compositus si (constet), (ex) anima scilicet et corpore; etiam alterum eorum ratione (vestigio) etiam duas nominavit res, suam utrique ad baptismi consilium, et visibilem quidem aquam et rationalem Spiritum, ut nempe hoc videntes.

ait: Quomodo potest homo nasci cum senex sit? Numquid potest in ventrem matris suae iterato introire et nasci? Quia secundae nativitatis adhuc nescius perseverabat . . quaerebat, ne hujus expers remanendo, vitae coelestis particeps esse nequiret. . . Et quia Nicodemus ad primam Domini responsionem sollicitus, quomodo sit intelligenda diligenter inquirit, meretur jam planius instrui, et quia secunda nativitas non carnalis est, sed spiritalis, audire? respondit namque illi Jesus: Amen amen dico tibi, nisi quis renatus fuerit ex aqua et Spiritu, non potest introire in regnum Dei. . . Natura spiritus invisibilis, carnis est visibilis; atque ideo carnalis generatio visibiliter administratur visibilibus incrementis. . . Quod ergo natum est ex spiritu, spiritus est; quia qui ex aqua et Spiritu regeneratur, invisibiliter in novum mutatur hominem, et de carnali efficitur spiritalis, *Comm. in Joan.* III. 3, 4, 5, in Migne, col. 778 f.

It will be observed that Alcuin, quoting the Vulgate, which speaks of a regeneration *denuo*, anew, none the less proceeds to consider the rebirth as *desursum*, upwards, into Heaven, into the spiritual sphere.[1] Alcuin was bound by the Vulgate text, while the Goths, following an old Spanish tradition, drew equally from Latin and Greek sources. Joannes Scottus, who, like Theodulphus, was not bound by the Vulgate tradition, is, therefore, in this passage in complete agreement with the Skeireins, for he points out that the Greek text distinctly

---

[1] "Nisi quis renatus fuerit *denuo* . . . quis *regnum* valet introire *coelorum?*" See p. lviii.

shows that one regeneration is terrestrial, the other celestial,[1] which is also Alcuin's theology.[2]

᠎ The remaining passages in the Skeireins contain no dogmatic ideas of importance, and so need not be discussed. But the beginning of page II is so strikingly like the corresponding passage in Alcuin that a mere chance resemblance is excluded: [3]

| Skeireins | Alcuin |
|---|---|
| Quia aquae multae erant illic. et veniebant et baptizabantur nondum missus fuerat in carcerem Johannes. Id autem dicens Evangelista ostendit, munus ei datum prope finem esse ᵖer Herodis consilium. | Quia aquae multae erant . . . Nondum enim missus fuerat Joannes in carcerem. Ideo hoc dixit Evangelista, ut intelligeretur, quae ante posuit, primo anno doctrinae Domini nostri Jesu Christi, quae incipiebat a baptismo suo, acta esse, *Comm. in Joan.* III. 23, 24, Migne col. 785. |

The writer of the Skeireins bears, in his methods, a striking resemblance to the author of the Augiensis MS. in his treatment of Alcuin. Here and there sentences have crept in almost in the form in which they occur in the original, but on the whole the wording is materially changed. The theology and the general concept have remained absolutely the same.[4]

---

[1] "Notandum, quod in codicibus Graecorum ἄνωθεν legitur, ubi in latinis codicibus denuo reperitur, ut sit sensus: nisi quis natus fuerit ἄνωθεν, hoc est desursum, ut desursum dicamus pro denuo; quod et facilius intelligitur, et duabus nativitatibus, terrenae videlicet atque coelesti, covenientius. . . Duae siquidem nativitates sunt, ut ait Augustinus; quarum una de terra, altera de caelo, hoc est desursum," *Comm. in Joan.*, in Migne, vol. CXXII, col. 315.

[2] "Coelestis namque est ascensio ejus ad vitam sempiternam," *Comm. in Joan.* III. 12, in Migne, col. 780.

[3] Note the very striking resemblance of "since he knew the heresy of these future men" to "sed etiam haereticorum perfidiam quam futuram praevidit" in the identical passage. See p. l and p. lii.

[4] "Für das Werk im ganzen und grossen gilt die Behauptung, dass er auf Alchuins Johanneskommentar beruht, und zwar so ausschliesslich darauf beruht, dass — ohne Übertreibung — nicht ein Gedanke anderswoher entnommen ist . . . der Bearbeiter hat durch einen grossen Theil seines Werkes zwar

Unfortunately Schönbach gives but a brief extract from this MS., and it is not possible to determine what relation it bears to the Skeireins. But so much is certain, — the Skeireins is based on Alcuin, hence it cannot have been written before 801, when Alcuin's Commentary on St. John first appeared. It is doubtful whether the Skeireinist utilised Joannes Scottus, for the few possible agreements with the latter have only to do with the use of the Greek original, which is not excluded in the case of Alcuin or any other Carolingian theologian. It is, however, likely that the Skeireins was not written before 813, for in that year Charlemagne demanded that homilies be written in the native tongue, and that would include the Gothic of Gothia and of Burgundy. As the Skeireins quotes passages from the Gothic New Testament with fair correctness, it is to be supposed that the Gothic Bible was written before that time. That it was not written before the end of the eighth century will appear from internal evidence.

den ganzen Inhalt der Darstellung seiner Vorlage entnommen, hat jedoch den Worthalt nicht beibehalten, er hat den Text Alchuins umstilisiert," Schönbach, *op. cit.*, p. 114.

# COMMENTARY TO THE GERMANIC LAWS
# AND MEDIAEVAL DOCUMENTS

## SOCIO FISCO

In the Theodosian Code there is mention of certain fines which are to be paid to the fiscus, and the formulae in which these fines occur run in stereotyped forms through the documents of the Middle Ages. The expression "Sinceritas tua reiectum quinque libras auri *fisco utilitatibus cogat inferre*," [1] to which the *Interpretatio* says "*quinque libras fisco inferre cogatur*," [2] has given rise to the formula *cogente fisco*. [3] Since it was a mere phrase without any very distinct meaning, it has been strengthened by the redundant *coactus*,[4] and for *cogente fisco* another equivalent phrase could be put, such as *distringente*,[5] *indiscutienti*,[6] *egenti*,[7] *posito* [8] *fisco*, which was still further expanded or corrupted into *cum fisco*,[9] *una cum*

[1] I. 9. 1. Similarly I. 11. 1, VI. 28. 4, VI. 30. 10, IX. 17. 4, IX. 21. 4, XIV. 3. 20.

[2] *Ibid.*, and II. 23.

[3] The ablative absolute is already to be found in *Cod. Theod.* III. 1: "*fisco vindicante*."

[4] "Deinde *cogente fisco* auri libras 15. argenti pondera 30. *coactus* exsolvat" (858), Ducange, sub *fiscus*.

[5] "Qui hoc agere temptaverit, inferat cum *distringente fisco* argenti pondera V, aurique libram unam *coactus* exsolvat" (813), Devic and Vaissete, *Histoire de Languedoc*, vol. II, Preuves, col. 79.

[6] "*Indiscutieni fisco* multa conponat" (764), *Urkundenbuch der Abtei Sanct Gallen*, Zürich 1863, vol. I, p. 43, and very often. "Inferat partibus vestris ... *fisco discutiente* multa conponat" (794), *Bibliothèque de l'École des chartes*, sér. 2, vol. III, p. 416.

[7] "Duplex satisfactione *fisco egenti* exsolvat" (627), *Bibl. d. l'Ec. des chartes*, vol. VI, p. 52.

[8] "Et insuper *posito fisco* ... *coactus* exsolvat," *MGH.*, *Formulae*, p. 107.

[9] "Inferat vobis *cum fisco* auri libras duas," Doniol, *Cartulaire de Brioude*, p. 107.

*fisco,*[1] *servanti una cum fisco,*[2] *una cum cogente fisco.*[3] Apparently the vague idea connected with such a formula was this: that one was to pay by compulsion of the fiscus, or, since the stipulatio duplae was divided up with the fiscus, that both the person in question and the fiscus were to be paid, as is frequently mentioned more specifically,[4] wherfore also the combination *inter tibi et fisco* is met with.[5]

In reality, however, all these combinations have resulted from another, *socio fisco,* which has been understood to mean *"*in company with the fiscus.*"* But *socio fisco* has arisen from the employment of *sociare* in the Theodosian Code in the sense of "to appropriate," [6] which, in the combinations "fisci viribus, fisco *sociare"* has the distinct significance of "to confiscate." [7]  In the Visigothic laws the expression "fisco, fisci partibus, fisci viribus *sociare"* is the usual technical term of confiscation,[8] which is also used in the other

---

[1] "Qui hoc egerit aut quicumque tentaverit *una cum fisco* auri libram unam persolvat," *ibid.*, p. 226.

[2] "Inferat parte statuta *servanti una cum fisco"* (626), *Bibl. d. l'Ec. des chartes*, vol. LI, p. 49.

[3] "*Una cum cogente fisco* multa conponat" (794), *ibid.*, sér. 2, vol. III, p. 418, "inferamus tibi *cum cogenti fisco* duplum," *MGH., Formulae*, pp. 89, 90.

[4] "Medietate palacio nostro, et medietate predictae congregationi" (818), *Historiae Patriae Monumenta*, vol. XIII, col. 176.

[5] "Inferit *inter tibi et fisco* soledus tantus vobis conponat," *MGH., Formulae*, p. 5: "inferat *inter tibi et fisco* soledus tantus, vobis conponit," *ibid.*, p. 6; "inferit *inter tibi et fisco* . . . exsolvat," *ibid.*, p. 11; "inferit *inter vobis et fisco*, conponere debiat," *ibid.*, pp. 13, 23, etc.

[6] "Si quis libertum emere ut servum, vel qualibet manumissione donatum inquietare voluerit, non solum bona sua largitionibus nostris iussimus *sociari*," *App.* XIX.

[7] "Fundum ipsum . . . fisci viribus *sociandum"* (403), VII. 18. 12; "fisco eius omne patrimonium *sociari* decernimus" (446), IX. 26. 4; "alioquin patrimonio suo fisco *sociato"* (401), IX. 42. 18; "proprietate privetur, ea videlicet fiscalibus calculis *socianda"* (404), X. 22. 5.

[8] "Omnem vero substantiam suam heredibus occisi iuxta legis superioris ordinem iubemus addici, aut etiam *fisco* . . . *sociari*," VI. 5. 18; "quisquis de Iudeis sub nomine proprietatis fraudulenta suggestione aliquid a precessoribus nostris visus est promeruisse . . . *fisco nostro faciatis sociari*," XII. 2. 13; "facultas predictorum omnimoda . . . *fisco nostro sociata* deserviat," XII. 3. 8; "m01edietatem rerum suarum *fisco sociandum* amittant"; XII. 3. 12, 13, and 17;

Germanic laws [1] and in Merovingian edicts. [2] From the formula *distringente fisco*, under the influence of *sociare*, has developed *sociante fisco*, [3] which has led to *socio fisco* with its many extravagancies. [4]

The Frankish documents record the variant *satiare*, *saziare* from the seventh century on. [5] In the ninth century we hear of a formula of arrest *prendere et saziare*, [6] which, however, is already used in the *Pactus Alamannorum* in the form *sisit et priserit*, [7] where *sisit* may have been influenced by "*exigere*." [8] That this *saziare* was developed from the form-

"decimam partem rei sue *fisci partibus sociandam* amittat," xii. 1. 3 and *Conc. Tolet.* xii; "totum *fisci erit viribus sociandum*," xii. 2. 18; "res eius *fisci viribus sociande* sunt," xii. 3. 4.

[1] "Alia medietas propter admissam violentiam *fisci viribus societur*," *Lex Burgund.*, *lex romana*, viii; "et res eius *in fisco socientur*," *Leg. Langob.*, *Lib. Pap.*, v ff.

[2] "Facultates eorum propinquis haeredibus *socientur*" (614), Bouquet, *Recueil des historiens des Gaules*, vol. iv, p. 119.

[3] "*Sociante fisco* multa conponat" (745), *Urkb. d. Abtei Sanct Gallen*, vol. i, p. 13; "*una cum sociante fisco* ... coactus exsolvat" (777), J. Tardif, *Monuments historiques*, Paris 1866, p. 62; "inferat ad ipsum sanctum locum heredum meam *sociantem fisco* auri libras quinquaginta" (739), C. Cipolla, *Monumenta novaliciensia vetustiora*, Roma 1898, vol. i, p. 37.

[4] "Inferat *socio fisco* auri liberas viginti" (671), Tardif, *op. cit.*, p. 16; "inter te et *socium fisco* ... conponat" (769), *ibid.*, p. 55; "*sotio fisco* ... coactus exsolvat" (833), *Gallia christiana*, vol. ii, Instrumenta, col. 165; "*una cum sotio fisco* ... quoactus exsolvat" (691), Tardif, *op. cit.*, p. 25; "inferat tibi *una cum sotio fisco* auri untias tantas esse multando," *MGH.*, *Formulae*, p. 186; "tunc inferat tibi *una cum sotio fisco* duplum tantum," *ibid.*; "inferat ei, cui litem intulerit, ista tota servante, *una cum socio fisco* untias tantas esse multando," *ibid.*, p. 188; "*una cum socio fisco distringente* ... coactus exsolvat" (766), Tardif, *op. cit.*, p. 49; "*una cum distringentibus sociis fisci*" (884), *Regesto di Farfa*, vol. iii, p. 34.

[5] "Si fuerit de facultate latronis ... *satiatur*," Bouquet, *Recueil*, vol. iv, p. 265; "*una cum satio fisco*" (833), ch. A. Trémault, *Cartulaire de Marmoutier*, Paris, Vendôme 1893, p. 276.

[6] "Ipsius hominis Rothberti *preserunt et saziaverunt* malo ordine et contra legem, unde legem subire et incurrere debent" (845), B. Guérard, *Cartulaire de l'abbaye de Saint Victor de Marseille*, vol. i, p. 33.

[7] "Si quis alterius ingenuam de crimina sea stria aut herbaria *sisit et eam priserit*," *Frag.* ii. 33, in *MGH.*, *Leg. Alaman.*, p. 23.

[8] "Multam iubemus *exigere*," *Leg. Burgund*, lxxvi. 1; "nec pulveraticum *prendere nec exigere*" (795), *Cartulaire général de Paris*, vol. i, p. 36.

ula *socio fisco* becomes clear from a document at Carcasson in the year 936, where *in sazina* is identical with the *in fisco* of other documents.[1] In the *Formulae* the usual form of this word is *sacire*. It is employed to express the seizure of land by lawful process, where the alodial holding was not certain.[2] The physical seizure of the land was necessary, in order to make the title good,[3] and in an immunity to a cloister specific mention is made of the fact that it has the right of holding the land (*sacire*) against all persons.[4]

Before discussing the further history of *socio fisco* I will show what has become of the first part of the confiscation formula, of the word *inferre*.[5] In the Langobard laws there is frequent mention of a fine *ferquidum*, which is there glossed by "simile." If a person carries fire from the hearth, causing a conflagration, he pays the *ferquidum*, "damnum componat

---

[1] "In tali conventu, dum ego Dodolinus vixero, teneam et possideam ista vinea ad usus fructuum per beneficium nostri Salvatoris et Sancti Nazarii cujus hereditas est, et accipiant *in sazina* sanctus Salvator per singulos annos solidos tres," Devic et Vaissete, *op. cit.*, vol. v, col. 170.

[2] "Repetebat adversus eum, dum diceret, eo quod rem suam in loco nuncupante illo, in pago illo, in centena illa, quam de parte genetoris sui illius legibus obtingebat conscriptas, ille predictam rem superius nominatam male ordine suprasedebat vel retenebat iniuste; sed ipse ille presens adherat. Interrogatum fuit ipsi illo ab ipsis viris quid contra haec dicere vellebat, per quem sibi de iam dicta re *sacibat* vel inantea *sacire* vellebat; sed ipse de presente taliter debit ei in responsis, quod ante hos annos genitor suos nomine illo ex alode conscriptam superius nominatam ei dimisisset. Dum taliter agitur, iudicatum fuit ipsi illo, ut apud duodecim homines suos consimiles in basilica sancti illius hoc coniuraret vel predictam rem *sacire* deberet. Sed veniens predictus ille ad eum placitum in noctis institutis, ingressus est in basilica illa, manu missa super sacrum et sanctum altare, coram ipsis missis vel racineburgis, quicquid indicatum fuit vel per suum fisticum habuit aframitum, hoc coniuravit vel legibus *sacibat*," *MGH., Formulae*, p. 251.

[3] "Dum pro malorum hominum consilium, quod non debueram, de terra vestra in loco nuncupante illo, quem excolere videor, revellare conavi et ipsa terra ad proprietate *sacire* volui et non potui, quod nec ratio prestetit, et vos vel agentes vestri eam ad parte vestra revocastis vel nobis exinde eiecistis," *ibid.*, p. 100.

[4] "Licentiam habeat ... per annis contra quemcumque *saciendi*," *ibid.*, p. 66.

[5] Based on my discussion in the *Zeitschrift für romanische Philologie*, 1913, p. 580 *ff.*

*ferquido,* id est similem." [1] Since the damage done by an accidental fire is assessed only to the amount of the property consumed,[2] while a wilful act of incendiarism is fined at its triple value,[3] this *ferquidum* must obviously be a double fine. The same is paid in case of a gift without launigild, of wilfully killing a dog or pig, of maiming a horse.[4] The old glossaries repeat the equation *"ferquidum* id est simile,"[5] without giving any further explanation, and the modern authors similarly explain *ferquidum* to mean "of equal value."[6] But *ferquidum* had acquired no definite meaning, as will soon be seen, for it arose from a misunderstood and miswritten clause, and, although a confusion has arisen between it and *simile* "of equal value," the comparison of the various fires due to carelessness, accidence, or wilfulness shows conclusively that it originally meant "a double fine."

Since the Germanic laws have generally arisen from a literal interpretation of legal formulae, we must investigate the latter first. So far as I know, the oldest reference to this word in a document is of the year 739, where it says that if the seller cannot legally defend the purchaser, he is to pay double the amount of what the improved land would fetch *"in ferquide* loco."[7] *Ferquide* cannot mean "similar," because it is sheer nonsense to talk of a valuation in a similar place, even as many documents correctly speak of a valuation in the same place.[8] But since the puzzling formula made

---

[1] *Rothar* 147.    [2] "Caput tantum conponat," *ibid.*, 148.

[3] "In treblum eum restituat sub stimationem rei cum omnia, quae intus cremata sunt," *ibid.*, 149.

[4] *Rothar* 186, 330, 337, 349 (*Liutp.* 151).

[5] *MGH., Leg.,* vol. iv, pp. 651, 653.

[6] F. Dahn, *Die Könige der Germanen,* Leipzig 1909, vol. xii, p. 148.

[7] "Si minime defensaro non potuero ego Petru, aut mei heredis tibi qui supra Aloin, aut tuis reprometto adque spondeo me esse conponiturum in duplu meliorata terrula, de quo agitur sub stemationem in *ferquede* loco," Troya, *Cod. dip. Langob.,* vol. iii, p. 650.

[8] "Omnia et in omnibus inintegro ab omni homine defensare quod si defendere minime potu . . . tunc sit conponituris ssto gaidualdi vel ad eius hhd.

no sense to the notaries, it was entirely omitted [1] or corrupted to *ferquidus et similis*,[2] *consimilis*.[3] It is not difficult to trace the origin of this *simili loco*. In a document of the year 572 we have the sensible reference to the double fine in case of breach of contract and also, "simili modo," for any improvements on buildings since erected.[4] Apparently the Langobard documents had erroneously spoken of a valuation in a similar place, where formerly the reference was to a valuation in a similar manner in the same place. Curiously a Spanish document of the year 823 shows how such a mistake may have arisen, for here *simili loco* is used in the sense of "in the same manner."[5]

aut cui gaiduald ipsum loc[um reliquerit] alium talem locum qualiter superius legitur sub extimatione intra *ipso* loco" (726), *Arch. stor. ital.*, ser. III, vol. XVII, p. 237; "in dupplo res meliorata, de quod agitor in *eodem* loco" (740), Troya, *op. cit.*, vol. III, p. 696; "in duplo meliorata qualem tunc fuerit in *eodem* loco" (761), *ibid.*, vol. v, p. 107; "in duplo meliorata in *ipso* loco qualis tunc fuerit" (762), *ibid.*, p. 174; "tunc componat pars parti . . . infra *ipso* locum . . . in dublo" (771), *Cod. dip. Langob.*, col. 84 *f.*; "tunc omnia vobis . . . in dublo componamus in *ipso* loco sub extimatione" (785), *ibid.*, col. 114; "conponamus, qualiter fuerit meliorata, ego et mei heredes tibi et heredibus tuis in *suprascripto* loco" (792), *ibid.*, col. 125.

[1] "In duplum rebus ipsius melioratis, sicut pro tempore fuerint sub estimationem restituamus" (769), *Cod. dip. Langob.*, col. 73; "promitto me vobis conponere suprascriptos iuges talis et alios talis una quoque inibi a vobis edificavit, aut melioratione fuerit in duplo" (772), *ibid.*, col. 88 *f.*; "ut in dublum restituat rem melioratam" (776), *ibid.*, col. 106, etc.

[2] "*Fer quidum* terra *et simile* in eodem locum bobis conponere debemus" (875), *Cod. cav.*, vol. I, p. 103; "et *ferquidum et simile* rebus in eodem loco bobis conponere spondimus" (877), *ibid.*, p. 104; "in duplo et alia tale casa et quantu aput vos meliorata fueru sup iu[sta esti]mazione *in ferquide et in consimile* loca" (1099), *ibid.*, p. 49.

[3] "Sub estimatione *consimili* loco" (753), *Cod. dip. Langob.*, col. 32; "*in consimiles locas*" (774), *ibid.*, col. 104; "*in consimile loco*," (936), Muratori, *Antiq.*, vol. II, col. 1136, (1014), *ibid.*, vol. I, p. 410, (1091), *ibid.*, p. 420; "*in loco consimili*" (1175), Camera, *Storia . . . di Amalfi*, vol. I, p. 361.

[4] "Quod . . . evictum ablatumve quid fuerit tunc quanti ea res erit quae evicta fuerit duplum pretium sstūm quinque solidorum a ssō venditore & ab ejusque hhbs. & successoribus eidem conparatori ss. ejusque hhbūs & successoribus cogantur inferre sed & res quoque meliorate instructae aedificateque taxatione habita *simili modo* omnia duplariae rei se qs. venditor hhdēsque suos reddere pollicetur," Marini, *I papiri diplomatici*, p. 184.

[5] "Reddat in quadruplum, et *simili loco* quantum inquietaverit Ovetensi

This *in ferquidum* (*locum*) is variously recorded, as *infer quidem*,[1] *fer quidem*,[2] *infer quide*,[3] *infer quede*,[4] *in ferquidi*,[5] *in ferquede*,[6] *in ferquide*,[7] *in ferquidem*,[8] *in ferquido*,[9] where the very spelling makes the word suspicious. It is obvious from the Langobard documents, even as it was from their laws, that *ferquidum* originally refers to double damages, wherefore it occurs, like the *simile* of the year 572, exclusively in the "stipulatio duplae," which guarantees the purchaser double damages in case of difficulties arising through the fault of the seller,[10] and is in the oldest document quoted by me correctly coupled with the "evictio,"[11] even as it is in a Langobard contract of the year 725.[12]

In the Theodosian Code the verb *inferre* is always employed to express the payment of the fine to the fiscus,[13] and the

Ecclesiae et cultoribus ejus, et insuper solvat auri talenta duo," *España sagrada*, vol. XXXVII, p. 322.

[1] "Conponamus nos . . . in duplu casa et res in melioratu, unde agitur, *infer quidem* locu sum estimationum qualis tunc fuerit" (759), Troya, *op. cit.*, vol. V, p. 56, and again pp. 279, 466, 542, 551, 556, 643, 704; vol. IV, p. 419 (752) *infer quidem* loco cum quid, aut qualis tunc fuerit" (769), *Mem. e doc. . . . d. duc. d. Lucca*, vol. IV¹, p. 116, and similarly pp. 135, 136, 138, 150, 167, 189; vol. IV², p. 49; vol. V², pp. 37 (759), 44, 52, 64.

[2] Troya, *op. cit.*, vol. V, p. 654; *Mem. e doc. . . . d. Lucca*, vol. IV¹, pp. 19 (753), 28; vol. V², p. 29.

[3] Troya, *op. cit.*, vol. V, pp. 58 (759), 333; *Mem. e doc. d. Lucca*, vol. IV¹, pp. 140 (779), 183; vol. V², pp. 26 (747), 38, 54.

[4] Troya, *op. cit.*, vol. IV, p. 429 (752), vol. V, p. 81; *Mem. e doc. . . . d. Lucca*, vol. IV¹, pp. 79 (744), 92.

[5] Troya, *op. cit.*, vol. V, p. 177: "*in ferquidi* loco et in ipso praedicto casale."

[6] *Ibid.*, vol. III, p. 650 (739).

[7] Muratori, *Antiq.*, vol. III, col. 1014 (783); *ibid.*, col. 1142 (1126).

[8] *Ibid.*, vol. V, col. 412 (793); vol. III, col. 1062 (964), col. 1086 (1058).

[9] *Ibid.*, vol. V, col. 1912 (752); vol. III, col. 1108 (1109), and again cols. 1152, 1154, 1158, 1168, 1169, 1170.

[10] For the "stipulatio duplae" read A. Bechmann, *Geschichte des Kaufs im römischen Recht*, Erlangen 1876, p. 375 *ff.*

[11] The citations in Roman law referring to this may be found in B. Brisson, *De formulis et solennibus populi romani verbis libri viii*, Halae et Lipsiae 1731, p. 483.

[12] "Et si pulsatus aut *aevectus* fuerit . . doblus solidos emptori suo restituat," *Cod. dip. Langob.*, col. 16.

[13] See notes on p. 1.

Justinian Code similarly uses *inferre fisco, aestimationem, argentum, pecuniam.*[1] Wherever the Latin document is used, this *inferre* has been preserved in the "stipulatio duplae," but, as a rule, in a misunderstood and much corrupted form. It will suffice to make a brief survey of the oldest sources. The double damages are mentioned in a Saint Gall donation of about the year 700,[2] while in another, of the year 741, the melioration formula appears, exactly as in the Langobard documents.[3] Beginning with 751 *inferre* is used almost exclusively.[4] The same has happened at Cluny, but the meaning of *inferre* was so obscure to the notaries that they added the words "componere, persolvere."[5] The Formulae, too, contain the "stipulatio duplae," with or without *inferre,* but generally very corrupt.[6]

The fate of *inferre* in the Spanish peninsula is interesting. In the Visigothic formulae we still have the sensible use of *inferre,* as in the Roman laws,[7] but in the later Spanish-Portuguese period the notaries no longer knew what to make

---

[1] B. Brisson, *De verborum quae ad jus pertinent significatione libri xix,* Lipsiae 1721, p. 457.

[2] "Si ego ipse aut ullus de heredis meos aut ulla opposita persona, qui contra hanc donationem istam agerit aut infrangere voluerit, inprimis iram Dei incurrat et tublum conponat," H. Wartmann, *Urkundenbuch der Abtei Sanct Gallen,* vol. I, p. 2.

[3] "Duplum tantum, quanta ipsa res meliorata valuerit, eis coactus exsolvat," *ibid.,* p. 7.

[4] "Qui contra hanc firmitate ita veniri timtaverit, *inferat* contra ipsus sanctus auro libra una," *ibid.,* p. 17; "qui contra hanc epistola donationis ambolale presumserit, *inferat* ad ipso loco sancto dubla repeticione" (752), *ibid.,* p. 18; "*inferat* parte custodiente dobla repeticione," *ibid.,* pp. 22, 23, 32, 37, *et passim.*

[5] "*Inferamus* vobis vestrisque eredibus, una cum tercio fisco auri uncia una *componat*" (870), A. Bruel, *Recueil des chartes de l'abbaye de Cluny,* Paris 1876, vol. I, p. 16; "*inferat* nobis una cum socio auro uncias IIII *componat*" (873), *ibid.,* p. 23; "tunc *inferamus* nos vobis uno cum tercio fisco auri uncia I *componat*" (874), *ibid.,* p. 24; "*inferamus* tibi cum tercia fisco auria libera *persolvat*" (874), *ibid.,* p. 25, *et passim.*

[6] See notes on p. 3.

[7] "Et insuper *inferat* vobis auri libras tantas," *MGH., Formulae,* p. 577.

of it. While the Spanish documents generally employ it correctly,[1] the Portuguese use what appears to be a totally inexplicable doubling *infer vel inferus*,[2] which in reality has arisen out of two persons of the verb, such as *inferat vel inferamus*, in a desire to agree, as in the first quotation, both with "aliquis homo" and with "nos." This *infera* has been in Portuguese and Spanish understood to mean "as far as," giving rise to *ferre in* "reach as far,"[3] *usque fer in, fer in* "up to."[4]

The Langobard formula *infer quidem* is based either on the preceding Ostrogothic or on the borrowed Visigothic documents. That such is the case is proved by the fact that the Lucca documents frequently have the same repetition as the

---

[1] "*Inferat* in cauto" (899), Berganza, *Antigüedades de España*, p. 372; "*conferat* tibi quidquid petierit in dupplo" (912), *ibid.*, p. 373; "*conferat* in cauto" (914), *ibid.*, p. 374.

[2] "Si quis tamen quo fieri non credimus aliquis homo uenerit uel uenerimus contra hac cartula inrumpendum de generis nostri uel de extraneis que in concilio post parte uestra deuindicare non potuerimus *infer uel inferus* quomodo pariemus uobis illa ecclesia et illa hereditate duplata uel triplata quantum ad uobis fuerit meliorata" (940), *PMH.*, *Dip. et chart.*, p. 31; "tunc *infera uel infera* pars nostra partique vestra" (949). *ibid.*, p. 34; "tunc *infera uel ininfera* pars nostra partique uestre" (952), *ibid.*, p. 38; "*infera uel infera* parie uobis" (964), *ibid.*, p. 54; "*infera uel infra* pars nostra" (964), *ibid.*, pp. 56, 57; "*inferam uel inferam* pars nostra" (971); *ibid.*, p. 65; "*infera uel infera* pariemus uobis" (984), *ibid.*, p. 89; "*inferat uel infera* pars mea" (985), *ibid.*, p. 94; "*infra uel infra* pars nostra" (1044), *ibid.*, p. 203.

[3] "Ad illum portum de Porrarium, et *feret in* illum riuolum de Homanum . . . et conclude per illum riuolum, descendit cum ille per Vaor, et idem per ripas et pergit per terminos de Populeros et *feret in* riuolum chane . . . usque *feret*, et item per illum portum de Ferraria . . . et *feret in* illa semita antiqua ad illas veredas de Mamonela, et pergit per illa vereda antiqua" (791), Fray Antonio de Yepes, *Coronica general de la orden de San Benito, Patriarca de Religiosos*, 1609–1621, vol. IV, p. 448 b "et pergit usque ad montem et *ferit in* illa mamola" (957), *PMH.*, *Dip. et chart.*, p. 42.

[4] "*Fer in* illa fonte" (873), *PMH.*, *Dip. et chart.*, p. 1; "et inde ad ille sumio usque *fer ad* illa uia trauessa . . . et per illa fonte *usque fer in* illo ribolum . . . et *fer in* illo molino . . et per illos collos ad illa petragosa *usque fer in* illo forno" (907), *ibid.*, p. 10; "et *fere in* suari" (960), *ibid.*, p. 50; "per riuulo homine et *fere in* suari . . . *usque fere in* homine . . . et inde ad fonte coua et *fere in* illo vallo" (960), *ibid.*, p. 51; "*usque fere in* comaro . . . et *fere* super canale" (961), *ibid.*, p. 52.

Spanish ones,[1] which is unprecedented outside of the older
Gothic countries. It is, therefore, necessary to assume that
*infer quidem* loco, which is the most common formula, must
stand for "*infer quid in* eo loco (simili modo sub extimatione
quale tunc fueret unde agitur)," or a similar phrase.

I will now show that *socio fisco* has given rise to the Gothic
*sagio*, *saio* and a number of similar important derivations.
Mommsen, who has so often pointed out in general outlines
the Roman origin of Ostrogothic institutions, has shown that
the *saio* is the Gothic equivalent for the Roman *agens in
rebus*, that is, that he is the executive officer carrying out the
decrees of his superior among the Goths as well as among the
Romans.[2] Cassiodorus once couples a *saio*, who is always a

---

[1] "Ispondimus vobis componere ipsa suprascripta sala, vel res, quos tibi
dedi in duplum *ferquidem, et infer quidem* loco sub extimationem quale tunc
fueret unde agitur" (773), *Mem. e doc. ... d. Lucca*, vol. IV[1], p. 131; "ipsa re
dupla, *fer quidem, infer quide* loco, sub extimatione cum quo, aut qualis tunc
fuerint" (774), *ibid.*, p. 132; "in tripum, *fer quide, et in ferquide* loco" (782),
*ibid.*, p. 143; "in duplum, *fer quidem, et infer quidem*" (779), *ibid.*, vol. V[2],
pp. 100, 101.

[2] "Theoderich hat aber den römischen *agens in rebus* nicht bloss sich an-
geeignet, sondern die Institution auch auf die Gothen erstreckt. Der *comitiacus* seiner Erlasse zwar ist immer ein Römer, aber zuweilen daneben und
dann an erster Stelle, häufiger allein tritt ein anderer Subalternbeamter auf,
gothisch bezeichnet als *saio* und ohne Ausnahme gothischer Nationalität.
Welche germanische Institution dabei zu Grunde liegt, muss dahingestellt
bleiben; *wie uns dieser Saio entgegentritt, ist er einfach der agens in rebus ge-
genüber den Unterthanen gothischen Rechts.* Wie die Soldateneigenschaft bei dem
*agens in rebus* schon durch die Nationalität ausgeschlossen wird, so kommt
sie auch dem Saio nicht zu; aber der Sache nach tritt der *agens* wesentlich
als Soldat auf und dasselbe gilt ebenso sehr, wenn nicht noch in höherem Grade
von dem Saio. Auch seine Thätigkeit besteht in der Uebermittelung der
königlichen Befehle jeglichen Inhalts an den oder die davon betroffenen Per-
sonen und der Ueberwachung ihrer Ausführung; bezeichnend für seine Stellung
ist es, dass er da verwendet wird, wo die Execution der Lokalbehörden nicht
ausreicht und dass bei Ladungen vor Gericht ihm der doppelte Betrag dessen
zukommt, was nach der von Theoderich aufgestellten Taxe dem Executor der
Provinzialbehörde an Sporteln zu zahlen ist. Mit dem Nebeneinanderstehen
des *agens in rebus* und des *saio* wird zusammenhängen, dass allgemeine juris-
dictionelle Anzeigen und Anordnungen, zum Beispiel die Anzeige der Ueber-
nahme einer Person in die spezielle königliche Tuition und die Anweisung zur
Ergreifung flüchtiger Verbrecher regelmässig an die die römischen Behörden

Goth, with a Roman *apparitor* [1] and a Roman *comitiacus*,[2] and Mommsen has shown that a *comitiacus, comitianus, ducicus,* or *ducianus* was an *apparitor,* hence officially identical with the *saio*.[3] Cassiodorus correctly says of a *saio* that he is the executor of the royal will,[4] but the word *executor* is also applied to a Roman,[5] who is a *comes*,[6] but, to judge from his title, *devotio tua,* and the mission on which he is sent, filled the duty generally exacted from a *saio*. *Devotio tua* is applied only to an *apparitor, exsecutor,* or *saio*,[7] while *vir devotus* is equally said of a *comitiacus* or *comitianus*.[8] It is, therefore, clear that *devotio tua* was the usual honorific title of an executive officer. It was already in use in the fourth century in regard to a prefect [9] and some other officer,[10] and *devotus* was in the Theodosian Code frequently employed to designate a soldier who paid his taxes promptly, so that it nearly corresponded to the term *fidelis,* with which we shall meet later on. It is, then, obvious that the *saio* was considered as the trusted servant of the king or judge,[11] whose chief duty consists in "taking away, confiscating" in the name of the judicial authority, as is specifically mentioned in the

gerichtet wurden. *Für die Gesammtauffassung der germanischen Reichsverweserschaft ist das Institut dieser saiones in hohem Grade belehrend.* Wer sich dem Augenschein nicht verschliesst, muss erkennen, dass so, wie Theoderich es gestaltet hat, es ebenso der praktische Ausdruck der personellen Omnipotenz des Herrschers ist wie das der *agentes in rebus* und also das Regiment Theoderichs über die Gothen eben dasselbe war, welches der Kaiser des Westreichs über die in seinem Dienst stehenden Ausländer übte oder doch üben sollte," *Ostgothische Studien,* in *Neues Archiv,* vol. xiv, p. 472 *ff.*

[1] "Triwilae *saioni* et Ferrocincto *apparitori*," iii. 20.
[2] "Dumerit saioni et Florentiano uiro devoto *comitiano*," viii. 27.
[3] *Variae,* p. 470.
[4] "Iussionis nostrae, cuius executor esse debuit," vii. 42; "in executore illud est pessimum, si iudicis relinquat arbitrium," xii. 3.
[5] i. 8.  [6] iv. 5.
[7] ii. 21, i. 8, iv. 47, v. 10, v. 27, xii. 3.  [8] ii. 10, viii. 27.
[9] *Cod. Theod.,* vii. 20. 1 (318).
[10] *Ibid.,* vii. 22. 2 (326).
[11] "Non *sayonis de rege* ingressio" (955), T. Muñoz y Romero, *Coleccion de fueros municipales,* p. 31.

ancient Gaudenzian fragment of the Visigothic laws.[1] Hence
the extended formula "*socio* fisco coactus exsolvat,*" which
we have so frequently met, was distinctly understood to
mean, "let him pay, having been compelled by the *socio*
fisci,*" that is, this *socio* produced the Gothic *sagio, saio,*
"confiscator."

From this *sagio, saio,* whose original form was *sacio,* as
preserved in Merovingian *sacibaro,* is derived the Spanish
*sacar* "to take away by force, confiscate,*" [2] hence, "to take
away from the country, export."[3] Similar meanings have
developed for the word in Portugal, where it means "to take
away, confiscate,*" [4] hence, "to collect the fine,*" wherefore

---

[1] "Qui ad iudicium iudicatum non reddiderit debitum et contempserit in
duobus mensibus, interpellet creditor regem et iudicem, qui transmittat
*sagionem* cum ipso, et *tollat sagio ille de substantia eius,* quod ipsum debitum
possit valere, quantum creditori suo restituere iussus fuerat, et reddat creditori," *MGH., Lex Visig.,* p. 470.

[2] "Villano pro pignos *sacare* per forcia" (955), Muñoz y Romero, *Coleccion
de fueros,* p. 31; "uilla de Tauroni medietatem, quomodo illa *saccauimus* pro
judicato de filios de Froila Osorizi" (988), *España sagrada,* vol. xl, p. 406; "et
post ea uenit domino açenare deosane et uoluit illa forçare de tota omnia sua
ereditate pro mentira . . . et non potuit illa ereditate *sakare*" (1044), *Coleccion
de documentos para el estudio de la historia de Aragon,* Zaragoza [1904], vol. i, p.
58; "si tale homine exierit de illa gente de ista domina que ad regi uoleant
*sakare* de ista binea quod istos fidiatores iam dictos ponant ad regi in alio loco"
(1061), *ibid.,* p. 170; "abuerunt contemtione vicinos de votaia cum abbate
domno blasco, dicentes quod partem aberent in supradicto monte et per lege
et iudicio de rege domno ranimiro et de suos barones *sakavit* eos exinde abbate
domno blasco," *ibid.,* p. 193; "quod nullus homo non *sacet* vos inde de illas
hereditates" (1147), *España sagrada,* vol. xxxv, p. 416; "et fuit ipso barrio
*sakato* a parte regalengo" (1071), *Indice de los documentos del monasterio de
Sahagun, de la Orden de San Benito,* Madrid 1874, p. 17; "et *saco* nobis de istas
hereditates" (1131), *ibid.,* p. 26; "et *saquo* inde saion et merinus et homicido
et roxum" (1137), *ibid.,* p. 28.

[3] "Estes ommes sobre dichos que son puestos en estos puertos cuenten todas
las mercadurias que quisieren por y *sacar*. . . Sy algund mercadero o otro omme
fuere fallado en todos mios rreynos *sacando* ninguno auer por mar nin por tierra
delos que yo defiendo, por ninguna parte fuera delos rreynos" (1268), *Cortes
de los antiguos reinos de Leon y de Castilla,* Madrid 1861, vol. i, p. 75.

[4] "Et damus uobis illos in oferzionem pro que nobis *sacastis* linpio de con-
zelio et sano pro parte de illo iudizio que noscum abuit aderedo" (991), *PMH.,
Dip. et chart.,* p. 99; "et si homo intrauerit in casa aliena per forcia quantum
inde *saccauerit* duplet et si nullam causam *saccauerit* quinque solidos ad pala-

*sacator* is the "collector of fines," that is, almost identical with *saio*.[1] In modern Spanish and Portuguese *la saca* is "export."

A passage in Ebn Khaldun shows that the custom of surrounding the sovereign with a bodyguard of *saiones* was imitated from the Spaniards, for it was first practiced by the Mowahhids of Spain, and the very name applied to such a bodyguard, *sâqah*, shows its derivation from *sagio, sacare*.[2] In the tenth century Arab. *sâqah* had the meaning of "rear guard." That it meant "a rear guard acting as a protection" is evident from Greek σάκα, which was in that century borrowed from the Arabs.[3] This σάκα was charged with the care of the sick and the feeble and their belongings,[4] wherefore it naturally carried off all the plunder, as is shown from the quotations in the Romance languages and from the use of *saccomannus* "plunderer," *saccomannum* "plunder" in

cium" (11. cent.), *ibid., Leg. et consuet.*, vol. I, p. 346; "qvi boues eiecerit de ero ubi ararent aut *saccauerit* la clauila aut desturbauerit quod non aren". (12. cent.), *ibid.*, p. 192.

[1] "Et quicumque contra decretum uel decreta mea que ibi sunt scripta uendiderit uel momparauerit . . . pectet duplatum illud quod magis uendiderit quam positum est in decreto. Et ad istos incautos *saquandos* mitto hominem meum Martinum Pelagii quod *saquet* eos ut dictum est per se uel per alios *sacatores* cum meis scribanis de uillis quos ipse ponere uoluerit," *ibid.*, p. 753.

[2] " (Les Mowahhids et les souverains de la famille de Zénata) restreignirent l'usage des drapeaux et des tymbales au sultan, et les interdirent à tous ses lieutenants: ils en firent le cortége spécial qui devoit accompagner le sultan quand il marchoit, et qu' on designoit sous le nom de *saka*. Le nombre en fut plus ou moins grand, suivant les usages particuliers adoptés par chaque dynastie: les uns se bornoient à sept, comme à un nombre qui porte bonheur; tel étoit l'usage des Mowahhids, et de la famille des Bénou' lahmar, en Espagne," S. de Sacy, *Chrestomathie arabe*, Paris 1826, vol. II, p. 266.

[3] "Ὁ δὲ ἄρχων τῶν ἑτέρων ἐξ τῶν ὀπισθίων, τῶν καὶ σάκα καλουμένων ἄνδρας καὶ αὐτὸς ἀφορίσας ἑκατὸν μεθ' ἡγεμόνος τινὸς ἐμπείρου, ἑάτω ἀπὸ διαστήματος περιπατεῖν ἐκ τῶν ὀπίσθεν ἕνα καὶ αὐτοὶ κατασκοπῶσι τοῦ μὴ κατὰ νῶτον τούτοις ἀδοκήτως ἐπελθεῖν τοὺς πολεμίους," Περὶ καταστάσεως ἀπλήκτου, iu R. Vari, *Incerti scriptoris byzantini saeculi X, Liber de re militari*, Lipsiae 1901, in *Index* sub σάκα.

[4] "Τὴν δὲ λοιπὴν διδόναι τοῖς τοῦ σάκα, ὅπως ἐκεῖνοι τοὺς πληγάτους τοὺς δὲ τὰ ἑαντῶν ἀπολωλεκότας ἄλογα καὶ μὴ δυναμένους πεζεῦσαι ἐκείνους τὲ αὐτοὺς δι' αὐτῶν βαστάζωσι καὶ τὸν φόρτον αὐτῶν," *ibid.*

Italian documents.[1] From the formula "*ponere ad sacco-manum*" has arisen the Spanish phrase "*dar saco mano,*" "to plunder," while Italian *saccardo, saccheggiare,* French *saccager,* have developed from the shorter *saccum* "plunder." But this *saccomannus,* which in the form *saccomanno* is common in Lombardy, is unquestionably of Langobard origin, even as it occurs as *sagibaro* in the Salic laws, and as *sagibaro* and *sagemannus* in the Anglo-Saxon laws. It does not appear clearly from the Salic law what the *sagibaro* was, but he is called a "puer regius,". that is, "servant or soldier of the king,"[2] hence he belongs in the same category as the *antrustio.*[3] One law, which is very obscure in language, says that there cannot be more than three of them at one malloberg, and that they are in some way connected with the collection of money,[4] hence it is obvious that they are in the same category with the *thungini.* This is proved conclusively from the Anglo-Saxon law where a *sagibaro* is considered as of equal rank with an alderman and is in Anglo-Saxon called "*gethungen,*"[5] which is in complete agreement with the Pithoean gloss "*sacebarone:* dicuntur quasi senatores." I shall show further on that certain cases at law could

[1] "Volebant et iam incoeperant *saccomanare* civitatem," Muratori, *Scriptores,* vol. XII, col. 481; "una nocte pernoctaverunt, multas pulchras domos et palatia cum aedificiis *saccomannando* et comburendo," *ibid.,* vol. XVI, col. 328; "nec de *saccomanno,* tamquam nobilissimus stirpe, curabat," *ibid.,* col. 348; "et ipsam Placentiam vi acceperunt post obsidionem 32. dierum, et ut asseritur ipsam ad *saccomannum* posuerunt," *ibid.,* vol. XI, col. 279; "deinde iverunt versus Pisaurum et quatuor castra posuerunt ad depraedationem seu ad *saccomanum,*" *ibid.,* vol. XIX, col. 894; "item, quia domum praefati dom. Cardinalis postea pergentes, Sanctitatis vestrae ultra omnem modestiam, posita fuit ad *saccamannum* in Luca," Martène & Durand, *Thesaurus novus anecdotorum,* vol. II, col. 1396.

[2] "Si quis *sacebarone* qui puer regius fuit occiderit," LIV. 2.

[3] "Qui antrusionem quo *puer regius* est occiserit," *Recap.* B. 32.

[4] "*Sacibaronis* vero in singulis mallibergis plus quam tres non debent esse, et si de causas de quod aliquid eis solvuntur, factum dixerint, hoc ad grafionem non requiratur unde ille securitatem fecerit," LIV, 4.

[5] "Si quis in domo aldermanni uel alterius *sagibaronis* pugnet, gif hwa on ealdormonnes huse gefeohte oðe on oðres geðungenes witan," *Ine* 6. 2.

not be introduced by the plaintiff in person, but only through the *thunginus* or *sacibaro*, hence *sacibaro*, *sacimannus* came to mean, not only "collector of money, confiscator," but also "spokesman, accuser,"[1] and hence the Germanic languages, with the exception of the Gothic, have developed from this *sagi-* the root *sag-* "speak." That it originally meant "to speak for the plaintiff, accuse" is proved by the Slavic languages where *sok* is "accuser," while in Russian it means "accuser, spy, denunciator" and the verb *sočit'* means "to find out, hunt up, chase," even as Lithuanian *sakiti* "to hunt," Finnish *sakka* "speech, announcement," OIrish *saig-* "tendere, petere, adire" are derived from this Germanic *sag-* "to prosecute at court."

On Romance territory *sag-* has stopped at the original meaning "to confiscate." From the eleventh century on the sources are abundant as to the fact that after a piece of property was adjudicated to the plaintiff, he had to "seize" the property by force, and that such seizure was by no means a mild affair is seen from the equation of *saisia* and *invasio*.[2] In Normandy private seizure was counted among the heavy crimes,[3] but it was prescribed by law if the courts had properly adjudicated the property, and even the king could not seize church property without due process of law.[4] Here we

---

[1] "In causis ubi iudex fiscalis aliquem inplacitet de socna sua sine alio accusatore, sine *sagemanno*, sine inuestitura," *Leg. Henrici* 63. 1; "non attraho mihi hoc N pro amicitia uel inimicitia uel pro iniusto lucro, nec uerius inde scio, quam mihi *sagemannus* meus dixit," *Oath formula* 4.

[2] "Invasionem, vulgari vocabulo *saisiam* dictam, propria manu facere," H. Morice, *Mémoires pour servir de preuves à l'histoire ecclésiastique et civile de Bretagne*, Paris 1742, vol. I, col. 591.

[3] "Si clericus raptum fecerit vel furtum, vel aliquem percusserit . . . aut assultum fecerit, aut aliquid *saisierit*" (1080), Teulet, *Layettes du Trésor des chartes*, vol. I, p. 27.

[4] "Si episcopi aliquid quod hic non sit scriptum in regis curia monstrare possunt se habuisse tempore Roberti comitis vel Willelmi regis, ejus concessione, rex eis non tollit quin bene habeant; tantummodo illud nullatenus *seisiscant*, donec in curia ejus monstrarent quod habere debeant. Similiter et laicis propter hoc scriptum rex nil tollit quod in curia regis monstrare possint

have not only *seisiscere* "to take possession," but also *disaisiscere* "to dispossess." Similar meanings are given to *saisire* and *dissaisire* in Norman England,[1] where on account of the forcible occupation of the land no other title than the one by *seisin* was valid.[2]

- An older form for this *dissaisire* has had a checkered career in the Italian formula of dispossession in Carolingian documents. In the Frankish werpicio the customary expression is "se *exitum* dicere, facere," [3] also "se *exutum* facere." [4] The whole formula, even as the werpicio itself, has arisen from the late Roman traditio, wherefore we find in the Ostrogothic documents "se *exisse* excessisse discessisseque dicere."[5] As the tendency was to substitute *foris* for *ex*,[6] we get the ex-episcopos non debere habere; tantummodo episcopos inde non *disaisscant*, donec in curia sit monstratum quod episcopi inde habere non debeant," *ibid.*, p. 28.

¹ "Si quis hominem habeat qui ei nolit esse ad rectum, si quid de eo tenet, post legittimam submonicionem *saisiri* faciat," *Leg. Henrici* 61. 18c; "postquam aliquis *dissaisitus* legem uel rectum domino suo uadiauerit et plegios, si opus est, addiderit, *saisitus* esse debet," *ibid.*, 53. 6.

² K. E. Digby, *An Introduction to the History of Real Property*, Oxford 1884, p. 92 *ff.*

³ "Per durpilum et festucam sibi foras *exitum*, alienum vel spoliatum in omnibus esse dixit, et omnia werpivit," *MGH.*, *Formulae*, p. 492, and similarly pp. 188, 190, 200, 210, 492, 547; "per mea fistuca de jamdicta rem illa *exitum* feci" (870), *Bibl. de l'Ec. des chartes*, vol. LXIX, p. 661; "se in omnibus dixit *exitum*," *ibid.*; "se in omnebus de ipso monasthyriolo . . . dixit esse *exitum*" (703), Tardif, *op. cit.*, p. 35; "sibi exinde dixit esse *exitum*" (750), *ibid.*, p. 44; "unde et ipse Gerardus ex praedictos teloneos se *exitum* dixit coram eis" (759), *Cartulaire général de Paris*, vol. I, p. 29; "se exinde in presenti dixit esse *exitum*" (703), Lauer and Samaran, *Les diplômes originaux des Mérovingiens*, Paris 1908, p. 21; "ut de ipsas villas se *exigere* fecisset" (782), Devic and Vaissete, *op. cit.*, vol. II, Preuves, col. 50.

⁴ "Supradictas rebus se *exutum* fecit" (870), *Bibl. de l'Ec. des chartes*, vol. LIX, p. 261.

⁵ "Inque bacuam possessionem rei ss. supra venditor eundem emptori actoresque ejus in rem ire mittere ingredi possidereque permisit hac (ac) suos omnes inde ex eadem rem *exisse* excessisse dissesseque dixit" (540), Marini, *I pap. dipl.*, p. 175; "omnes solidos (suous) inde *exisse* excessisse dixique dixit" (540), *ibid.*, p. 180; "se suosque omnes inde *exisse* excessisse descessisseque dicxerunt" (539 or 546), *ibid.*, p. 173; "suos omnes inde *exisse* et excessisse discessique dixit" (572), *ibid.*, p. 184; "se suosque omnes exinde *exisse* excessisse discessisseque dixit" (end of 6. cent.), *ibid.*, p. 185.

⁶ "Dico me meosque omnes exinde a presenti die *foras exissent*" (769), *HPM.*, vol. XIII, col. 71.

pression *forisfacere*, which originally had the meaning "to commit a misdemeanor," but now acquired the additional meaning "to forfeit."[1]   But far more popular was *absacire* for "to give up possession," and this word not being clearly understood it has assumed a large number of extravagant forms.[2] *Sacire* never became very popular in Italy. Although *sasire, sagire, saxire, xasire* are recorded since the twelfth century[3] and *dissagire, resagire* were used in the south,[4] these forms give way to the much more frequent *staggire*, which, however, has arisen in an entirely different manner.

In 361 the Romans promulgated a law of *hospitale ius*,[5]

---

[1] "De qua suprascripta et predesignata proprietate terre et case cooperte et discoperte ex toto per omnia et in omnibus, et etiam desuper omnia me *foris facio* et ipsam in tua potestate relinquo et refuto" (1218), F. Cornelius, *Ecclesiae Venetae*, Venetiis 1749, vol. IX, p. 388. The notary of this document has raised the notarial style to an art by quoting every known formula of antiquity. The whole document is unique.

[2] *Absacito* (814), *HPM.*, vol. I, col. 40; *absasito* (890), *ibid.*, vol. XIII, cols. 576, 910, 912, 1033; 1078, 1079, vol. I, cols. 165, 169, 183, 189; *absasita* (991), *ibid.*, vol. I, cols. 288, 306, 610; *absascito* (990), *ibid.*, vol. XIII, col. 1502; *abasasito* (903), *ibid.*, col. 1332; *absito* (976), *ibid.*, col. 1357; *absasisito* (973), *ibid.*, col. 1306; *absaxito* (928), *ibid.*, col. 895, vol. I, cols. 302, 505; *absarcito* (986), Ughelli, *Italia sacra*, vol. IV, col. 843; *absarsito* (966), *HPM.*, vol. I, col. 209; *apsasire* (980), *ibid.*, col. 258; *absititum* (995), Ughelli, *op cit.*, vol. III, col. 39; *adsasito* (999), *HPM.*, vol. XIII, cols. 1758, 1761; *assassito* (999), *ibid.*, col. 1763, vol. I, col. 592; *ausasito* (967), *ibid.*, col. 1222; *autsasito* (966), *ibid.*, col. 1213; *hautsasito* (936), *ibid.*, vol. I, col. 140; *absesi* (979), U. Pasqui, *Documenti per la storia della città di Arezzo*, Firenze 1899, p. 109; *asentam* (963), *HPM.*, vol. XIII, col. 1157; *asentem, ibid.*, vol. I, cols. 614, 669; *absentes, ibid.*, cols. 551, 566, 585, 600; *apsente, ibid.*, cols. 558, 637.

[3] L. Frati, *Statuti di Bologna*, vol. III, in the Vocabulary. "Iura et bona ad prefatum monasterium pertinentia sepissime occupavimus, *seysivimus*, perturbavimus per bannum et per alias oppressiones innumeras . . . omnem vim cuiuscumque oppressionis, occupationis, *seysicionis* inferende in homines" (1212), *Bullettino dell' istituto storico italiano*, vol. XVIII, p. 113.

[4] "Iniuste et sine ratione inextitit *dissagitus*" (1185), Camera, *Storia* . . . *di Amalfi*, vol. I, p. 368; "Goffridus iniuste et sine indicio sola auctoritate sua *dissagivit* ecclesiam sancti Nicolai de quibusdam terris suis de ecclesia sancti Petri de scavezulis . . . eandem ecclesiam *resagiri* facias de ipsis terris sicut inde prius *sagita* fuerat" (1180), *Cod. dip. barese*, vol. V, p. 250; "Goffridus Gentile *dissagivit* ecclesiam beati Nicolai auctoritate et vi sua de quibusdam terris . . . Goffridus Gentile *resagivit* predictam ecclesiam" (1196), *ibid.*, vol. VI, p. 5.

[5] *Cod. Theod.* VII. 8. 1.

according to which soldiers and servants of the state were to be billeted in private houses. This was merely an extension of a previous usage, for in 333 teachers were exempted from the burden of keeping *hospites*,[1] and ten years later the clergy were included in this immunity.[2] With these exceptions no one could be freed from the obligation,[3] by which a third of the house was turned over to the *metatores* or *mensores*, as the billeting officers were called. The Germans, as is well known, appropriated to themselves a third of the Roman possessions, where they considered themselves to be the *hospites*, or two thirds, where they looked upon the Romans as in their service. To this I shall return later. Here I shall only mention that the right of quartering, *hospitaticum*, *hospitalitas*, *hospitium*, is asserted throughout the Middle Ages, when it was frequently attended by violence.[4] The Germans correctly translated *hospitium* by *heriberga* "soldiers' quarters,"[5] which has produced English *harbour* "protection," *harbinger* "metator, billeting officer." In Anglo-Saxon the word is lacking, and Norse *heriberga* is obviously borrowed from the German.

As *hospes* was a person who was quartered upon another, it naturally lent itself as a synonoym for "surety, warrantee,

[1] XIII. 3. 3.    [2] XVI. 2. 8.

[3] "Ab *hospitalitatis* munere domum privatorum nullus excuset," VII. 8. 3.

[4] "Quando etiam Episcopos, Abbates, vel Comites, seu fidelium nostrorum quempiam in propria villa morari contigerit, cum suis in suis maneant domibus, *ne sub obtentu hospiti vicinos opprimant, vel eorum bona diripiant*," *Synodus Tycinensis* ann. 855; "ut in domibus Ecclesiarum neque missus, neque comes, vel judex quasi pro consuetudine neque placitum, *neque hospitium vindicent*," *Concilium annonym.* ann. 904; "preterea concedimus predictis civibus (Luccae), ut nostrum regale palatium intra civitatem vel in burgo eorum non hedificent aut inibi *vi vel potestate hospitia capiantur*" (1081), J. Ficker, *Urkunden zur Reichs- und Rechtsgeschichte Italiens*, Innsbruck 1874, p. 125; "at vero homines Uchezoni, canonico super ipsam terram *bis quiete hospitato, tunc tercio per vim eiecerunt*" (1138), *ibid.*, p. 153; "nullaque imperii nostri magna vel parva persona . . . molestare, divestire, angariare vel violenter *hospitare . . . audeat*," *ibid.*, p. 270.

[5] "*Hospitalitatem* quem vulgo *herbergiam* vocant," J. Laurent, *Cartulaire de Molesme*, p. 151.

hostage." In the *Cronicae* of Fredegar *hospes* is used exclusively for "hostage,"[1] and the same expression is employed in the letters of Paul I. to Pipin.[2] In the eleventh century the Frankish documents suddenly begin to substitute *hostis* for *hospes* in the threefold meaning of "guest, renter, and surety," so that there can be no doubt as to their identity. Fortunately we have the documentary history of this change. In 904 Berengarius issued for the church at Asti an immunity, which has been very frequently repeated until late into the eleventh century. Here the phrase occurs, "nulla denique magna parvaque publica persona eos *hostaticum* facere compellat,"[3] where *hostaticum* can be nothing but *in hostem ire*, "to take part in military expeditions," of the older documents. The ending *-aticum* was generally used for taxes, hence the incomprehensible word of the much quoted immunity was transferred to the exemption from certain obligations,[4] where it apparently had no definite meaning. In

---

[1] "Quam plures *hospitibus* ab eis accepit," *MGH.*, *Scrip. rer. merov.*, vol. II, p. 177; "*hospites* dederunt mutuo," p. 196; "dederunt invicem mutuo *hospites*," p. 197; "receptis *hospitibus*," p. 197; "datis *hospitibus* et mutuo acceptis," p. 198. Krusch (*Neues Archiv*, vol. VII, p. 513), who did not see the relation between *hospes* and *hostis*, said as follows: "Sehr merkwürdig ist ferner die Verwechslung von 'obsides' und 'hospites'; Geiseln nennt der fränkische Verfasser der Origo stets 'hospites.'"

[2] "Ut nostros ad tuam Excellentiam dirigere debeamus Missos, et suos *hospites*, quos ibidem ad vos habere videtur, recipere debeat ... ut jubeas ipsos *hospites* praedicto filio nostro Desiderio Regi restitutere" (762), Troya, *Cod. dipl.*, vol. V, p. 193 f.; "neque praelatos hospites permittitis parti Langobardorum restituere" (764 or 758), *ibid.*, p. 264.

[3] L. Schiaparelli, *I diplomi di Berengario I.*, Roma 1903, p. 148; *ostaticum* (918), *ibid.*, p. 310; *ostiaticum* (1037), *Codice diplomatico padovano dal secolo sesto a tutto l'undecimo*, p. 151; *ostaticum* (1047), *ibid.*, p. 184.

[4] "Et sint liberi et soluti cum omnibus suis adiacentiis, vineis, campis, olivetis, cultis et incultis, mobilibus et immobilibus, Toloneis Ripaticis *Hostiaticis*" (969), Odorici, *Storie Bresciane*, vol. IV, p. 96; "et nullus potestative in eorum mansionibus ingredi temptet, nemoque illos de eorum proprietatibus absque imperiali iudicio audeat investire, Ripaticum, tholoneum, *hostiaticum*, aut aliquam publicam functionem ab eis aliquid exigat" (1155), *ibid.*, vol. V, p. 107; "et cedimus illis per hanc nostri precepti vel concessionis paginam portaticum toloneum ripaticum et *opstaticum* et absque aliqua publica functione quiete vivere" (969), *MGH.*, *Diplomata regum*, vol. I, p. 511.

France, where this immunity must have originated, *hostaticum* was in the eleventh century considered a synonym for *hospitaticum*, and was used wherever derivatives from *hospes* had been employed before, that is, for "surety"[1] and for the taxes of the *hospes*, the emphyteutic peasant.[2] To this was soon added *hostis* for *hospes*, and thus arose the modern French *hôte*, *ôtage*, *hôtel*, etc., while in Italy *ostaticum*, *ostagium*, under the influence of *sagire*, produced *stazire*, *stagire* "confiscate," *stasina* "confiscation."[3] This *stazire* was understood as *extasire*, and to this was formed *intesire*, *intensire*, *tesire*, *tensire*.[4]

[1] "Miserunt se in *ostaticum* de jamdictis comite et comitissa et illorum filiorum apud Gerundam . . . inde omnes istos *ostaticos* praedictos aut unum aut duos ex illis, faciant emendare ipsum omne malum . . . et si aliquis de praedictis *ostaticis* mortuus fuerit, jamdicti vicecomes et vicecomitissa mittant alium *ostaticum* vel alios non minus valentes in potestatem jamdicti comitis" (1070), Devic and Vaissete, *op. cit.*, vol. v, col. 577 *ff.*; "dabit *ostaticos* decem, quales ipsa comitissa voluerit, de ipso onore que non l' al tolla ni l'al anpar" (1083), Teulet, *op. cit.*, vol. I, p. 29; "dans, post se, octo *ostacios* per fides suas . . . Isti siquidem tenebunt tamdiu *ostagium* suum secundum mansiones suas . . . quamdiu unusquisque moras habuerit in reddendum centum solidos" (1093), G. Musset, *Cartulaire de Saint-Jean d'Angély*, in *Archives de la Saintonge et de l'Aunis*, vol. xxx, p. 235.

[2] "De *hostagiis* autem, id est censibus domorum, quoniam inolevit nequitia ut plerumque post longos temporum decursus et generationum permutationes hi qui *hostagia* debent ea ab Ecclesia abalienare et sciscitantes unde ea debeant libertatem quam nec habent nec habere debent, sibi usurpare contendunt, dignum ac necessarium duxi, loca ipsa in quibus et de quibus debentur, eos quoque qui debent nominatim discernere," Van Drival, *Cartulaire de l'Abbaye de Saint-Vaast d'Arras*, Arras 1875, p. 102 *f.*

[3] "*Staziri* vel sequestrari," F. Bonaini, *Statuti inediti della città di Pisa*, vol. I, p. 232; "*stasina*," *ibid.*, p. 232, etc.

[4] "Praedari vel *intesiri*, vel in praedam aliquo casu concedi," *Statuta Lucensis civitatis* 1539, lib. I, cap. CLIX, "*Intensina* seu sequestrum *intensire*," *Liber statutorum Arretii* 1580, p. 104; "Teneatur potestas in continenti facta accusatione vel documentatione de aliquo maleficio perpetrato vel commisso ab aliqua persona, invenire vel facere et *tesire* (*tensire*) vel *tesiri* facere bona omnia accusate persone," L. Zdekauer, *Statutum potestatis comunis Pistorii*, p. 115 *f.*

# DUCENARIUS

THE chief judge of the Salic and the Ribuarian Franks is called *comes* or *grafio*. In the early Merovingian documents the two terms are not identical, because the *grafio* is mentioned after the *comes*.[1] The *grafio* has arisen from the merging of a number of different offices to which the honorific title "tua *gravitas*" was attached. In the Theodosian Code this refers to the *praefectus praetorio*,[2] *praefectus urbi*,[3] *vicarius*,[4] *praeses*,[5] *dux*.[6] Cassiodorus thus addresses senators and magistrates,[7] and in several documents in Ostrogothic times high acting city officials receive this title.[8] Now the Theodosian Code classes the following officers together, *praefectus praetorio, vicarius, rector provinciae*, and places them before the minor judges, hence we get for them very nearly the rank of the Frankish *grafio* of early times. But it is in England where this *grafio*, a contraction of *gravitas*, has been preserved in all the various offices to which the title rightly belonged. The Latin *praepositus, praefectus, vicecomes* are given as equivalents of AS. *grefe, greve*,[9] and the compounds *portgrevius* "city provost," *tunesgerefa* "praefectus de villa," *weardgerefa* "prepositus custodum" show that *greve* and *gravitas* are identical as regards the duties they had to perform.

---

[1] *MGH., Dipl.*, p. 58 (693), and in other documents, even in Carolingian times: "virisque inlustribus, ducibus, *comitibus*, domesticis, *grafionibus*, vicariis, centenariis eorumque iunioribus" (816), *MGH., Formulae*, p. 307.

[2] VII. 4. 9, VIII. 5. 3, XIV. 3. 20.     [3] XIV. 4. 2.     [4] VI. 35. 4.

[5] II. 6. 2, VI. 31. 1.     [6] VIII. 4. 4.     [7] *Variae*, in *Vocabulary*, sub *gravitas*.

[8] "Una cum vestra *gravitate* oportet praesentibus actoribus traditionem fieri" (489), Marini, *I pap. dipl.*, p. 129; "vestram Reatinae Civitatis municipes *gravitatem* . . . fidejussorem vestrae praebeo *gravitati*" (557), *ibid.*, p. 122 *f.*

[9] Liebermann, *Die Gesetze der Angelsachsen*, in *Vocabulary*.

In the Ribuarian law *grafio* is the translation of "iudex fiscalis,"[1] but he is once distinguished from the *comes*,[2] even as he is several times mentioned along with the *comes* in the Salic law,[3] but in the latter case the two seem already to be confounded, for while certain laws speak of the *comes*,[4] corresponding laws mention him as *grafio*. The *comes* or ·*grafio* was the higher judge, but by his side there existed a judge sitting in minor cases, whose duty finally deteriorated into that of an executor, a confiscator. That was the *tunginus*, who developed out of the Roman *ducenarius*.

Suetonius tells us that Augustus introduced a new order of *ducenarii* who sat in minor cases,[5] and from Eusebius and Cyprian we learn that the dignity was coveted by many,[6] since, as we are told by Suetonius, the *procurator ducenarius* was invested with consular dignity,[7] and St. Jerome placed him immediately after the senator.[8] In the fourth century the *ducenarius* is mentioned by the side of the *centenarius*, while his office is called *ducena*,[9] and the dignity of the *ducenarius* was still recognized in the fifth century.[10] The

---

[1] LI, LIII, LXXXIV.                    [2] LXXXVIII.

[3] "In mallo iudici, h. e. *comite aut grafione*," Cap. II. 3; "sic debet iudex, hoc est *comes aut grafio*, ad loco accedere," III. 1.

[4] *Cap.* IX. 1, *Extravag.* B. 1, 2.

[5] "Ad tres judicum decurias quartam addidit, ex inferiori censu quam *Ducenariorum* vocaretur, judicaretque de levioribus causis," *In Augustum*, cap. XXXII.

[6] "Sublatusque fuit mundanis dignitatibus: *ducenarius* potius quam episcopus vocari volens," Cyprianus I *Epis.* IV; Eusebius, *Historia ecclesiastica*, VII. ·30.

[7] "Ornamenta consularia etiam procuratoribus *ducenariis* indulsit," *In Claudium*, cap. XXXIV.

[8] "Post tribunum primicerius, deinde senator, *ducenarius*, biarchus, circitor, eques," *Ad Pammachum*.

[9] "Primipilaribus post emeritam militiam, perfectissimatus, vel *ducenae*, vel centenae, vel egregiatus dari potest" (317), *Cod. Theod.* VIII. 4. 3; "Caesarianos in actu dumtaxat constitutos, ad perfectissimatus, vel *ducenae* bel centenae, vel egregiatus dignitates non opportet admitti" (317), *ibid.*, X. 7. 1, and XII. 1. 5.

[10] "Sumentibus *ducenariis* principatum hanc tribuimus facultatem, ut his pro se liberos ac fratres suos in eadem militia serenitatis nostrae nutu liceat

*ducenarii* were apparently somewhat arbitrary in their methods, for their transgressions in executing orders called forth severe measures against them, and it was especially provided for that they could not summon a debtor without due warrant, and in case of false arrest they were severely punished.[1]

The Frankish *tunginus, thunginus* is in every particular identical with the *ducenarius*. He is mentioned with the *centenarius*, but obviously as occupying a higher position.[2] The Pithoean glosses say that the *thunginus* is the judge who comes after the count and who elsewhere is called *decanus*.[3] The *thunginus*, like the *ducenarius*, collects debts, but only with a due warrant, and, mindful of the severe punishment meted out to him in case of false arrest, is very slow in bringing the debtor into court. The law of the year 315 completely explains the procedure in *De fides factas*. If a freeman or letus has loaned money to a person and cannot collect it, he summons him to court *nexti canthichius*, saying, "I ask you, *thunginus, nexti canthichus gasacio meo* him who owes me the money." Then the *thunginus* must say, "*nexthe*

conlocare" (396), *ibid.*, VI. 23. 8; "qui ex agentum in rebus numero, militae ordine ac labore decurso, *ducenae* dignitatis meruerit principatum, aut qui viro inlustri magistro officiorum, ut probatus fuit adiutor, eo tempore quo iam honoratis viris coeperit adgregari, eorum, qui vicariam egerint praefecturam honore potiatur" (426), *ibid.*, VI. 27. 20, 21.

[1] "Si quis se a *ducenariis*, vel centenariis, ac precipue fisci advocatis, laesum esse cognoscit, adire iudicia ac probare iniuriam non moretur, ut in eum qui convictus fuerit conpetenti severitate vindicetur" (315), *ibid.*, VIII. 10. 1; "*ducenarios* ab exactione provincialium secundum constitutionem sacrae memoriae Constantini sinceritas tua iubebit arceri" (364), *ibid.*, XI. 7. 9; "*ducenarii*, et centenarii, sive sexagenarii, non prius debent aliquem convenire, quam a tabulario civitatis nominatim brevis accipiant debitorum. Quam quidem exactionem sine omni fieri concussione oportet, ita ut, si quis in iudicio questus, quod indebite exactus est, et aliquam inquietudinem sustinuit, hoc ipsum probare potuerit, severa in exactores sententia proferatur" (315), *ibid.*, XI. 7. 1.

[2] "Ante *thunginum* aut centenario," *Lex salica* XLIV. 1; "*Thunginus* aut centenarius mallo indicant," XLVI. 1; "mallo quem *thunginus* aut centenarius indixerit," XLVI. 4.

[3] "*Thunginus*: iudex qui post comitem est. *degan.* sollensib."

*ganthicio* I him, as the Salic law demands." Still the *thunginus* does not dare to collect the debt, but sits with a posse before the house of the debtor, allowing the debt to grow larger by fines. Finally the *grafio*, after similar ceremonial delays, dares to proceed against the defendant.[1]

We shall first ascertain what the mysterious words *nexte canthichius*, about which so much learned nonsense has been written, mean. First we shall put down all the readings in the various codes preserved for the queer formula, in order to see whether some approach to intelligibility may not thus be gained.

1. *nexti canthichius, nexticantigyus, nestiganti huius, sicti cantidios, sicum nestigante, nestigante huius, nestigantio sic.*

2. *nexti canthichus gasacio, nexticantigyus gasacium, nestiganti his sagatio, instigante cuius cassatium, nestigantio cassahone, nestigante gasationum, ne istigante gassachio.*

3. *nexthe ganthichio, nexticantigium, nestigante, instigante, nestigatio, instigante ego sagatium, nestigantio gasachio.*

The only intelligible word one gets out of this chaos is the Latin *instigante*, and this is a correct and important reading. Among the Ostrogoths the warrant of the *saio* contained the

[1] "Si quis ingenuus aut letus alteri fidem fecerit, tunc ille cui fides facta est in xl noctes aut quomodo illius cum testibus uel cum illo qui praecium adpreciare debent accedere debet. Et si ei noluerit fidem facta soluere, mał thalasciasco, hoc est sol. xv super debitumquod fidem fecerit culp. iud. Si adhuc noluerit conponere debet eum ad mallum manire et sic *nexti canthichius* malare debet: Rogo te, *thungine*, ut *nexti canthichus gasacio meo* illo qui mihi fidem fecit et debitum debeat unde ei fidem fecerat. Tunc *thunginus* dicere debet: *nexthe ganthichio* ego illo in hoc quod lex salega ait. Tunc ipse cui fides facta est testare debet ut nulli alteri nec soluat nec pignus donet solutionis, nisi ante ille impleat quod ei fidem fecerat. Et festinanter ad domum illius illa die antequam sol collocet cum testibus ambulare debet et rogare sibi debitum soluere. Si hoc noluerit facere, solem ei collocet. Tunc si solem collocauerit, cxx dinarios qui faciunt solidos iii super debitum adcrescant. Istud usque ad tres vices per tres nondenas fieri debet, et in tercio ista omnia facta si noluerit conponere, usque ad ccclx dinarios h. e. solidos novem adcrescat, id est ut per singulas admonitiones vel solem collocatum terni solidi super debitum adcrescant," l.

words *te compellente, te imminente*,[1] that is, the sovereign gave the *saio* the right to compel, hence *imminens* itself became the equivalent for "confiscator, saio."[2] We can now see how *saio*, that is, *socio*, came to take the place of "exactor." The documents show that the usual formula of confiscation was rather "*socio fisco coactus exsolvere*" than "*te imminente coactus exsolvere*," because the usual confiscation was by order of the fiscus and not by special edict of the sovereign, even as we have recorded in Cassiodorus. But if *te imminente* has produced *imminens* "confiscator," *socio fisco* must similarly produce *socio, saio* "confiscator," as has actually happened.

Among the Visigoths the warrant reads *iudice insistente*,[3] that is, "by authority of the judge." The Frankish and other Germanic laws occasionally employ such phrases, but *socio fisco* or a similar combination, as has already been shown, generally takes their place. But in the mysterious formula of the Salic law there can be nothing but a corruption of *instigante iudice causacio mea (audiatur)*, as may be judged from the recorded Ostrogothic "*te imminente causa legibus*

---

[1] "Ad iudicium comitis Dudae saepe dictus saio *te compellente* veniat audiendus," Cassiodorus, *Variae*, IV. 27; "*te* debeat *imminente* construi," II. 39; "mox ei praedium cum alio eiusdem meriti *vobis imminentibus* a pervasore reddatur," III. 20; "*te imminente* cogantur exsolvere debitas functiones," IV. 14; "ut coram partibus positis *te imminente* censeatur," IV. 32; "*imminente* Duda saione nostro," IV. 39; "*te imminente* causa legibus audiatur," IV. 46; "ad iudicium competens *te imminente* conveniant," V. 31.

[2] "Proinde factum ut curiales . . . *imminentum* sollicitudine coacti gravia damna sentirent," II. 25; "ipse enim *imminentem* necessarium facit, qui sollemnia praebere distulerit," XII. 8.

[3] "Et si potentior fuerit, *insistente iudice* quartam partem facultatum suarum amittat," II. 4. 14; "mox iubente principe vel quolibet *iudice insistente* non solum castrationem virium perferat, sed insuper illam in so iacturam excipiat ultionis," III. 5. 7; "*insistente iudice* cogantur exsolvere," V. 6. 6; "ad integrum ipso *(iudice) insistente*," VII. 4. 4; "eundem servam pro facti temeritate *insistente iudice* ei, cuius res invasit vel abstulit, serviturum tradere non desistat," VIII. 1. 5; "ut, si Goti de Romanorum tertiam quippiam tulerint, *iudice insistente* Romanis cuncta reforment," X. 1. 16; "*iudice insistente* heredibus mortui cogatur exsolvere," XI. 2. 1.

audiatur," for it is only by a proper warrant that the *thunginus* could cause any arrest. The *thunginus* did not survive long among the Franks, for in the later period we hear only of the count as a judge. In the Ribuarian law he is not mentioned at all, but the phrase of the appeal to the *thunginus*, which in intelligible language was, "rogo te, *tungine*, ut insistente iudice causacio mea audiatur," is employed in the corrupted form, "ego te *tangano* ut mihi legem dicas."[1] Precisely the same phrase is used in the identical case in the Salic law, so we shall investigate the latter.

If the rachinburgii, sitting in the malloberg, refuse to hear a case, then the plaintiff says, "I *tangon* you to hear my case according to the Salic law." If the rachinburgii still refuse, they pay three solidi by distress, and if they refuse once more they are once more distrained and pay fifteen solidi.[2] The derivation of this law from the *De fides factas* is obvious. The rachinburgii are placed in a position of debtors who refuse to pay their just debts. A warrant has to be sworn out for distress, and the procedure is the same as in the former case. The incomprehensible address to the *tunginus* is here turned into a verb *tangonare*, which has survived in the French *tangonner* "to urge on, prod," and this word *tangono* is taken as an expression for a distrainable action, hence in the Ribuarian law it is distinctly provided that interpellations in court are not distrainable, "sine *tangano* loquitur."[3]

---

[1] "Si quis causam suam prosequitur, et raginburgii inter eos secundum legem Ribuariam dicere noluerint, tunc illi, in quem sententiam contrariam dixerit dicat: Ego vos *tangano* ut mihi legem dicatis," LV.

[2] "Si qui rachineburgii in mallobergo sedentes dum causam inter duos discutiunt, legem dicere noluerint, debet eis dicere ab illo qui causa prosequitur: hic ego vos *tancono* ut legem dicatis secundum legem Salegam. Quod si ille dicere noluerint, septem de illos rachineburgios cxx dinarios qui faciunt solidos III ante solem collocatum culpabiles iudicentur. Quod si nec legem dicere noluerint nec de ternos solidos fidem facerent, solem illis collocatum, DC dinarios qui faciunt solidos xv culpabiles iudicentur," LVII.

[3] "Quod si quis in iudicio pro servo interpellatus fuerit, quod si servos tales non fuerit, unde dominus eius de fiducia securus esse posset, in iudicio re-

Just as *socio fisco* has produced *saio* "confiscator," and *distringente fisco* has given English *distrain*, so *tungine* of the warrant for distress has produced *tangono* "I appeal for a warrant to levy distress, I urge action, compel."

We can now determine what became of the *centenarius* of the Theodosian Code and the Salic law. In the *Pactus pro tenore pacis*, variously dated from 511–558, Chlotar complains that the night watches failed to catch the thieves, that, therefore, *centenae* be established. The rest of the decree is puzzling, but it is clear that if the thief is caught by a *trustis*, the latter gets half of the fine.[1] The conclusion of the *Pactus* makes it clear that the *centenarii* are those who are called *in truste*.[2] Some manuscripts have the word *antrustio* for *in truste*,[3] and there are recorded many variant forms *antrutio*, *antrusio*, etc. For *in truste* we get once the significant reading *ex truste*.[4] If we now turn to *Edictum Chilperici*, of the year 561–584, we find that the *antrustiones* are

spondeat ad interrogationes: 'Sta tu,' et liceat ei sine *tanganu* (*tangano, tancano, tagano, tangno*) loquere et dicere: 'Ego ignoro' ", xxx. 1; "hoc etiam constituemus, ut nullum hominem regium, Romanum vel tabularium interpellatum in iudicio non *tanganet* (*tangat, tangenet*) et nec alsaccia requirat," lviii. 19; "absque *tangano* coniurent," lviii. 29; "si quis in iudicio interpellatus cartam per manibus habuerit, nulle ei male ordine vel invasio requeratur; quia dum interpellatus respondit ad interrogationes Sta. tu, et sine *tangano* loquatur et dicat; non malo ordine sed per testamentum hoc teneo," lix. 8.

[1] "Quod si post (per) *truste* inuenitur, medietate conpositione *truste* (*trustis, trustes*) adquirat," J. Hessels and H. Kern, *Lex salica*, p. 417.

[2] "Pro itinere pacis iubemus ut in *truste centenariae* ponantur, per quorum fide atque sollicitudine pax praedicta seueritas. Ut *centenariae* latro licet prae esse caritatis indisrupta uinculum ut *centenariae* inter communes prouintias licentiam habeant latrones sequi uel uestigia adsignata minare aut *in truste* qua defecerat, sicut dictum est causa remaneat, ita ut continuo capitalem ei quem perdiderat reformare festinet, et latronem perquirat, quem sine (si in) *truste* peruenient, medietate sibi uindicet uel dilatura si fuerit de facultate latronis ei qui damno pertulerit sartiatur," *ibid.*, p. 418.

[3] "Qui *in truste* dominica (*antruscione* dominico) fuit," xli. 3; "sine *truste* dominica (*andruscio* dominicus) fuit," xlii. 1.

[4] "Si quis hominem in hoste occiserit, triplici conpositione conponat sicut in patria conponere debuit, excepto si *ex truste* (*truxte*) regale non fuerit ille homo. Nam si *ex truste* regale fuerit," etc., lxiii. 1, 2 *Lex emendata*.

mentioned after the *obtimates*, that is, they rank with the *agentes in rebus*, the confiscators. This is proved by the statement that the graphio goes with seven rachinburgii *antrustionis* to confiscate property.¹ Indeed, this very passage contains the word from which *trustis* is derived. It is the word *extrudere* "to evict, confiscate,"² in which sense it is classical Latin and is used as a legal term by Ulpian. Instead of the participle *extrusus* we have here the form *extruste*, which the other manuscripts have changed to *intruste*, *antrustio*, even as Visigothic *ex squalido* was in Italy changed to *in gualdo*.³ But that *extrudere* is the correct word from which this *trustis* is derived is proved conclusively by the *Lex ribuaria*, where the identical law has *strude* or *trude* for "confiscation"⁴ and *in strute regia*, corrected to *in truste regia* for the Salic *trustis*.⁵

In the Theodosian Code we frequently find *solatium* used in the sense of "pecuniary aid," almost the same as "salà-

¹ "Pertractantes in Dei nomine cum uiris magnificentissimis obtimatibus uel *antrustionibus* et omni populi nostro . . . et graphio cum vii rachymburgiis *antrutionis* bonis credentibus, aut quis sciant accionis, a casa illius ambulent et pretium faciunt, et quod graphio tollere debet . . . nam agens et qui mallat ipsum ad nos adducant, et *adtrutionis* secundum legem consecutus habuerit inter octuaginta et iiii noctes ipsa inuitatio et lex faciat sicut superius scriptum est," *ibid.*, p. 409 *f.*

² "Et si rachymburgiis nec vii nec iii dare potuerit nec dat graphio et ille qui accepit res illius quem contra legem et iustitiam *extruderit* et ille qui male inuitauit soluat, cui res fuerunt . . . et si dixerit illi cui res tolluntur quod male eum *destruat*, et contra legem et iustitia," *ibid.*, p. 410.

³ See p. 84 *ff.*

⁴ "Quod si ad septimo mallo non venerit, tunc illi, qui eum manit, ante comite cum septem raginburgiis in haraho iurare debit, quod eum *ad strude* (*istrudem, trude*) legitima admallatum habet; et sic iudex fiscalis ad domum illius accedere debet, et legitima *strude* exinde auferre et ei tribuere qui eum interpellavit . . . quod si ipsam *strudem* (*trudem*) contradicere voluerit, et ad ianuam suam cum spata tracta accesserit, et eam in porta sive in poste posuerit, tunc iudex fideiussores ei exigat, ut se ante regem repraesentit, et ibidem cum arma sua contra contrarium suum re studeat defensare," xxxii. 3, 4; "si quis iudicem fiscalem ad res alienas iniuste tollendas, antequam ei fidem fecerit, aut ad *extrodo* (*extrudo, exdrote, exstrudem, strude*) admallatum habuerit, invitare praesumpserit, bis vicinos et quinos solidos multetur," li. 1.

⁵ "Si quis eum interficerit qui *in strute* (*truste, dustria*) regia est," xi. 1.

rium." Throughout the sixth century and later it has the meaning of "support, help,"[1] hence *solatium collectum* is "a posse,"[2] though I shall show later that it has arisen from an entirely different phrase. From this application of *solatium* to the duty of the *antrustiones* have developed the various connotations of *trustis*. Since *trustis* is a synonym of *solatium*, it itself means "solatium, auxilium, consolatio, spes,"—meanings which appear in German *trôst*, etc., while *trustis* has also the connotation of *fides*.[3] An *antrustio* is the equal of a *fidelis*, and so we have the Ribuarian form *drudus* "trusted friend," in the phrase "*solatium* drudorum," recorded in 858.[4]

If we now turn to the Visigothic laws, we find another equivalent for the exactor or confiscator. The ancient law of Theudis calls him *compulsor vel executor*.[5] The later laws employ *compulsor exercitus, servus dominicus*,[6] or *thiufadus*.

[1] "Experientia itaque tua praefato supplici ecclesiastica non desinat impertire *solacia*," Gregorii I *Registri*, IX. 209; "Bonifatium notarium evocatus ad *solatium* Chlodovechi," Gregorii Turonensis *Historia Francorum*, in *MGH*. p., 104; "Theudoricus autem, Chlothacharium fratrem et Theudobertum filium in *solatio* suo adsumptos, cum exercitu abiit," *ibid.*, p. 115.

[2] "Qui vero edictum nostrum ausus fuerit contempnere, in cuiuslibet iudicis pago primitus admissum fuerit, ille iudex *collectum solatium* ipsum raptorem occidat" (596), *Childeberti Secundi Decretio*, in *MGH., Capitularia*, vol. I, p. 16; "agentes igitur episcoporum aut potentum per potestatem nullius res *collecta solacia* nec auferant, nec cuiuscumque contemptum per se facere non praesument" (614), *ibid.*, p. 23.

[3] "Rectum est, ut qui nobis fidem pollicerentur inlesam, nostro tueantur auxilio. Et quia illi fidelis, Deo propitio, noster venens ibi in palatio nostro una cum arma sua in manu nostra *trustem* et fidelitatem nobis visus est coniurasse: propterea per presentem preceptum decernemus ac iobemus, ut deinceps memoratus ille inter numero *antruscionorum (antrustionorum, andrustionorum)* conputetur," *Marculfi Formulae*, I. 18.

[4] "Sine adiutorio uxoris ac filiorum et sine solatio et comitatu *drudorum* atque vassorum nuda et desolata exibit," *MGH., Capitularia*, vol. II, p. 429.

[5] "Simili hetiam *compulsores vel executores* decreto prestringimus, ut non pro sua conmoda exigant volumtate, sed ab eis, quos propria evectione conpulerint, subvectum tantum super eum accipiant caballorum. Nec illi prius conmoda *conpulsionis* exigant, quam suas in iudicio exerent actiones," *MGH., Lex Visig.*, p. 468.

[6] "*Servi dominici*, id est *compulsores exercitus*, quando Gotos in hostem ire compellunt, si eis aliquid tulerint . . . restituere non morentur," IX. 2. 2; "*servi dominici*, qui in hoste exire conpellunt," IX. 2. 5.

The latter, who is not only a military official, but also a judge,[1] rates directly after the comes or vicarius,[2] that is, he occupies precisely the same position that the *thunginus* does in Merovingian times, even as the *servus dominicus* is the same as *puer regius* of the Salic law. It is generally assumed that Gothic *thiufadus* is derived from *thusundifaths* "millenarius," but that is impossible by any criterion one may choose. Such a contraction is simply impossible, and the *thiufadus* is not identical with the *millenarius*, for the *millenarius* is mentioned with and above the *thiufadus*. It is quite true, in the military hierarchy the *thiufadus* was identified with an officer above the *centenarius*, hence naturally he stood somewhere near and may even have been identified with the *millenarius*. As a judge the *thiufadus* occupied a position below the count, hence is absolutely identical with the *ducenarius* of the Theodosian Code and the *thunginus* of the Franks, even as the Codex Parisinus Lat. 4670[3] correctly glosses *thiufadus* with "vassus regis," an exact rendering of the Salic "puer regius." I have already pointed out that the *compulsor*, in fact all the *agentes in rebus*, of which the *thiufadus* is one, were known as *devoti*.[4] Hence *thiufadus* can

---

[1] "Cum ceteris negotiis criminalium etiam causarum *thiuphadis* iudicandi concessa licentia, criminosos a legum sententiis ipsi vindicare non audeant, sed debita in eis, ut conpetit, censura exerceant. Qui *thiuphadi* tales eligant, quibus vicissitudines suas audiendas iniungant, ut ipsis absentibus illi causas et temperanter discutiant et iuste decernant," ɪɪ. 1. 16.

[2] "Si quis iudicem aut comitem aut vicarium comitis seu *thiuphadum* suspectos habere se dixerit," ɪɪ. 1. 24; "dux, comes, vicarius, pacis assertor, *thiuphadus*, millenarius, quingentenarius, centenarius, defensor, numerarius," ɪɪ. 1. 27; "ducibus vel comitibus, *tiufadis* atque vicariis," ɪv. 5. 6; "dux aut comes, *thiufadus* aut vicarius," ɪx. 2. 8; "ducibus, comitibus, *thiufadis* vicariis," *ibid.;* "admonitio ducis vel comitis, *thiufadi*, vicarii seu cuiuslibet curam agentis," ɪx. 2. 9; "dux, comes, *thiufadus*," *ibid.*; "dux, comes, *tiuphadus*, numerarius, villicus," *Edictum Ervigii* (683), *MGH., Lex Visig.*, p. 479; "quod si ego Ermengaudus comes, aut vicharius, aut vilicus, aut *tuifadus*, aut aliqua persona venerit contra ista scriptura" (1029), Devic and Vaissete, *op. cit.*, vol. v, col. 384.

[3] *MGH., Lex Visig.*, p. xxii.

[4] "Bei den Subalternbeamten erscheint seit der zweiten Hälfte des vierten

be nothing but *thiwadus*, that is, Lat. *devotus*, the honorific title of the executive officer who, as we have seen from the Ostrogothic documents, was generally a Goth. We can now proceed to the determination of the origin of the Burgundian confiscator, the *wittiscalcus*. To do this we must first establish the proper meaning of *senior* in the Visigothic laws. Here we have the *seniores palatii, aulae*,[1] who represent the higher officials at the court, in which sense *seniores* is used elsewhere.[2] These references are all from laws promulgated in the second half of the seventh century. In the *Antiquae* this word is nowhere employed, but in the subscriptions of illustrious men to the acts of the Third Council of Toledo (589) the reading "similiter et omnes *seniores Gothorum* subscripserunt"[3] follows after the signatures of the clergy and "viri illustres." "Omnes *seniores* Gothorum" was still used in a law of the first half of the seventh century,[4] where it apparently is secondary to "primates palatii," and this is borne out by the use of "*seniores* loci" for officials be-

Jahrhunderts der Titel *vir devotissimus*, der auch in den Inschriften häufig, meist *v. d.* abgekürzt, auftritt. Dieser Titel, der das nahe Treuverhältniss zum Kaiser bezeichnet, ist daher vorzugsweise den zu ihm in näherem Verhältniss stehenden Soldaten, insbesondere den *domestici* und *protectores* und den militärisch organisierten *agentes in rebus*, sodann aber auch den kaiserlichen Kanzleibeamten beigelegt worden," O. Hirschfeld, *Die Rangtitel der römischen Kaiserzeit*, in *Sitzungsberichte der Berliner Akademie der Wissenschaften*, 1901, p. 607 *f*.

[1] "Sane duces omnes *senioresque palatii* ad huiusmodi sententiam obnoxii tenebuntur ... qui aut de bello refugiunt, aut in bellica profectione constituti extra *senioris* sui permissum alibi properasse reperiuntur," variant to IX. 2. 9; "quod serenissimo nostrae celsitudinis iussu a venerandis patribus et clarissimis *palatii senioribus* discreta titulorum exaratione est editum" (681), *Concilium Toletanum* XII, in *MGH., Lex Visig.*, p. 476; "hoc solum vos, honorabiles Dei sacerdotes, cunctosque *aulae regiae seniores* ... adiuramus" (639), *Conc. Tolet.* XVI., *ibid.*, p. 483.

[2] "Ununquisque (arma) a *seniore* vel domino suo iniuncta ... principi, duci, vel comiti suo presentare studeat," IX. 2. 9; "conventus sacerdotum atque etiam *seniorum*," XII. 1. 3.

[3] *MGH., Lex Visig.*, p. 485.

[4] "Quicumque ex palatii nostri primatibus vel *senioribus gentis Gotorum*," III. 1. 5.

low the comes or iudex.[1] Obviously we here observe in the seventh century the development of *senior* in the sense of *dominus*, but in the sixth century it seems to have had an inferior meaning, the "*seniores* Gotorum" standing below the highest officials. Beginning with the Council of Toledo of the year 653, for which we have a series of signatures, the "viri illustres officii palatini" consist of the good Byzantine hierarchy of "comes cubiculariorum, notariorum, patrimoniorum, spatariorum, thesaurorum, stabuli," and of the mysterious *comes scanciarum*,[2] but of the "*seniores* Gotorum" there is not a trace. We know from the Germanic root of this *scancia* that it must mean "butlery." Ducange has no early quotations for the word, but the only two recorded quotations from the Latin documents for *scalcus* give it the meaning of "butler,"[3] hence there can be no doubt that the two are identical in origin. This may be shown in another way.

In the beginning of the seventh century the Frankish kings promulgated their decrees in the name of their bishops, dukes, counts, domestics, and *agentes in rebus*,[4] and this formula was again used in the beginning of the eighth century.[5] In the second half of the seventh century the list is more pretentious, the place of the *agentes* being occupied by domestici, refendarii, siniscalci, comes palati,[6] but occasion-

---

[1] "Denuntiet aut sacerdoti aut comiti aut iudici aut *senioribus* loci aut etiam in conventu publico vicinorum," VIII. 5. 6.

[2] *MGH., Lex Visig.*, p. 485 f.

[3] "Pincernae seu *scalchi; scalcus*, id est, architriclinus", Ducange, sub *scalchus*.

[4] "Viris inlustrebus Vuandelberto duci, Gaganrico domestico et omnibus *agentibus*" (632), Lauer and Samaran, *op. cit.*, p. 5; "duci . . . grafioni vel omnebus *agentebus*" (639), *ibid.*, p. 8; "episcopis . . . ducibus . . . comiti, vel omnibus *agentibus*" (640), *ibid.*, p. 19.

[5] "Viris apostolicis, patribus episcopis, necnon inlustribus viris: ducibus, patriciis, comitibus, vel omnibus *agentibus*" (727), *ibid.*, p. 85; "viris inlustribus, gravionibus atque omnibus *agentibus*, vel iunioribus eorum" (743), *ibid.*, p. 86; "viris apostolicis patribus nostris, necnon et imperatoribus omnibus comitibus vel omnibus *agentibus*" (744), *ibid.*, p. 87.

[6] "Grafionibus . . . *siniscalcis* . . . comite palati" (657), *ibid.*, p. 9; ". . . *seniscalcis* . . . refendariis . . . comite palati" (657), *ibid.*, p. 10; "episcopis

ally the older form with *agentes* is employed, and from the
exclusion of *domestici* it is clear that *agentes* refers to the
*siniscalci* and possibly some others mentioned after them.[1]
The *siniscalci* stand in the same relation to the optimati,
comites, graviones, in which the *seniores Gotorum* are to the
comites, iudices of the Visigothic laws, and obviously the
*comites scanciarum* of the Visigothic signatures are identical
with the *siniscalci*. This is conclusively proved by a statement in the St. Gall Codex of the *Lex romana raetica curiensis*
to the effect that the *seniores ministri* included the camara-
rius, butiglarius, *senescalcus*, iudex publicus, and comes-
tabulus.[2] As we have already come across the *iuniores* in connection with the *seniores*, it is interesting to observe from the
same passage that a iunior was a vassal, either a freeman or
slave, who by the favor of his lord was allowed to hold a
ministerium, apparently a special office like that of the
*agentes in rebus*, but of less importance, since the composition
for the death was smaller.[3]

We now can easily determine the Roman office from which
the Gothic *scancia* and the Frankish *siniscalcus* are derived.
Mommsen has shown that the bodyguard of the emperors,
called *schola*, was originally recruited almost exclusively from
among the Germanic tribes and that they did not perform
field duties, but personally attended on the sovereign.[4] In the

... optimatis ... gravionebus ... *seniscalcis* ... comite palati" (691), *ibid.*,
p. 14; "episcopis ... optematis ... comitebus ... grafionibus ... domesticis
... referendariis ... *seniscalcis* ... comite palati" (693), *ibid.*, p. 16; "episcopis ... majore domus nostro ... optimatis ... comitebus ... domesticis
... *seniscalcis* ... comite palati" (697), *ibid.*, p. 19.

[1] "Viris inlustribus ducibus, comitibus, domesticis, vel omnibus *agentibus*"
(675), *MGH., Dip.*, vol. I, p. 41; "patriciis et omnebus ducis seu comitebus vel
*actorebus publicis*" (667), *ibid.*, p. 44.

[2] "Si quis de *senioribus quinque ministribus* occiderit, de qualecumque linia
fuerit, ad cxx solidos fiat recompensatus," *MGH., Leg.* v. p. 442.

[3] "Si vassallum domnicum de casa sine ministerio aut *iunior* in ministerio
fuit, et domnus eum honoratum habuit, si ingenuus fuit, fiat conpositus ad
solidos xc, si servus ad lx," *ibid.*

[4] *Hermes*, vol. XXIV, p. 223 *f.*

fifth century the commander of such a bodyguard was known as *comes scholarum* and the soldiers themselves as *scholares*. There were several *scholae* stationed in the East and the West, a distinction being made between *seniores* and *iuniores*, even as many auxiliary troups had this double appellation. The *seniores* of the Goths and in the St. Gall Codex include all the higher soldiery of the bodyguard, the comites of which are nearest to the person of the sovereign; but the guard doing personal service, the *senior scholaris*, must, from the beginning of the fifth century have attended to the sovereign's food or drink, for it is specifically stated in a law of the year 413 [1] that the *comes scholae* was admitted to the emperor's table. This *senior scholaris* has produced *seniscalcus* even as *scholaris* has given *scalcus*, Goth. *skalks* "servant." The *scholae, scholares sacri palatii*, or *collegii gentilium* are several times mentioned in Italian documents of the sixth and seventh centuries,[2] and the combination "*schol. collē. gentilium*" is particularly interesting, since it may explain the Visigothic term "*seniores* Gotorum." Two of these recorded *scholares* have the honorific title *vd.*, that is, *vir devotus*, hence they were in the same class as the apparitores, and so were equal to the "servi dominici." This, then, explains why *scholaris* came to mean "servant." As a Burgundian name *Guidiscalus* is found,[3] it is not easy to determine whether *scalus* or *scalcus* is the older form, but the derivation of either from *schola, scholaris* is certain.

In the Burgundian laws the confiscator is called *wittiscalcus* or *puer noster*.[4] Unfortunately the word *wittiscalcus*

---

[1] *Cod. Theod.* VI. 13. 1.

[2] "Cautio Valeri *Schol*," Marini, *I pap. dipl.*, p. 205; "*vd. scol. collē. gentilium*," *ibid.*, p. 170; "Johannis *vd. schol. sacr. pal.* "(639), *ibid.*, p. 148.

[3] *MGH., Lex Burgundionum*, p. 199, note.

[4] "De *wittiscalcis*. Comitum nostrorum querela processit, quod aliqui in populo nostro eiusmodi praesumptionibus abutantur, ut pueros nostros, qui iudicia exsequuntur, quibusque multam iubemus exigere, et caede conlidant et sublata iussum comitum pignora non dubitent violenter auferre. Qua de re

occurs but twice in any document, and so it cannot be ascertained whether it was ever popular. But it can be shown that it is a badly corrupted form of an older word, for in the dozen manuscripts preserved, none of them of a period earlier than the ninth century, the spelling varies so much that it obviously was not understood. In the title we have the variations *deouitis calcis, de widis calcis, deuitiscalcis, de vitis calcis, de victis calcis, de uitiis caballijs, de utis calcis, de vuittiscalcus, de uuitiscalcis, de uicis calcis,* which all seem to be variations of an original *devotis scalcis;* that is, the name of the "puer noster" was *devotus scalcus,* in which the *de-* was thought to be a preposition, producing *votis, vutis, vuitis, witis scalcis* of the text. This *devotus scalcus* is precisely the same as the *vd. schol.,* that is *vir devotus scholaris* of the Italian documents, hence the first part, *devotus,* is identical with the *thiufadus* of the Visigothic laws, and this again is in meaning identical with the Frankish *thunginus.* The conclusive proof of this identity is given by the gloss "in mallobergo ante *teoda* aut *thunginum*" of the Salic law,[1] where *teoda* can be only our *thiufadus, devotus,* the equal of *thunginus.*

We can now proceed to investigate the philological and cultural effects of the employment of Germans as *agentes in rebus,* who later in the Germanic states became the important officers of the courts. The *thunginus* of the Salic laws is also found in England in the form *gepungen* "emeritus, prouectus, prefectus, veteranus miles,"[2] which at once indicates that

presenti lege decernimus: ut quicumque post hac *pueros nostros* ceciderit et insolenter abstulerit, quod ex ordinatione iudicis docebitur fuisse praesumptum, tripla satisfactione teneatur obnoxius, hoc est: ut per singulos ictus, pro quibus singuli solidi ab his inferuntur, ternos solidos is qui percusserit, cogatur exsolvere .... Mulieres quoque, si *wittiscalcos* nostros contempserint, ad solutionem multae similiter tenebuntur," LXXVI.

[1] "Ista omnia illi iurati dicere debent et alii testes hoc quod in mallo publico ille qui accepit in laisum furtuna ipsa aut ante regem aut in mallo publico b. e. in mallobergo ante *teoda aut thunginum,*" XLVI.

[2] Th. Wright, *Anglo-Saxon and Old English Vocabularies.*

it was a veteran soldier who was invested with the dignity
of a "prefectus," a splendid confirmation of the edicts of the
Theodosian Code in which the office of the *ducenarius* is
mentioned. That this dignity was considerable we have seen
not only from the fact that *geþungen* was mentioned in the
same connection as the ealdermon, that is, as the senior of
the Roman and Visigothic laws, but also from the abstract
noun *geþungenness* "dignitas, honestas, excellentia, fastig-
ium, elatio, arrogantia," recorded in the Anglo-Saxon glosses.
If *thunginus* has produced AS. *geþungen*, with the back formation *þeón* "thrive, flourish, grow, increase," *tunginus* has
produced AS. *dugan* "to profit, avail, be virtuous, good,"
*duguð* "manhood, multitude, troop, army, nobles, nobility,
majesty, glory, virtue, excellence." Both groups are represented in the other Germanic languages. We have Goth.
*dugan* "to be of avail," *þeihan* "to flourish," OHG. *tûgan*
"valere, pollere, prodesse," *toht* "bonus, utilis, valens,"
*tugad, tugund* "virtus, nobilitas," *dîhan* "proficere, pollere,
florere, crescere, excellere," ONorse *þungr* "heavy, weighty."
    If we turn to the Slavic languages, we again find both
groups represented. We have the root *dong-* "strong (Pol.
*duży* "large," Lith. *daug* "much") and the far more important root *tong-* [1] which has developed a variety of meanings.
It will suffice to quote *tuga* "oppression, weight, sorrow, grief,
exhaustion, misfortune, oppression," *tyaža* "lawsuit, quarrel,
disagreement, enmity," *tyagati sya* "to go to law," *tyagati*
"to pull," in order to show that we are dealing with direct
derivatives of *tunginus* "exactor." But they show us much

---

[1] "*Teng-* eine wurzel, aus deren grundbedeutung 'ziehen' sich theilweise
mit hilfe von praefixen, eine fülle von schwer zu vermittelnden bedeutungen
entwickelt hat, die unter die folgenden schlagworte gebracht werden können:
(1) ziehen, dehnen, spannen; (2) binden; (3) fordern, streiten; (4) leiden; (5)
arbeiten; (6) erwerben; (7) schwer sein; (8) lästig sein; (9) bangen. Die wurzel
nimmt durch steigerung die form *tong-* an," Miklosich, *Etymologisches Wörterbuch der slavischen Sprachen*.

more, namely that AS. *þing, þinc* "council, office, gift, thing," *þingian* "to intercede, ask forgiveness, plead, address," *þingung* "pleading, intercession, mediation," *þingere* "interceder, mediator, advocate," OHG. *ding* "conventus, concilium, mallum, forum, causa, res," *gadingon* "pacisci, judicare, convenire, contendere, fedus pangere," *gadingi* "placitum, pactum, conditio, spes," *gadingo* "patronus," and other similar forms are directly derived from the same *thunginus, tunginus,* and that, therefore, OHG. *dûhjan* "premere," *ziuhan* "pull" etc., are equally back formations of the same root *thung-, tung-.*

From the Salic *trustis* are derived not only OHG. *trôst* "confidence, security, etc.," but also, by a back formation, AS. *treow* "troth, trust," OHG. *triuwa* "true," Goth. *trauan* "to trust," OPrussian *druwis* "faith," Slavic *druh, drug,* "companion, friend, other." Gothic *triggwa* "true" was obviously formed at a time when OHG. *triuwa* had already produced OFrench *triues* "truce, compact," LLatin *tregua* "peace of God." Far more important are the derivatives from *devotus.* As the Goths were the chief apparitors and nearest servants of the Roman emperors, they were considered not only as "servi dominici," but also as the "devoted people," as which they were frequently addressed,[1] hence *devotus* produces not only the connotations "servant," but also "people, gentiles." We have Goth. *þiwadw,* AS. *þeowot, þeowet* "servitude," from which come AS. *þeow* "servant, bondsman, slave," *þeowe, þeowen, þeowin, þeown* "a female servant," and Gothic has *þius* "slave," *þiwi* "female slave," *þewisa* "servants," while OHG. has exclusively *diu, diwa* "female servant," *diorna* "girl, maid." From the OHG. is derived OSlavic *dêva, dêvaya* "girl," while OHG. has lost the masculine from which

---

[1] "Aequabili ordinatione disponas populumque nobis *devotum* per tuam iustitiam facias esse gratissimum," Cassiodorus, *Variae,* IX. 8; "nec moram fas est incurrere iussionem, quae *devotos* maxime noscitur adiuvare," *ibid.,* 1. 17.

*diu* "female servant" was formed, the Slavic *děti* "children,"
Russ. *ditya* "child," originally "puer noster, regius," as
used in old documents, prove that a form *diot, diet,* now preserved only in OHG. in the sense of "people," originally
meant "puer noster," and this is proved conclusively by
Finnish *dievddo, divdo* "mas, vir," which has preserved both
the old form *devotus* and the meaning attached to it. Similarly the OHG. *dionôn* "to serve," ONorse *þjónari* "servant," ORussian *tiun, tivun* "servant, officer, ruler," have
lost a *d*, as is again proved conclusively by the Finnish
*teudnar* "servus, famulus."

Goth. *þiuda*, OHG. *diota, diot, diet*, AS. *þioda, þiod* "people," Goth. *þiudans* "ruler" have been referred to Umbrian
*tota-, tuta-* "urbs," Sabinian *touta* "community," Oscan *touto*
"civitas, populus," *túvtíks* "publicus," but that is totally
impossible, since the dialectic Italian words proceed obviously from a meaning "common, whole," that is, from Latin
*totus*, while the Germanic words cannot be separated from
the meaning "servus," a connection which has arisen only
through the employment of the German people as "servi
dominici." This is further shown by the fact that the *seniores Gotorum*, with which we have already met, were derived from the *schola gentilium seniorum*, wherefore *þiuda*
was identical with "gentiles," producing Lettish *tauta* "foreign country, Germany," OSlavic *tuždĭ, čuždĭ* "foreign,"
*čudŭ* "giant;" but these words may have developed directly
from the connection of *þiuda* with the Germans. In addition
to derivatives from *devotus* we have also others, such as AS.
*þenian* "to serve," *þen, þegn, þaegn* "servant, attendant,
valiant man, soldier knight," ONorse *þegn* "subditus, homo
liber," OHG. *degan* "masculus, herus, miles," which have
arisen from Latin *decanus*, which was confused with *ducena,
ducenarius*, as is specifically stated in the Pithoean glosses.

The Celtic languages have also this confusion, for from *devotus* are derived Irish *tuath*, Welsh *tûd*, Cornish *tûs* "nation, people, men," while *decanus* has given Breton *dên*, Cornish *den*, Welsh *dyn*, Irish *duine* "man."

# SCULCA

In the *Notitia dignitatum* there is a reference to *exculcatores, excultatores, exculeatores Brittaniciani*, that is, to British scouts. Ammianus Marcellinus uses the word *proculcatores*, and Vegetius refers to this word as being new.[1] The form *exculcator* is obviously popular etymology, as though it were from *exculcare* "to press out."[2] In the sixth century *sculca* was used by Gregory the Great,[3] and in Byzantium σκοῦλκα, σκοῦλτα "scout" σκουλκεύειν "to do scout duty" were freely employed. But the Greeks also used the shorter form κοῦλκα, which also appears in LLatin, as we shall soon see. The form *exculeatores* of the *Notitia dignitatum* must have arisen from a shorter form *culeatores*, and this is actually found in Welsh and Cornish, that is, in British, until the present day. We have Cornish *golyas, gollyaz, golzyas, colyas, gologhas* "to watch, keep awake," *guillua* "a watch, vigilia," Welsh *gwyl, gwel* "a sight, a show, holiday, festival," that is, "vigilia" in the Christian sense, *gwyliad* "a vision, watching," *gwyliadur* "a sentinel," *gwyliaw* "to watch, be vigilant, look out." The Irish has only *feil* "festival, holiday," but all of these words are directly derived from Lat. *vigilia*, and Welsh *gwyliadur* at once explains Lat. (*ex*)*culcator*, which the *Notitia dignitatum* distinctly associates with the Britons.

This *culcare* has an interesting history on Frankish territory. The Salic law has a curious phrase "solem *collocare*," which has given rise to a lot of extravagant ideas about "primitive" Germanic law. A man was not allowed to re-

[1] "Post hoc erant ferentarii et levis armatura, quos nunc *exculcatores* (*scultatores, exscultatores*) et armaturas dicimus," xxvii. 10. 10.

[2] E. Böcking, *Notitia dignitatum*, Bonnae 1839–1853, vol. ii, p. 228.

[3] *MGH.*, Gregorii i. *Registri*, vol. i, p. 130.

gain stolen property as his own unless he had legally claimed
it by the act known as "solem *collocare*."[1] A master refusing
to punish his guilty slave at the request of a third party, that
party could not take the master to court except by the act of
"solem *collocare*" for the period of three times seven days.[2]
Any refusal to pay a debt, to appear in court brings about
the summons to court by a preceding "solem *collocare*."[3]
One law has *solsatire*[4] instead of *solem collocare*, and that
this is not merely a misprint or mistake is proved by a
reading *collegato sol sista* and by the stereotyped phrase "legibus custodire et *solsadire*" of the Merovingian documents[5]

[1] "Si ille uero quod per vestigio sequitur, quod si agnoscere dicit, illi alii
proclamantem, nec auferre per tertia manum voluerit nec *solem* secundum
legem *colocauerit* (*collegauerit, colecauerit, culcauerit, calcauerit*) et tulisse con-
uincitur, MCC din.," XXVII. 3.

[2] "Si dominus serui supplicia distulerit et seruus praesens fuerit, continuo
domino illo qui repetit *solem collegere* (*colecare, culcare, collocare*) debet. Et
eadem septem noctes placitum facere debet ut seruum suum ad supplicium
tradat. Quod si ad septem noctes seruo ipso tradere distulerit, *solem* ei qui
repetit *collecit* (*colecit, culcet, collicet, collocet*); ed sic iterum ad alias septem
noctes placitum faciat id est ad XIIII noctes de prima admonitione conpleantur.
... Tunc repetens *solem* ei cum testibus *collegare* (*colecit, culcet, collecit, collicet,
colocare, collocet*) debet," XL. 7 *ff.*

[3] "Si aliquis alteri aliquid prestiterit de rebus suis et noluerit reddere ...
sic ei *solem collocit* (*colecit, culcet, collecit, collicet, culcauerit, collocet*)," LII; "si
quis ad mallum uenire contempserit ... tunc eum debet manire ante regem,
hoc est an noctes XIIII, et tria testimonia iurare debent quod ibi fuerunt ubi
eum manibit et *solem collocauit* (*collegato sol sista, culcat solem, sola legauit,
collicet ei solem, collocent ei solem*)," LVI; similarly LVII. 1, 2; CVI. 7, 8.

[4] "Et is si ibidem non conueniret aut certe si uenire distulerit, qui ipsum
admallauit ibi eum *solisacire* (*solsatire, sole latere*) debet, et inde postea iterata
uice ad noctes XIIII eum rogare debet, ut in illo mallobergo respondere aut con-
uenire ubi antrusciones mitti iure debent," CVI.

[5] "Sed venientis ad eo placitum ipsi agentis jam dicto abbati, Noviento, in
ipso palacio nostro, per triduo seo per plures dies, ut lex habuit, placitum eorum
vise sunt custudissent, et ipso Ermenoaldo abbati abjectissent vel *solsadissent*
... testimuniavit quod ... placitum eorum ligebus custudierunt, et super-
scriptus Ermenoaldus abba placitum suum custudire neclixeit" (692), Sauer
and Samaran, *op. cit.*, p. 15; "sed veniens ad eo placeto praedictus Chrotcharius,
Valencianis, in ipso palacio nostro, et dum placetum suum ligebus custodibat,
vel ipso Amalberctho *sulsadibat*, sic veniens ex parte filius ipsius Amalberctho,
nomene Amalricus, *sulsadina* sua contradixissit ... Et postia memmoratus
Chrotcharius per triduum aut per amplius, placitum suum, ut lex habuit, cus-
todissit, et ipso Amalberctho abjectissit vel *sulsadissit*" (693), *ibid.*, p. 16.

and of the Formulae.[1] Twice we have *solatium collectum* for "the posse that lies in distress,"[2] and in the Ribuarian law *alsaccia* is used for "distress."[3]

That the ceremony of sitting from morning until sunset for a series of days before proceeding with the case in court was a real act is proved not only by specific statements,[4] but especially by the enormously exaggerated development of this Frankish law among the Irish in their law of distress as laid down in the Brehon Laws. In either case we have nothing but a development of the corresponding Roman law of the year 382, according to which the severer cases were not to be proceeded against at once, but the defendants were to be watched by a guard for the period of thirty days.[5] The very phrase which contains this injunction, "reos sane accipiat vinciatque *custodia*, et *excubiis sollertibus* vigilanter obseruet," or "*sollicitis* obseruet *excubiis*,"[6] became the stereotyped sentence from which has developed our legend of watching until the sun went down. That this phrase is

---

[1] " Noticia *solsadii*, qualiter vel quibus presentibus illi homo placetum suum adtendit Andecavis civetate. . . Qui ipsi iam superius nomenati placitum eorum legebus a mane usque ad vesperum visi fuerunt custodisse," *Form. Andec.*, 12; " et ipsi illi ad placetum suum adfuit et triduum legebus custodivit'et *solsadivit*," *ibid.*, 13; "qui illi ad placitum adfuit una cum antestis suis, per legibus triduum custodivit et *solsadivit*," *ibid.*, 14; " qui illi et germano suo illi placito illi de manum usque ad vesperum placitum suum legibus custodivit et *solsadivit*," *ibid.*, 53; " a quo placito veniens memoratus illi in palacio nostro, et per triduo seu amplius, ut lex habuit, placitum suum custodisset vel memorato illo abiect-isset vel *solsatisset* . . . antedictus ille placitum suum legibus custodivit et eum abiectivit vel *solsativit*," *Marculfi form.*, I. 37; " sed memoratus quidem ille per triduum suum custodivit placitum et iam dicto illo secundum legem obiectivit vel *solsativit*," *Form. Turon.* 33.

[2] See note 2, p. 29.                  [3] See note 3, p. 26.

[4] " Iniuriosus tamen ad placitum in conspectu regis Childeberthi advenit et *per triduum usque occasum solis* observavit," Greg. Turon. *Hist. Franc.*, VII. 23.

[5] " Si vindicari in aliquos seuerius, contra nostram consuetudinem, pro causae intuitu, iusserimus, nolumus statim eos aut subire poenas, aut excipere sententiam, sed *per dies XXX. super statu eorum sors et fortuna suspensa sit : reos sane accipiat vinciatque custodia, et excubiis sollertibus vigilanter observuet*" (382), *Cod. Theod.* IX. 40. 13.

[6] *Cod. Theod.* XIV. 27. 1.

significant is proved by its occurrence in Gregory, "certe *sculcas* quos mittitis, *sollicite* requirant, ne dolens factum ad nos recurrat," "carefully employ the watches which you send, lest the crime should fall back upon us." Obviously the *sulsadina* of the Salic law, which was necessary before the judge could proceed with the case, contained the words to the effect that the watches had carefully been employed for the period of three days, that is, three times seven days, since the distress was repeated each week. The *sulsadina*, no doubt, contained some abbreviation, such as *sol. culc.*, that is, *sollicite culcatum*, and as this contraction was not understood, it developed into *solatium collectum, solem collocare, solsadire, alsaccia*. This *solem collocare* has brought about the formal sitting each day until sunset. In any case, if we compare the formula of the *sulsadina*, "triduum legibus custodire et solsatire" with the Roman "per dies triginta ... custodia, et excubiis sollertibus vigilanter obseruet," the derivation of the first from the second is obvious beyond a shadow of a doubt.

It is this *solem culcare* which has helped Lat. *collocare* to assume in the Romance languages the special meaning of "to lay down in bed," hence French *se coucher* "to go down (of the sun), lie down"; Ital. *coricare*, old *colcare*, Venetian *colegar* "to sit down, lie down, go to bed." In the Germanic languages *sculca* has given Engl. *sculk, skulk* "to lie in wait," Danish *skulke* "to lie in hiding, shirk," MLG. *schūlen* "to be hidden, to look furtively," dial. Swedish *skula, skjula* "to walk stooping," dial. Norwegian *skjula, skulka, skulma, skylma* "to look furtively, scowl," Dan. *skjule*, Swed. *skyla*, ONorse *skŷla* "to protect," OHG. *scūlinge* "hiding place," Engl. *scowl*. So long as the meaning is "to lie in wait" one may safely assume a derivation from original *sculca*, but when the idea of protection is added, there is frequently a confusion with native German words related to Lat. *scutum*, or with words directly derived from it.

The *scutarii*, frequently mentioned as *gentiles*, are of common occurrence in the writers of the fifth and sixth century. They were a bodyguard of the emperors, forming a separate schola, and did not materially differ from those whom I have described as *scholares*. They occupied approximately the same position and by a philological transformation became the *sculdasii* of the eighth and later centuries. A Goth, Witterit, is mentioned in a document of 539 or 546 as a *scutarius;* that he was an *agens in rebus* is proved by his honorific title *vd.*, i.e., *vir devotus.*[1] In the Langobard documents of the eighth century we find the transitional form *sculdhoris*,[2] and only in the Langobard laws and later do we get the customary *sculdais, sculdhais, sculdasius*. We get the forms *scutarius*,[3] *schultarius*,[4] *schuldarius* [5] in the tenth century, the latter two in the south of Italy, where they may well have preserved an older spelling, and so the development of the word is obviously *scutarius > scultarius > sculdarius > sculdharis > sculdhais > sculdais*. That this *sculdais* is identical, or nearly identical, in his functions with the Gothic *scutarius* is proved by his occupying a position after the vicecomes [6] and before the centenarius,[7] hence it is at once to be inferred that, like the *wittiscalci* of the Burgundians, the

---

[1] Marini, *I pap. dipl.*, p. 172.

[2] Troya, *op. cit.*, vol. v, p. 132 (762), 241 (763), 711 (773).

[3] Ughelli, *Italia sacra*, 2. ed., vol. II, col. 103.

[4] *Ibid.*, 1. ed., vol. VIII, col. 602.        [5] *Ibid.*, col. 605.

[6] "Dux comes uicecomes *sculdacio* gastaldio decanus" (904), *HPM., Chartæ*, vol. I, col. 108; "dux comes uicecomes *sculdatio* decanus saltarius vicarius" (926), *ibid.*, col. 128; "dux marchio comes vicecomes *sculdatio* gastaldius aut ullus reipublicae exactor" (969), *ibid.*, col. 222; "dux archiepiscopus marchio episcopus comes vicecomes *sculdacius* gastaldus" (992), *ibid.*, col. 290; "dux marchio comes vicecomes *sculdascius* locopositus aut quislibet publicus actor" (894), L. Schiaparelli, *I diplomi di Berengario I*, p. 45; similarly p. 51 (896), 79 (899), etc.; "dux comes vicecomes *scutarius*" (904), Ughelli, *Italia sacra*, vol. II, col. 103; "dux marchio comes vicecomes *sculdaxio*" (950), *ibid.*, col. 104.

[7] "Praecipiunt ad *sculdahis* suos, aut ad centenarios, aut ad locopositos" (747), *MGH., Leg. Langob., Rat.* 1.

*thungini* of the Franks, the *saiones* of the Visigoths, he was an executor, a collector of debts, even if we did not have in the laws[1] the specific reference to him in this capacity and to his being a "vassus regius."[2] Hence his chief duty consisted in summoning to court and catching thieves, that is, in superintending the *sculca* or *sculta*, that is, the *solis collocare* of the Franks. For this reason *scutarius* has here and in Germanic countries changed to *scultarius*.

The Gothic Bible translates "debtor" by *dulgis skula* and "creditor" by *dulga haitja*. The first literally means "debt ower," the second "debt compeller." This Goth. *dulgs* "debt" is related to OSlavic *dlŭgŭ* "debt," OIrish *dliged* "law, right, duty," *dligim* "I owe, have a right," Cornish *dylly* "owing," Breton *dle* "debt," etc. These are all derived from LLatin *dulgere* "to release," from Lat. *indulgere* "to forgive." The Edict of Chilperic provides that when a slave has killed a freeman, his master should swear that he had nothing to do with the killing, and then he should turn the slave over or release him, *"dulgat,"* to the relations of the slain man.[3] *Dulgere* is several times recorded in this sense in the eighth century,[4] especially in connection with obsides, hospites, because deserting the hostages was tantamount to breaking vows and starting a rebellion.[5] In the *Formulae* the usual formula of cession is (concedere et) *indulgere*.[6] In-

---

[1] "Si homo liber qui debitor est, alias res non habuerit nisi caballos domitos aut iunctorios, seu vaccas, tunc ille qui debitum requirit, vadat ad *sculdahis* et intimet causam suam, quia debitor ipsius alias res non habet, nisi quae supra leguntur. Tunc *sculdahis* tollat bobes et caballos ipsius et ponat eos post creditorem, dum usque ei iustitia faciat," *Roth.* 251.

[2] "Ingelrico *sculdassio* uassum eidem odolrici comis et ancione qui *sculdassio* uassum eidem comis" (887), *HPM., Chartae*, vol. I, col. 75.

[3] "*Dulgat* seruum hoc est de licentia parentibus coram parentes qui occisus est, et do ipso quod uoluerint faciant, et ille sit exolutus," *Lex sal.*, LXXVIII. 5.

[4] "Quantum in ipsa donatione continet, et a die praesente trado, *dulgo*, atque transcribo," in Ducange, sub *dulgere*.

[5] "Cupiebat supradictus Haistolfus nefandus rex mentiri, quae antea pollicitus fuerat, obsides *dulgere*, sacramenta irrumpere" (756), in Ducange.

[6] "Volemus esse translatum atque *indultum*," *Form. Andec.* 46; "probamus

dulgences of two kinds were granted by the Roman emperors in the fourth and fifth centuries, those in regard to debts, under the name of *indulgentiae debitorum*,[1] for which the edicts run from the year 363 to 436, and those in regard to crimes, under the name of *indulgentiae criminum*,[2] from 322 to 410. The remission of debts refers to those in any way due to the state. The remission in regard to crimes took place on particular occasions, more especially on Easter day.[3] At first poisoners, murderers, adulterers were excluded from the indulgence,[4] then this exception was increased to include five crimes leading to capital punishment,[5] and this list kept growing[6] until it included all but petty crimes.[7] Hence (*in*)-*dultum* came to mean not only "remission of crimes," but

esse *indultum*," *Marc. form.*, I. 4; "omnia ex omnibus . . . habeant *indultum*," *Form. Turon.* 21; "ex nostra indulgentia visi fuimus concessisse atque *indulgisse*," *Cart. Senon.* 36; "in omnibus habeat concessum atque *indultum*," *Form. Sal. Bignon.* 2; "sibi habeat concessum atque *indultum*," *Form. Cod., E. Emmerani frag.* II. 9.

[1] *Cod. Theod.* XI. 28.     [2] *Cod. Theod.* IX. 38.

[3] "*Ob diem Paschae* (quam intimo corde celebramus) omnibus quos reatus adstringit, carcer inclusit, claustra dissoluimus" (367), IX. 38. 3; "*Paschae celebritas postulat*, vt quoscunque nunc aegra expectatio quaestionis, poenaque formido sollicitat, absoluamus" (368), IX. 38. 4; "*paschalis laetitiae dies* ne illa quidam tenere sinit ingenia, quae flagitia fecerunt: pateat insuetis horridus carcer aliquando luminibus" (381), X. 38. 6; "*religio anniuersariae obsecrationis hortatur*, vt omnes omnino periculo carceris metuque poenarum eximi iuberemus" (384), IX. 38. 7; "vbi primum *dies Paschalis* extiterit, nullum teneat carcer inclusum, omnia vincla soluantur" (385), IX. 38. 8.

[4] "Praeter veneficos, homicidas, adulteros" (322), IX. 38. 1.

[5] "Exceptis quinque criminibus, quae capite vindicantur" (353), IX. 38. 2.

[6] "Adtamen sacrilegus, in maiestate reus, in mortuos veneficus, siue maleficus, adulter, raptor, homicida, communione istius muneris separentur" (367), IX. 38. 3; "ne temere homicidii crimen, adulterii foeditatem, maiestatis iniuriam maleficiorum scelus, insidias venenorum, raptusque violentiam sinamus euadere" (368), IX. 38. 4. A still longer list in the succeeding laws.

[7] "Quis enim 1. sacrilego diebus sanctis indulgeat? quis 2. adultero, vel incesti reo tempore castitatis ignoscat? quis non raptorem in summa quiete et gaudio communi persequatur instantius? 5. Nullam accipiat requiem vinculorum, qui quiescere sepultos quodam sceleris immanitate non siuit; patiatur tormenta 6. veneficus, 7. maleficus. 8. adulteratorque monetae: 9. homicida, quod fecit semper expectet: 10. reus etiam maiestatis, de domino aduersum quem talia molitus est, veniam sperare non debet" (385), IX. 38. 8.

also "holiday," hence Goth. *dulþs* "holiday," *dulþjan* "to celebrate," OHG. *tult, dult* "festival," *ostertuldi* "Easter," *tuldjan* "to celebrate." There are two series of crimes which are principally included in the amnesty, those arising from debt, and those arising from such pretty crimes as do not call for serious criminal prosecution, hence we get from.(*in*)*dulgere* in Goth. *dulgs* "debt" and in OHG. *tolg, tolc,* OFrisian *dolg,* AS. *dolg, dolh* "wound," such as does not cause death, for then it would become "homicidium" and would not have been included in the indulgence. From this OHG. *tolg, tolc* comes an enormous group of words in Slavic, represented by the root *tolk-* "to beat, strike, thrash" and, at the same time, like OHG. *dult, tult,* represented in Polish *tłoka* "voluntary work with dancing and eating," Lettish *talka, talks, talkus* "an evening entertainment for the workers" and from this ultimately comes, through the Norse, English *talk.*

The conception of "debt" has arisen in the Germanic, Slavic, and Celtic languages through contact with Roman law. Now the root *dulg-,* while universal in Europe, has not left any traces with that connotation in any of the Germanic languages outside of Gothic, and even the Gothic uses the other root *skul-, skuld-,* to express the idea of debt. Before proceeding to show how this has arisen from Lat. *sculta,* I shall show how another Latin term has produced the idea of "obligation" in the Germanic and Romance languages. The Roman laws called down heavy punishments upon the *plagiator,* the man who by solicitation inveigled boys and slaves to his house and later sold them beyond the sea. In the beginning of the sixth century we find, therefore, in Theodoric's Edict, *plagiare* "sollicitare" and *plegium* "the crime of detaining a boy or slave by solicitous actions." [1] The Visigothic laws have a whole series of enact-

[1] "Qui ingenuum *plagiando,* id est sollicitando, in alia loca translatum aut vendiderit, aut donaverit, vel suo certe servitio vindicandum crediderit, occidatur," 78. .

ments against the evil of plagiarism, from which it appears that it differed from stealing in that the respective person was coaxed, "sollicitatus," to enter one's service.[1] At a later time *plegium, plevium, plebium,* etc., occur in the sense of "solicitude, care," in Frankish documents,[2] and are recorded since the sixth century in the sense of "security," but it is only since Norman times that *plegium, plevium* "pledge" became really popular in France and in other countries. The AS. has preserved the word in all the successive stages of its semantic evolution. We have seen that *plagiare* meant "to solicit, entice, coax," hence AS. *plegan, plaegan* "to mock, deride, applaud, play, dance"; similarly *plegium* meant "the crime of soliciting, extreme penalty for such a crime," hence AS. *plio, pleo, pleoh* "danger, injury, fault," *pliht* "danger," *plihtan* "to expose to danger, pledge." Similarly we have OHG. *phlëkan, phlëgan, plëgan* "curare, ministrare, regere," *phlicht* "cura," ONorse *plega* "to exercise," *plaga* "to take care, guard, love," etc. From this group cannot be separated OSlav. *plensati* "to dance," Boh. *plésati* "plaudere, exsultare, saltare," Gothic *plinsjan* "to dance." The early recorded *plevium* has produced OFrench, Provençal *plevir* "pledge," Fr. *pleige* "surety," etc.

All the words connected with the idea "debt, guilt, pledge" have in the European languages arisen from the correspond-

[1] "Quicquid ad discum nostrum dare debet, unusquisque iudex in sua habeat *plebio* qualiter bona et optima atque bene studiose et nitide omnia sint conposita quicquid dederint" (800), *MGH., Cap.,* vol. I, p. 85; "et ferramenta, quod in hostem ducunt, in eorum habeant *plebio* qualiter bona sint et iterum quando revertuntur in camera mittantur," *ibid.,* p. 87; "quicquid ipsi in pace violanda delinquerint, ad ipsius debet *plivium* pervenire" (823), *ibid.,* vol. II, p. 305.

[2] "De seruum ecclesiae aut fiscalinis uel cuiuslibet si aliquo quicumque in potestatem ad sorte aut ad *plibium* (*pleuium, plebeium, plebium*) promouatur, ut ipse precius dominum reformetur," *Decretio Chlotharii regis:* "si quicumque homo alienum servum de capitale crimine amallaverit, et ei ad sacramentum non crediderit, nisi subscribere eum vult, de presente *plebat,* hoc est subscribat suum servum alterum talem, qua ille est, cui reputat," *Lex romana raet. curien.,* IX. 4.

ing Latin terms, as the whole criminal procedure of the Germanic laws is but an evolution of the edicts of the Theodosian Code. Hence it would be extremely strange if OHG. *sculd* "facinus, crimen, reatum, debitum, causa" should have proceeded from a native word. I have already shown the confusion between *scutarius* and *scultarius*. It can be shown that this confusion was universal on Germanic ground. It is generally assumed that Lat. *scutum* "shield" is derived from a root *sku-* "to cover," which is very likely if we consider Gr. σκῦτος "hide, leather," but one thing is certain and that is, that it is only in the Latin that the idea "shield" has developed in this group, although a similar relation of "hide" and "shield" is found in the Sanskrit *čarma*. Now, all the other European languages have derived the word for "shield" from Lat. *scutum*. We have Albanian *sk'üt, sk'ut*,[1] OIrish *sciath*, OWelsh *scuit*, OBreton *scoit*, Cornish *ysguydh*, OSlavic *štitŭ*. Hence it would again be extremely strange if Goth. *skildus*, ONorse *skjoldr*, AS. *scyld*, OHG. *scilt* were not derived from the same *scutum*, even because *scutarius* has by documentary evidence become confused with *scultator*.[2] The universal umlaut found in these words would indicate that they were derived through a source borrowing not from Latin, but from the Greek, where the identical word etymologically, σκῦτος, was confused with it; but that Lat. *scutum* was at an early time borrowed back into Greek, that is proved, not only by the later σκοῦτον, but also by σκουτάριος, recorded in the second century.

There cannot be the slightest doubt that *scultarius*, derived from the older *scutarius*, and quite correctly in the

---

[1] G. Mayer, *Etymologisches Wörterbuch der albanischen Sprache*, Strassburg 1891, p. 388. Mayer thinks that Lat. *scutum* should have given *šk'üt*, not *sk'üt*, but he contradicts himself immediately by admitting that *skutér* "chief herdsman" is from Gr. σκουτάριος, Lat. *scutarius* "shield bearer, famulus, domesticus."

[2] The very form *sculdhor*, which I have found twice recorded, may be a direct corruption of *scultator*.

OHG. form *sculdhaizo, sculdheizo* glossed as "praefectus, tribunus, procurator, quinquagenarius, praeco, exactor populi," was popularly understood to be the compeller of those crimes which demanded distress, that is, a *sculta* or *sculca*. Such crimes, as we have seen, were debts and those leading to capital punishment. Thus *sculta* came to mean those crimes themselves, precisely as *dulgere* "to remit the petty crimes or debts" led in all the European languages to the meanings "petty crime" and "debt." *Sculta,* then, meant "guilt, debt, compulsion, that which one owes." Indeed, OHG. *gasculdôn* is glossed by "exigere (culpa), promerere," *gasculdan* by "exigere (iram judicis)," *sculdon* by "promerere," and *sculdan* by "condemnare," the latter in the significant phrase "*sculdante* za gelte," "condemning to pay the fine." The underlying meaning is invariably "the compulsion in cases of debt or crime," hence Goth. *skuldō* "that which one owes, a debt, due," *skulds* "owing," and from this we get the back formations *skula* "debtor, liable to, in danger of," *skulan* "to owe, to be obliged to, to be about to." The Germanic philologist, who makes his facts fit in with his abstract laws, will be shocked at finding a preteropresent verb among those borrowed from a Latin root. It must not be forgotten that these verbs are for the greater part not found outside of the Germanic languages, that no Indo-Germanic root from which *skulan* may be derived has been discovered, and that this group, like Goth. *daugan*, which is also a preteropresent and borrowed from the Latin, entered the Germanic languages before the sixth century, even before the Anglo-Saxons had settled in Britain, and while the Germanic tribes had not yet separated.

The other Germanic languages need not detain us, except the Anglo-Saxon, where we have not only *scyld* "sin, crime, guilt," but also *gylt* "crime, sin, fault, debt, guilt," which is, no doubt, developed directly from Welsh *gwyliad, gwyliat,*

OBreton *guiliat* "a watching." The Slavic languages do not seem to have any derivatives from this group, having borrowed from the older root *dulg-*. Lithuanian has *skola* "debt," *skylu, skilau* "to fall into debt," *skeliu* "to owe," but also words without an initial *s*, such as *kalte* "debt, crime," *kaltas* "guilty."

# HOMOLOGUS

In the Visigothic laws we hear of a *buccellarius*, a free man who could change his patron, to whom he had sworn fealty, by surrendering all his arms and half of his acquisitions while in the service of his patron, and provisions were made for the daughters of the *buccellarius*, whereby they obtained a dowry from the property surrendered, if they married according to the patron's will.[1] An identical law substitutes the *saio* for the *buccellarius*,[2] hence the two could not have differed much in their capacities, if they were not entirely the same. The usual conception about the *buccellarius* in the Middle Ages was that he was a cut-throat retainer, a parasite,[3] and this opinion is well founded, if one considers the Roman law of the year 468, according to which people were not permitted to keep bands of armed *buccellarii* on their estates.[4] But,

---

[1] "Si quis *buccellario* arma dederit vel aliquid donaverit, si in patroni sui manserit obsequio, aput ipsum quae sunt donata permanenat. Si vero alium sibi patronum elegerit, habeat licentiam, cui se voluerit commendare: quoniam ingenuus homo non potest prohiberi, quia in sua potestate consistit: sed reddat omnia patrono, quem deseruit. Similis et de circa filios patroni vel *buccellarii* forma servetur, ut si ipsi quidem obsequi voluerint, donata possideant: si vero patroni filios vel nepotes crediderint reliquendos, reddant universa, quae parentibus eorum a patrono donata sunt. Et si aliquid *buccellarius* sub patrono adquesierit, medietas ex omnibus in patroni vel filiorum eius potestate consistat: aliam medietatem *buccellarius*, qui adquaesivit, obtineat: et si filiam reliquirit, ipsam in patroni potestate manere iubemus: sic tamen, ut ipse patronus aequalem ei provideat, qui eam sibi possit in matrimonio sociare. Quod si ipsa contra voluntatem patroni alium forte elegerit, quidquid patricius a patrono fuerit donatum vel a parentibus patroni, omnia patrone vel heredibus eiun restituatur," *Euric. Frag.* cccx and *Lex Visig.* v. 3. 1.

[2] *Euric. Frag.* cccxi and *Lex Visig.* v. 3. 2, 3, 4.

[3] "*Buccellarius* assecula, satellites, galearius, parasitus, scurra," *Corpus glossariorum latinorum;* "Βουκελλάριος ὁ ἀποστελλόμενος καὶ φῶν τινά," Ducange.

[4] "Omnibus per civitates et agros habendi *buccellarios* vel Isauros armatosque servos licentiam volumus esse praeclusam. Quod si quis, praeter haec

while it is quite true that the *buccellarii* during the latter days
of the Roman Empire formed private bodyguards, swearing
allegiance to their patrons under whom they fought, and during the fall of the Empire resolving themselves into companies
of freebooters,[1] it also appears from the Gothic enactments
that they had a certain legal standing, which can hardly
have arisen from a condition of lawlessness, but rather must
have preceded it.

The earliest reference to *buccellarii* is in the *Notitia dignitatum*, where "comites catafractarii *bucellarii* iuniores" are
mentioned, and almost contemporaneously with it comes the
statement by Olympiodorus that in the time of Honorius not
only Romans, but also Goths, bore the name of *buccellarii*.[2]
The derivation of this word from Lat. *buccella*, suggested
by Olympiodorus and accepted by many modern writers, is
mere popular etymology and of no use. All we know is that
the word was employed for certain Roman and Gothic soldiers or private retainers. In the Visigothic laws the relation
subsisting between the *buccellarius* and his patron is called
by the familiar terms *obsequium* or *patrocinium*, which is a
free agreement entered upon by the servant loyally to support his master from whom he received his arms and his sustenance. Guilhermoz has ably shown that the *patrocinium*
and the *buccellarii* of the Visigoths are of Roman origin,[3]
and I will now try to show what the origin of the word *buccellarius* is.

We know of the *patrocinium* chiefly from the many enact-

---

nostra mansuetudo salubriter ordinavit, armata mancipia seu *buccellarios* aut
Isauros in suis praediis aut juxta se habere temptaverit, post exactam centum
librarum auri condemnationem vindictam in eos severissimam proferri sanci-
mus," *Cod. Just.* IX. 12. 10.

[1] Mommsen, in *Hermes*, vol. XXIV, p. 233 *ff.*, and C. Lécrivain, *Les soldats
privés aus Bas Empire*, in *Mélanges d'archéologie et d'histoire*, vol. X, p. 267 *ff.*

[2] "Τὸ Βουκελλάριος ὄνομα ἐν ταῖς ἡμέραις Ὁνωρίου ἐφέρετο κατὰ στρατιω-
τῶν οὐ μόνων Ῥωμαίων, ἀλλὰ καὶ Γότθων τινῶν," Lécrivain, *l. c.*, p. 277.

[3] *Essai sur l'origine de la noblesse en France au moyen âge*, Paris 1902, p. 13 *ff.*

ments against it in the Theodosian Code. It appears that in the fourth and fifth centuries farmers, especially in Egypt, entered into a kind of servitude to a patron, in order to avoid paying taxes.[1] A few years before, Libanius had addressed a letter to Theodosius, in which he gave a terrible picture of the ravages committed by those farmers who left the villages and their masters and entered the service of officers stationed near by.[2] In 415 these farmers, called *homologi*, were ordered to return to the villages which they had left, the patrons receiving back what they had spent on them.[3] These farmers were obviously free men, for it was specifically stated that the law against the *patrocinium* referred only to those who had property of their own.[4]

The *patrocinium*, as a military institution, which, however, can hardly be separated from its mere economic form, put the *buccellarius* under obligation to defend the master rightly or wrongly against all men. The Visigothic laws are full of references to this evil. Judges would favor a case of a man to

[1] "Omnes ergo sciant, non modo eos memorata multa feriendos, qui clientelam susceperint rusticorum, sed eos quoque qui fraudandorum tributorum causa ad *patrocinia* solita fraude confugerint, duplum definitae multae subituros" (399), XI. 24. 4.

[2] "Εἰσὶ κῶμαι μεγάλαι πόλλων ἑκάστη δεσποτῶν. αὗται καταφεύγουσιν ἐπὶ τοὺς ἱδρυμένους στρατιώτας, οὐχ ἵνα μὴ πάθωσι κακῶς, ἀλλ' ἵνα ἔχωσι ποιεῖν. καὶ ὁ μισθὸς ἀφ' ὧν δίδωσιν ἡ γῆ, πυροὶ καὶ κριθαί καὶ τὰ ἀπὸ τῶν δένδρων ἢ χρυσὸς ἢ χρυσίου τιμή. προβεβλημένοι τοίνυν τὰς τούτων χεῖρας οἱ δεδωκότες ἐώνηνται τὴν εἰς ἅπαντα ἐξουσίαν. καὶ νῦν μὲν κακὰ καὶ πράγματα παρέχουσι τοῖς ὁμόροις γῆν ἀποτεμνόμενοι, δένδρα τέμνοντες, ἁρπάζοντες, θύοντες, κατακόπτοντες, ἐσθίοντες," Libanius, *De patrociniis*, 4.

[3] "Hii sane, qui vicis quibus adscripti sunt derelictis, qui *homologi* more gentilitio nuncupantur, ad alios seu vicos, seu dominos transierunt, ad sedem desolati ruris constrictis detentatoribus redire cogantur: qui si exsequenda protraxerint, ad functiones eorum teneantur obnoxii, et dominis restituant, quae pro his exsoluta constiterit," *Cod. Theod.* XI. 24. 6.

[4] "Excellentia tua his legibus, quae de prohibendis *patrociniis* aliorum principum nomine promulgatae sunt, seueriorem poenam nos addidisse cognoscat: scilicet, ut si quis agricolis vel vicanis propria possidentibus *patrocinium* reppertus fuerit ministrare, propriis facultatibus exuatur. His quoque agricolis terrarum suarum dispendio feriendis, qui ad *patrocinia* quaesiti confugerint," XI. 24. 5.

whom they were related by patronage,[1] and rich men relied
on their retinue to impede the course of justice,[2] having recourse to riotous clamors,[3] while the *Lex romana raetica
curiensis* meted out severe punishment to those who did not
apply to their judges for the law, but to the "milites qui in
obsequio principum sunt."[4] It is, therefore, clear that the
*buccellarius* was a free Goth who entered into a compact to
serve another in return for certain advantages. The important point in this relation was the contract which specifically
declared what the forfeit would be if such a free man,
having entered into an agreement to work for another, chose
to change masters or break the contract.

In Byzantine Egypt a contract was called ὁμολογία, from
the formula ὁμολογεῖ "he promises, spondet," which is the
essential part of such a contract.[5] In the Coptic contracts [6]

[1] "Si quis iudici pro adversario suo querellam intulerit, et ipse eum audire
noluerit aut sigillum negaverit et per diversas occasiones causam eius protrax-
erit, pro *patrocinio* aut amicitia noles legibus obtemperare," II. 1. 20.

[2] "Quicumque habens causam ad maiorem personam se propterea contulerit,
ut in iudicio per illius *patrocinium* adversarium suum possit obprimere, ipsam
causam, de qua agitur, etsi iusta fuerit, quasi victus perdat, iudex autem mox
viderit quemcumque potentem in causa cuiuslibet *patrocinari*, liceat ei de
iudicio eium habicere. Quod si potens contemserit iudicem et proterve resistens
de iudicio egredi vel locum dare iudicanti noluerit, potestatem habeat iudex
ab ipso potente duas auri libras auri exigere et hunc iniuria violenta a iudicio
propulsare," II. 2. 8.

[3] "Audientia non tumultu aut clamore turbetur . . . nullus se in audientiam
ingerat . . . quod si admonitus quisquam a judicem fuerit, ut in causa taceat
hac prestare causando *patrocinium* non presumat, et ausus ultra fuerit parti
cuiuslibet *patrocinare*, decem auri solidos eidem iudici profuturos coactus exol-
vat, ipse vero, in nullo resultans, contumeliose de iudicio proiectus abscedat,"
II. 2. 2. It is interesting to notice here that the Bavarian law has used this
*clamore*, which naturally means "riotous noise, sedition," in the same sense in
the form *carmulum*, "si quis seditionem suscitaverit contra ducem suum, quod
Baiuvari *carmulum* dicunt," I. 2. 3, and this leads to Slavic *kramola* "sedition."

[4] "Quicumque homo, qui suos iudices, qui in sua provincia commanent,
postposuerit, et *ad milites, qui in obsequio principum sunt*, suas causas agere
presumserit: ipse qui eam causam inquirit, in exilio deputetur; et ille miles, qui
ipsam causam iudicat, x libras auri solvat," II. 1. 7.

[5] M. J. Bry, *Essai sur la vente dans les papyrus gréco-égyptiens*, Paris 1909,
p. 131 *ff*.

[6] W. E. Crum, *Catalogue of the Coptic Manuscripts in the Collection of the
John Rylands Library*, Manchester 1909, in the *Vocabulary*.

*homologei, hamalogi* occurs numberless times in such contracts in the sense "we agree, promise." The agreement of a sailor, who distinctly mentions the fact that he is a free man, runs as follows: "I, John, the sailor, son of the late George, of Shnoum, write to George, the sailor, son of Melas, likewise of Shnoum. Seeing that I have agreed to embark with thee as sailor upon the little ship 'Apa Severus,' and to receive hire the 10th Indiction, henceforth, until the fulfilment of its year, namely the month of Paope, in God's will, of the 11th Indiction; now therefore I undertake (*homologei*) to remain as sailor on this ship, in all freedom, without sloth or neglect. It is agreed that we will conceal nothing, one from the other, of what God shall bring to us; and we will give to each other the proportion fixed from the takings of 'Apa Severus' from to-day henceforth, until the fulfilment of its year. And if its year be fulfilled and we agree together, we will set sail again together. But if I wish to part from thee, while I am a sailor with thee upon the little ship, thereupon I will pay 2 gold solidi as fine, all that I have being at thy disposal. . . . For thy assurance, therefore, I have drawn up this agreement (*homologia*) for thee and do consent thereto by my signs, and I have begged other freemen and they have witnessed it."[1]

In Langobard times such a contract was called *libellus*, and a freeman promising to work the land of a patron for a series of years or for life distinctly stated the conditions, under which he worked, in such a *libellus*,[2] and the usual phrase for

---

[1] W. E. Crum, *op. cit.*, p. 76.

[2] A typical *libellus* would run something like this: "Manifestum mihi Luitpert *homo liber*, et filio qd. Teuderici, quia *per cartulam* ad resedendo confirmasti me et filius et nepotibus meis tu venerabili domno Peredeo Episc. in casa Eccl. vestre in loco Ligori, ubi antea residet qd. Ursulo, et in omnem res ividem pertenent. Proinde *per hanc cartula repromicto me una cum filiis seo nepotibus meis, ut diebus vite nostre in ipsa case abitare debeamus, et ipsa casa et omnes res ibidem pertenent in omnibus meliorare debeamus, et in alio loco aut in alia casa peculiarina facere non debeamus* Et per singulo anno tibi et successoribus tuis reddere

such land holding, was "*libellario* nomine."[1] If *homologus*, *homologites*,[2] came to mean "the farmer who works for another by a contract,"[3] and in the West *libellarius* had the same significance, it must be obvious that *buccellarius* must have been formed in some similar way. Now, in Gothic *bôka* means "letter, document," from which are derived German *buch*, Russian *bukva* "letter," etc., and our *buccellarius* is derived from this word. But *bôka* itself is of Latin origin. Before the sixth century *libellus* was not the only word for "book, written document." Far more often they employed *pugillar*, in Greek πύκτιον, πύκιον, to express "document," while *libellus* designated the complete book.[4] It is this stem *pug-*, πυκ-, which has produced Goth. *bôka*, and from *pugillar* has been formed *buccellarius*, the synonym of the later *libellarius*, and the Roman equivalent of the Greek *homologus*.

Another word, which was almost identical in meaning with *buccellarius* has proceeded from a Latin word meaning "book," namely *vassallus*. Since Pliny's time *vasarium* pub-

debeamus de ipsa res duo modio grano, et duo modia farre, vino anforas quinque, olivas medietate, animale bono magese, in Pascha uno pullos, ovas decem, et angaria vobis facere debeamus, sicut est consuetudo facere alii massarii de ipso loco," etc. (764), *Mem. e doc . . . di Lucca*, vol. v², p. 51.

[1] "*Libellario titulo*," Cassiodorus, *Variae*, v. 7 (523); "sed et terrulam ecclesiae nostrae vicinam sibi . . . *libellario nomine* ad summam tremissis unius habere concede" (590), Gregorii I *Registri*, ii. 3; "volumus ut securitatis *libellos* de pensionibus facias" (591), *ibid.*, i. 42.

[2] W. E. Crum, *op. cit.* (*mologites*), p. 237.

[3] The *homologi* are several times recorded in the second century in Egypt, and Wilcken (*Griechische Ostraka aus Aegypten und Nubien*, Leipzig und Berlin 1899, vol. i, p. 253 ff.), agreeing with Gothofredus, at first considered them to be peasants who accepted the patronage by some kind of *homologia* "agreement," but he later somewhat modified his views in M. Rostowzew's *Studion zur Geschichte des römischen Kolonats*, in 1. *Beiheft zum Archiv für Papyrusforschung*, p. 219 ff. But for our purposes the precise status of the *homologi* is immaterial, for all we are concerned with is the fact that these *homologi* entered *in patrocinium* and, as we shall later see, retained the name of *homologi* in the West.

[4] "Venere in manus meas *pugillares* libellique cum quibusdamn otissimis versibus ipsius chirographo scriptis," Suetonius, *Nerva* 52.

## 58    COMMENTARY TO THE GERMANIC LAWS

*licum* was the usual name for a "liber censualis," a book in
which the amount of tax the farmers had to pay was precisely recorded.[1] In the earliest Ostrogothic document of the
year 489 the new owner of the estate says that he is ready
each year to pay the fiscal dues for it, and so he asks the authorities to have the name of the former owner erased from
the polyptic and his own inserted instead, to which the answer of the officer granting the request is that he will have
the name erased from the *vasaria publica*, etc.[2] What these
polyptics were is best seen from a capitulary of Charles the
Bald in 864, where it says that they contain a precise statement of the corvée due by each colonus,[3] and this is borne out
by the polyptic of Irminon and similar lists.

That derivatives *vasarinus* "free serf," *vasarinium*, *vasa-
risiscum* "corvée due from the free serf" existed is proved
by the corrupted forms *warcinus* "free serf," *warcinium*,
*warciniscum* "corvée due from the free serf," recorded in
736,[4] and *varcinaticum* "animalia exacta ad mensam principis," used in a document of the year 816.[5] The Langobard

---

[1] Plinius, vii. 49, *Cod. Theod.* xiii. 11. 12, Cassiodorus, *Variae* vii. 45.

[2] "Parati sumus singulis annis pro eadem praedia conpetentia solvere unde
rogamus uti jubeatis a *polypthicis publicis* nomen prioris domini suspendi et
nostri dominii adscribi . . . Unde erit nobis cura de *vasariis publicis* nomen
prioris dominii suspendi et vestri dominii adscribi," Marini, I *pap. dipl.*, p. 130.

[3] "Illi coloni, tam fiscales, quam et ecclesiastici, qui sicut in *polypticis* con-
tinetur et ipsi non denegant, carropera et manopera ex antiqua consuetudine
debent," *MGH., Leg.* sec. ii. 2, p. 323.

[4] "Faichisi seo Pasquale, fratris germani, filii quondam Beninato, qui fuet
aldio vestrum S. Saturnini . . . tu predicta Pasquale et Faichisi in casa S.
Saturnini resedire diveatis in Diano casa, vel in omni res patris nostro, quondam Veninato, quia manifestum est quod *de livera mater natis sumus*, et de
istato nostro nulla condicione bovis redivibamus, nisi tantum bonis de ipsa
casa vel omni res patris nostro, *warcinisca* facere diveamus, sic ut bovis pater
nostrum quandam Veninatus usum facere fuet, ad pratum sicandi stabulum
faciendi in via ubi vovis opum fuerit, sicut unum de *warcini* vestri . . . Si nos
Pasquale et Faichisi vel nostros heredes de ipsa casa exire voluerimus, aut
ipsas *warcinia* facere minime voluerimus, exeamus bacui et inanis et insuper
conpunamus pine nomini auri sol. 20," Brunetti, *Codice diplomatico Toscano*,
vol. i, p. 488.

[5] "De quibus una est donatio quam Lupus Dux ad praedictum sanctum

document which has preserved the word *warcinus* shows that he was a free man of the same type as the *libellarius*. There occurs in it the expression "*warcinisca* facere," that is, "to do the work prescribed in the polyptic or *vasaria publica*," where the *libellarius* promises not to do *peculiarina*, that is, work on the property of another, even as the *buccellarius* forfeited his rights if he worked for another master. In the eleventh century we for the first time meet with the *guarthones*, that is, *warciones*, in France, where they are represented as a lawless lot, not unlike the *buccellarii*,[1] and from this *guarthones* we ultimately get French *garçon*, etc.

The form *vasarinus* is found in Visigothic in the form *gasalianus*. The seizure of uncultivated land could take place with the help of one's familia, servitores, or servi, that is, by those who did not have land of their own but were dependent on their patron from whom they received oxen and working tools. In return they promised to serve their master in a stated way. We have here that class of coloni who in Italy would be registered in the *vasaria publica*. In 804 we find the same class of free serfs in Spain under the name of *gasaliani*.[2] A similar class of free serfs in patrocinio were the Langobard *gasindi*, which is obviously from *vasini*, as *gasalianes* is from *vasalini*, *vasaliani*. Like the *warcini* the *gasindi* were free to change their patrons, and that these in

locum fecit de *varcinatico*, id est animalia, quae exigebantur ad mensam Principis Ducatus Spoletani," Muratori, *Scriptores*, vol. I², p. 369: "obtulit quoqu, praeceptum . . . et de clausura in Marsis, et de *vuarcinatico*, id est, animalia-quae exigebantur ad mensam Ducis Spoletani," *ibid.*, p. 372.

[1] "Solent enim venire *guarthones* et scutarii et servientes de Morteriolo in domos villanorum et furtim aliquid capere de domibus eorum" (1055), E. Le-long, *Cartulaire de Saint-Aubin d'Angers*, Paris 1903, vol. I, p. 271.

[2] "Ego Ihoannes episcopus sio ueni in locum que uocitant Ualle Conposita et inueni ibi eglesia deserta uocabulo Sancte Marie Uirginis et feci ibi fita sub regimine Domino Adefonso principe Obetau, et construxi uel confirmabi ipsam eglesia in ipso loco et feci ibi presuras cum meos *gasalianes* mecum comorantes . . . et construxi ibi cenobium cum meos *gasalianes* et tenui eas iure quieto, sub regimine iam dicto Domino Adefonso," *Chartes de l'église de Valpuesta*, in *Revue hispanique*, vol. VII, p. 282 *ff*.

their turn are identical with the Visigothic *buccellarii* as to
their status is proved by the fact that gifts reverted to the
donor if the *gasindus* left his patrocinium.[1] *Gasindus* is an old
word, for it occurs in a Merovingian document of the year
546[2] and is found in Gothic as *gasinþa, gasinþja* "companion." So, too, *gasalianus* is recorded in Gothic *saljan*
"to harbor, live," *saliþwos* "inn, dwelling," as though *ga-*
were a prefix. But this *ga-* is a corruption of the original
*va-* as preserved in Frankish *vasallus, vassalus, vassus.*

*Vassus* occurs in the *Leges Alamannorum*,[3] and in the Salic
laws,[4] although used in the connection "*vassus* in ministerio," for which several readings are "puer in ministerio,"
hence almost in the sense of *gasalianus*, but this unique
occurrence of the word may be due to a late introduction.
There can, however, be no doubt that *vassus* was well known
in the eighth century, for it is recorded in authentic documents from the year 762 on,[5] and in 757 *vassallus* is a free
serf who may change his master at will, but may not take his
wife along, if she is a gift of the master,[6] that is, he is precisely under the same obligation as the *gasalianus* or *buccellarius*. Even at this early period *vassus, vassallus* has the
general meaning "servus" and he may hold a beneficium,[7]

[1] "Et si aliquid in *gasindio* ducis, aut privatorum hominum obsequium,
donum munus conquisivit, res ad donatore revertantur," *Ed. Roth.* 225. See
Guilhermoz, *op. cit.*, p. 46 *ff.*
[2] "Una cum omnibus rebus vel hominibus suis, *gasindis*, amicis, susceptis,"
*MGH., Dip. imp.*, vol. I, p. 6; also pp. 12 and 45.
[3] XXXVI, LXXIV.                                    [4] X (XXXV. 6).
[5] *MGH., Dipl. Karolina*, vol. I, p. 23; also (771), p. 74, p. 95, etc.
[6] "Homo Francus accepit beneficium de seniore suo, et duxit secum suum
*vassallum*, et postea fuit ibi mortuus ipse senior (i. e. homo Francus) et dimisit
ibi ipsum *vassallum;* et post hoc accepit alius homo ipsum beneficium, et pro
hoc ut melius potuit habere illum *vassallum*, dedit ei mulierem de ipso beneficio, et habuit ipsam aliquo tempore; et, dimissa ipsa, reversus est ad parentes
senioris sui mortui, et accepit ibi uxorem, et modo habet eam. Definitum est,
quod illam quam postea accepit, ipsam habeat," *Decretum compendiense*, in
*MGH., Capitularia*, vol. I, p. 38.
[7] "Similiter et *vassus* noster . . . beneficium et honorem perdat" (779),
*ibid.*, p. 48.

hence the original meaning "free serf" must be considered older; thus there is no break between the serfs of the *vasaria publica* of the sixth and the *vassalli* of the eight century.

*Homologare* "to make a vow to God" is not uncommon among the early Christian writers. _The term was, no doubt, when transferred from the legal contract, expressive of that devotion, that condition "in patrocinio," which subsisted between the believer and his God. If the *homologus* made promise to serve his master without fail, he at the same time took upon himself to defend him, to represent him, be his surety, "agere pro patrono." Before entering upon the discussion of this aspect of the *homologus* in the West, I shall point out to what important results the Roman legal term "*gerere pro patrono*" has led. In the Roman law we have *gerere curam* "to administer," more particularly *se gerere pro* "to act in the capacity of," *gerere pro domino* "to represent the master." While we occasionally get a similar phrase in the Middle Ages,[1] we far more often have *quirens, quarens, quaritor, garens, warrantis*, etc. "surety, fideiussor, warrantee,"[2] hence *querire* "to protect, hold safe."[3] The earliest reference to a word derived from *gerere* in this legal sense we get in a document of the year 954, composed at Cerdagne or Urgel, that is, not far from Toulouse, where the earliest other forms are recorded. We have here *giregar* "to

---

[1] "Patronos vel *gerentes se pro patronis*" (1257), *Les Olim*, vol. I, p. 18.

[2] "Arnaldus Maurinus vendidit suam partem per se et per suum fratrem, Willelmum Maurinum; et debet esse *quirens* de hoc suo fratre," C. Douais, *Cartulaire de l'abbaye Saint-Sernin de Toulouse*, p. 21; "debent esse *quirentes* de omnibus eorum hereditariis" (1155), *ibid.*, p. 26; "et erimus eis legales *quaritores* de omnibus amparatoribus," *ibid.*, p. 78; "filii sui debent esse inde legales *quarentes* Deo et ecclesie Sancte Constantie de omnibus hominibus," *ibid.*, p. 150; "et habeas ibi *quarantes* tuos qui *quarentizent* tibi feoda . . . praecipio quod justicia mea faciat ei habere considerationem meae curiae secundum quod audierit *warantos* tuos" (1181), V. Bourienne, *Antiquus cartularius ecclesiae Baiocensis*, Rouen, Paris 1902, vol. I, p. 15.

[3] "Uxorem sua et infantes sui debent hunc casalem legaliter *querire* Deo . . . de omnibus hominibus," C. Douais, *op. cit.*, p. 155.

hold safe, defend." [1] But *garîr*, pl. *gurrân* "security, warn-
ing, bail" is recorded in Arabic as early as the middle of the
ninth century, and that this is borrowed from the Latin or
Greek is proved not only by its utter unrelatedness to anything in Arabic, but also by the Greek gloss γεριτεύειν
"gerere, administrare, διοικεῖν," given in Ducange as taken
from the Glossae Basilicωn. Now, we have *gerere pro herede*
translated by "ὡς κληρονόμος διοικειῖν καὶ δεσπόζειν," [2]
while *pro herede gestiones* is left in Greek as "πρὸ αἱρέδε
γεστίονες," [3] so that there cannot be any doubt as to the
presence of *gerere* in Graeco-Roman law from the time of the
Justinian Code on. The almost exclusive appearance of
*garens* at Toulouse and at a comparatively late time is, no
doubt, due to its borrowing from the Arabic, which, in its
turn, received it from the Greeks.

*Garens, guarens* "protector, defensor, warrantee" produced the very popular *garantia, garandia, garentia, guar-
entia*, etc., "guarantee, protection, defence, prohibition,"
hence *garenna, guarenda, varenna* "a forest or river in which
none but the king may exercise his rights, warren." The
Latin documents record a large number of verbs from this
group, *garire, gariscere, garentare, garandiare, garandire*, etc.,
"cavere, spondere, praestare, defendere, sanare." The forms
with *n* are very old, for we find in the capitularies of Charlemagne *warnire* "to prepare for war, defence." [4] The Ro-

---

[1] "Siamus tibi adjutores de ipsa honore quod haberetis vel in antea habere potueris cum nostrum consilium a tener et a *giregar* et a defendre contra cunctos homines vel feminas per fidem rectam sine engan," Devic and Vaissete, *op. cit.*, vol. II Preuves, col. 422.

[2] B. Brisson, *De verborum quae ad jus pertinent significatione, libri XIX*, sub *gerere*.

[3] *Ibid.*, sub *heres*.

[4] "Unusquisque infra patriam cum pace et sine oppressione pauperum ... et in hostem vel ad placitum, sive ad curtem veniens, de suo sit *warnitus*, et de domo sua moveat ut cum pace ... venire possit," *MGH., Capitularia*, p. 158; "nobis in adjutorium, prout citius potuerint, veniant, et de hoc omnes semper *warniti* sint," *ibid.*, p. 360.

mance languages have borrowed their respective terms from the French or Provençal, where there is an enormous number of derivatives of this group. We have Prov. *garen* "surety, witness, helper," *garensa* "salvation, protection, cure," *garentia* "witness, proof," *garana, garena,* "warren," *garandar* "to observe, enclose, surround," *garanda* "reliability, measure," *garar* "to observe, look out, pay attention, suspect," *garir* "save, cure, ward off," *garida* "salvation, help, protection," *garnir* "fit out with every thing necessary, equip, prepare, adorn"; similarly OFrench *garant* "protection, defence," *gare* "ambuscade," *garer* "to furnish," *garir* "to guarantee, preserve, save, protect, defend, furnish, resist," *garison* "defence, protection, safety, sustenance," *garnir* "to fortify, prepare, defend," etc.

The Germanic languages have similarly adopted this group of words. We have Goth. *warjan* "to prohibit," *wars* "wary," OHG. *wara* "intuitio, consideratio, cura," *biwaron* "servare, providere," *warjan, werjan* "prohibere, cohibere," *weren* "to grant, warrant," *warnon* "munire, prospicere, admonere, instruere," AS. *waer* "ware, aware, having knowledge, prepared, on guard, careful, wary, cautious, prudent," *waru* "watchful care, observance, keeping of command," *werian* "to hinder, check, restrain, defend, resist attack, defend at law, protect, guard from wrong or injury," *warenian, warnian, wearinan* "to take heed, beware, be on guard, abstain," etc. Similarly the Slavic languages have a very large quantity of derivatives from the root *var-* with the underlying meaning "to guard, protect." We have already seen from the Provençal sources that *garire* is generally connected with "de omnibus hominibus," that is, that this verb has the distinct meaning "to protect, by fighting against all men." We have also in French *gare gare* "hunters' call in the pursuit of the stag," hence *gara, guerra* was early associated with "strife, tumult, war," OHG. *werra* "scandal, quarrel, sedition,"[1] while the popular Provençal forms *giregare, guerregare, guerrigiare* produce later the MHG. *krîg*, German *krieg* "war," *kriegen* "to make war, obtain."

This root *gar-, war-* has become confused with the root *gard-, ward-*, which has arisen in an entirely different manner. In the Visigothic laws we find an officer, *gardingus*, who is also a "compulsor exercitus." He is mentioned after the *thiufadus*, but apparently not as an integral part of the military and judicial hierarchy,[2] for he is only mentioned in connection with sudden military expeditions. But the *gardingi* are near to the royal person, for they figure with the seniores or optimates palatii, after the high priesthood, once, as confirming a law,[3] another time, as being subject to the same punishment.[4] They either take part in the expedition or stay at home and do duty in the *guardia* "the home guard,"[5] hence *gardingi* unquestionably is related etymologically to

---

[1] "Rixas et dissensiones seu seditiones, quas vulgus *werras* nominat" (858), *MGH., Capitularia*, vol. II, p. 440; "de ista die in ante Karoli Hludowici imperatoris filii regnum illi non forconsiliabo, neque *werribo*" (860), *ibid.*, p. 298; "si *werra* in regno surrexerit, quam comes per se comprimere non possit" (877), *ibid.*, p. 360.

[2] "Dux et comes, thiufadus aut vicarius, *gardingus* vel quelibet persona, qui aut ex ipso sit commissu, ubi adversitas ipsa occurrerit, aut ex altero qui in vicinitate adiungitur, vel quicumque in easdem provincias vel territoria superveniens infra centum milia positus, statim ubi necessitas emerserit, mox a duce suo seu comite, thiufado vel vicario aut a quolibet fuerit admonitus, vel quocumque modo ad suam cognitionem pervenerit, et ad defensionem gentis vel patrie nostre prestus cum omni virtute sua, qua valuerit, non fuerit," IX. 2. 8; "iam vero, si quisquis ille admonitus, et tamen qualibet cognitione sibimet innoescente non nescius, aut progredi statim noluerit, aut in definitis locis adque temporibus prestus esse destiterit: si maioris loci persona fuerit, id est dux, comes seu etiam *gardingus*, a bonis propriis ex toto privatus exilii relegatione iussu regio mancipetur," IX. 2. 9.

[3] "Videntibus cuncti sacerdotibus Dei senioribusque palatii atque *gardingis*," II. 1. 1.

[4] "Secundus est canon de accusatis sacerdotibus seu etiam optimatibus palatii atque *gardingis*," XII. 1. 3.

[5] "Quicumque vero ex palatino officio ita in exercitus expeditione profectus extiterit, ut nec in principali servitio frequens existat, nec in *wardia* (*guardia*) cum reliquis fratribus suis laborem sustineat, noverit se legis huius sententia feriendum," IX. 2. 9.

*guardia*, and it is possible to ascertain the Latin equivalents from which the two are derived. In the fifth century the *militia cohortalis* is opposed to the *armata* or *legionaria militia*,[1] apparently because it represented a home militia doing guard duty. But *cortis*, the briefer form of *cohortis*, produces *gard-* in the Romance and Germanic languages,[2] and *gardia, guardia, wardia* represents here *cortis* in the sense of *militia cortalis* "guard." Such a militiaman is called *cohortalis apparitor*[3] or *cohortalinus*,[4] and in Gothic we get similarly, derived from guardia, the word *gardingus*. Thus we get Goth. *wardja* "guard," OHG. *warta* "speculatio, cura, custodia, excubiae, statio, spectaculum," *warten* "videre, spectare, adspicere, speculari, excubare, sperare," AS. *weard* "watch, ward," etc. The Slavic languages have also this root *vard-, vart-*, with which the other root *var-* has become confused.

I have assumed Arabic, rather than Greek, influence in the late appearance of *garens*, because there is in Gothic another unmistakeable Arabic word, which entered about the same time.[5] In a Carolingian document of the year 794 we meet for the first time the verb *gurpire* "to abandon."[6] It is also used in the sense of "abandon, turn over" in a formula of Marculfus,[7] but as it has been shown that this collection of formulae could not have been made up before 741, we have no datable case before the end of the eighth cen-

---

[1] A. v. Priemenstein, in Pauly Wissowa, *Real-Encyclopaedie*, vol. VII, col. 358. Also as *cohortalina* opposed to *castrensis militia, Cod. Theod.* XVI. 5. 65. 4.

[2] Of this I treat in full under the history of the *curtis*.

[3] *Cod. Theod.* VIII. 4. 30.

[4] *Cod. Theod.* VI. 35, 14. 1. etc.      [5] See Preface, p. viii.

[6] "Necnon omnem iustitiam et res proprietatis, quantum illi aut filiis vel filiabus suis in ducatu Baioariorum legitime pertinere debuerant, *gurpivit* atque proiecit et, in postmodum omni lite calcanda, sine ulla repetitione indulsit et gratia pleniter concessit et in sua misericordia commendavit," *MGH., Capitularia*, vol. I, p. 74.

[7] "Villas nuncupatas illas, in pago illo, sua spontanea voluntate nobis per fistucam visus est *werpisse*, vel condonasse," I. 13.

tury. As the abandonment or cession of property, in Salic law at least, could not take place except by the throwing of the festuca from the hand, this *gurpire, werpire* came to mean "to throw," a fact amply proved by hundreds of quotations.[1] That the original meaning was "to abandon" is proved, not only by OF. *guerpir, gerpir, werpir, gepir, gurpir, curpir, guepir* "quitter, laisser, abandonner," Prov. *gurpir, guerpir, grupir* "déguerpir, abandonner, délaisser, separer," but also by LLat. *arbus, garbus, gerbus,* frequently recorded in Italian documents in the sense of "abandoned (land)."[2] As there is not a trace of this word to be found before the eighth century, its appearance and universality can be accounted for only by some event which took place in that century. This is amply explained by the Arabic invasion the very progress of which was characterized by the abandonment of land by the Goths and Franks. We have in Arabic *ḥariba* "it was, or became, in a state of ruin, waste, uninhabited, depopulated, deserted, desolate, uncultivated, or in a state the contrary of flourishing," *ḥarib, ḥarab* "in a state of ruin, etc.," *ḥarab* "a ruin, waste, a place, country, place of abode, in a state of ruin, etc." The Franks did not inherit the word from their German ancestors, for there is no reference to it in any of the older Germanic laws, nor anywhere else in the documents or in literature, hence the Franks could have acquired it only directly or indirectly from the Arabs, and the fact that the Goths have the word *wairpan* only in the

---

[1] "Absolvere eum nolebat, nisi prius dimissionem manu propria (quod et vulgo *werpire* dicitur) faceret calumniam super hoc *guipivit* in manu mea; et si tunc eam habuerit, mox ei abrenuntiet, quod lingua Francorum *gurpire* dicimus (1031); ingenuitatem illorum et alodem manibus *gurpierunt;* Odo, Brunellus dictus, ecclesiam de Evorea quam dudum haereditario quidem, sed injurioso jure, laicus possederat, *guerpo* in manu mea posito, sanctae ecclesiae per me restituit," in Ducange, sub *guerpire.*

[2] "Terra *arba*" (976), *Codice diplomaticc padovano dal secolo sesto a tutto l'undecimo,* p. 87; "terras arabiles et prata et *garbas* et buscalivas" (1100), *ibid.,* p. 458; "terris arabilis et *gerbis*" (10. cent.), *ibid.,* pp. 4, 230. See Ducange, sub *gerba, gerbida, gerbina, gerbum.*

meaning "to throw" shows that they could have acquired it only from their Frankish neighbors who lived under the Salic law, that is, in the second half of the eighth century, when a large number of Goths settled in the southwest of France in the territory known as Gothia, or somewhere else on French territory.

The Langobard laws give an interesting illustration of the late appearance of the word among the Germanic nations. In the very late Cartularium to the Langobard laws, of about the year 1000, it is specifically mentioned that the formula *warpi te* was employed by Romans, Salics, Ribuarians, Goths, Alemanians, Bavarians, and Burgundians alike in the complete cession or tradition.[1] But there are certain acts where *warpi te* is used in Salic documents exclusively.[2] In the text of the Langobard law the word does not occur, but in ninth century manuscripts a law dealing with the crime of throwing a man from a horse is entitled *De marahworfin*,[3] while another, speaking of the desecration of graves, is entitled *De crapworfin*. But these titles are lacking in the older codices and wherever they appear are not repeated in the text, hence they are obviously later additions. Thus it is clear that the Salic law has forced the word on all the Germanic nations, without itself containing a trace of the word before the end of the eighth century, which once more establishes the Arabic origin of the word.

Before *gerens* took the place of *agens*, and before *buccellarius* meant "private apparitor," *homologus* was the popular word for *agens* among the Teutons, hence where the Langobard law uses *auctor*[4] and the Interpretations translate this

---

[1] "Si est Romanus, similiter dic; sed si est Salichus, si est Riboarius, si est Francus, si est Gothus vel Alemannus venditor . . . Et adde in istorum cartulis et Baioariorum et Gundebadorum. . . Et in omnium fine traditionis adde . . . 'warpi te '," 2 (*MGH., Leges*, vol. IV, p. 595). Similarly 13 (p. 598).

[2] *Ibid.*, p. 600 (Nos. 17, 18, 24).

[3] "Si quis hominem liberum de caballo in terra iactaverit," *Roth.* 30.

[4] "Si quis caballum emerit et *auctorem* ignoraverit," *Roth.* 232.

by *warens*,[1] all the other Germanic laws use a derivative of *homologus*. The Langobard law in question deals with the surety which the purchaser receives from the seller of a horse to guarantee the seller in case the horse was stolen. The *Edictum Theoderici* simply says that a question raised about the sale of a thing must be answered by the seller before the buyer's judge, and that the seller cannot refer the buyer to his own *auctor*, the person from whom he himself got the thing, but that he may summon that *auctor*, to defend him in court.[2]

The *Lex Burgundionum* says more explicitly that if a person recognizes a thing to be his own, he may ask for a surety or, failing to get one, may seize his property, except that in case he has made a false claim he must pay back double the amount.[3] The *auctor* of the Edict is here confused with any surety, a most natural mistake, for the *auctor* who guarantees the sale is eo ipso a surety for that sale. The Salic law has elaborated enormously upon its predecessors. "If a person recognizes his property he puts it into the hands of a surety, both parties swearing. All parties concerned in the transaction are warned and must appear in court within 40 days. If the person warned does not appear, the person who has had dealings with him sends three witnesses to summon him and three other witnesses are furnished to prove that he has

t

[1] In the *Liber Papiensis*. Compare also: "debet esse: *auctor* et bonus *garenz* de omnibus amparatoribus" (13. cent.), Cazauran, *Cartulaire de Berdoues*, Paris 1905, p. 347.

[2] "*Auctor* venditionis, etiamsi privilegium habeat sui iudicis, tamen defensurus venditionem suam, forum sequatur emptoris," 139. "Qui de re comparata pertulerit quaestionem, ipse petitori respondere compellitur, nec ad *auctorem* suum proponentem repellit: quem necesse est hoc tantum ipse commoneat, ut factum suum in venditione defendat," 140.

[3] "Quicumque res aut mancipium aut quodlibet suum agnoscit, a possidente aut fideiussorem idoneum accipiat, aut si fideiussorem petitum non acceperit, res, quas agnoscit, praesumendi habeat potestatem. Si vero falsus fuerit in agnoscendo, rem, quam male agnovit, et aliud tantum cogatur exsolvere," LXXXIII.

had dealings with him, thus freeing himself of the charge of theft. The person failing to appear stands out as a thief to him who has recognized his property, pays the price back to him with whom he has had his dealings, and he pays the penalty according to law to him who has recognized his property. All this is to be done in court where the surety lives, that is, where the thing has been put into a third hand." [1] The *Lex ribuaria* has the same provision, except that the guilty person is brought before the king's scaffold or to the place where the surety is.[2]

In spite of the elaborate accessories the law is essentially the same as in Theodoric's Edict, except that the supposedly stolen thing is left in a third hand. Even as in the older law, the seller has to answer in the court of the buyer or, rather, of the claimant's surety, and the seller has to defend himself against the charge of receiving stolen goods. The surety is called *hamallus*, *hamallatus*, the other forms of which are badly corrupted. That *hamallus*, for *homologus*, means "surety, witness" is proved by a Merovingian document of the year 679, where *hamallatus* is corrupted to *hamedius*. A woman, Acchildis, accuses Amalgarius of illegally holding a piece of property which belongs to her by inheritance. To

[1] "Si quis seruum aut caballum uel bouem aut qualibet rem super alterum agnouerit, mittat eum in tertia manu. Et ille super quem cognoscitur debeat agramire; et si cis ligere aut carbonariam ambo manent et qui agnoscit et apud quem cognoscitur in noctis XL placitum faciant, et inter ipso placito qui interfuerit qui caballo ipso aut uenderit aut cambiauerit aut fortasse in solitudinem dederit. Omnes intro placito isto communiantur, hoc est ut unusquis que de cum negotiatoribus alter alterum admoneat. Et si quis commonitus fuerit et eum sunis non tenuerit et ad placitum uenire distulerit, tunc ille qui cum eum negotiauit mittat tres testes quomodo ei nunciasset ut ad placitum ueniret. Et alteros tres quod publicae ab eo negociasset; istud si fecerit exuit se do latrocinio. Et ille qui non uenerit super quem testes furauerunt, ille erit latro illius qui agnoscit et precium reddat ille qui cum illo negociauit, et ille secundum legem conponat ille qui res suas agnoscit; ista omnia in illo mallo debent fieri ubi ille est *gamallus* (*hamallus, amallus, rhamallus*) super quem res illa primitus fuit agnita aut intertiata," XLVII.

[2] "At regis staffolo vel ad eum locum, ubi *amallus* (*amallatus, mallatum, mallus*) est, auctorem suum in praesente habeat," XXXIII.

this Amalgarius replies that he and his father have held the
property for thirty-one years. Amalgarius is requested to
bring with him six sponsors, that is, *homologi,* who are all to
swear over the chapel of St. Martin that he and his father
have lawfully held the estate for thirty-one years. Amalgarius appears with his *hamedii* and, complying with the
law, gets the estate.[1] That *hamedii* was actually in use is
proved not only by the gloss "*hamedii,* id sunt coniuratores,
quos nos geidon dicimus,"[2] but also by the short form *medius, medicus* "witness," of extremely common occurrence in
the *Lex Alamannorum.*[3]

The whole proceeding in the above-mentioned case is in
accordance with the Ribuarian law, which in this particular
may have been the same as the Salic law. In any case, the
Ribuarian law provides that the swearing should take place
in the chapel together with six witnesses.[4] That *hamallus,*

[1] "Cum ante dies in nostri vel procerum nostrorum presencia, Conpendio,
in palacio nostro . . . ibique veniens fimena, nomene Acchildis, Amalgario
interpellavit dum dicerit eo quod porcione sua, in villa noncobanti Bactilione
valle, quem de parti genetrici sua Bertane quondam, ligebus obvenire debuerat,
post se malo ordene retenirit. Qui ipse Amalgarius taliter dedit in respunsis, eo
quod ipsa terra in predicto loco Bactilione valle, de annus triginta et uno, inter
ipso Amalgario vel genetore suo Gaeltramno quondam, semper tenuerant et
possiderant. Sic eidem nunc a nostris procerebus ipsius Amalgario fuissit
judecatum, *ut de nove denomenatus aput sex, sua mano septima,* dies duos ante
istas Kalendas julias, in oraturio nostro, super cappella domni Martine, ubi
reliqua sacramenta percurribant, hoc dibirit conjurare, quod antedicta terra,
in predicto loco Bactilione valle, inter ipso Amalgario vel genetore suo Gaeltramno, de annus triginta et uno semper tenuissint et possedissint, nec eis diger
numquam fuissit, nec aliut exinde non redebirit, nisi edonio sacramento. Sed
veniens antedictus Amalgarius ad ipso placito Lusareca, in palacio nostro, una
*cum hamedius suos,* ipso sacramento, justa quod eidem fuit judicatum, et nostros equalis preceptionis locuntur, in quantum inluster vir Druetoaldus, comes
palati noster, testimuniavit, ligibus visus fuit adimplissit, et tam ipse quam et
*hamediae suae* diliguas eorum derexsissent. Propteria jobimus ut ipsa porcione,
in predicto loco Bactilione vualle, unde inter eus orta fuit intencio, memoratus
Amalgarius contra ipsa Acchilde vel suis heredibus omne tempore abiat evinde-
cata," Lauer and Samaran, *Les diplômes originaux des mérovingiens,* Paris 1908,
p. 12.
[2] *MGH., Capitularia,* vol. I, p. 91.    [3] "Cum 12 *medicus* electus iuret."
[4] "Sibi septimus in haraho coniurit," xxxiii. 2.

*hamedius* is the same as *agens* is proved by the presence of the word *mallato* in this sense in Spain.[1] This connotation "agent, representative, advocate," which the word obviously has, has led to the verb *homallare*, with its variants, *omallare*, *obmallare*, *admallare*, *mallare*, in the basic sense of "to represent a person in court." The formula "prosequire, adsumere, respondere vel *homallare*" is quite common in the documents,[2] and since *homallare* means "to represent a case through a competent speaker, attorney," [3] it also means "to carry to court, denounce," [4] in which sense it is even found in Portugal.[5] The corresponding term for "to summon, appear in court" in Theodoric's Edict [6] and in the Visigothic laws [7] is *convenire*. But *convenire* is closely as-

[1] "Direxerunt ad Regem ad Legionem suo *mallato* Bera" (934), *España sagrada*, vol. XL, p. 400.

[2] "Fidelis, Deo propicio, noster ille ad nostram veniens presentiam, suggessit nobis, eo quod propter simplicitatem suam causas suas minime possit prosequire vel *obmallare* (o-, ad-, ho-,)," *Formulae Marculfi* (in *MGH.*, *Formulae*), I. 21; "iobemus, ut memoratus pontifex, aut abba, vel abbatissa, seo advocatus eius in vice adsumendi vel *omallandi* (ho-) ... cum aequitatis ordine respondendi vel *omallandi* (ho-)," I. 36; "ut ipsa causa suscipere ad *mallandum* vel prosequendum in vice mea debeas," II. 31; "oc coniuravit uel legibus custodivit, quomodo se contra illum sibi *obmallavit*," *Formulae Salicae Merkelianae*, 28; "rogo, preco, supplico atque iniungo per hunc mandatum ad meam vicem hominem nomen ille, quem ego beneficium ei feci argento uncias tantas, ipsum meum ubi et ubi eas vel meas prosequere et *admallare et* adcausare facias," *Formulae Andecavenses*, 48; "ad vicem meam prosequere et excausare, *admallare* eas facias," *Formulae Turonenses*, 45; "per omni iure investigare, inquirere, prosequi et *admallare* debeas," *Formulae Senonenses recentiores*, 10.

[3] "Homo nomen ille alico homene nomen illo *mallavit* pro res suas," *Form. Andec.*, 43.

[4] "Unde me ille homo in *mallo* publico *malabat*," *Form. Senon.*, 21; "unde me ille ante vir magnifico illo vel aliis bonis hominibus *malavit*, quae ego herbas maleficas temporasse vel bibere ei dedisse," *Cart. Senon.*, 22.

[5] "Et filauit nostro porto et parauit ibidem suo barco et nameabit nostros homines et *maliauit* nostro barcario et exiuit nobis inde multa superbia et malefactoria super nostros homines" (999), *PMH.*, *Dipl. et chart.*, p. 112.

[6] "A die qua per auctoritatem *conventus* est," 11; "iudicis praeceptione *conventus*," 46; "*conventus* legibus," 56; "uxor pro marito non debet *convenire*," 153.

[7] "Si tali admonitione conventus aut se dilataverit aut ad iudicium venire contemserit," II. 1. 19; "postquam *conventus* fuerit a iudice," VIII. 1. 7.

sociated with *conventus* "assembly, synod, court." So, too, *homallare*, in its abbreviated form *mallare*, leads to *mallus* "assembly, court." However, this term has no concrete reference to a definite court, least of all to a Germanic court, hence it is not found in the Formulae Andecavenses, Marculfi, Turonenses, Bituricenses, nor in the distinctly German laws of the Frisians, Thuringians, and Saxons.

The *Lex romana raetica curiensis* is a modernisation of the Breviary of Alaric and so aids us in getting at the exact equivalent of *mallare*. *Mallus* does not occur there at all, while *amallare*, never *mallare*, renders the older "in iudicium vocare, repetere, litigare, accusare, convenire, in iudicium deducere,"[1] that is, it means "to summon, denounce." In the Ribuarian law *admallare* means "to summon,"[2] while in the *Lex Alamannorum* and *Baiuwariorum* it means "to prosecute in court, plead."[3] The Salic law has two expressions for "to summon," *manire*[4] and *mallare*. The first is

[1] "Si ille miles illum privatum patrianum *amallaverit* (in iudicium vocauerit)," II. 1. 2; "si privatus homo illum fiscalem *admallaverit* (si privatus fiscum repetat)," II. 5; "et si de presente, quo *ammallatus* fuerit, ipsas res reddiderit (et eo die, a quo de tali re coeperint litigare)," IV. 15. 1; "si quiscumque homo alienum servum de capitale crimine *amallaverit* (si servos alienos accusandos esse crediderit)," IX. 4; "quod si forsitan terciam vicem *amallati* fuerint et ante iudicem venire noluerint, sicut alii contumaces pene feriundi sunt (quod si tertio conventi)," XVIII. 11; "qui post longum tempus alterum hominem de quale cumque causa *amallare* voluerit (in iudicium deduci non potest)," XXVII. 10.

[2] "Sicut in presente legitimi *malatus* fuerit," LVIII. 19; "quod eum ad strude legitima *admallatum* habet," XXXII. 3.

[3] "Et si quis alium *mallare* vult de qualecumque causa, in ipso mallo publico debet *mallare* ante iudice suo . . . in uno enim placito *mallet* causam suam," *Lex Alem.*, XXXVI. 2; "ille homo qui *mallatur* ante eum de causa illa," *ibid.*, XLII. 1; "*mallet* eum ante plebem suam," *Lex Baiuw.*, I. 10, 13. 2; "et si qui se *malliet* de eadem re iustitiam faciat," III. 14. 6.

[4] "Si quis uero commonitus fuerit et sumis eum pro non detinuerit et ad placitum uenire distulerit, tunc ille cum quo negotiauit mittat tres testes quomodo ei *maniauerit* quod ad placitum ueniat," XLVII (cod. 10); "si quis ad mallum legibus dominicis *mannitus* fuerit," I. 1; "et ille qui alium *mannit* cum testibus," I. 3; "tunc *maniat* eum ad mallum et testes super singula placita qui fuerunt ibi praestos habeat," XLV. 2 b; "*manire* eos cum testibus debet," XLVIX. 1; "si adhuc nolierit conponere debet eum ad mallum *manire*," L. 2; "ad regis praesentia ipso *manire* debet," LVI. 1. 1; "tunc eum debet *manire* ante regem,

used almost exclusively for summoning privately by means of witnesses, not for the legal summons by order of the judge, hence the gloss has it correctly *"mannitus: vocatus tribus testibus praesentibus."*[1] The distinction is the same as is made in Latin between *admonere* and *convenire*, the first referring to a private summons, although it may also be used in regard to the judge's summons,[2] while *convenire* means only "to summon directly to court." Obviously *manire* is the corrupt form for *(ad)monere*, which is equally used in the Salic law for it.[3] The more common word is *mallare, admallare, obmallare.* Thus *mallus* was derived to express all those actions with which the summoning is connected. It is either the legal court of any count, thunginus, iudex, etc.,[4] or it only refers to the legal three summonses, when it means "a period of seven days."[5]

hoc est in noctes XIIII, et tria testimonia iurare debent quod ibi fuerunt ubi eum *manibit* et solem collocauit," LVI. 1. 4, etc.

[1] J. Hessels and H. Kern, *Lex salica*, in *Vocabulary*.

[2] "Necesse eot hoc tantum ipse *commoneat*, ut factum suum in venditione defendat," *Ed. Theod.*, 139; "iudex cum ab aliquo fuerit interpellatus, adversarium *admonitione* unius epistule vel sigilli ad iudicium venire conpellat, sub ea videlicet ratione, ut coram ingenuis personis his, qui a iudice missus extiterit, illi qui ad causam dicendam conpellitur, offerat epistulam vel sigillum," *Lex Visig.*, II. 1. 19.

[3] "Omnes intro placito isto communiantur, hoc est unusquisque de cum negotiatoribus alter alterum *admoneat*," XLVII. 1; "tunc ad que *manitus (monitus, admanitus)* est extra sermonem suum ponat eum," LVI. 5; "tribus testibus praesentibus, *admonere* debet, ut seruum suum infra VII noctis praesentare debeat," XL. 10.

[4] "*Mallus* publicus," *Lex. sal.*, XIV. 4; "legitimus *mallus* publicus," *ibid.*, XLVI. 6; "*mallus* comitis," *ibid.*, *Capit.* 1. v; "*mallus* thungini aut centinarii," *ibid.*, XLIV. 1, XLVI. 1; "*mallus* iudicis, hoc est comitis aut grafionis," *ibid.*, LXXII. 1, etc.

[5] "*Tribus malos (mallis)* parentibus offeratur, et non sic redemitur, uita charebit," *Lex sal.*, *Pact.* 2; "et si inter ipsas VII noctes fidem facere nec componere noluerit, tunc *in proximo mallo* . . . sic inuitetur graphio," *ibid.*, LXXVIII. 7; "*in alio mallo* iterum minare debit, et ibi tres testes debit collegere. Edonius a *tercio uero mallo* similiter faciat," *ibid.*, XXXVI (LXV cod. 7); "quam si uero nec ipse habuerit unde tota persoluat, tunc illum qui homicidium fecit qui eum sub fidem habuit *in mallo* praesentare debent, et sic postea eum *per quattuor mallos* ad suam fidem tollant," *ibid.*, LVIII. 6; "sin autem manitus fuerit ad

There is a strange psychological phenomenon which causes such words as "astronomy" and "prodigy" to become popularly "astromony" and "progidy." By a similar psychological law the consonant groups *h-m-l*, *g-m-l* show in all the European languages a tendency to turn into *m-h-l*, *m-g-l*. Thus the Arab. *hamal* "carrier" is found in Roumanian and the Slavic languages as *mahal*, while Albanian has side by side *gamule* "glebe," *magul'e* "hill," OSlav. *gomila*, *mogyla* "tomb," Roum. *gămălie*, *măgălie*, Slav. *gomolya* "clod." It may be that this group is derived from Lat. *cumulus* or *grumulus* (witness Croatian *gromila* = *gomila*) "heap," or it may, after all, be the same Greek ὅμιλος, which is not unlikely, when we consider Russ. *gomola*, Boh. *homola* "pyramis, cone" and Croatian *gomila*, which generally means "a mass of human beings." Whatever the case may be, which for our purpose is immaterial, the fact remains that the groups *h-m-l*, *g-m-l* become *m-h-l*, *m-g-l*. If we now turn to the Langobard laws, we there find the earliest Germanic derivative of *homologus*, namely a verb *hamalôn*, *mahalôn* "confabulari," hence *gahamalus*, *gamahalus* "confabulatus." But the text is certainly tampered with, for what it intends to say is this: "If one of the fideiussores or sacramentales dies, the plaintiff has a right to substitute another in his place." Here, as in the Salic and Ribuarian texts, the word *hamallus* was used, but a later scribe, knowing the current meaning of *gahamalus*, *gamahalus* "sponsor, sponsatus," added "aut de natus, aut de *gahamalus*, id est confabulatus," which by the very equation (which, besides, is not contained in all the texts) betrays its later origin.[1]

---

*secundo mallo, aut a tertio, seu ad quarto, vel quinto, usque ad sexto* venire distullerit, *pro unoquemque mallo* . . . culpabilis iudicetur," *Lex rib.*, xxxii. 2.

[1] "Et si aliquis de ipsos sacramentalis mortus fuerit, potestatem habeat ille qui pulsat, in locum mortui alium similem nominare de proximus legitimus, aut de natus aut de *gamahalos* (*gahamalos, gaamaalos, gamelos, gamalos*) id est confabulatus," *Roth.* 362.

In OHG. we have *mahalôn* "postulare, causas, agere, interpellare," *mâlon* "contendere," *gamahaljan* "despondere," *mahalo* "concio, foedus," *gamahalo* "sponsus, vir, conjunx." If we now consider that *mallus* "conventus" was a fictitious term, referring to the legal summonses which had to be repeated each seven days, we at once see how the "primo, secundo *mallo*, tribus *mallis*" of the quotations produced OHG. *zeinemo male, ze andermo male, ze driu malen*, hence *mâl* "legal term, time." Furthermore, the Roman law generally spoke of summonses "trinis litteris" or "trinis epistulis," since the summonses were not legal if not given in writing, and this was also the case in Visigothic law,[1] hence *mâl* was also a "written document" and OHG. *mâlôn* "to paint," i. e., "to write." This appears even more directly from the Goth. *mēl* "time, hour, space of time," plural *mēla* "writing," *mēljan* "to write," AS. *mael, mal*, Icel. *mâl* "a part, portion measure, term of anything, space of time," etc., AS. *maelan* "to say, speak, converse," *mal*, Icel. *maeli, mâl* "speech, discourse, multitude, assembly, place of meeting." At the same time the form ὁμολογητής, which produced LLat. *hamallatus*, of which *hamedius* is obviously a corrupt form for *hamedlus* or *hameldus*, has led to Crimgothic *malthan*, Goth. *mapljan*, AS. *maeðlan* "to speak, discourse," Goth. *mapl* "conventus, agora," AS. *meðel* "discourse, speech, council," OHG. *madal* "concio, sermo." Since the *hamallus, hamallatus* was the real informer and *amallare*, therefore, acquired the meaning "to denounce, inform," we get OHG. *meldôn*, AS. *meldian, ameldian* "to discover, betray, make known, inform against," AS. *meld* "evidence, proof, discovery," OHG. *melda* "delatura, proditio." The Slavic languages have the roots *modl-*, *mold-*, *mol-*, to express the idea "to request, pray," Lith. *malda* "prayer," and that this group is derived from the same

---

[1] II. 1. 19. See note 2 on p. 73.

source is proved by Judaeo-Spanish *meldar* "to read the prayers, to pray." It may also be possible that Russ. *molvit'* "to speak" is derived from it, for this root occurs only in the eastern Slavic languages and is, therefore certainly borrowed. Ducange records even as late as the thirteenth century *homologare* "to make a vow, promise,"[1] which may have survived in the language of the church. From this *homologare* was formed the feudal term *homolegius* "a vassal,"[2] which was popularly related to *homo* and *allegare* and produced the feudal terms *homagium* and *allegancia,* OFrench *homage* and *lige, liege,* etc.

[1] "Pro se et hominibus suis voluerunt et *homologaverunt* Deo et B. Mariae praedictas decimas" (1268), also *amologare.*

[2] "Sed si voluerit unum locare, poterit de suis vassallis seu *homolegiis,* et coram illo secundum terminos praefixos parare potest" (1156), in Ducange.

# EX SQUALIDO AND VASTA

Soon after the Spanish expedition of 778 Spaniards and other fugitives from the Arabic West began to settle in Septimania and southern Aquitaine. At the end of the eighth century Charlemagne presented a certain Johannes with the Villa Fontes in the Mark of Narbonne and with other lands, which Johannes was to hold by right of *aprision*, working them with the aid of his own men.[1] In 812 all lands held by the immigrants by the right of *aprision* for 30 years were turned over to them free from taxes.[2] In a decree of January 815 Louis the Pious confirmed the privileges of the Spanish settlers in the waste lands, and a year later he expanded the law in such a way as to grant the same immunities to the commoners.[3] Charles the Bald in 844 expanded the grant so as to include the Spanish Mark, Septimania and Aquitaine, and mentioned specifically that the Spaniards could preserve their local customs in the territory of *aprision*.[4]

In all these decrees the Carolingians refer distinctly to the *aprision* as a Spanish custom, which is correct, for it may

[1] "Nos vero concedimus ei ipsum villarem et omnes suos terminos et pertinentias suas ab integro et quantum ille cum hominibus suis in villa Fonteioncosa occupavit, vel occupaverit, vel *de heremo traxerit*, vel infra suos terminos sive in aliis locis vel villis seu villare occupaverit, vel *aprisione fecerit cum hominibus suis*," E. Mühlbacher, *Die Urkunden der Karolinger* (in *MGH.*), vol. I, p. 241 f.

[2] "Demandamus, ut neque vos neque iuniores vestri memoratos Ispanos nostros, qui ad nostram fiduciam de Ispania venientes per nostram datam licentiam *erema loca sibi ad laboricundum propriserant et laboratas habere videntur*, nullum censum superponere presumatis neque ad proprium facere permittatis, quoadusque illi fideles nobis aut filiis nostris fuerunt, quod *per triginta annos habuerunt per aprisionem*, quieti possideant et posteritas eorum .et vos conservare debeatis," *ibid.*, p. 290.

[3] *MGH., Capitularia*, vol. I, p. 261 ff.

[4] "In portione sua quam *aprisionem* vocant," *ibid.*, vol. II, p. 259.

be shown by documentary evidence that the Frankish kings
in the eighth century had in mind the Visigothic method of
colonisation which, in its turn, was based on the Roman procedure. Alfonso I of Asturias ascended the throne in 739 and
was the only Gothic ruler who maintained himself against
the victorious Arabs. After these had devastated Galicia,
he strove to repeople the devastated region, as we learn from
the wills and donations of Bishop Odoarius and his men. In
745 Odoarius returned with his followers from Africa, immediately setting out to found abbeys and resettle the country about Lugo. Several of his people (famuli, servitores,
familia), guided by Aloitus, petitioned Odoarius to turn over
to them, for services which they promised, some of the villas
which he had seized (quas ipse prendiderat). Of this property, held by *presura*, Aloitus gave one fifth to the Church.[1]
Two years later Odoarius wrote his will, making over to the
Church all his possessions which he had acquired by *presura*
and had worked with his *familia*.[2] In a donation of 757 Auza-

[1] "Nos homines humillimi, ego videlicet, Aloitus, et uxor mea nomine Ka,
et propinqui mei . . . qui omnes simul cum caeteris plurimis ex Africae partibus
exeuntes cum Domino Odoario Episcopo, (cujus eramus famuli, et servitores)
cum ad Lucensem Urbem Galleciae Provinciae ingressi fuissemus, invenimus
ipsam Civitatem desertam, et inhabitabilem factam cum suis terminis. Prae-
fatus vero gloriosus Odoarius Praesul ipsam Urbem, ut universam Provinciam
studuit restaurare, ac *propria familia* stipavit. Nos vero supra nominati, qui
ex ejus eramus familia, perseverantes in illius servitio per multorum curricula
annorum petivimus cum omni subjectione, ut nobis concederet, et donaret
unam Villam, ex ipsis, *quas ipse prendiderat*, quod facere misericordia motus non
distulit; et dedit nobis unam Villam prenominatam Villamarci, *quam ipse prendiderat* . . . Hanc itaque Villam nobis donavit pro servitio quod ei fecimus; et
veritate, quoniam ei tenuimus sub tali tenore, et pacto, ut cunctis diebus vitae
nostrae tam nos nominati, quam etiam successores nostri jussionem ejus et
voluntatem successorum ejus, qui in eadem Urbe fuerint, faciamus in per-
petuum . . . Ego ipse Aloytus quintam de omni mea hereditate, quam *de manu
ipsius Pontificis per presura acceperat* die dedicationis super altare offero," *España sagrada*, vol. XL, p. 353 *ff*.
[2] "Ego supra taxatus verens, et timens, ne me incauta vitae fallente inaniter
rapiat, decrevi, ut post obitum meum de paupertacula mea quicquid potui
*ganare vel applicare atque apprendere, et familia mea populare*, prout valui . . .
Deo et Patrono meo aliquid presentare. Offero . . . ipsam praedictam Civita-

nus tells of his return with his sons from Africa, in order to take up land on the basis of the Alfonsinian *presura,* whereby we learn that the latter was of three kinds, *de escalido, de ruda silva* and *de suco mortuorum.*[1] A still better account of the whole colonisation scheme is found in a donation of Odoarius, of the year 760. He tells how Alfonso's representative, Pelagius, had invited him to come to Lugo, where he seized government land (praesimus loca Palatii) and planted vine-yards and gardens. He allowed his men to become proprietors (possessores) and gave them work-oxen and other cattle. He settled them on the banks of the Miño, where he had found villages in ruin *de succo mortuorum* and *de ruda silva,* and seized the land as his *presura.*[2]

tem ab omni integritate conclusa intus in circuitu murorum, quam ex radice restauravi: Villas praenominatas, quam *ex presuria adquisivi, et ex stirpe, et familia mea populavi . . .* Monasterium Sancti Stephani vallis Athanae, *quod ex propria familia extipavi,* et ex radice fundamentavi, et ex aliis Ecclesiis dotavi, quo *a me et a mea familia sunt fundamentata per presuria . . .* quas omnes sunt in ipso territorio Liziniano, et Sabiniano a me *possessae per presuria . . .* Ecclesia Sancto Felice de Raymundi cum adjunctionibus ejus *stipata de familia mea . . .* Ecclesia S. Eolalia et S. Maria Alta, et ejus familia ab integro, et Ecclesia S. Joannis de Mera, *quos predivit* germanus meus Ermiarius *de Escalido . . .* Item in dexteris Lucense Villa de Benati *de mea pressura stipata de mea familia," ibid.,* p. 356 *ff.*

[1] "Nos omnes pressores degeneris hereditarios nominibus Auzano una cum filios meos Guntino, et Desterigo venientes de Africa *ad pressuram* ad Gallecia terra sicut et alii populi ceteri ingenui per jussionem Domini Adephonsis Principis, et *presimus* Villas, et *hereditates de Escalido et de Ruda Silva, de Suco Mortuorum . . .* idem terris quae pro justo pretio emimus, et *per nostras pressuras presimus, et juri possessa retinemus," ibid.,* p. 362 *f.*

[2] "In territorio Africae surrexerunt quidam gentes Hismaelitarum, et tulerunt ipsam terram a Christianis, et violaverunt Sanctuarium Dei; et Christicolas miserunt in captivitatem, et ad jugo servitutis, et Ecclesias Dei destruxerunt, et fecerunt nos exules a patria nostra, et fecimus moram per loca deserta multis temporibus. Postquam Dominus per servum suum Pelagium in hac Religione respicere jussit, et Christianos in hac patria ditavit; sive etiam, et divae memoriae Princeps Dominus Adephonsus in Sedem ipsius sublimavit qui ex ipsa erat de stirpe Regis Recaredi et Ermegildi. Dum talia audivimus perducti fuimus in Sedem Lucensem cum nostris multis familiis, et cum caeteris populis tam nobiles quam innobiles; et invenimus ipsam Sedem desertam et inhabitabilem factam. Nunc denique laboramus ibidem, et aedificamus domum Dei, et Ecclesiae Sanctae Mariae et *praesimus loca Palatii,* et ipsam Civitatem restauramus eam intus et foris; et plantavimus vineis et pomiferis. Postea

The German *bifanc* is obviously identical with this *presura*, even as the Latin terms *comprehensio, porprisum, captura* frequently occur in German documents,[1] and *porprisum* is older than *bifanc*, for it occurs in the sense of "seizure of property" in the Germanic laws.[2] However, it is obvious from the attitude of the Frankish kings to the Spanish *presura* that the center of Europe at that time possessed no such extensive territory for colonisation as existed in the region newly settled by the Spaniards. We shall now investigate the procedure of the aprision.

The "seizure" of land took place in a solemn manner, in presence of the royal banner and accompanied by flourishes of the trumpet,[3] and the land thus seized had to be worked by the prospective proprietor or his men[4] for thirty years. The proof had to be given that land had been reclaimed from the wilderness;[5] thus, in a lawsuit at Gerona in 844, the wit-

---

vero fecimus de nostra familia possessores pro undique partibus, et dedimus illis boves ad laborandum, et jumenta ad serviendum eis. Tunc exivimus per gyro Civitates, Villas, et hereditates ad inquirendum, ut laborassent illas: et invenimus in Ripa Minei Villas destructas *de Succo Mortuorum*, et *de Ruda Silva*, ubi posuimus nostra familia ad portum Minei, quae dicunt Agari. Super ipsum portum misimus ibi Agario: et in illa villa posuimus Avezano, et misimus ad eam nomen Avezani de nostra *praesura*," *ibid.*, p. 364 *ff.*

[1] W. Arnold, *Ansiedlungen und Wanderungen deutscher Stämme*, Marburg 1875, p. 259 *ff.*

[2] "Nullus praesumat alterius res *proprendere*," *Lex Bajuw*. II. 12; "si quis caballum, hominem, vel quamlibet rem in via *propriserit*," *Lex ribuar*. LXXV.

[3] "Edificauimus *cum cornam et albende* . . . contestamus ad ipsa eclesia illa hereditate per suis terminis que habuimus de *presuria* que preserunt nostros priores *cum cornu et cum aluende*" (870), *PMH.*, *Dipl. et chart.*, vol. I, p. 3.

[4] They are called *familia, famuli, servitores, homines*, and they are also known as *gasalianes*. Of these I have already treated.

[5] "Villare *eremum* ad laborandum" (795), Devic and Vaissete, *op. cit.*, vol. II, Preuves, col. 60; "manifeste verum est quod ipsas res ego retineo, set non injuste quia *de eremo eos tracxi in aprisione*" (852), *ibid.*, col. 228; "qui fuerunt per illorum aprisione vel ruptura quod illi homines hoc *traxerunt de heremo* ad culturam" (875), *ibid.*, col. 380, and often; "quae deinceps *ex locis eremis* atque incultis ad eorum usus adpriserint" (823), Marca, *Marca hispanica*, col. 768; "res quas genitor eorum per concessionem patris nostri Caroli praestantissimi Imperatoris *ab eremo* in Septimania *trahens* ad villam construxit" (833), *ibid.*, col. 771; "terras quas sui homines *ex eremo traxerunt*" (840), *ibid.*, col. 776;

nesses swore that they "had seen and heard and been present" when Emperor Charles had given fiscal land to the abbot and when the abbot, after the death of certain Saracens, had "seized" the land.[1]

Gothofredus has long ago pointed out that this aprision was nothing but the occupation of the *agri occupatorii*, as legalized in 423 by Honorius and Theodosius. According to this law the veterans were to possess the buildings and fenced-in lots on state land if they were not claimed by previous owners.[2] Such public land was called *ager occupatorius*, because it was occupied after the expulsion of the enemy, as Siculus Flaccus thinks,[3] but his own use of *occupare* shows that it was a technical term for the seizure of land for cultivation.[4] Long before the law of 423 veterans could seize vacant lands,[5] and in a decree of 364 the veterans were per-

"aprisiones quas *ex eremi vastitate traxerunt*, simul cum iis deinceps quae proprii laboris sudore trahere et excolere ipsi successoresque eorum potuerunt" (850), *ibid.*, col. 784; "*de eremi solitudine* ad culturam perductam" (869), *ibid.*, col. 791; "cum omnibus apprehensionibus quas ipsi monachi propriis manibus *de eremi vastitate traxerunt*" (869), *ibid.*, col. 793, and similarly cols. 763, 769, 782, 783, 787, 790, etc.; "stirpes, vel ut vulgo dicitur exartes quosdam, quos ex rebus Tricassinensis comitatus ipsi proprio labore *de heremo* ad agriculturam perduxisse noscuntur" (864), Ch. Lalore, *Cartulaire de l'abbaye de Montiéramey*, Paris, Troyes 1890, p. 6.

[1] "*Nos vidimus et audivimus et presentes fuimus* quando domno gloriosissimo Carole Imperatore dedit de fischo suo Libentio Abbate, et ad suo germano Assenario monacho Castro Tolon cum fines et adjacentias eorum tali pacto, ut in ipsas valles Leocarcari plantent et edifficent monasterium Sancti Cirici et Sancti Adree. Item postea *vidimus et audivimus et presentes fuimus* quando Libentius Abba una cum Assenario monacho prendiderunt primi homines post mortem Galaffre et Biuxan filio eius et aliorum Sarracenorum dicto castro Tolon cum fines et adjacentias eorum, et ibi dictas valles plantaverunt," etc., J. Villanueva, *Viage literario á las iglesias de España*, vol. XIII, p. 226.

[2] *Cod. Theod.* II. 23. 1, to which Gothofredus attaches a long discussion on the aprision.

[3] "*Occupatorii* autem dicuntur *agri* quos quidam arcifinales vocant, quibus agris victor populus occupando nomen dedit," Lachmann and Rudorff, *Gromatici veteres*, p. 136.

[4] "Quoniam non ex mensuris actis unus quisque miles modum accepit, sed quod aut excoluit aut in spem colendi *occupavit*," *ibid.*

[5] *Cod. Theod.* VII. 20. 3 (320).

mitted to take their servants along with them,[1] from which it may be concluded that the land worked by the servants was "seized" for the proprietor, exactly as in Visigothic law. A few years later *loca absentium squalida*, i. e., deserted lands that had reverted to the state, were thrown open to colonisation.[2] *Loca squalida* is not by any means a mere poetic expression, but a technical term, for *loca squalidiora* are opposed to cultivated land;[3] and even Isidor derived *squalidus* from "excolitus," because the field was not "cultivated."[4] A law of 421 added the estates (under the name of *caduca mortuorum bona*) which were left without heirs or had been confiscated from criminals to those which might be seized for occupancy.[5]

If we compare the laws of the Theodosian Code with those of Alfonso, we at once perceive that the latter contain slavish, but peculiarly corrupted, imitations of the Roman formulae. *Caduca mortuorum* has changed to *de succo mortuorum*, the well known technical term *rudis ager*[6] appears here as *ruda silva*, while *loca squalida* has been transformed into *terra de escalido*. Thus the *hereditates de escalido* are lands reclaimed from the wilderness, and the legal seizure of these is called *presa, presura, proprisum, bifanc*, etc.; hence, for ex-

---

[1] *Cod. Theod.* vii. 20. 8.

[2] "Conmoneat Tua Sinceritas hoc sanatione Veteranos, ut *loca absentium squalida* et situ dissimulationis horrentia, de solita fructuum indemnitate securi, quantum vires uniuscuiusque patientur, exerceant. Namque decernimus, ut his qui soli relicti terras sulcaverint, sine molestia praeiudicioque dominorum provectum emolumenta quaerantur: nihilque illis, qui messum tempus adsolent aucupari, agratici nomine deferatur," *ibid.*, vii. 20. 11.

[3] "*Squalidiora* adque ieiuna, (in)culta adque opima," *ibid.*, xiii. 11. 3.

[4] *Gromatici veteres*, p. 369.

[5] *Cod. Theod.* x. 10. 30. "*Vacantia mortuorum bona,*" *Cod. Just.* x. 10. 4. "*Caduca bona* fisco nostro competere legum cauta decreverunt," Cassiodorus, *Variae*, v. 24; "*caduca bona* non sinis esse vacantia," *ibid.*, vii. 7; "quorundam etiam *substantias mortuorum* sine aliqua discretione iustitiae nomine *caduci* perhibent titulo vindicare," *ibid.*, ix. 14.

[6] "Id ius datur quod est lege Hadriana comprehensum *de rudibus agris* et iis qui per x annos continuos inculti sunt" (117–138), F. Girard, *Textes de droit romain*, 4⁰ éd., Paris 1913, p. 876.

ample, *presa* may as well refer to a mill-pond, in so far as it has been formed on land that has been "seized."[1] When, therefore, Charles the Bald wrote "quicquid de heremi *squalore* excolere potuerint" and "ex deserti *squalore* habitabiles fecerunt,"[2] he was conscious of using a technical term, even as *ex squalido* had long before led to a verb *exsqualidare, scalidare* "to clear the wilderness for cultivation," which lives in the Spanish *escaliar*, Navarrese *escachar*, French *deschaller*.[3]

[1] "Sed ad aprehendendam illam aquam pro ad illos molinos intra ipsos terminos et ultra istos terminos aprehendam ipsam aquam pro ad ipsos molinos per cujuslived hereditatem tam de rege quam de infanzone quam de quodlibed sicut ego jure meo usque hodie tenui" (904), R. Escalona, *Historia del real monasterio de Sahagun*, Madrid 1782, p. 377; "et adhuc damus vobis medietatem de illas acenas et de illas *piscarias, quae nos apprehendiuimus* apud uos pro facere in illo fluuio" (1102), A. de Yepes, *Coronica general de la Orden de San Benito*, vol. VI, p. 495a; "si quis *presas* suas aut aquas istas frangere aut uetare presumpserit" (1168), Mariano, Trigita y Lasa, *Colección de documentos inéditos para la historia de Navarra*, Pamplona 1900, p. 11; "dua *presa* in ipsu flumine ubi faciat clausuria pro pisci capiendum" (1047), E. Gattola, *Historia abbatiae cassinesis*, vol. I, p. 43; "*prense* noue si in aliquo *presis* ueteribus impendimentum fecerint, siue sint superius siue inferius ... non ualeant ... si uero aqua de *prensa*, aut de molino, aut de calice emanauerit" (1176), *Forum Turolij*, in *Colección de documentos para el estudio de la historia de Aragon*, vol. II, p. 147 f.; "frangebant violenter *presam* de villa Salit ad episcandum" (1139), *Indice de los documentos del monasterio de Sahagun, de la Orden de San Benito*, Madrid 1874, p. 28.

[2] "Placuit etiam nobis illis concedere, ut, quicquid *de heremi squalore* in quolibet comitatu ad cultum frugum traxerint aut deinceps infra eorum aprisiones excolere potuerint, integerrime teneant et possideant," *MGH., Capitularia*, vol. II, p. 259; "quas siquidem aprisiones praefatorum Hispanorum progenitores per licentiam seu concessionem avi nostri Karoli ac post obitum illius genitoris nostri Ludovici *ex deserti squalore* habitabiles frugumque uberes proprio labore fecerunt," Devic and Vaissete, *op. cit.*, vol. II, Preuves, col. 228.

[3] "Per manus nostras *excalidavimus* et domos fecimus et presimus in montibus et fontibus" (775), Berganza, *Antigüedades de España*, vol. II, p. 370; "ipsas terras omnes *descalido* donamus" (902), *ibid.*, p. 372; "molinos ... quod fecerunt factos de stirpites de *scalido*" (968), *ibid.*, p. 404; "hunc locum *squalidum* nomine habitante irrumpimus" (781), *España sagrada*, vol. XXXVII, p. 310; "terras quas de *exqualido* primitus prehenderunt, egessierunt, vel adhuc cum Deo juvamine prehendere vel egesiere potuerint" (835), *ibid.*, vol. XL, p. 380; "quidquid *squalidavit* dominus Seniorinus tius meus" (842), *ibid.*, p. 382; "de *squalido* aprehendistis neminem possidentem" (875), *ibid.*, vol. XXXIV, p. 431; "presa in *scalido* jacente" (878), *ibid.*, vol. XVII, p. 244; "quantumcumque in ispa villa per ordinacione dominica de *squalido* apprehendimus" (909), *Indice de documentos del monasterio de Sahagun*, p. 109; "nos illut *de-*

If we now turn to Italy, we find here the royal domain expressed by *gualdo* or *galo*. Italy had long lacked extensive public lands fit for colonisation,[1] hence the state could come into possession of territory only through its abandonment by owners, that is, of territory *ex squalido*. Indeed, in the documents of the Benedictine Order at Benevento,[2] which go back to the sixth century, we frequently hear of the domain in which abbeys are founded under the name of *gualdo* and *galo*.[3] Since there is mention of a forest which lies in the *galo*,[4] the two are not identical and *galo* does not mean "forest," but only includes the word. We similarly hear of

*squalido* de gente Barbarica manu propria cum pueris nostris adprehendimus tam cultam quam etiam incultum" (909), R. Escalona, *Historia . . . de Sahagun*, p. 379; "Suprafactum locum in vetustatem reductum, pene obliuioni deditum, vepribus, seu densissimis siluis opertum, etqui magnis arboribus ex immensitate annorum adumbratum, auxiliante Domino cum fratribus restauraui, aedificia instruxi, vinea et pomares plantaui, terras de *scalido* eieci, horta, et omnia quae ad vsum Monasterii pertinent imposui . . . omnem solitudinem, omnemque industriam, erga supradictum terenum exercens, Ecclesiam Sancti Petri, quam dudum restauraueram, miris reedificaminibus reboluens ampliaui, et in melius, ut potui erexi" (915), Yepes, *Coronica*, vol. IV, p. 447 b; "neque pascere neque scindere uel *scaliare* nisi de uolunta prioris jamdicti" (1036), *Colección . . . de Aragon*, vol. I, p. 13; "augmentare, comparare, et *scalidare* vel acaptare" (1048), *ibid.*, p. 43; "augmentare acaptare comparare et *scalidare*" (1044), *ibid.*, p. 54; "comparare examplare et *excalidare*" (1044), *ibid.*, p. 56; "comparare *scalidare* augmentare" (1045), *ibid.*, p. 64; "in *scalio* quantum possunt rumpere" (1083), *ibid.*, vol. III, p. 61; "et que podades *escaliar* en la dicha Bardena ho á vos pluguiere en los hyermos" (1062), T. Muñoz y Romero, *Coleccion de fueros municipales*, p. 329; "et in antea adquisierit sive emtione sive et *eschalido*" (1134), Villanueva, *Viage literario*, vol. XV, p. 360; "en allant icellui suppliant ainsi exemplir, essarter et *deschaller* les terres de son maistre" (1477), Godefroy.

[1] E. Baudouin, *Les grands domaines dans l'empire romain*, Paris 1899, p. 9.

[2] Ughelli, *Italia sacra*, vol. VIII, 1. ed.

[3] "Ecclesia quae aedificata est in *galo* . . . quae sita est in *galo nostro* Paline," *ibid.*, col. 573; "quae aedificata est in *ialo nostro* Noceto . . . quae fundata est in *ialo nostro* Casa Polluci . . . ex ipso *galo* Motula . . . in *galo nostri palatij* . . . de *galo nostro* territorium . . . in *galo nostro* Manere," *ibid.*, col. 574; "concessimus in eodem *galo* pascuum ad peculia," *ibid.*, col. 575; "in *gualdo* in fine Consina," *ibid.*, col. 577; "in *galo nostro* . . . in praedicto loco de *galo nostro* . . . necnon *gualdum* in monte Virgineo" (774), *ibid.*, col. 578, and similarly cols. 581, 585, 587, 597, 598.

[4] "Sylva cum terra vacua, quae fuit de *galo nostro* in nominata platea," *ibid.*, col. 621.

fishing in the *gualdo*, and in this case Troya has pointed out that at the time mentioned there could have been no forest in the region indicated.[1] The *gualdo* is generally referred to as "noster" or "dominicus," i. e., it is considered as belonging to the prince of the realm. We get a complete picture of the constitution of the *gualdo* by limiting ourselves to its mention in the *Regesto di Farfa* previous to the middle of the ninth century.

Lupo, the Duke of Spoleto, in 746 turned over to the abbey of St. Mary in Sabinian territory a piece *"ex gualdo nostro qui dicitur ad sanctum iacintum,"*[2] and somewhat later the whole of the *gualdo*[3] and the land of the colonists to whom this *gualdo* belonged,[4] either because the property was part of the *gualdo* without having become private or, as appears from a later lawsuit, because the colonists remained in possession of their lots, but from then on had to pay to the abbey their dues and for the common use of the *gualdo*. All kinds of misunderstandings immediately arose between the colonists and the abbey, and these had to be ventilated before the courts. The colonists asserted that they were in full possession of their casalia in the *gualdo publico*, partly because they had been preempted, not in the *gualdo* of St. Giacinto, but in the adjoining one of Turre. Arnolus declared that he had himself cleared (mundavit) his casale in the *gualdo* and that he owed the abbey but five modii. Mizicus and Lupulus and other public colonists in the *gualdo*

---

[1] "Simul etiam et concessimus in nostrum venerabile locum *waldum nostrum* de fluvio Calore, hoc est usque Vadum Carrarum Sancti Marciani, et usque sub casa Valerii, ut annue et semper homines de ipsa Ecclesia piscationem faciant, et nullus sine permissu Sacerdotis nominatae Ecclesiae in ipsum *waldum* habeat licentiam introire ad piscandum," Troya, *op. cit.*, vol. III, p. 117.

[2] *Regesto di Farfa*, vol. II, p. 29.

[3] "*Gualdum* qui nominatur ad sanctum iacintum, qui est terminatus usque riuum currisem, et pertransit recte in aquam transuersam, deinde in *gualdum* pontianum, per riuum de ipso pontiano usque in tyberim," *ibid.*

[4] "Cum terris de colonis qui ipsum *gualdum* possederunt, seu omnia ad ipsum *gualdum* pertinentia," *ibid.*, p. 30.

received, in exchange for the land donated to the abbey, other land measured out to them with the rope in the following manner: for each 105 feet of the old they received 83 of the new land, because it was cultivated and 80% of it was considered an adequate exchange; on the other hand, Lupulus received 100 feet for each 92 feet of his former lot, because it was less productive. The casale of Teodices was not changed, but he had to pay the public taxes to the abbey. Similar action was taken in the case of two other proprietors, while the public colonist Campolus had to turn over his casale to the abbey. Rinculus Coccus had a piece of land in the *gualdo*, but, being very poor, was allowed to fence in another lot that produced 22 modii.

This extremely important document makes it clear that we are dealing in the *gualdo* with precisely the same conditions as confronted us in the Spanish *ex squalido*. As in the aprision, so the colonist is here given land which he must himself clear and cultivate, and the *gualdo* is not only forest but also possesses barren and cultivated land which in some way has reverted to the state. This is confirmed by later documents. The same abbey is presented with one half of a *gualdo* and a chestnut grove in the other half that is left for public use.[1] This public use consists in the right of pasturage [2] and hunting, which the king may reserve for

---

[1] "Ut uobis, uel uestro monasterio cedere deberemus medietatem de *gualdo nostro* qui est positus in finibus ciculanis, et dicitur ipse *gualdus* ad sanctum angelum in flumine . . . ipsam medietatem de nominato *gualdo* cum ipsa aecclesia sancti angeli quae ibi est, cum omnibus adiacentiis et pertinentiis suis in integrum, qualiter ad publicum possessum est, in ipso sancto loco concedimus possidendum. simul et concedimus uobis medietatem de castaneao jui dicitur sessiale, quod est in reliqua medietate praedicti *gualdi*, quam nobis ad publicum reseruauimus" (761), *ibid.*, p. 54.

[2] "Turmae decem debeant aestiuo tempore communiter cum iumentis publicis reatinis pabulare, ubi ubi per *gualdos publicos*, quo consueta sunt ipsa iumenta publica ambulare. Similiter et duo millia pecora de suprascripto monasterio, cum nostris peculiis publicis reatinis communiter omni tempore debeant pabulare in monte caluo, et in riuo curuo, postquam inde iumenta uel peculia monasterii praefati, ut diximus amodo in suprascriptis *gualdis* uel monti-

his own use.[1] In place of *gualdo* may stand *terra populi*,[2] *curtis*,[3] and *pascua publica*,[4] and *gualdo* soon disappears entirely, apparently because no public lands were left, while for "forest" there creep in the expressions *cagio*[5] and *gaio*,[6] which had long been in use at Modena [7] and at Lucca,[8] where also the longer forms *gahagio*, *cahagio*, *cafagio* are indiscriminately used for them. It is obvious that in case of these we are no longer dealing with the ownerless wilderness, as in Spain, but with the enclosed common, though the combination *gahagium* (*gahaium*, *gaaium*, *gaium*, *gagium*) *regis* in Rothar's laws [9] shows that the fundamental idea was the same as in the case of *gualdo* at Benevento and Reate. This *gualdo* had existed in Lucca, but in the eighth century it was superseded by the *gaio* forms, to survive only in local names.[10]

bus, cum nostris iumentis publicis siue peculiis, absque alia datione securius debeant pabulare" (767), *ibid.*, p. 73.

[1] "De ipso suprascripto *gualdo* alegia concessimus in ipso sancto loco, uel ad cunctam congregationem, omnia in integrum quanta ad ipsum *gualdum* pertinere uidentur . . . excepta uenatione de ipso *gualdo*, quam nobis reseruauimus faciendam" (772), *ibid.*, p. 76.

[2] "Et ista terra est secus *terra populi*, quem in mea reseruaui potestate". (803), *ibid.*, p. 145.

[3] "In ipso sancto monasterio donauimus a die praesenti medietatem de *curte* seu *gualdo* " (808), *ibid.*, p. 153.

[4] "Ut in *pascua publica* omni tempore debeant pabulare uel nutrire" (840), *ibid.*, p. 238.

[5] "Portionem meam de *cagio* agonis" (840), *ibid.*, p. 240.

[6] "Alpibus, *gais*, molendinis" (829), *ibid.*, pp. 224, 229.

[7] "Silvam unam in *gajum* Lamese" (75 .), Marini, *I pap. dipl.*, p. 103; "concedimus . . . curtem nostram, quae dicitur Zena, territorio Motinensi, silva jugis numero quingentis, coherentes ibi a tribus partibus *gajo nostro*" (752), Muratori, *Antiquitates*, vol. II, col. 152.

[8] "Parte mea de *cahagio* sub monte" (747), *Memorie e documenti . . . di Lucca*, vol. V[2], p. 27; "parte mea de casa et *cagio*" (761), *ibid.*, p. 43; "portionem meam de *gahagias*" (796), *ibid.*, p. 150; "parte mea do *cafagio nostro*, quem de jure parentorum nostrorum habere videmur" (778), *ibid.*, vol. IV[1], p. 138; "una petia de terra mea, quod est *gahagio* illo meo" (747), Troya, *op. cit.*, vol. III, p. 250; "*gagiolo* illo prope ista curte ora presepe circumdatum". (730), F. Brunetti, *Codice diplomatico toscano*, vol. I, p. 487.

[9] *Leg.* 319, 320.

[10] "Ubi vocabulum est *Ad Waldo*" (783), *Mem. e doc. . . . di Lucca*, vol. IV[1], p. 17; "ubi ejus corpus requiescit in *Gualdo*". (770), *ibid.*, vol. V[2], p. 68.

In a donation of 772 we find a *waldeman*, "forester," in the *gagio*, but with the Latin name Bonus,[1] even as three other *waldatores* at Volturno in 778 bear the good Latin names Rodulus, Albus, and Crispus.[2] I shall at another time show that the whole system of land measurement in the Middle Ages and almost all the agrimensorial expressions have arisen from the Byzantine gromatic method. Here I wish only to point out that the Langobard *waldeman, waldator* has survived until the present time. In Reggio and Modena he was called *gualdemano*,[3] in Ravenna and Pesaro *gualdario*,[4] and elsewhere *gualdaro, guallaro, guallario*.[5] The confusion of *gualdator* with *guardator*, from *guardia* "watch" was too natural, hence we hear at Bologna and Carpo of *guardatorii, guardatores* "foresters," and at Pisa the *cafadiarius* is glossed as *guardianus*.[6]

[1] "Largimur in Jura de ipso Monasterio ex *gagio* nostro Regiense, quae nuncupatur Terra, Siua, Roncora, et Prata insimul ad misura iusta, iuges numero quatuor millia, per designata, et determinata loca, a Bono *Waldeman* supra scripti *Gagij nostri*," Troya, *op. cit.*, vol. v, p. 657.

[2] "Et propterea venerunt *waldatores* ante nos Rodulus, et Albus, et Crispus, qui ab antiquis guiratores fuerunt, et dixerunt quod supradicta loca, quae cum Episcopo giravimus, semper de *waldo* fuerunt," Muratori, *Scriptores*, vol. 1², p. 363.

[3] "Castaldus, Bubulcus, *Gualdemanus* siue custos cuiuslibet ciuis Mutinae," *Statuta civitatis Mutinae ad iudices Aquarum pertinentia*, Mutinae 1575, fol. 78; "et qui custodes, Camparij et *Gualdemani* teneantur, et debeant custodire omnes, et singulas terras, res, et loca existentia intra eorum custodiam, congrue referendo, tam die, quam de nocte," *Statuta magnificae communitatis Regii*, Regii 1582, fol. 202 *ff*.

[4] "Item quod *gualdarij* constitutij a Comune montis Columbi super Rippa, Circuitu et Casaro et aliis bonis teneantur acusare omnes dapnum dantes ab eis inventos in predictis bonis Comunis et aliis infra octo dies Consulibus dicte terre sive nuntio curie; alioquin teneantur emendare dapnum de eorum proprio, et habeant predicti *gualdarij* quartam partem condempnationum factarum de eorum acusis" (1276), A. Tarlazzi, *Appendice ai Monumenti Ravennati*, Ravenna 1869, vol. 1, p. 309; "*gualdarii* Pisauri teneantur et debeant bene custodire et guardare de die et de nocte res et bona possessionum et fructus omnium possessionum existentium in curte et in contrata eis designata, ne deuastentur et tollant per personas et animalia," *Statuta ciuitatis Pisauri*, Pisauri 1531, fol. 72 *ff*.

[5] Rezasco, *Dizionario del linguaggio italiano storico ed amministrativo*, sub *gualdario*.

[6] "Salvo quod potestas possit dare licentiam comunis *Guardatoriis* (*guarda-*

In Tuscany *cafagium, cafaium* is universal, in the tenth
century to designate the ancient public domain, hence one
later finds at Florence a number of localities named *Caf-
fagio, Cafaio*,[1] by the side of *Gaio, Gualdum*.[2] In Lucca a
*Cafajario* is mentioned in 975 [3] and the *cafadiarius* at Pisa
proves that this means "a forester." The older writers explained this *caggio* as an abbreviation of *campo del faggio* [4]
or *casa del faggio*,[5] because place names *Faggia* occur, but
they are far from the mark. *Cafaggio, Gafaggio* was conceived by the Langobards as derivations in *ga-*, and this led
to *faia* "forest,"[6] and in the thirteenth century to *fagiae* in
Milan, to designate certain localities which obviously, like
the *cafagii* at Lucca, had been reclaimed from the public
domain.[7]

*toribus*), saltuariis et custodibus prexonum cum erunt exercuerint eorum officia
portando cultellos" (1259), L. Frati, *Statuti di Bologna*, vol. III, p. 281; "per
consilium generale de carpo elligantur saltarij et *guardatores* suficientes . . . ad
custodiendum ne dampnum detur per personas uel bestias in bonis campestribus
hominum de carpo nec super terratorio de carpo . . . item quod ipsi exercendo
officium saltarie per suam *guardam* possint portare arma" (1353), *Monumenti
di storia patria delle Provincie Modenesi, Statuta Carpi*, Mutinae 1887, p. 9;
"*Guardianos* sive *cafadiarios* pisani districti, per nos vel per alium iurare
faciemus, quod guastum sive dampnum quod fuerit factum in campis aut vineis,
sive sediis vel pratis, aut aliis locis et in quibuscumque bonis infra guardiam
in qua ipsi sunt *guardiani*, a bestia, animali, vel pullis aut antheribus alicuius
civis vel foretanei, vel a persona aliqua, renuntiare et debeant" (1286), F.
Bonaini, *Statuti pisani*, vol. I, p. 243.
    [1] "*Gafaggio*" (1187), G. Lami, *Sanctae ecclesiae florentinae monumenta*,
Florentiae 1758, p. 1448; "in loco dicto *Cafaggio*" (1297), *ibid.*, p. 404; "in
quodam petio terre posite in *Cafaggio* apud Burgum Sancti Laurentii" (1223),
*ibid.*, p. 804; and often; "*Cafaio*" (1097), *ibid.*, pp. 30, 1448.
    [2] "Et in *Gaio* villam quae dicitur Aspo" (1161), *ibid.*, p. 1159; "Ad *Gual-
dum, gualdum* nemus significat," *ibid.*, p. 540.
    [3] "Quae modo regere videtur per ipse *Cafajario*" *Mem. e docum* . . . *di
Lucca*, vol. V[2], p. 352.
    [4] G. Lami, *Lezioni di antichità toscane*, Firenze 1766, p. xc.
    [5] F. L. Del Migliore, *Firenze città nobilissima illustrata*, Firenze 1684, p. 263.
    [6] "Et de silva nostra qua vulgo appellatur *Faia* praepositalis," Ducange
sub *faia*.
    [7] "Statuerunt, providerunt et ordinaverunt quod locus de Villiono plebis
de Locate *fagiarum* Porte Vercelline, qui modo non est locus, sed est grancia
monasterii Carevallis Mediolani et tantum per ipsum monasterium teneatur,

All the Slavic countries possess derivatives from Ital. *gaio*, to express the enclosed domain. In Dalmatia *gaium* occurs early in the sense of "common pasture where formerly there was a forest."[1] In Servian the verb *gajim* means "to fence in, clear the ground, clean the forest."[2] In Poland *gaj* had the primary meaning of a field, forest or water domain, and the *gaiowe* was the revenue from such a domain,[3] while *gaić* means "to open up a forest, to cut it down," and similarly Bohemian *hájiti*, Russian *gait'*, and "the forest" is in OBoh. *hay, hag, hayg, háj*, Russ. *gay*, Lith. *gojus*. In the Slavic sources frequently occur the forms *gades, gadus*, for *gaium*. In the Servian documents *gadi* and *gai* interchange indiscriminately,[4] while in Poland *gades* means more nearly "enclosure, fence."[5] Precisely the same significance is at-

tollatur et canzelletur de libris et actis Communis Mediolani" (1286), L. Osio, *Documenti diplomatici tratti degli archivij milanesi*, Milano 1864, vol. I, p. 37; "in molendino Credentie *fagierie* Communis Mediolani seu domini Mathei Vicecomitis capitanei Mediolani" (1296), *ibid.*, p. 49; "coram domino Gabardo Scroxato jurisperito consule justitie Mediolani, camere civitatis, et omnium *fagiarum* Mediolani" (1372), *ibid.*, p. 153.

[1] "Dictus Laurentius habere debeat quartam partem totius pasculi sive *gai* . . . si dictus Laurentius probare poterit coram ipso, quod a tempore domini Albertini Mauroceno, olim comitis Jadre, citra quo tempore facta fuit divisio pasculorum et *gaiorum* positorum in districtu Jadre, ipse terre fuerint pasculum sive *gaium* et disboscate fuerint, idem Laurentius debeat libere eas habere quemadmodum essent pasculum sive *gaium*," *Monumenta spectantia historiam Slavorum meridionalium, Listine*, vol. I, p. 405.

[2] "*Gajim* extirpo, expurgo sylvam, foveo nemora, conservo lucum collucando, ramos inutiles decidendo ac frutices noxios amputando et evellendo . . . impedio, arceo aquam ne exundet . . . arceo ab ingressu foenilis interposito aliquo signo baculi signati," P. Budmani, *Rječnik hrvatskoga ili srpskoga jezika*, u Zagrebu 1887–91, sub *gaj*.

[3] "Adiungimus eciam scultet predicto et suis successoribus legittimis de nostra gracia speciali in omnibus siluis et fluuijs, in frucetis omnibus et fructibus nobis pertinentibus, quod dicitur *gaiowe*, terciam partem" (1360), *Monumenta medii aevi historica res gestas Poloniae illustrantia*, vol. III[1], p. 301; "scoltetis et successoribus eorum damus quartum denarium de pascuis et siluis wlgariter *gayowe*, racione cuius easdem siluas tenebuntur custodire" (1421), *ibid.*, vol. VIII[3], p. 471.

[4] "*Gadorum* Dolgnae Blatae, *gai* in Dolgna Blate," J. J. Hanel, *Monumenta historico-juridica Slavorum meridionalium*, Zagrabiae 1877, vol. I, p. 91.

[5] "Kosciol cum *gadibus* suis inter Dobrzycza et Kosciol, incipientes a Do-

tached to *gades* in the German documents,[1] but the word is neither specifically German nor Slavic, since *gadi* "fence, protection," *gadier* "forester" are also recorded in the Provence.[2] As Ital. *cafagiario* has led to *cafadiario*, *gagiarius* has produced *gadiarius*, *gagium* has given Prov. *gadi*.

Before investigating the fate of *gaium* on German territory, we shall discuss a Gaulic gloss

caio breialo siue bigardio

ascribed to the fifth century. Zimmer[3] says of it: "Hier ist das erklärte Wort (*caio*) seinem Ursprung und der Bedeutung nach für uns fast klarer als die zu seiner Erklärung (breialo siue bigardio) verwendeten. An der Hand liegen nämlich, wie Stokes sah, für das erstere altbret. *caiou* gl. *munimenta*, kymr. *cae* 'inclosure, hedge, field,' mittelbret. *quae* 'haye despines' (Catholicon), neubret. *kaé* (plur. *kaé-ou*) 'haie clôture faite d'épines; petit mur, moitié pierres, moitié terre.' Dieses kymr.-bret.Wort gehört, wie Rhys, *Rev. Celt.* I. 370 sah, zu ahd. *hac*, ags. *häg*, *haga*, altn. *hagi*, ags. *hege* (engl. *hedge*), die sowohl den eingehegten Zaun oder Wall als auch Alles, was eingehegt wurde (septum, urbs, Weide, junger Wald), bezeichnen. Die Verwandschaft macht klar, wie zu demselben keltischen Stamm *kagjo*- auch alti. *cae* 'Haus' in *cerdchae* 'Schmiedehaus (gl. officina) sowie mittellat. *cayum* 'domus' gehören ... Das an erster Stelle zur Erklärung von *caio* verwendete *breialo* ist offenbar das im Mittellatein gebräuchliche *broialum*, *brogilus*, *broylus*, *bruillius*, als dessen

---

brzycza que *gades* ordinarie currunt per terram, per rubetos, per paludines, per silvas usque ad Maluina, cum pratis que sunt in *gadibus* dicte ville Kosciol" (13. cent.), *Codox diplomaticus Mujorts Poloniae*, Poznaniae 1877, vol. I, p. 45; "termini autem sive *gades* earundem villarum" (1237), *ibid.*, p. 175.

[1] Ducange, sub *gades*.

[2] "Item sobre la forma ... de metre *gadis* e bans els ortz, els blatz, els verdiers, e elas terras ... e sobre lo sagramen de baile e dels *gadiers* prestador,"∙ Levy, *Provenzalisches-Supplement-Wörterbuch*.

[3] H. Zimmer, *Keltische Studien*, in *Zeitschrift für vergleichende Sprachforschung*, vol. XXXII, p. 230 *ff*.

92    COMMENTARY TO THE GERMANIC LAWS

Grundbedeutung 'campus arboribus consitus et muris aut sepibus cinctus' angenommen wird, was ja zu der für *caio* unter Vergleich der brittanischen Wörter und der Etymologie zu erschliessenden Bedeutung stimmt. Dieses *breialo, broia- lum, brogilus* ist vermuthlich selbst gallischen Ursprungs und geht auf einen Stamm *brogilo-* deminutiv zu *brogi-* zurück." In this statement there are several inaccuracies, as we shall soon see from an investigation of documents bearing on *breialo*.

In Greek, περίβολος is frequently used in the sense of "enclosure, wall,"[1] and in the sixth century the formula ἐκτὸς ἁγίων περιβόλων is frequently employed, to designate the property lying outside the church enclosure.[2] In Can. 76 of the Trullan Synod it says ' οὐ χρὴ ἔνδον τῶν ἱερῶν περιβόλων καπηλεῖον, ἢ τὰ διὰ ἀρωμάτων εἴδη προ- τιθέναι," and Balsamon[3] is certainly mistaken in referring περίβολοι merely to walls of the church building. In the old glosses we have "περίβολος consaeptum, maceria, moenia, territorium" and "*peribulus* est murus extrinsecus, *peribulus* id est in circuitu domus, *peribulum* deambulato- rium." This agrees with the Modern Greek use of περιβό- λιον, as repeatedly recorded in mediaeval documents.[4] The current use of this word in Italy, hence among the Lango- bards, is attested by the Greek documents of Sicily and southern Italy. In the south of Italy περιβόλαιον was also written περιαύλιον, as though it were "that which lies around

---

[1] " Γείτονες νότου ἀμπελὼν Ταθώτιος τῆς Φίβιος, βορρᾶ γῆ Πατοῦτος τοῦ Ὥρου καὶ τῶν ἀδελφῶν, ἀπηλιώτου περίβολος τῶν ἀμπελώνων " (104 B.C.), L. Mitteis, *Griechische Urkunden der Papyrussammlung zu Leipzig*, Leipzig 1906, vol. I, p. 3.

[2] " Παραδώσω σοι ἐν δημοσίῳ τόπῳ ἐκτὸς ἁγίων περιβόλων καὶ θείων χαρακ- τήρων " (566), F. Preisigke, *Griechische Papyrus . . . zu Strassburg*, Leipzig 1912, vol. I, p. 166.

[3] Ducange, sub περίβολος.

[1] "Περιβόλαιον τὸ πλήσιον τοῦ οἴκου, τὸ εὑρεθὲν νῦν λιβάδιον ἐν ᾧ ἵστα- νται συκέαι δύο καὶ ἀπιδέα μία" (1073), Miklosich and Müller, *Acta et dip- lomata graeca*, vol. I, p. 6.

# EX SQUALIDO AND VASTA 93

the house," [1] and the garden was named περιβόλης, in Sicily περιβόλιτζον.[2] When Charlemagne wrote in his *Capitulare de villis* "ut lucos nostros quos vulgus *brogilus* vocat, bene custodire faciant," he had in mind the Greek περίβολος, which becomes still clearer in the account of the Langobard Luidprand who in the tenth century used indiscriminately *brolium, briolium, perivolium,* and explained it as being a deer park.[3]

In Italy *brolium* is recorded since the eighth century.[4] Beginning with the tenth century it signifies the ducal or municipal palace with its surrounding garden. In Brescia we hear in the thirteenth century of such a *broletto,*[5] and, as here, so there existed at Milan a new and an old *broletto,* and a still older *brolio.*[6] These Milanese *broletti,* with their market

[1] "Εἰς το χωρίον το καλούμενον λαννιάνον περαύλοια χωραφιέοι τόποι in villam quae cognominantur lanniano *Clausurie* territorie" (1000), F. Trinchera, *Syllabus graecarum membranarum,* Neapoli 1865, p. 11.

[2] " Ο περιβόλης του πρεσβυτερου λεοντος νοταριου," *ibid.,* p. 94; "Καλλίεργον αὐτοῦ περιβόλιτζον" (1234), S. Cusa, *Diplomi greci ed arabi di Sicilia,* Palermo 1868, vol. ι, p. 92; " μετὰ καλοῦ ἡμῶν θελήματος πεπράκαμεν τὸ ἡμέτερον περιβόλιτζον σὺν τῶν μετ' αὐτοῦ ἐντὸς φυσκίας καὶ φρέατος " (1239), *ibid.,* p. 95, and similarly pp. 116, 557, 559, 679.

[3] "Sed et idem Nicephorus in eadem coena me interrogavit, si vos *perivolia,* id est *briolia,* vel si in *perivoliis* onagros vel caetera animalia haberetis? Cui cum, vos *brolia* et in *broliis* animalia onagris exceptis, habere, affirmarem: Ducam te, inquit, in nostrum *perivolium,*" *MGH., Scriptores,* vol. ιιι, p. 355.

[4] "Cum vineis *brolijs*" (724), Troya, *op. cit.,* vol. ιιι, p. 376; "vineis *brollis* pascuis" (768), *ibid.,* vol. v, p. 376; "sala cum ipso *broilo* ibidem adherente" (896), Muratori, *Antiquitates,* vol. ι, col. 154; "casa nova, cum curte et area in qua stat, cum *brolio* uno tenente, cum muro circumdata, seu arboribus et petras infra stante" (913), *HPM.,* vol. xiii, col. 782; "sedimen unum cum *broilo* uno tenente" (941), *ibid.,* col. 951.

[5] "Ut quinque porte pallacii seu *broletti* claudantur et aperiantur omni die et de die stent aperte ita quod non possint claudi occasione consilii" (1245), F. Odorici, *Storie bresciane,* vol. vii, p. 109; "tenear non posse facere fieri aliquam iustitiam corporalem seu vindictam in *broletto* novo et veteri" (1285), *ibid.,* p. 129.

[6] "Tunc temporis prope murum civitatis consitum fuit pomerium quod dicitur *brolium,* ex omni genere arborum et fructuum in tanta densitate, quod nemoris densitatem incurreret, ubi nullae personae nec habitare nec arare licitum fuit, in medio fuit fons vivus ... In processu temporis parvum pomerium constructum fuit, qui diminutione per respectum ad *brolium magnum* dictum est *broletum*" (14. cent.), *Miscellanea di storia italiana,* vol. vii, p. 452.

places and avenues, were carefully described by Flamma, an author of the fourteenth century,[1] who, in doing so, quoted an old poem that, like Luidprand's report, told of onagers kept in the park.[2] As early as the eleventh century palaces and courts of justice were located there,[3] and in the twelfth century they are mentioned at Como, Pavia, Mantua, Vercelli, Venice,[4] while at Novara the park and palace are called *bloretum*.[5]

These *brolii* are confined almost exclusively to Lombardy and Venice. In the old Liguria and on the western side, from Lucca to Salerno, one frequently comes across a *perilassium*, *berolais*, which has heretofore been wrongly identified with the Roman amphitheater and learnedly derived from a Germanic *bero-laz* "bear den"[6] or a Greek περιειλάς.[7] In the Florentine documents of the eleventh and later centuries reference is frequently made to a *perilasium majus* and a *perilasium minus* or *picculum*, as the name of some locality.[8]

[1] *Miscellanea di storia italiana*, VOL. VII, p. 452 ff.

[2] "*Brolettis* binis vetus novatur ab imis,
Excedit meniis faustis in coclea fanis,
Distinctis horis onager miratur in illis."

[3] "Cum in Dei nomine Civitate Mediolanium a *Brolito* Domui Sancti Ambrosii . . . in judicio residerent Dominus Ugo Marchio, et Comes Comitatu istius Mediolanensis, singulorum hominum justiciam faciendam ac deliberandam" (1021), G. Giulini, *Memorie . . . di Milano*, Milano 1854, vol. II, p. 112 f.

[4] *Statuti del comune di Vicenza 1264*, Venezia 1886; G. Robolini *Notizie tenenti alla storia della sua patria*, Pavia 1826, vol. II, p. 238 ff.

[5] A. Ceruti, *Statuta communitatis Novariae anno 1277 lata*, Novariae 1879, p. 8.

[6] Friedländer, *Darstellungen aus der Sittengeschichte Roms*, Leipzig 1910, vol. II, p. 561 ff.; R. Davidsohn, *Forschungen zur älteren Geschichte von Florenz*, Berlin 1896, p. 15 ff.

[7] C. Lupi, *Sull' origine e significato della voce Parlascio*, in *Archivio storico italiano*, Ser. 4, vol. VI, p. 492 ff.

[8] "Excepta quadam parte terrae, in qua hortus esse videtur, et est posita prope *Perilasium maius*, et iuxta hortum nostri Monasterii" (1070), Lami, *Lezioni di antichità toscane*, p. 81; "prope *Perilasio picculo*" (1071), *ibid.*, p. 96; "terrae peziam unam, totam ad unam tenens, quae posita est in loco, qui nominatur *Perilasium*, et iuxta ipsum *Perilasium*, quae terra decernimus, de una parte decurrit ei via, et finis praedictum *Perilasium*" (1085), *ibid.*, p. 81; "prope *perlasio*" (1018), Davidsohn, *l. c.*; "prope *perilasium majorem*" (1031)

*Pirolascio,* *Perilascio* occur often at Lucca, from 963 on,[1] and "prope *Perilasium*" is used at Arezzo as early as 936,[2] while at Reate "ad *Perilasium*" is recorded in 791.[3] In the south are given the forms *Burlasco, Borlasco, Vorlasco, Virlasco,*[4] at Salerno one hears in 994 of a *Mons Berolasi* or *Berolasi,*[5] and in Capua a quarter of the city, which Herchempert identified with the amphitheater, was in the ninth century called *Berelais.*[6]

The assumption that *perilasium* is identical with the amphitheater is invalidated by the existence of two *perilasia* at Florence, and Davidsohn's identification of *perilasium minus* with the dramatic theater is not proved by documentary evidence, in fact, Lupi has shown[7] that in some places the *perilasium* was too far away from the city ever to have served such purposes. There cannot be the slightest doubt that *perilasium, berelais* are merely corrupted forms of Greek περίβολος, which was in common use in Italy and which is even to be found in Aramaic *parvíla* "the open space about a city which generally served as a pasture." Herchempert was not entirely wrong in his equation of *berelais* and amphitheater, for the first generally arose there where originally stood a Roman public building. In Langobard times the Roman theaters were in ruins, and the space they occupied was taken by the city for public parks and municipal halls. Thus, for example, the Milan *brolium* arose where formerly

*ibid.;* "prope *perilasium* quod dicitur *picculo* iuxta civitate Florentia" (1069), *ibid.* A large number of quotations for the forms *pratolasei, pratolascio, perlascium, pierlascium, pierlasium, perlasium, perlagium, piarlagio, parlagio, parlascio* may be found in Lupi, *l. c.*

   [1] Lupi, *l. c.*
   [2] U. Pasqui, *Documenti per la storia della citta di Arezzo,* Firenze 1899, pp. 85, 95.
   [3] *Regesto di Farfa,* vol. II, p. 125.        [4] Lupi, *l. c.*
   [5] *Codex dipl. cavensis,* vol. III, p. 15.
   [6] "Veniens *Berelais,* hoc est Amphitheatrum," Muratori, *Scriptores,* vol. II, p. 247.
   [7] *Op. cit.,* p. 499 *f.*

stood the amphitheater and ergasterium,[1] and the *brolium* in northern Italy was not only the park, but also the public buildings in it.[2]

In Lombardy, Venice, and Ravenna, where the old buildings could easily be destroyed, in order to use the stone for the new palaces, the memory of antiquity was easily obliterated, and *brolium* remained only as the name for the new garden and buildings; but in the south, where the amphitheaters had occupied steep and inaccessible hillsides, the ruins survived for a longer time, and *berelais, perilasium*, derived from περιβόλης or περίβολος, was not only the name for the hill where the amphitheater had been located, as in Capua and Salerno, but was intimately connected with the amphitheater in the memory of the people. The identity of *perilasium* and *brolium* becomes an absolute certainty from the use of the word *parlascio* at Pisa for "city garden where the municipal building stood,"[3] in which sense it is also recorded in the other Ligurian cities,[4] while at Ivrea *parlacium* was a park surrounded with hedges and moats.[5]

In Germany, *brogilus* originally meant "grove," but it has produced German *Brühl* "a well watered meadow," the

---

[1] "Erat autem istud hedifitium (amphitheatrum) fundatum ubi nunc est *brolium*. Ergasterium fuit hedifitium altissimis muris circumseptum diversis cameris et stabulis distinctum, in quibus erant tauri indomiti, leene, ursi et tygrides. . . . In isto loco nunc est ecclexia sancti Nazarii in *brolio*." *Misc. di storia ital.*, vol. VII, p. 468.

[2] "*Broletum* est edifitium quadrum alto muro circumdatum," *ibid.*, p. 452; "in alia parte civitatis est alia curia comunis, que dicitur *broletum* vetus," *ibid.*, p. 453.

[3] "Corse scapigliata e come forsennata al *Parlascio*, dove abitavano i consoli e gli altri che reggevano la repubblica" (for the year 1005), R. Roncioni, *Delle istorie pisane libri XVI*, Firenze 1844, p. 61.

[4] Rezasco, *Dizionario del linguaggio italiano storico ed amministrativo*, sub *parlagio*. From a confusion of this *parlagio* with *parlare* "to speak" has arisen the vulgar Latin *parlamentum*, originally "city council," then "parliament."

[5] "Cum toto *parlacio* inter et foris et omnibus fossatis et pendinis in circuitu ipsius *parlacii*; coheret a monte uia que currit ante iam dictam ecclesiam et ipsum *parlacium*; a meridie carectum qui est in plano subter costadum iamdicti parlacii" (1075), *HPM.*, *Chartae*, vol. I, col. 649.

semantic change of which has been correctly stated by
Staub and Tobler: [1] "place or suburb where formerly there
was a grove or pasture, but which has either been transformed into a meadow or has been thrown open for building
purposes." The word occurs in OHG. as *broil, bruil* and
is used early in England, where it is written *broel* and conceived, not as an Anglo-Saxon, but as a Latin word meaning
"deer park." [2] We find it in Raeto-Roman *bröl* "garden,"
Prov. *bruelh, bruelha, bruoilla* "grove, bush," OFr. *broil,
broel, broal, bruel* "deer park," *broillet, bruillet, breullet,* etc.,
"small forest."

If we now turn to the Gaulish gloss "*caio* breialo bigardio" we conclude, since *breialo* is obviously our περίβολος,
that *caio* must also designate an enclosed place, especially a
grove. This is made certain by *kahei, kaei, kei, kahai, kahe,
kabei* (?) of the Bavarian [3] and *gahagio* (*gahaio, gaaio, gaio,
gagio*) *regis* of the Langobard laws. If we now compare
Bavarian *kahei* with Carolingian *brogilus*, we get the same
equation as in *caio breialo*. The additional gloss *bigardio* is
easily explained. At Bayonne and Bordeaux *cayum, caya*
has survived in the sense of "outhouse, cellar," but the
identical OHG. *cadum, gadum* "domus, aedes, septa," *obiz-
gadem* "pomarium," Low German *gadem, gâm* "appendix,
booth" show that the original is again "enclosure." These
words all express "penthouse attached to a house, enclosure
next to the house," hence *bigardio* is nothing but OHG.
*bîgard* "enclosure next to another." Thus the Gaulish gloss
is, with the exception of the last word, nothing but Low Latin,
and cannot possibly be of the fifth century. It is not earlier
than of the seventh century.

---

[1] *Schweizerisches Idiotikon*, Frauenfeld 1905, vol. v, sub *brüel*.
[2] "*Broel* edisc deortuun," Th. Wright, *Anglo-Saxon and Old English Vocabularies*, col. 9; "*broel* hortus cervorum, deortuun, uel edisc," *ibid.*, cols. 196,
275; "*broelarius* ediscweard," *ibid.*, cols. 275, 359.
[3] "Si vero de minutis silvis, de luco vel quacumque *kaheio* (*kaeio, keio,
kahaio, kaheo, kabeio*) vegitam reciderit," XXII. 6.

Thus it appears that the Byzantine περίβολος has given way to Gothic *gualdo* and Langobard *gaio*, and we shall now see how this change has taken place.

In OHG. the word *wald* does not mean only "forest"[1] but also "wilderness,"[2] hence *wuast-waldi* is glossed with "desertum."[3] ONorse *völlr* "unworked field," AS. *weald*, Engl. *wold*, *weald* "forest, field" show that the fundamental idea was *ex squalido* and not "forest," even as *gualdo* in Italy referred to the royal domain in general, inclusive of cultivated ground. The *gualdo nostro* or *publico* of the earliest documents and the *gaio regis* of the Langobard laws prove conclusively that the basic idea of *gualdo*, according to its derivation from *ex squalido*, was that of *dominium* "royal domain." In Frankish documents *gualdo* appears only after Charlemagne's Italian conquest, hence this word became popular in Germany in the sense of "forest" only through Langobard influence, although it must popularly have been present in the sense of "domain" long before. In Spain, where *ex squalido* has survived in its original form and meaning, *gualdo* is totally wanting. So, too, in Gothic there does not exist a similar word for "forest," because this idea has developed at a comparatively late time, but *waldan* has the original meaning "to rule, exercise dominion," because *gualdo* meant "dominium, royal possession." This *waldan* has been derived from Lat. *valeo*, but Uhlenbeck has pointed out the impossibility of this connection on account of Lith. *galéti* "to be able," which corresponds to Lat. *valeo*, while Goth. *waldan* corresponds to Lith. *valdýti*.[4] The only objection that could be brought against such a derivation from *ex squalido* would

---

[1] Steinmeyer and Sievers, *Althochdeutsche Glossen*, vol. I, p. 298, vol. III, p. 91.

[2] "In eremi vastitate in des *uualdes* uuasti," *ibid.*, vol. I, p. 469, and Graff, *Althochdeutscher Sprachschatz*, sub *wald*.

[3] Graff, *l. c.*

[4] *Kurzgefasstes Etymologisches Wörterbuch*, Amsterdam 1900, p. 166.

be the appearance of the names Cariovalda, Catualda in the first century,[1] but this objection would be valid only if one knew what the ending *ualda* in these words meant. Slav. *vlad-*, which goes back to an older *vald-*, means "to rule," Lith. *valdýti* "to rule, wield, direct," OPrussian *waldnika* "king." In none of these languages can a trace of the meaning "forest" for this group be found, while *gaio* in all of them has that connotation, which at once shows that the former is by far the older word and must have entered into the Balto-Slavic family of languages before the seventh century. But *gaio* is wanting in Gothic; the word arose independently from it and at a later date. German *walten* cannot be separated from Goth. *waldan* and *gualdo* "forest," because in OHG. names *-walt* and *-wald* interchange indiscriminately. But if Goth. *waldan* has arisen from *ex squalido*, then Goth. *wilþeis*, OHG. *wildi* "wild" is a derivative from it, with an even closer approximation to the original meaning than in *waldan*. Precisely the same semantic relationship is to be found in the Celtic, where we have Welsh *gwyllt* "wilderness, overgrown place, wild, insane," OBret. *guelenes* "waste island," Corn. *gwylls* "wild," *guelfôs* "desert," *guel* "field," Ir. *geilt* "terror, wild," while the form *vlad, vlat* expresses the idea "dominium," Welsh *gwlad* "country," Corn. *gulat* "fatherland," Bret. *gloat* "kingdom," Ir. *flaith* "prince, dominion," but the change from *vald* to *vlad*, which is parallel to the transformation in Slavic, is of the same nature as the one from *farst* to *frast*, of which I speak later on.

Bavarian *kahei* has survived as *Gehai* and *Kai*, not only in the sense of "forest," but also of "meadow, fishpond,"[2] and OHG. *hac* "urbs, saeptum," *hagjan* "to enclose," which occur only late, have developed from *gahagio* by dropping what appeared to be a prefix, *ga-*. ONorse *hagi* "pasture,"

[1] E. Forstemann, *Altdeutsches Namenbuch*, Bonn 1900, col. 1496.
[2] Schmeller, *Bayerisches Wörterbuch*, vol. i, col. 1022.

Dan. *have* "garden," AS. *haga* "fence, house, villa"[1] have
been borrowed from OHG. In the Romance languages only
French *haie* "hedge" has been derived from the German;
Provençal and Italian know only derivatives of *gaio*. We
have seen how *gaio* has in the Langobard documents successively lengthened into *gaaio, gahaio, gahagio, gafagio,*
finally to produce the briefer forms *fagia, faia,* and we have
been able to observe the gradual disappearance of the royal
domain from the eighth to the eleventh century, when the
place names *Cafaggio, Fagia* alone were left to indicate the
existence of such public lands. It now remains to be shown
how *ex squalido* may have given *gaio, caio.*

It may be assumed that the word *galo* of the documents
at Benevento is a miswritten *gaio,* but as it occurs very frequently this is not probable. That a *galo* should have existed
by the side of *gualdo* is not to be wondered at, for we have
not only the phrase *ex squalido* but also *ex squalore,* which
would produce a form *gualora, galora,* for which a singular
*galo* would be a back formation. But this is merely hypo-
thetic and so must be omitted from our consideration. We
shall, therefore, have to show that *gaio* may have proceeded
from *ex squalido* independently from such an assumed transformation, that is, we shall have to show that *squalido* or
*qualido* may have produced *gaio, caio.* Now, the Spanish
*scaliar, scalio* show that a form *squalio* must have existed at
an early time. Fortunately we have another Spanish word,
*cayo* "sand bank," Fr. *quais* "quay," where its derivation
from a word *scalio* may be proved by documentary evidence.
Lat. *scala,* Gr. σκάλα has from the beginning of the Chris-

[1] "Se *haga* binnan port the aegelric himsylfan getimbrod haefde" (1044),
J. Earle, *A Handbook to the Land-Charters, and other Saxonic Documents,* Oxford 1888, p. 244, and similarly pp. 194, 239, 289, 294; "dabo unam villam,
quod nos Saxonice an *haga* dicimus" (855), *ibid.,* p. 336, and similarly pp. 374,
447; "nouem praefatae ciuitatis habitataculis, quae patria lingua *Hagan* ap-
pellari solent" (996), *ibid.,* p. 403.

tian era been used for "quay," and the Byzantines called the
landing dues σκαλιάτικον. In the pacts made between the
Venetians and Pisans on the one hand and the Byzantine
emperors on the other there is frequent mention of *scala* [1]
and *scalaticum, scaliaticum,*[2] and the Genoese have also derived their wharf system from Constantinople.[3] In modern
Genoese *scâ* is "quay," which form obviously passed through
a previous *scaia*, from a still older *scaria, scarius* [4] recorded
at least since 1001.[5] This *scala* passed early into Arabic
*kallâ'* [6] and *iskâla, isqâla*. We have at Barcelona *scharum,*[7]
at Marseilles *scare,*[8] which leads to Ital. *squero* "wharf." In
France we get in the twelfth century *caium* for it,[9] while

---

[1] "Ad hoc donat eis et ergasteria . . . et maritimas III *scalas*" (1082), Tafel
and Thomas, *Urkunden zur ältern Handels- und Staatsgeschichte der Republik
Venedig*, vol. I, p. 52, and again pp. 110, 191, 208, and G. Müller, *Documenti
sulle relazioni delle città toscane coll' oriente fino all' anno MDXXXI*, Firenze
1879, p. 57.

[2] "Naves omnes venientes de Pisa permanent in *scala* Pisanorum sine
scalatico usque ad duos menses, si vero plus morari voluerint dent *scalaticum*
ad voluntatem *scalarii*" (1162), G . Müller, *op cit.*, p. 10; "pro commercio, uel
passagio, uel samariatico, uel *scaliatico*" (1199), Tafel and Thomas, *op. cit.*,
p. 272, also p. 257.

[3] *HPM., Leg. iur. reip. genuen.*, vol. I, col. 499 *f.*

[4] "Redditum de ripa et de *scariis* comunis ianue" (1149), *ibid.*, col. 141 *ff.*;
"novi *scarii*" (1163), *ibid.*, col. 215 *f.*; C. Desimoni, *Statuto dei padri del Comune
della Repubblica Genovese*, Genova 1885, p. 321; A. Jal, *Glossaire nautique*,
Paris 1848, sub *scarium*.

[5] "Tota ipsa plagia de regiminis Minoris, quantum continet de cantu in
cantum ubi *scaria* fuerunt," E. Pansa, *Istoria dell' antica repubblica d'Amalfi*,
Napoli 1724, p. 45; "si nave o legno . . . sia varata o levata da *scario*," *Tab.
Amalf.*, in N. Alianelli, *Delle antiche consuetudini e leggi maritime delle provincie
napolitane*, Napoli 1871, p. 132.

[6] "*Kallâ'* a station of ships, near the bank of a river; the bank of a river,"
Lane.

[7] A. de Capmany y de Montpalau, *Memorias historicas sobre la marina
comercio y artes de la antigua ciudad de Barcelona*, Madrid 1779, vol. II, p. 25.

[8] L. Méry et F. Guindon, *Histoire analytique, et chronologique des actes et des
délibérations du corps et du conseil de la municipalité de Marseille depuis le X^ma
siècle jusqu' à nos jours*, Marseille 1842, vol. II, p. 325.

[9] "Consuetudines *caiagii*" (1145), A. Thierry, *Recueil des monuments inédits de l'histoire du tiers état*, Premiere série, vol. I, p. 57; "redditum, quem in
portu fluminis Somene de navibus obtinebat, vulgo appellatum *caiagium*"
(1149), *ibid.*, p. 58; "porro Johannes de Cruce in predicto portu terram con-

in England *scaliaticum* appears as *scavagium*, as though from the AS. *sceawian* "to show."

Spain has preserved more clearly the tradition of the Roman law, so, while it possesses direct derivatives from *ex squalido*, it has neither *gualdo* nor *gaio*. In a similar way Spain has been free from the corruption of another technical term which is placed in the Theodosian Code by the side of *ex squalido* and which has produced a remarkable series of words in the rest of Europe. In 390 Valentinianus published an edict relegating the monks to the "vast" solitudes, *vastae solitudines*.[1] The sentence "deserta loca et vastae solitudines" which is used in it is based on the classical juxtaposition of "desertum et vastum," but, although the law was partially repealed in 392, this *vastum* remained as the expression for monastic solitudes. *Vastae solitudines* occurs with great frequency during the founding of monasteries [2] and similar expressions may be quoted in endless number.[3] Most

tiguam flumini habebat, quam postmodum, ecclesia jam per elemosinam possidente, ad naves recipiendas idem Johannts preparabat, et ibi *caium* facere disponebat ... et redditus ipsorum *caiorum*, sive multi sive pauci sint, sive quocunque modo diminuti, communes in alterutrum concesserunt ... custos redditum tam *caiagii* quam granariorum communiter eligetur" (1151), *ibid.*, p. 60.

[1] "Quicucque sub professione Monachi repperiuntur, deserta loca et *vastas solitudines* sequi, adque habitare iubeantur," xvi. 3. 1.

[2] "Est praeterea locus silvaticus in heremo *vastissimae solitudinis* in medio nationum praedicationis nostrae, in quo monasterium construentes, monachos constituimus sub regula sancti patris Benedicti viventes" (751), *S. Bonifati epistola*, in *MGH.*, *Epistolae*, vol. III, p. 368; "apparuit eidem Saviniano angelus Domini, qui demonstravit locum *vaste solitudinis* coherentem fluvio Sivolis, ubi deberet proficere amore matris, sororis et caste coniugis caste Menelei, sicut consilium dederat, domum orationis," *Vita Menelei*, in *MGH.*, *Scrip. rer. merov.*, vol. V, p. 142.

[3] "Quod cenubium aliquo infra regna nostra *vasto* in loco que dicitur Haireulfisfelt super fluvium Fulda monasterium aedificasset" (775), *MGH.*, *Dip. Karol.*, vol. I, p. 129; "huius tempore per Galliarum provincias agmina monachorum et sacrarum puellarum examina non solum per agros, villas vicosque atque castella, verum etiam per heremi *vastitatem* ex regula dumtaxat beatorum patrum Benedicti et Columbani pullulare coeperunt" (9. cent.?), *ibid.*, *Scrip. rer. merov.*, vol. V, p. 54; "observabam quodam per *vaste* Vinciacensis silve lucos" (11. cent.?), *ibid.*, p. 151; "arrepto itinere, cum iam per *vastam* heremum

popular was the expression *vastina*,[1] hence *vasta* "uncultivated territory subject to settlement" [2] gives way to *wastina*,[3] of which the largest, the *Wastina* of Vendôme, is mentioned as early as 834,[4] while a great number of localities in France are named *Gastina, Gastinetum, Gastinesium, Gastineti, Vastina, Vastum*.[5]

The words *vasta, vastina* have entered into OHG. in almost unchanged forms,[6] but there are also many variant forms, *wuostî, wôstî, wuostinna, wuastinna, wôstinna, wuostunna, wôstenja, wostinnî, wôstunnja*, OSaxon *wôsti, wôstunnia*, OFrisian *wôste, wôstene, wêstene*, AS. *wêste, wêsten*. From OHG. *wuostî, wôstunnja*, etc., we get OSlavic *pušta, pustyni, pustynja* "wilderness," to which belongs a large group of words in all the Slavic languages, including the verb *pustiti* "to let." Lettish *pōsts* "devastation," Prussian *pausto* "wild" show that OHG. *wuôsta* must have had an intermediate form *fôsta*, to produce *post-, pust-* of the Balto-Slavic languages. That such a form actually existed is proved

Vosacum nomine iter caperet" (before 11. cent.), *ibid.*, p. 237; "quod ibidem gaudii fuerit, quod tale miraculum per famulum suum Preiectum in heremi *vastitatem* subito aeger recepisset salutem," *ibid.*, p. 238; "cum sanctus Filibertus semper desideraret heremi *vastitatem*" (9. cent.), *ibid.*

[1] "Dono . . . et castrum ipsum de Monteplano cum toto monte et ecclesia ibi dicata S. Laurentio cum omni jure, mancipiis, *vastinis*, molendinis, censu, silvis, aquagiis altis et bassis" (863), Ducange, sub *vastum*.

[2] "*Vasta* Ardinna" (770), *MGH., Dip. Karol.*, vol. I, p. 71; "*vasta Bochonia*" (775), *ibid.*, pp. 148, 149, 190, 191, 196.

[3] "Extirpare fecit de foresta, quae dicitur *Wastina*" (1007–1050), Ch. Métais, *Cartulaire de l'abbaye cardinale de la Trinité de Vendôme*, Paris 1893, vol. I, p. 3; "cum veniret ad forestam de *Wastino*, videns eam pluribus in locis extirpatam" (1032), *ibid.*, p. 16, and often; "dimidium habeamus pasnatici is silva *Guaslinensi*" (1050), Trémault, *Cartulaire de Marmoutier*, Paris, Vendôme 1893, p. 128, and again pp. 193, 335.

[4] "*Wastina* in Windoninse pago," *Gesta Aldrici*, Ch. Métais, *op. cit.*, p. 16.

[5] Chevin, *Dictionnaire Latin-Français des noms propres des lieux*, Paris 1897.

[6] Steinmeyer and Sievers, *op. cit.*: "Uastantes *uastanti*," vol. I, p. 294; "uasta solitudine *uuastemu* einotte," p. 295; "uastabat *uuosta*," p. 356; "deuastantes *uuostinti*," p. 383; "uastitas *uuasti*," p. 468; "in eremi uastitate in des uualdes *uuasti*," p. 469; "uastans *uuostandi*," vol. II, p. 21; "vasta *uuostin₁*," p. 59.

by the Celtic languages. In OIr. *fás* "desert" shows its direct descent from *vasta*, but in the other Celtic languages the long *a* has caused the insertion of an *r*. In Welsh we have *gorest, gores* "what lies open, unenclosed, waste," in Breton *frost, fraost* "deserted, waste, uncultivated." That *forst, frost* is very old in Celtic is proved by Frankish *forestis* which is first recorded in the year 556 in a donation of Childebert I, where *forestis* refers, not to the forest, but to the fisheries [1] and is, like *gualdo* and *gaio*, connected with *nostra*.[2] The *forestarii* who held sway in the *forestis*, however different they may have been from the *gualdatores*, like these had the same charge of the fisheries, the capture of poachers, supervision of borders.[3] *Gualdus* made its appearance in Germany only after Charlemagne's Italian expedition in 776, and at first in a document written at Vicenza,[4] after which it took the place of *vasta* and *forestis*.[5] Like *gualdus*, so also *forestis* became finally identical with "forest."

The Germanic languages have no words derived from *forestis* except OHG. *forst, uorst*, which in itself shows that it is a borrowed word. From OHG. it has passed into all the Slavic languages, OSlav. *hvrast* "sarmentum, bush, oak," Bulg. *hrast, hrastalek, hraste* "bush," *fraste* "noise," Pol. *chrost* "noise, bushes, faggots," *chwrastać* "to rustle," hence Magyar *haraszt* "oak forest," Rum. *hrêst* "bush."[6]

---

[1] "Has omnes piscationes, quae sunt et fieri possunt in utraque parte fluminis sicut nos tenemus et nostra *forestis* est, tradimus ad ipsum locum," *MGH., Diplomatum*, tom. I, p. 7.

[2] The quotations for *forestis* in Merovingian and Carolingian documents are given in full in H. Thimme's *Forestis* (*Archiv für Urkundenforschung*, vol. II, pp. 101–154), to which I refer the reader.

[3] Thimme, *l. c.*, p. 120 *ff.*

[4] "Predictus Hildebran dus dux*gualdum* ad prefatum monasterium tradidisset," *MGH., Dip. Karol.*, vol. I, p. 157.

[5] "In *ualdo* Bochonia" (779), *ibid.*, p. 169; "infra *ualto* qui vocatur Vircunnia" (786), *ibid.*, p. 206; "infra *waldo nostro*" (791), *ibid.*, p. 227.

[6] F. Miklosich, *Etymologisches Wörterbuch der slavischen Sprachen*, Wien 1886.

On Romance territory France is especially rich in such
derivatives. Breton *frost, fraost* is strongly represented in
the north,[1] occurring in the Latinized form *frostum* in the
eleventh century[2] and somewhat later as *frussatum* in England.[3] Since the fourteenth century we have the French
forms *fro, frau, fros, froc, frox, frouz, flot, flos,* etc. "terre inculte et abandonnée, chemin rompu, large chemin public
près d'une ville, place communale plus large que le chemin
mais soumise à la même police,"[4] and *frestiz, fraitis* "terre
en friche, terre qui n'est pas cultivée."[5] Fr. *floc* has produced Spanish *llueco, lleco* in the same sense. In northern
Italy we in the eighth century meet with *frascarium* "uncultivated, overgrown land"[6] and later with *frascata, fras-
chetum* in the same sense, while *frasca,* both in Italy and the
Provence, is equivalent to "faggots."[7] The change from
*frast-* to *frasc-* is the same as from *frostum* to *frusca.*[8] In
France there is a great variety of derivations from this *frasc-,*
*frescherium, frescheium, fresceium, freschium, frecum, frichia,
frichium, friscum, fresca,*[9] which have survived in Fr. *friche*

---

[1] "Les maisons *frostés* et desherbregées," *Archives de Bretagne,* vol. VI, p. 171.
Similar combinations: "*froustes et inhabitées,*" *ibid.,* vol. V[2], p. 132; "*frost et
inhabité,*" *ibid.,* pp. 214, 37, 40, 116; "sallines, fossez, vasseres, *frostz,* baulles,"
*ibid.,* pp. 41, 54. I quote them from E. Ernault, *Glossaire moyen-breton,* Paris
1895. See also Godefroy, sub *frost.*

[2] "Aimericus Saporellus dedit absque censu, in alodo, vineale quod fuit
Gosleni prefecti, et ipse Aimericus quiete possidebat quia a prioribus possessoribus in *frostum* deciderat," *Archives historiques du Poitou,* vol. II, p. 36.

[3] "Quod venit de *frussato* praedicti Rogeri" (1196), Jones and Macray,
*Charters and Documents illustrating the History . . . of Salisbury,* London 1891,
p. 58.

[4] Godefroy, sub *fro.*                        [5] *Ibid.,* sub *fraitis.*

[6] "Cum pratis vineis silvis *frascareis* molendinis" (710), *Cod. Langob.,* col.
7; "Expensum predeis rusticis, idest *frascario* in casale Oaualiunano" (735),
*Bullettino dell' istituto storico italiano,* vol. XXX, p. 53.

[7] "Ligna exinde excidere, aut animalia ibidem pascere, vel *frascas* aut perti-
cas aut circla exinde tollere" (944), B. Capasso, *Monumenta ad Neapolitani
Ducatus historiam pertinentia,* vol. II[2], p. 7; "aliquam personam incidentem
arborem vel *frascas*" (1170), *HPM., Leg. Gen.,* p. 22; "sive sit accusatio de
guastis vel incisione arborum et *frascarum,*" *ibid.,* p. 25.

[8] Ducange, sub *fraustum.*                     [9] Ducange.

"uncultivated ground," but the old *vastum, guastum,* changed to *gascum,* has produced the more popular *gascaria, gascheria, gasquerer,* now *jachière, jacherer.* The dialects have a very large number of words which are derived from *frast-, frasc-* [1] and Jura *frachous* "bois cassant pour allumer le feu," Morvan *freucher* "battre, froisser, rouler," Ital. *frascare* "to strike," *esser per le fratte* "être dans la frape," show that Fr. *fracas, frapper* are developments of this group, semasiologically evolved from the idea of beating the bush, and identical with the Slavic group, where *hvrast* mean both "bush" and "noise."

The connotation "fresh" has been evolved from this group in an interesting manner. The public domain and private forests had since earliest times been used for the pasturage of swine and sheep, the owner of such domain or forest claiming for this right a yearly tithe. The Visigothic laws speak of the swine tithe in the seventh century in a law quoted as *Antiqua,* [2] and as early as the sixth century this *decima porcorum* was turned over by the Merovingians to the Church, [3] while in 653 it was distinctly mentioned that this

[1] "*Frâte* branchages d'un arbre, usité dans les exploitations forestières du pays, Bourg. *frat* fragile, Poitou *frette* petite branche, *fréter* clore avec des branches entrelacées, Jura *frachous* bois cassant pour allumer le feu, Suisserom. *fratzi, fratschi, frachi* rompre, briser, couper, Ital. *fratta* broussaille, haie, buisson, *esser per le fratte* être dans la frape; *frâteiller* faire du bruit en marchant ou en remuant dans les feuilles sèches, *freuche* friche, terre inculte, couverte de bruyère de genévriers, Berry *frau, frou, défrau* terre inculte, Norm. *frau* place publique, emplacement libre, vide, Champ. *friez* friche, Guernesey *frie* gazon, *friquet* préau, *fro* lieu inculte; *freucher* battre, froisser, fouler, Pic. *frusser* presser, Berry *froucher* battre, froisser, à Metz *freuchie* se dit d'un léger piétinement d'un bruit continu et sourd; *frocher* froisser, Wallon *frohî* frayer en brisant, action de frayer, Wallon de Mons *froncher,* Luxembourg *frouchir,*" E. de Chambure, *Glossaire du Morvan,* Paris, Autun 1878.

[2] "Qui porcos in silva sua tempore glandis invenerit, primum custodi aliquid velut pigneris tollat indicium et domino pastoris vel parentibus mandet, ut, si convenerit, *usque ad tempus decimarum porcos in silva sua permittat . . .* ut porcos suos in silvam eius, si voluerit, introducat et *decimum* juxta consuetudinem *solvat,*" VIII. 5. 1, 2, 3, 4.

[3] "Agraria, pascuaria, vel *decimas porcorum* Ecclesiae pro fidis nostrae de-

*decima porcorum* of the Church was collected from the swine pasturing in the *forestis*.[1] This tithe was levied on the increase of the flock, as is distinctly mentioned in the emphyteutic contracts at Lucca, where the pigs and lambs so delivered were to be one year old.[2] If we compare the obligations of the peasants of Saint Gall with those of the Lucchese documents, we find a very close resemblance, only that instead of "porco annotino" we here get the expression *friskinga*.[3] The etymologists derive this *friskinga* from G. *frisch*, but the latter is entirely wanting in Gothic, occurs but late in OHG. as *frisc*, in AS. as *fersc*, is in ONorse *fersk*, *frisk* unquestionably borrowed from the German, just like Lith. *prëskas*, Slavic *prës'n* "fresh, unleavened." At the same

votione concedimus, ita ut actor et decimator in rebus Ecclesiae nullus accedat" (554), Bouquet, *Recueil des historiens des Gaules et de France*, vol. IV, p. 116.

[1] "Ut de omnes fructus terre infra pago Spirense quantumcumque fiscus noster continet, tam de annona quam de vino, mel, sive jumenta, de porcos, quam de omni reliqua solucione ad nos aspiciencia sic et homines fisci faciant *decimas porcorum qui in forestis insaginantur*," Pardessus, *Diplomata*, vol. II, p. 424.

[2] "Uno porco et uno animale *annotino* et angaria ad curtem vestram . . . facere debeamus" (777), *Mem. e doc . . . di Lucca*, vol. IV ¹, p. 18; "gregis equorum, armentorum, ovium seu porcorum, omnia *qui nati fuerent a callendas Januaria*, inditione quarta in ipso sancto loco idem *decimas* dare debeas" (721), *ibid.*, p. 68; "cum jam dictas decimas in ipso supra scripto loco permaneant, et *perennis temporibus mihi offerantur* a nobis, vel heredibus atque actoribus nostris" (729), *ibid.*, p. 71; "ad misso vestro, seu ad actorem vestrum de curte vestra in ipso loco, tempore consueto, reddere debemus grano modio quattuor, vino puro decimatas sex, *porco annotino*, angaria quanta utilitas ad ipsa curte vestra facienda" (770), *ibid.*, p. 118; "et *porco uno per omnes Nativitates Domini*" (798), *ibid.*, p. 176; "uno animale *annutino* in mense magio, *porco uno annutino* in octammio . . . et ipse animal nos et porco usque in Rosellas minare debeam" (762), *ibid.*, vol. V ², p. 48; "in omnem mense magio uno *annotino*" (776), *ibid.*, p. 147.

[3] "In anno reddamus carram de vino et *friskingam*" (720), H. Wartmann, *Urkundenbuch der Abtei Sanct Gallen*, vol. I, p. 3; "et pro istas res proservire volo annis singulis, hoc est XXX seglas cervisa, XL panis, *frischenga* tremesse valiente et XXX mannas et arare duos juchos in anno et recollegere et intus ducere et angaria, ubi obus est" (754), *ibid.*, p. 22; "et annis singulis persolvam censum inde, id est cervisa siclas XXX, panes XL, *friskinga* trimissa valente" (759), *ibid.*, p. 28, and often.

time OHG. *friscing, fruschinc, frinscing, frinskinga,* etc., means "victima, hostia, holocausta," where there is not the slightest reference to "fresh." *Friscing* is the "fresh," one year old pig, offered as a tithe to the owner of the forest and later, when the tithe was turned over to the church, as "offering to the church." Its name was derived from *frisca, frusca,* etc., "wasteland," (which, as we have seen, took the place of *forestis,*) because, according to the law of 653, the *decima porcorum* was collected from the pigs pasturing in the *forestis.* But *friscing,* a German derivative from *friscum* "wasteland" is identical with *annotino* of the Lucchese documents, that is, it was at the same time considered to mean, "one year old, fresh pig." Thus *frisco, fresco, frasco* (Fr. *frais*) came to mean "fresh," not only in the Romance languages, but also in German.

# ARBUSTUM VITATUM

PLINY tells in his *Natural History* the following about the cultivation of the vine: "The experience of ages has sufficiently proved that the wines of the highest quality are only grown upon vines attached to trees, and that even then the choicest wines are produced by the upper part of the tree, the produce of the lower part being more abundant; such being the beneficial result of elevating the vine. It is with a view to this that the trees employed for this purpose are selected. In the first rank of all stands the elm, with the exception of the Atinian variety, which is covered with too many leaves; and next comes the black poplar, which is valued for a similar reason, being not so densely covered with leaves. Most people, too, by no means hold the ash in disesteem, as also the olive, if it is not overshadowed with branches. . . . They must not be touched with the knife before the end of three years, and the branches are preserved, on each side in its turn, the pruning being done in alternate years. In the sixth year the vine is united to the tree. In Italy beyond the Padus, in addition to the trees already mentioned, they plant for their vines (arbustat agros) the cornel, the opulus, the linden, the maple, the ash, the yoke-elm, and the quercus; while in Venetia they grow willows for the purpose, on account of the humidity of the soil." [1]  Columella is more specific as regards the purpose of planting certain kinds of trees: "The Atinian elm thrives much better, and is much taller, than our Italian elm; and yields a sweeter leaf, and more agreeable to oxen; which if you feed cattle

[1] XVII. 35. I quote from Bostock and Riley's translation (London 1855, vol. III, p. 512).

constantly with, and afterwards begin to give them leaves of that other kind, it makes the oxen nauseate their food. Therefore, if it can be done, we will plant all our land with this one kind of the Atinian elm; but, if this cannot be done, we will take care, in laying out our rows, to plant an equal number of our own Italian, and of Atinian elms alternately: so we shall always make use of mixt leaves; and the cattle, being allured by this seasoning, as it were, will more eagerly eat up that due quantity of food, which is allotted them. But the poplar tree seems to nourish the vine most of any; next to that the elm; and, after that, the ash tree also. The poplar tree (opulus) is rejected by most people, because it yields a thin leaf, and not proper for cattle. The ash tree, which is most acceptable to goats and sheep, and not useless for oxen, is rightly planted in rough, rugged, and mountainous places, where the elm thrives but indifferently. The elm is preferred by most people, because it both suffers the vine without any inconveniency to it, and yields a most agreeable fodder for oxen, and comes up and thrives very well in various kinds of soils. Therefore let him, who has a mind to plant a great number of trees for supporting vines, prepare nurseries of elms and ashes in that manner I have described." [1] "The vines must be set in the farthermost part of the trench, and their firm-wood stretched along the trench, and erected to the tree, and fenced with rails against the injuries of cattle." [2]

Such a plantation was known as *arbustum*, and, because of its use in trailing vines, it is very frequently mentioned together with *vitis*.[3] The same method is still pursued in Italy,

[1] *De re rustica*, v. 6. Quoted from L. Junius Moderatus Columella *Of Husbandry*, London 1745, p. 226 f.

[2] *Ibid.*, p. 231.

[3] "*Arbusta*, ubi traduces possent fieri *vitium*," Varro, *De re rustica*, I. 8. 3; "cum me *arbustum* videre . . . atque . . . *vitis* incidere falce novellas," Vergilius, *Eclogae*, III. 10; "jam vinctae *vites*, iam falcem *arbusta* reponunt," Vergilius, *Georgica*, II. 416; "De *arbustivis vitibus* . . . si *arbustum* te habere delec-

and up to the twelfth century *arbustum vitatum* remained a common expression in the documents of southern Italy as a description of a vine-covered grove.[1] That this is not merely a stereotyped phrase, such as is common in the documents of that time, is proved by the very definite description of the duties required from a tenant who took possession of land on the basis of an emphyteutic contract. Not only was he to take care of the existing trees, of whose fruits he was to furnish the owner a certain part, but he was also to plant new groves and take care of them.[2]

About Naples we find since the tenth century the expressions *terra arbustata, pecia de arbusto*, originally in exactly the same connotation as *arbustum vitatum*,[3] but in the eleventh

tat," Palladius, III. 10. More quotations are to be found in the *Thesaurus linguae latinae*, sub *arbustum* 2.

[1] "*Arbustu vitatu*" (801), *Codex diplomaticus cavensis*, Neapoli 1873, vol. I, p. 5 (803), p. 6; "terra mea qui est *arbustu* et *vitatu*" (824), *ibid.*, p. 15; "cum *arbustu bitatu*" (848), *ibid.*, p. 34; "terra mea qui est *arbustu bitatu*" (848), *ibid.*, p. 35 (850), p. 40; "ipsa terra cum *arbustu vitatu*" (853), *ibid.*, p. 45, etc.

[2] "Ut a die presenti incipiamus exinde cappilare ipsos arbores et laborare eos, et ipsum laborem quod exinde fecerimus demus vobis exinde medietatem in predicto loco. ipsa vero alia ligna que non sunt de laborem quodcumque exinde fecerimus medietatem vobis exinde demus. ipsa vero terra incipiamus *cultare et pastinare adque implere eos totum de tigillis* et insurculare debeamus de ipsa zinzala." (10. cent.), Camera, *Memorie storico-diplomatiche dell' antica città e ducato di Amalfi*, Salerno 1871, vol. I, p. 164 *f.*: "quomodo vinea, et terrua vacua se meruerit laborare, et cultare, et ipsi *arborea vitati* qui jam. ibidem plantati sunt, quomodo *arbores vitati* se meruerint cultare et conciare . . . Et presente debeant *arbustare* integra superius dicta indicata prima petia de terra juxta rationem, et *arbores ipsae vitare vites arbusti*, excepta ipsa praefata Curte. Et amodo usque in decem anni completi nostri Monasterii integra jam dicta de terra prima petia *arbustata* rationabiliter, et *arbores ipsos vitatos*, excepto ipsa praefata Curte, cum ipsis arbores in ipsa vinea levaverint licentiam et potestatem habeant incidere. Etiam in antea vinum, quod de ipsum arbustum Deus annualiter dederit, et frugium de subter dividere debeant cum parte suprascripti nostri Monasterii" (973), Muratori, *Scriptores*, vol. I², p. 457; and similarly pp. 454, 455; "et siat factum et plenum amodo et usque ad completis annis tres et factus siat *arbustus* seu ipsa . . . nemus et pergula et ubive terre de dicto *pastinemus tigillos et insurculemus eos de ipsa castanea zenzala*" (1104), C. Minieri Riccio, *Saggio di codice diplomatico formato sulle antiche scritture dell' archivio di stato di Napoli*, Napoli 1878, vol. I, p. 16.

[3] "Quale tempore ipse *arbustum* fuerit totus pastenatus et *vitatus*," *Regii Neapolitani archivi monumenta*, Napoli 1849, vol. III, p. 158; "vene et diligenter

century they are used more generally in the sense of "woodland," as opposed to fields,[1] while in the north of Italy we never hear of *arbustum, arbustata*, but only of *buscalia, buschiva*, which is there common from the beginning of the tenth century.[2] *Boscalea* is already mentioned in a document of the year 753, but this document is from an apograph of the eleventh century and certainly spurious.[3] In the documents of the tenth and eleventh centuries *buscalia* refers to plots that are neither fields, forests, nor wastelands, and since a *terra buscoliva* is especially mentioned as being wooded, it is certain that *buscalia* is a generic name for a brush grown tract of land.[4]

lavorare et excolere debemus . . . et vites in memorata petia de *terra arbustata* omni annuo ponere et plantare," *ibid.*, p. 157: "laborandi et *arbustandi* quamque seminandi cacuminas et *vites* ibidem ponendi et plantare," *ibid.*, p. 32.

[1] "*Terra arbustata* et campores" (1015), *ibid.*, vol. IV, p. 75; "*petia arbustata* et campese" (1021), *ibid.*, p. 157.

[2] This in itself should suffice to prove the derivation of the first from the second, but the law-mad philologists do not recognise documentary evidence. They insist that Ital. *bosco* is to be derived from Gr. βοσκή, which is not only at variance with documentary facts, but also contradicts the phonetic laws which they maintain. Βοσκή means "fodder, grazing ground" and never "grove." In a Byzantine papyrus of the year 616 βοσκή stands for "meadow grass," "μήτε μην δυνασθαι τον αυτον ιωαννην φαγειν εκ της βοσκης των αυτων αρουρων σποριμων γηδιων αλλ επι τω τα κτηνη του αυτου μοναστηριου φαγειν την αυτην βοσκην" (F. G. Kenyon, *Greek Papyri in the British Museum*, London 1898, vol. II, p. 238 *f.*), and this prohibition is strikingly like the very ancient one from Amorgos "πρόβατα δὲ μὴ βόσκειν εἰς τὸ τέμενος μηδέν" (Dareste, Haussoulier, Reinach, *Recueil des inscriptions juridiques grecques*, Paris 1895, p. 205 n.). In the *Basilica* the caption "De pascuis publicis et privatis" is once rendered by "Περὶ βοσκῶν καὶ λιβάδων, καὶ λειμώνων," and once by "Περὶ νομῶν ἤτοι βοσκῶν." (G. G. E. Heimbach, *Basilicorum libri* LX, Lipsiae 1850, vol. V, p. 147), and it is clear from the juxtaposition of βοσκή and λειμών, λιβάς, νομή that the reference is to meadows, even as βοσκή and λιβάδι are identical in Modern Greek. Besides, the Greek word having entered the west only in the ninth century, it should have appeared there as *vosca*, not as *boscus*. Hence the derivation of *bosco* from βοσκή is a sheer impossibility.

[3] *Cod. Langob.*, col. 30 n.

[4] "Silvas stalarias et *busgeas*" (910), *ibid.*, col. 751; "petiola terre cum *buscalia* super se" (961), *ibid.*, col. 1107; "cum aeris suarum seu terris arabilis et pratis silvis et *buscaleis* atque gerboras" (1009), *Codex diplomaticus Cremonae* (*HPM.*, ser. II, vol. XXI), Augustae Turinorum 1895, vol. I, p. 45, and again pp. 48, 49, 59 (*boscalea*) et passim; "de silvis e stellariis seu castanetis, *bus-*

Another form for it is *buscaria*,[1] and at the same time *busco*,
*bosco* makes its appearance in Sardinia and in the north,[2]
and the juxtaposition of this with "silva" shows that it again
means "brush grown land." But as there is also mention
of plowed land lying in the *bosco*, it apparently was sometimes reclaimed, but the usual reference is to "*bosco* comuno," the common pasture land.

In pre-Carolingian times not the slightest trace of *bosco*
is to be found anywhere in Italy. It is first recorded in the
north in 910 and slowly spreads as far as Naples. In the beginning of the tenth century the word was still new, and in
904–5 we hear for the first time of certain obligations in the
*arbustum* called *arbustaria*, *arbustericia*.[3] It is clear that
these produced the chronologically later recorded *buscaria*,
*buscalia*, *busco*, *bosco*, but this may be proved even without
the presence of these laws. The laws being written in Frank-

*caliis* adque gerbosas" (941), *Bullettino dell' istituto italiano*, N° 21, p. 160;
"de silvis e stellariis seu gerbosas, *busgalias*" (943), *ibid.*, p. 158; "de silvis et
stellareis et *buscaleis*" (1015), *Codice diplomatico padovano dal secolo sesto a
tutto l'undecimo*, Venezia 1877, p. 135, and again pp. 140, 155, 197; "petia una
de terra *buscoliva* cum silva superabente" (1096), *ibid.*, p. 343; "terras arabiles
et prata et garbas et *buscalivas*" (1100), *ibid.*, p. 358; "una pecia de terra cum
*buscalia* super se" (961), F. Odorici, *Storie bresciane*, vol. v, p. 14; and again
pp. 38, 51 et passim; "petiam terrae aratoria, olivatae, et *buschivae*" (1221),
*ibid.*, vol. vii, p. 97; "terris arabilibus cultis et incultis silvis *buschilibus*" (991),
*MGH.*, *Dip. reg. et imp. Ger.*, vol. i, p. 447; "vineis *buscalibus* pratis" (1016),
*ibid.*, p. 497 and again p. 585.
   [1] "Silvis insulis *buscariis*" (969), *MGH.*, *Dip. reg. et imp. Ger.*, vol. i, p. 540;
"prata salecta *buscaria*" (1020), *ibid.*, vol. iii, p. 549; "silvis frascariis *buscariis*" (1038), Muratori, *Antiq.*, vol. i, col. 447.
   [2] "Cum terris cultis et discultis, *buschis* et silvis" (1002), *Codex diplomaticus
Sardiniae* (in *HPM.*, vol. x) vol. i, p. 147; "terris cultis et incultis, agrestis et
domesticis, silvis sive *boschis*" (1009), *ibid.*, p. 148; "in parte aratoria in parte
*bosco*" (1005), Odorici, *op. cit.*, vol. v, p. 21; "*bosco* comuno" (1005), *HPM.*,
*Chartae*, vol. ii, col. 92; "pecia una de *bosco*" (1040), *ibid.*, col. 137.
   [3] "Venationes ac *arbusta*," L. Schiaparelli, *I diplomi di Lodovico III e di
Rodolfo II*, Roma 1910, p. 60; "nec ullas publicas *arbustarias* aut redibitiones
vel illicitas occasiones sive angarias super inponere audeat vel inferre presumat,"
L. Schiaparelli, *I diplomi di Berengario I*, Roma 1903, p. 139; "atque districtum
seu *arbustericiam* aut quamcumque redibitionem publicam quoque modo exigere," *ibid.*, p. 176.

ish style, we shall have to look to France for the origin of the words and the development of their meanings.

In a French document of 870 we find a locality *Arbustellum*[1] and soon after *Ad illum Boscum, Alboscum*,[2] while in the tenth century and later mention is almost exclusively made of places *Bosco, Boscaria, Boschetto*,[3] not only in France but also in Spain.[4] *Ad illum Boscum* is merely an amplification of *Alboscum*, and this is a corruption of *Arbustum*, but this cannot be insisted upon, since local names *ad illum* (*locum*) are not uncommon. These localities lay in or near the *arbustum*, and we must now ascertain how *-bustum* came to be changed to *boscum*.

Abbo, of the Church of S. Germain of Paris, wrote towards the end of the ninth or in the beginning of the tenth century, a poem "De bellis Parisiacae Urbis," where, referring to the year 886, he speaks of the enormous masses of cattle which were gathered in the aula of S. Germain, which was thus turned into a *bostar*. The aula here means the yard or enclosure of the church, and what Abbo means to say is that the yard was changed into a cattle enclosure.[5] *Bostar* stands for *bustaria*, as a result of a confusion with *bos* "ox" and

---

[1] Bouquet, *Recueil des historiens des Gaules et de la France*, vol. VIII, p. 628.

[2] "Villam nostram quae vocatur *Ad illum Boscum*" (893), M. Deloche, *Cartulaire de l'abbaye de Beaulieu*, Paris 1859, p. 217; "in loco qui dicitur *Ad illo Bosco*" (891), *ibid.*, p. 210; "*Alboscum*" (970), A. Bernard, *Cartulaire de l'abbaye de Savigny*, Paris 1853, p. 184.

[3] "Villa quae vocatur *Boscus*" (1059), Deloche, *op. cit.*, p. 135; "*Bosco*" (1061), *ibid.*, p. 152; "mansum de *Bosco*" (1100), *ibid.*, p. 74; "*Boscaria*" (960), Devic and Vaissete, *op. cit.*, vol. v, col. 238; "*Boscheto*" (961), *ibid.*, col. 245.

[4] "Locum de *Bosco* Tellentis" (963), A. de Yepes, *Coronica general de la orden de San Benito*, vol. VIII, app. 2a; "aplicat ad *Busco* de Corteças" (1010), F. Sota, *Chronica de principes de Asturias y Cantabria*, Madrid 1681, p. 654.

[5] "Haec oculis equidem petii sistens super urbis
Moenia, nec visu claudebantur neque ritmo:
At quoniam cingi nequeunt pratis, nec ab agris,
Efficitur *bostar* Germani Antistitis aula,
Completur tauris, suculis, simisque capellis,"
Bouquet, *Recueil*, vol. VIII, p. 15.

*stare* "to stand" and Greek βουστάσιον,[1] while Papias confused *bostar* with *bustum* "a place where cattle are burned,"[2] but Matthew of Paris in the thirteenth century employed *bostar* correctly in the sense of "cattle yard."[3] In Spain we occasionally find in the eighth century *arbusta* for such an enclosure,[4] but far more frequently we meet there with *bustum* and *bustellum,* a forest enclosure on the outskirts of the estate,[5] generally surrounded by a hedge[6] and used as a cattle yard.[7] The herds pasturing in such a corral were of a given size, for the tax for pasturing was figured by the *busto.*[8] There were, however, also very extensive *bustos,* with

---

[1] "*Bostar,* créche Gallice, a bos et stare. Bouverie, *bostar,* estable a buefs. *Bostar,* stabulum, quasi boves stantes," Ducange, sub *bostar.*

[2] "*Bostar,* locus ubi comburebantur corpora boum, vel statio boum."

[3] "In vallibus videlicet Moriani quaedam villae, scilicet quinque, cum suis *bostaribus,* caulis, et molendinis adjacentibus, obrutae sunt," *Chronica majora* (in edition of H. R. Luard, vol. v, p. 30).

[4] "*Arbusta* cum suis hibernales" (862), R. Escalona, *Historia del real monasterio de Sahagun,* Madrid 1782, p. 631.

[5] "De fonte Sombrana usque ad foz de *busto,* de foz de *busto* usque ad pinnam rubeam" (804), *España sagrada,* vol. xxvi, pp. 442, 445; "cum montibus, fontibus, azoreras, *bustis,* pratis, aqueductibus, etc." (823), *ibid.,* vol. xxxvii, p. 321; "Eclesiam Sancti Emeterii cum Sernis et *Bustis* de monte Pelio . . . et *Bustos* praenominatos Loarrio, et Longe Braneas, et Arrium, et Translectum; in Riosa Ecclesiam Sanctae Mariae, seu *Bustos* praenominatos tam de tempore verani, quam de tempore iberni usque Portum" (827), *ibid.,* p. 324 *f.;* "*bustello* in illa carrale antiqua" (891), *ibid.,* p. 338; "addicimus etiam Ecclesiae vestrae *busta* praenominata, in territorio Asturiensi, id est, in monte Aramo *bustum* quod dicunt foios, etc." (891), *ibid.,* p. 341; "item in portus de Caso adsignamus eglesie uestre *bustum* quem dicunt Troniscum . . . et alium *bustum* in fonte Fascasia" (905), *Indice de los documentos del monasterio de Sahagun, de la orden de San Benito,* Madrid 1874, p. 2; "*bustum* . . . Tronisco in summa portaria . . . id est terminos de parte orientali *bustum* Mencii" (923), *ibid.,* p. 4; "*bustum* quem uocitant Pinzon qui iacet circa alium quem dicunt Troniscum" (934), *ibid.,* p. 5; "in loco quod dicunt *busto* de Picones" (930), *ibid.,* p. 113; "in loco quod dicunt *busto* de Dulcidio" (956), *ibid.,* p. 137; "in *Bustello* in Villa noua" (1181), *ibid.,* p. 387.

[6] "*Bustello* medio de sepe" (906), *PMH., Dipl. et chart.,* p. 9.

[7] "*Bustos* in monte Lene duos cum bacas tres, *bustos* in Nalare a Sancto Martino in Lotani quatuor, *busto* in Monte Nigro cum vaccas" (998), *España sagrada,* vol. xl, p. 409.

[8] "Et omnes qui quesierint pausar cum suo ganado in terminos de Elbora prendant de illis montadigo de grege das oues iiii or carneiros, de *busto* de

116    COMMENTARY TO THE GERMANIC LAWS

their own appurtenances and lands.[1] We also find the forms
*bustare*,[2] *bustaria*,[3] and *bustarega*,[4] and in the latter case it is
distinctly mentioned that they were enclosed pastures.

If we now compare the Spanish forms *bustum*, *bustare*,
*bustello*, *bustariega* with the Italian *busco*, *buscaria*, *buscalia*,
and with *arbusta*, *arbustaria*, *arbustericia* of the Italian documents of 904–5, the identity of these becomes at once obvious, and it is clear that *arbustaria*, *arbustericia* refer to the
tax for pasturing which the proprietor of the forest may exact. Fortunately we possess in the *Fuero general* of Navarra
a detailed account of the organisation of such a pasture.
Although the Fuero was written down in the thirteenth
century, the laws and practices described there refer to Visigothic times. The first title of the sixth book deals with the
pasture, which is here called *vedado* and *bustalizia*.[5]

A *vedado* was a horse or cow pasture in what formerly had
been meadow land. It was laid out by common consent of
the infanzons and peasants, by measuring off the land twelve
times in all four directions with the perch "of the royal see."

uaccas I uaca" (1166), *PMH.*, *Leg. et consuet.*, vol. I, p. 392, et passim. See
*Index generalis*, sub *busto.*
  [1] "In portu de casso adsignamus Eclesiae vestrae *Bustum*, quem dicunt
Troniscum, cum suis pascuis vel paludibus, et suis furnis ratione servata"
(905), R. Escalona, *op. cit.*, p. 378; "juxta Pireneum quoque *bustum* vaccalem
quod de Regenda nuncupatur; alium *bustum* quod Caulinos dicitur cum suis
propriis terris; alium *bustum* vaccalem quod Maccabes nuncupatur, cum suis
pisceis, furnis, et utilitatibus suis; etiam quartum *bustum* ovile juxta ipsam"
(951), *España sagrada*, vol. XXXIV, p. 454.
  [2] "Serra *bustare* de hac Torubio" (912), Yepes, *Coronica general de la orden
de San Benito*, vol. I, p. 38.
  [3] J. Santa Rosa de Viterbo, *Elucidario*, Lisboa 1865, sub *busto.*
  [4] "Et si fluvius Sancti Dominici levaverit *bustaregas* abbatis vel espinare,
integret se abbas pro eo, et aliud remaneat pro pasto, et dominium sit abbatis"
(1209), M. Férotin, *Recueil des chartes de l'abbaye de Silos*, Paris 1897, p. 123;
"que habia antes soto y *bustariegas* en que solian pacer" (1253), *ibid.*, p. 203;
"que el soto con las otras *bustariegas* queden enteramente al abad para siem-
pre" (1254), *ibid.*, p. 207.
  [5] "Aqui conpieza el libro VI° en quoal fabla de paztos," P. Ilarregui y Lapuerta, *Fuero general de Navarra*, Pamplona 1869, p. 123 *ff.*

Such a perch was seven cubits and a clenched fist long, and was at the end provided with an iron point weighing two pounds.[1] If the land was really measured with the perch, it produced an enclosure of about an acre; but if *echar* means "to throw," the enclosure would become many times larger. Such a *vedado* was closed from beginning of February until the end of December and afterward was open for all cattle. The common ground in the forest between two villages where the pigs and the cattle pastured was called puerto, and the enclosure itself was known as *busto* or *bustalizia*, which was produced in the same way as the *vedado*, only that it was determined by the hammerthrow in the following manner: The measurer sat down in the middle of the space set aside for an enclosure and threw a sharp axe with a handle a cubit long twelve times in each direction. It is not likely that each throw netted more than twenty feet for it was accomplished under the acrobatic feat of holding the right ear with the left hand and casting the axe from between that arm and the breast.[2]

The hammerthrow has been frequently recorded in Germany since the twelfth century, and since Grimm[3] a poetic, religious or legal German custom has been theorised out of it. The identical Navarrese custom goes back to a sensible

[1] "Si todos los vezinos quisieron fer *vedado* de nuevo, vayan a la sed del Rey et retiengan el amor del iuvero del Rey et ganen la piertega con su fierro . . . Toda piertega de sied deve ser vii cobdos rasos, et ocheno el puyno cerrado en luengo; et deve aver en el fierro dos libros, en el fust de espesura quanto i ombre puede alcanzar con el dedo somero el pulgar cabo el fierro. Et aqueylla piertega sea daveyllano, drecha et lisa et sin corteza, como nasze en el mont; et aqueilla piertega deven aver por los prados de cavayllos et de los buyes. Este ombre que ha a echar la piertega, nos deve remeter nin mover el un pie del logar onde tiene," *ibid.*, p. 124.
[2] "Toda *bustalizia* deve ser al menos quoanto i ombre puede echar xii vezes a iiiiº partes la segur, devese asentar arecho en el medio de la *bustalizia*; et esta segur que es a echar deve aver el mango un cobdo raso, et el fierro deve aver de la una part agudo et de la otra part esmochado, et teniendo la oreylla diestra con la mano siniestra, deve passar el brazo diestro entre el pezcuezo et el brazo siniestro, et eche quoanto mas podiere echar esta segur, come dicho es de suso,". *ibid.*, p. 128.
[3] *Deutsche Rechtsaltertümer*, pp. 55 ff., 527 ff.

Roman method of measurement by the *decempeda pertica*. Twelve perticae of ten (or twelve) feet square formed in Rome the unit of surface, two of which were equal to a iugerum.[1] In the Navarrese custom we have, therefore a survival of the Roman law which was intended for the provinces. Here as there the "decempeda" had to be "cast" twelve times, as in the Roman measurement, and seven cubits were just about ten feet. In Navarre the perch had to be obtained from the *sied del Rey* "the royal see," but in reality this is a popular transformation of the Roman *regio*, the local court, where the land questions were settled.[2] Where the ignorant peasants could not help themselves with straight measurements, in the forest or the swamp, there they had recourse to the hammerthrow, and by the employment of the acrobatic feat they managed to obtain a fairly equitable mensuration. Hence the hammerthrow is as much a Roman institution as the Scandinavian *solskipt*, which has been shown to be the Roman *solis divisio*.[3]

We have an Aragonese law of the year 1247 which coincides with the law of the *busto*, but here *busto*, understood as *bostar*, has further been corrupted to *boalare*,[4] that is, *bostar* "a place for oxen," has produced *boale* and *boalare*. In the Limousin this *boalare* has in the ninth century given rise

[1] Blume, Lachmann, und Rudorff, *Die Schriften der römischen Feldmesser*, Berlin 1852, p. 355, and C. Lachmann, *Gromatici veteres*, Berolini 1848, p. 367 f.:

"Actus quadratus undique finitur pedibus cxx, ita cxx $\boxed{\phantom{cxx}}^{cxx}$ cxx. Actus duplicatus iugerum facit . . . iugerum autem constat longitudine duocentorum xl, latitudine cxx; ita cxx $\boxed{\phantom{cxx}}^{ccxl}$ cxx."

[2] "*Regiones* enim dicimus intra quarum fines singularum coloniarum aut municipiorum magistratibus ius dicendi coherdendique est libera potestas," *Gromatici veteres*, p. 135.

[3] *Atti del Reale i stituto veneto*, vol. LXII, p. 1039; *Vierteljahrschrift für Sociologie und Wirtschaftsgeschichte*, vol. II, p. 421 ff.

[4] *Fueros y observancias del Reyno de Aragon*, Zaragoça 1667, p. 56b.

to *baccalaria*,[1] as though it were a place for cows. These *baccalariae* naturally lay far away from the village and were left in charge of the poorer or unmarried peasants, hence we get *baccalarius* "bachelor," which has spread over Europe from the south of France. That this derivation is the real one is proved by the synonymous German *Hagestolz*, OHG. *hagustalt*, AS. *hagusteald* "bachelor," ONorse *haukstalda* "famulus, mercenarius, agricola liber," where the first part of the word has distinct reference to "forest," that is, the "bachelor" was he who lived in the forest, where the *busto* was located. It is not easy to ascertain what the second half of the word is derived from, but it looks as though in German it proceeded from the same Spanish *bustalizia* which produced a form *bustalt*, understood as *bus-stalt*, in which the first part, for *buscus*, gave way to the popular *haga*. It is certainly remarkable that there should be in German a similar confusion as there is in the Romance *busto*, *bustal*, *bostar*, *boale*, *boalaria*, *baccalaria*.

Thus it appears that the Roman institution of the *arbustum vitatum* has survived in Spain only as an enclosure which was not thrown open to all in the summer. *Arbustum*, here contracted to *bustum*, has the special meaning of "closed vineyard," because any other pasture was free for all neighbors, according to the Roman custom, while the vineyard could be held against others so long as the grapes were not yet gathered in. This institution of "enclosures" has been of enormous economic consequences in Spain, whence it passed over to the rest of Europe, bringing with it an exceedingly large linguistic family. Unfortunately there are, in this group, a number of contaminations which make it the most prolific and the most difficult of any to treat. I shall confine myself only to the most obvious derivations.

---

[1] "*Baccalaria* indominicata" (866), Deloche, *Cartulaire de l'abbaye de Beaulieu*, p. 10, and again pp. 73, 202, 210, 270.

In Basque we have *bost-*, *brost-*, *brosk-* for "bush"— "*bosta*
buisson, *brosta* haie, broussaille, et aussi fourré, lieu couvert
de broussailles de bruyeres, *broka* détritus, debrit d'objets
sans valeur, qu'on passe dehors avec le balais." Here and in
the Romance languages we find not only the original *bust-*,
but also *brust-*, etc. This latter form may have arisen in the
same way as *frost* from *vast*, or from *arbust-* by metathesis.
We shall now turn to the Latin sources in France. We have
already seen that *buscus*, *boscus* here takes the place of Span.
*bustum*, and to this must be added *buschus*, *buschetus*, *boccus*,
*bochetus*, which appear only late. There arose very early the
necessity of distinguishing the standing, green timber from
the firewood and the faggots, since one of the privileges in the
forest consisted in the permission to cut a certain number of
trees a year for building purposes and to gather dead wood for
fuel. Hence such a right is called *boscairare*, *buscare*, *buscal-
hare*, *boscare*.[1] The building timber was called *boscus viridis*
or *vivus*, to distinguish it from the faggots, *boscus siccus* or
*mortuus*, which also included certain standing trees that were
used for fuel,[2] hence we get the specific statement, "*boscus*

---

[1] "Qui in bosco *boscauerint* possint pascere in ea prata" (1145), *HPM.*, *Lib.
jur. reip. gen.*, vol. I, col. 108; "piscari uenari et *boscare* usque in riuum" (1219),
*ibid.*, *Chartae*, vol. I, col. 1255; "teneantur ipsi potestates quod per aliquos vel
aliquibus sue potestacie non faciant trahi seu *boschari* aliquod lignamen ad opus
ipsorum potestatum et iudicum vel scribarum" (13. cent.), *ibid.*, *Leg. gen.*, col.
23; "et tenent vasalli ipsius Ogerii communem et pasculare et *buscare* in ipsa
curte Plazano" (1129), C. Vignati, *Codice diplomatico laudense*, Milano 1879,
vol. I, p. 121; "tagliando buscum scilicet frascas et ramas . . . pascere debent
et segare et *buscare* . . . *buscare* de ramis et foliis omni tempore eis liceat, omnes
tamen erba scilicet et ligna ad dorsum, non cum plaustro ferant" (1156), *ibid.*,
p. (1151), p. 165 *f.*; "ne debeant . . . paschare *buschare* nec pischare" (1215),
P. Sella, *Statuta comunis Bugelle*, Biella 1904, vol. II, p. 3; "ut extranea persona non debeat *boscare* seu pascare super terra communis," A. Valsecchi, *Gli
statuti di Albenga*, Albenga 1885, p. 29; "interrogatus qualiter scit, quod homines Arelatis visi fuerint *boscairare* in dicto territorio, dixit quod vidit ibi
Stephanum Gaillardum, qui faciebat inscidi ligna in deffenseto . . . dixit quia
vidit homines Castillonis lignerare sive *boscairare*, et laborare et pascere animalia sua, et ejicere avere de Arelate, et *boscadeiros* " (1265), Ducange.

[2] "Dedi etiam domui et omnibus pertinentiis suis, quantascumque habuerit,
in silva mea de Lesga usuarium ad omnia necessaria sua etiam tam *viridi* quam

*vivus* ad aedificandum, *mortuus* ad calefaciendum, comburendum, ardendum."[1] The laws distinctly mention that the dead wood is carefully to be "sought" with wooden hooks, in order to break down the dead branches, hence we get in Spain *buscare* "to seek." To separate more clearly and briefly the standing timber from the dead wood, *boscus* was employed only for the first, while the latter became known in the feminine, as *bosca, busca, buschia, buca, bucha, buchia, buga,* but more commonly *bruscale, bruscia, brozia, brossa, brossia, brucia, broca, bruga, brua, broa, bruera, brueria, brugeria, brugaria,* and even *bronda, branda, bropa, branca, branchia.* It is not difficult to explain this great variety of forms.

From the tenth century on we find *bruscus* and *brusca*[2] for *buscus* and *busca,* but in the northwest of Italy *bruca* and *bruga* became the most popular words for "faggots, fuelwood, twigs," while in France we have the fuller forms *bruscia, broca,* etc. Where formerly *buscalia, buscaria* was used, we find in the south *brucaria, bruguera, bruaria, brueria* for "brush grown country." This group, spreading to the north into regions where there was no forest, has been applied to heathergrown land. The Welsh *brwg* "forest, brush, ferns," which is borrowed from the English, shows the meaning "forest" and "fern" side by side, because the underlying meaning is deserted land, brush grown land, etc. The early loss of *s* in *bruscus, brusca* is explained by the influence of Lat. *brocchus, broncus, bronchus* "provided with teeth," while Lat.

in *sicco*" (1083), M. Prou, *Recueil des actes de Philippe I<sup>er</sup>*, Paris 1908, p. 278; "quoniam a predecessoribus suis tres cotidie quadrigatas in suis nemoribus de *bosco mortuo* ad opus coquine sive pistrini et elemosine ibidem monachi possidebant, hoc ille cupiens majorare, quartam quoque de *vivo bosco* perpetualiter concessit" (1101), *ibid.,* p. 354.

[1] Ducange, sub *boscus mortuus.*
[2] "*Brusca* Marcofeldis" (949), Bouquet, *op. cit.,* vol. IX, p. 382; "Pumar cum toto caverso usque in *toto Brusco*" (1042), Muñoz y Romero, *Coleccion de fueros municipales,* p. 191.

*branca* "paw" produces *branca, branchia* "fuelwood, fag-gots"[1] and then "branch." Similarly *bropa* results from a crossing of *brosca* with Lat. *scopa* "thin twig,"[2] and under the influence of Lat. *frondem* arises *bronda*.[3] But *brusca* "firewood" has produced *bruscare, bruxare, brusare*, and French *brûler*, from an older *brusculare*.

We now can treat the Romance representatives of' the group in a summary manner. We have "OFr. *boschaille* bois, *boscheer, bouchoyer, bocheyer* couper du bois, *boschel, bochal*, etc., buisson, bosquet, bocage, petit bois, *bouche* botte fagot, *bouchage* tas de fagots, *boissier boisier, boichier* qui travaille le bois, *buschier* abattre du bois et en faire des bûches, couper des branches d'arbres, *busche, boize* buche." If we keep in mind that *boscare* was the act of finding and knocking down the dry branches with the wooden stick, we see at once why we get "OFr. *buschier, busquer, bucquier, bucquer, busser* frapper, heurter, *boucheter* émouter, battre, mal traiter, *busquer* chercher." Forms with inserted *r* are: "*broce, broche, brousse, brouce, brouse*, etc., broussailles, hal-lier, petit bouquet d'arbres, *broceron, brocheron* petite branche courte, *broçon*, touffe, *broçonner* bourgeonner, reverdir, *broisson* rejeton." As early as the tenth century *brustum* means "forest fodder, young leaves, food for goats,"[4] and from this comes "OFr. *brost*, brout, jeune pousse des arbres

---

[1] "*Brancas* etiam de Leia, quantum necesse fuerit ad focum monachorum" (1073), Prou, *Recueil des actes de Philippe I^er*, p. 168; "in saisina habendi usagium suum subscriptum, videlicet percipiendi *brueriam*, fulgeriam, et folium quod cecidit de arboribus, pasnagium ad 3, denarios pro porco, pasturam ad animalia sua in vallibus, secando herbam a festo S. Joannis usque ad Assump-tionem B. Mariae virginis in defensis etiam forestae . . . percipiendi etiam *branchas* siccas cum croceo ligneo sine ferro" (1271), Ducange, sub *branca*.

[2] "Statutum est, quod aliquis laborator . . . non audeat aportare aliquas sarmentas, vel *bropas*, vel alia ligna absque expressa licentia illius cujus la-borat," Ducange, sub *bropa*.

[3] "*Brondae* olivariorum, vel aliarum arborum," Ducange, sub *bronda*.

[4] "Capreae quoque ad sotularia monachorum facienda *brustum* habeant per totum boscum," Ducange.

au printemps, *broster* brouter, *brotage* droit qu'on payait pour faire brouter ses bêtes quelque part, *brotel*, *broteau* taillis, *broterie*, *brouterie* lieu ou broutent les animaux." From *brusculum* are derived "OFr. *bruliau* fagot, broussaille, *brûlis* portion de foret incendiée, de champs dont les herbes ont été brûlées, *brusler* brûler." *Burjon* "bourgeon," like "Prov. *burca, burga, burja* fourgonner, tisonner, aiguilloner, pousser, taquiner, cogner, heurter, *bourjouna, broujouna, brouchona, brounchouna* fourgonner, patrouiller, bousculer, Centre *broquer, bruquer* heurter, choquer" owes its origin to a contamination with Lat. *brocchus, bronchus*.

A similar wealth of forms is to be found in the Provençal: "*bos, bosc, boch, boi, bo*, etc., bois, *bousca* rechercher, quêter, gagner les bois, déguerpir, *bouscaia, bouscalha* ramasser du bois, *bouscaio, bouscalho* bois en général, toute sorte de bois, *bouscaren, bouissaren* forestier, *bouscas* grand bois, futaie, épaisse forêt, forêt affreuse, mauvais bois, sauvage, bâtard, *bousco* recherche, bois en général, *bousquet* bosquet, petit bois, *bousa* boiser, couvrir de bois, bâtonner, rosser, *boustiga* remuer, fouiller, bouleverser, *busc* broutilles ou brussailles épineuses, *busca* busquer, bûcher, *buscaia* glaner des buchettes, *buscaio* broutille, brindille de bois mort, *busqueja* ramasser du bois, *bussa* cosser, heurter de la tête; *bro, broc, brot, boc* branche morte, scion, bûchette, épine, dard, buisson, bâton, *broco* bûchette, broutille sèche, *brous* broussaille, *broussa* balayer, *broussaio* broussailles, bruyère en général, *brousso* bruyère à balais, touffe de broyère, *broust* brout, pousse d'un taillis ramée, *brousto* pousse, ramée, branche, taillis, pousse de chou, chou brocoli, *brout* brout, jeune pousse des arbres et des plantes, *brouta* pousser, vegeter, *brouto* rejeton, nouvelle pousse, *broutouna* pousser, bourgeonner, *brusc* bruyère commune, tige de bruyère, *brusqueirolo* petit champ de bruyère, *brusquié* taillis de bruyères, *brusquiero* champ couvert de bruyère, bruyère, *bruga* taillis de bruyères; *broundas* rameau dont on se sert en guise de balai, *brounditoun, broutihoun* petite broutille, petit rameau, *brounca, abrounca, brouncha, brunca, bruca, breca, ruca* broncher, heurter, *bruia, brulha, broulha* pousser germer, reverdir, *bruioun, brulhou, brellou, broulhou, bourlhou, orboulhou* bourgeon, rejeton de chou, *brula, brusla, brunla, burla, bourla, brouda* brûler, incendier, *bruscla, baruscla, bourouscla, brucla, bristoula, brounzi, brousi, brausi, abrausi, brusi, brui, broui* haler, brûler, *brusa, bruza, bruisa* brûler."

Since the corresponding Italian words have evolved out of the French terms, we naturally find them at first in the north. Beginning with the twelfth century we find recorded *broco* "twig, faggot" [1] and crossing with *frasca* we get *frusca*,[2] so that later Ital. *bruscolo, fruscolo fuscello* are synonymous, while *broco* develops further into *sbrocco, sprocco*. The forms with and without *r* interchange in the dialects, hence Genoese *busca bûsca = buscare* "to seek" and *bruscare* "to brush," while Friul. *busca = busca, busco, brusco, bruscolo*, and *bruschâ and buschâ = dibruscare, bruscare, buscare*. If we now consider that Ital. *busso, buscio, fruscio* at the same time mean "noise," it becomes at once clear that not only all these belong to the *busco* group, but that also French *bruit* is to be included in it. The development of "noise" is universal in Europe, as has been seen under *vasta*. Spanish *brotar* "to form buds," *brote* "bud," *bruza* "brush," *buscar* "seek" have developed from the French, and a careful search will in the Romance languages reveal a much larger number of words that belong to this group.

I now turn to the second part of the expression *arbustum vitatum*. In Langobard Italy *terra vitata* is opposed to "terra

---

[1] "Ramos et *brochas* cuidam alboris pini" (1289), P. Monti, *Vocabolario dei dialetti della città e diocesi di Como*, Milano 1845; "fructus a *brochis* separatis" (1176), *ibid*; "pecia una campi cum *brugis*" (1269), *ibid*.

[2] "*Fruscas* vel ramos de arboribus" (1313), *Statuti di Brescia*, in *HPM.*, vol. xvi, col. 1720.

campiva, aratoria, prativa, ortiva," to field and garden land, and also to "terra olivata, selvata," olive grove and forest.[1] Much older and much more popular is the use of *vitis* in the sense of *terra vitata*, "*vites* meas petia una in fundo bonate quem ego emmi" (745).[2] Although now and then the combination *terra cum vitibus* occurs,[3] from which may be assumed that it has the original meaning of vine-covered land, such expressions as "ipsa petiola est de *uites* et uacua terrola,"[4] "petiola una de terrola cum *uite* et uacuum,"[5] show that *vites* means "brush grown land."

This *vitis*, which occurs in Langobard documents since the beginning of the eighth century, occurs at least as early in Frankish documents. In a spurious Merovingian document of the sixth century, which is, no doubt, not earlier than of the eighth century, the pertinence runs as follows, "haec

---

[1] "De suprascripta *terra vidata* me nihil reservo" (785), *Cod. Langob.*, col. 113; "pecia prativa . . . pecia *vidata*, pecia campiva" (857), *ibid.*, col. 337; "estas cum curte, orto, area et *terra vidata*" (859), *ibid.*, col. 346; "una *vitata* et alia campiva et *vitata* uno tenente" (867), *ibid.*, col. 405; "terra campiva et prativa, *vitata* et silvata" (915), *ibid.*, col. 803; "terrola aratoria seo et *vidata*" (869), Muratori, *Antiq.*, vol. I, col. 721; "petia una de *terra vitata* cum campo" (878), F. Odorici, *Storie bresciane*, vol. IV, p. 65; "duas pecias terras uni in parte *vidata* et in parte aratoria et alia aratoria" (961), *ibid.*, vol. V, p. 14; "pecias septe de terra tres *vidates* cum quadtuor arbores olives supabete, et tres aratorias setima ortiva" (1016), *ibid.*, p. 27; "una pecia terre arative *vidate* et prative" (1104), *ibid.*, vol. VI, p. 14; "terrae aratoriae, *vitatae*, et olivatae et vegrae" (1221), *ibid.*, vol. VII, p. 98.

[2] *Cod. Langob.*, col. 26. "Curtes terras *vites* pratas et silvas . . . terra *vitis*, prata" (761), *ibid.*, col. 49 f.; "terra aratoria seu *vitis*" (768), *ibid.*, col. 69; "media juge de terra aratoria" (769), *ibid.*, col. 76; "campis pratis *vidibus* et selvis" (799), *ibid.*, col. 130; "secunda petiola *vitis* cum castenellum in simul se habente" (812), *ibid.*, col. 163; "petia de *vites*" (867), *ibid.*, col. 411 f.; "quarta pecia de *vites* jacet ad vinea Vicana" (974), *ibid.*, col. 1314; "*vites* et oliveta" (983), *Cod. dip. pad. dal sesto*, etc., p. 66, and similarly pp. 85, 116, 117, 124, 136, 218, 278; "vineis . . . et ortos duos duasque petias de *vite*" (1033), *ibid.*, p. 162; "pecia una de terra cum *vitibus*" (1073), *ibid.*, p. 245; "terra una de *vite* et alia de terra arva" (795), M. Lupi, *Codex diplomaticus civitatis et ecclesiae Bergomatis*, Bergomi 1784, vol. I, p. 606.

[3] Troya, *op. cit.*, vol. IV, p. 469 (753).

[4] *Bullettino dell' istituto storico italiano*, N° 30, p. 64 (758).

[5] *Ibid.*, p. 69 (762).

omnia cum mancipiis desuper manentibus, mansis, domibus, aedificiis, curtiferis, *widis, campis*, vineis, silvis, pratis, pascuis, aquis aquarumve decursibus,"[1] and again, "tam mansis, colonicis, aedificiis, silvis, ingrediciis, *widis, campis*, pratis, pascuis, aquis aquarumve decursibus."[2] Pardessus reads incorrectly for it *unidis, campis*,[3] while Quantin has the significant reading *vuidis, campis*.[4] In another, most likely spurious, document, which is said to be of the year 499, but which exists only in a copy of the thirteenth century, we find the same pertinence, "haec omnia cum mancipiis desuper manentibus, mansis domibus aedificiis cultiferis *mudiscapis* vineis silvis campis pratis pascuis aquis aquarumve descursibus,"[5] where, of course, *mudiscapis* is a misread *vuidis campis* or *widis campis*. The position of this *vuidis campis* between curtiferis and vineis does not permit any doubt that we are dealing here with some kind of a plantation, and the identical juxtaposition of *vitis* and *campum* of the Langobard documents shows that what in Italy formed two distinct words and concepts here begins to be conceived as one idea, so that in the last quoted document, but not in the first two, *campis* is once more repeated before *pratis*. The constant use of *vuidis campis* in the pertinence has led to regarding this as a compound. Now, as *vasta* has led to *forestis*, and *bustum* to *bruscus*, etc., and *uacatum* to *vacartum*,[6] so *widis campis* has changed into *widriscapis*,[7] *wadriscapis*,[8] *watris-*

<hr/>

[1] *MGH., Dipl. imp.*, vol. I, p. 133.     [2] *Ibid.*, p. 134.

[3] J. M. Pardessus, *Diplomata*, vol. I, p. 132.

[4] M. Quantin, *Cartulaire général de l' Yonne*, Auxerre 1854, vol. I, pp. 3 and 4.

[5] *MGH., op. cit.*, p. 116.

[6] "Que conjacet in *vuacatis* ipsius villae" (954–986), C. Ragut, *Cartulaire de Saint-Vincent de Mâcon*, Mâcon 1864, p. 179; "que conjacet in *vacartis* ipsius villae," *ibid.*, p. 178.

[7] "Hoc sunt sessi cum *widriscapis*, casis" (722), Martène and Durand, *Veterum scriptorum et monumentorum collectio*, vol. I, col. 19.

[8] "Cum domibus, edificiis, curtiferis, cum *wariscapis* (*waris campis*), terris," *MGH., Formulae*, pp. 266, 268, 269, 270, 175, 179, Martène and Durand, *op. cit.* (837), vol. I, col. 127, D. Haignéré, *Les chartes de Saint-Bertin*, Saint Omer 1886, vol. I, p. 20 (975), *Monumenta Boica*, vol. XXVIII, p. 59 (796). ·

*capis*,[1] *watriscafis*,[2] *vatriscafis*,[3] *wardi scampis*,[4] *uuatriscapud*,[5] *wardriscapis*,[6] *warescapiis*,[7] *wariscapiis*,[8] *quadriscapis*,[9] *quadris campis*,[10] *wastris campis*,[11] *votris campis*.[12] Ducange also records *wadiscabum* and *waskium*. From this variety of forms have arisen OFr. *warescais, warescait, warescape, wareschel* "tierres vagues, lieux destinés à la pâturage publique,"[13] and to these are to be added Wallon. *warechais, wareschaix,* Liège *wercha,* Mont. *warescaix, waréchaix, wareskaix* "pâturages communaux, vaines pâtures."

All these words belong to the north of France. Otherwise the older form *widis, vuidis* has spread over a very large territory. In the *Chanson de Roland* we have once *voide place*,[14] and once *voide terre*.[15] In the latter case we have a precise rendering of Ital. *terra vidata,* and from a large number of documents of the thirteenth century we know that *wide, voide terre* was the technical expression for "wasteland." This is also the case in the *Chanson de Roland,* where the word never occurs again, although one would expect it, if it already had the current meaning of "empty." Besides, the last quoted verses sound like an imitation of the documentary

---

[1] Pardessus, vol. II, p. 289 (711).  [2] *Ibid.*, p. 293 (713).
[3] *Ibid.*, p. 291 (712).
[4] F. Dahn, *Die Könige der Germanen,* Leipzig 1905, vol. IX, div. 2, p. 85.
[5] Warnkoenig (Gheldolf), *Histoire de la Flandre,* Paris 1835, vol. I, p. 326 (839).
[6] Ch. Piot, *Cartulaire de l'abbaye de Saint Trond,* Bruxelles 1870, vol. I, p. 2 (741).
[7] *Ibid.*, p. 5.  [8] *MGH., Scriptores,* vol. X, p. 371 (745).
[9] D. Haignéré, *op. cit.,* p. 9 (800).
[10] D'Achery, *Spicilegium,* vol. III, col. 342 (850), J. B. Mittarelli, *Annales camadulenses Ordinis Sancti Benedictini,* Venetiis 1755, vol. I, col. 22.
[11] W. Ritz, *Urkunden und Abhandlungen zur Geschichte des Niederrheins und der Niedermaas,* Aachen 1824, p. 7 (824).
[12] *Ibid.*, p. 14 (895).
[13] Godefroy gives an extremely large number of citations for these words.
[14] "Que mort l'abat en une *voide place*" (v. 1668).
[15] "Il n'en i ad ne veie ne senter,
   Ne *voide terre* ne alne ne plein pied
   Que il n'i ait u Franceis u paien." (v. 2399–2401).

pertinence "cum viis et semiteriis et *vidis terris* et arboribus et planis." Godefroy quotes several passages in which *wide terre* means "pasturage."[1] However, the *wides terres* are not exactly pastures, but fallow land overgrown with brush, used as pastures. They are opposed to *pleines terres* "cultivated lands," as may be seen from a discussion of Philippe Beaumanoir in the thirteenth century.[2]

For *vuide terre* we also find *vaine et vuide*.[3] This *vaine* is only a learned adaptation to *vana*, but has in reality arisen from *gain*.[4] *Gain* means "extraordinary, unexpected gain." In Godefroy there are a number of quotations in which he falsely translates *gain* by "fruit de la terre, recolte," where it should have been rendered by *"regain,* rowen." In the lines

> Si a veu en une pleigne
> Berbiz qui paissoient *gain* (*Renart* VIII. 175).

*gain* can refer only to "grass." For "autumn" Godefroy records *waym, wain, vain, win, gayn, gain, vayng, gaain,* and

---

[1] "Les pasturages de toutes les *wides terres* qui sient (1284); de laquelle *wide terre* vendue si com dit est li dis venderes se devestit en la main du prevost de Maisieres (1336); asqueles III. quartiers il ne prist nul pourfit a le premiere anee, et les doit laisier a *wides* (1360)."

[2] "S'il avient que li mors muire avant que le blé soient semé, mes les terres ont leur roies ou aucunes de leur roies, ou les vignes sont fouïes ou taillies ou provignies, mes les grapes n'i aperent pas encore, en teus cas ne vienent pas des despeuilles qui puis i sont mises en partie, mes li labourages tant seulement de tans passé: si comme se les jaschieres sont fetes au vivant du seigneur et li douaires a la dame li est assis en *terres vuides*, se les jaschieres furent fetes du sien et du son seigneur it est bien resons que ce qui i fu mis de sa partie li soit rendu de ceus qui en portent les jaschieres toutes fetes. Voir est quant il convient que li douaires soit essieutes de la partie as oirs, la coustume est tel que la dame qui veut avoir le douaire, fet la partie et, quant ele a la partie fete, l'oirs du mort prent laquele partie qu'il li plest; et pour ce est il bon a la dame, s'ele met les *terres vuides* d'une part et les pleines d'autre, qu'ele face retenue que, se li oir ou li executeur prenent les terres pleine (*terres wides* ou pleines), que sa partie de muebles li soit sauvee; car s'ele lessoit courre la partie simplement sans fere retenue, ele n'avroit nul restor des terres pleines, pour ce qu'il sembleroit qu'ele avroit tout avalue l'un contre l'autre," Am. Salmon, *Philippe de Beaumanoir, Coutumes de Beauvaisis*, Paris 1899, vol. I, p. 220 f. (chap. XIII, 458 and 459).

[3] In Gaston Phebus, quoted by La Curne de la Sainte-Palaye, sub *vuit*.

[4] See the chapter on *Quovis genio*.

he adduces a large number of forms from the dialects.[1] As the original meaning of *gain* was forgotten and it meant any kind of a gain, there was formed in French, first recorded in Littre in the sixteenth century, the pleonastic *regain* for "rowen," for which we have the dialectic, Picard. *reguin, rouain,* Wallon *rigain.* To these are to be added Morvan *"regâmer* repousser, pousser de nouveau, Normand *revouin* regain, *revouiner* possuer comme le regain, *revoiner* reverdir, Comtois (Fourges) *ruwain,"*[2] Berry *"reguiner* pousser en regain."[3] From the Norman *revouin* comes Engl. *rowen.* later popularized to *roughings.*

The distribution of this word in the south is particularly interesting, because it shows to what wild transformations, utterly baffling philology and phonetics, a word may be subjected. Levy records *gaim* in the Provence. In Berry we already find *regouiver* for *reguiner.* In the south the case is much worse. In Lyons we get the forms *reviouro, revioulo, revuro, revivro, revioro, reviula* "regain."[4] After this one will not be surprised at the extravagances recorded in Mistral. Here we get *revieure, rouibre, rouire, rouibre, rebouibre, reboulbre, roubibre, roudibre, gouibre, reboulibre, rebouribre, reboulume, relubre, rebouchouire, reboujouire, reboussouire, rourieu, bourieu, abourieu, aurieu, bouirieu, vourieu, vouri, voueiri.*[5] One

---

[1] "Lorr., Fillieres *wayin,* culture d'automne pour semer le blé. S.-Dizier, semer le *vain:* 'Quand nous serons en *vain* nous payerons les domestiques.' Apres le *vain,* on fait le chien. Fr.-Comté, *vahin, vaihin, vouaihin, vouain, vain,* automne; *vahin, voyain, vouyain,* regain. *Gain, guien,* synonyme de regain dans le departement des Deux-Sèvres et dans le H.-Maine. Centre de la France, Issoudoun, aller au *gain,* aller en vendanges. Poitou, *gain, guiain,* regain, seconde coupe des prairies." Besides, Godefroy cites *gaaigneau, gaigneau, gaynau, ganneau, guimeau, guimau, waymal,* "qui se joint habituellement avec le mot pré pour designer un pré à regain, un pré qui se fauchait deux fois par an" and "en Touraine, l'on disait *gaimau,* en Saintonge *gueymaulx.*"
[2] E. de Chambure, *Glossaire du Morvan,* Paris, Autun 1878.
[3] H. Moisy, *Dictionnaire de patois normand,* Caen 1887.
[4] N. du Puitspelu, *Dictionnaire étymologique du patois lyonnais,* Lyon 1890.
[5] To these must be added Vosges. *woye, woeye, r'woye,* N. Haillant, *Dictionnaire phonétique et étymologique,* Epinal 1885.

sees plainly how, beginning with *gain* in the north of France, the forms get worse and worse as they proceed south. If we turn to the *Atlas linguistique de la France* (N° 1139), one can get a clear idea how it has happened. *Gain* occurs only sporadically in the northwest, in Côtes-du-Nord, Orne, D.-Sèvres, while in Belgium forms arising from *wain* are universal. If a straight line is drawn from Bordeaux to Châlons-sur-Saône, we get to the north of it the *regain* group. From Belgium, where the *rewain* forms are exceptional, the *rewain* words go straight south, here and there alternating with *wain*. Towards Switzerland begin the corruptions which produce the Provençal forms. In Doubs *regain, rewain, wain* meet. In the southwest of Switzerland we get *rekwai*, while in Jura and Doubs we have *rewain*. Towards the east rise the forms *rekwa, rekwar, rekor, reko*, and these go south to Savoie and Ain. In Isère *rekor* stands side by side with *revur*, and the latter explains the other corruptions of the south. In the south, along the coast, and along the Pyrenees, in Landes and Gironde, that is, at the periphery, derivations from *regain* are exceptional. Here we have the freely formed *reprin* or *retaille*, and Covarubias was certainly right when he derived Span. *retoño* from the synonymous *retallo*. If this map may be safely trusted as representing a historic tradition, and there is nothing to contradict such an assumption, the whole group must have had its birth in the north, spreading in two streams, one directly to the south, the other along the western border, equally to the south and towards Switzerland, taking from there a westerly direction. We are, therefore, compelled to assume that an intensive use of the rowen proceeded from the north. French *gaim, waim* has entered Italy in the form *guaime*, and *guimeau, waymal* has produced there *gomireccio, grumereccio*, again proving the assumption that the group proceed from the north of France. The same confirmation is found in Germany. MHG. *amat, üemet*, Swiss *amad*, German *Emde, Oehmd, Ohmet, Ohmt* "rowen" are transformations of the French *waim*, with a leaning towards MHG. *mat* "mowing," and as Fr. *guimeau* has led to Ital. *grumereccio*, so it has also produced German *Grummet*, with a possible popular derivation from "grün" and "Mahd."

The expression *terre vaine et vague*, which becomes more and more popular, contains a tautology. In Normandy *terra vacua* was originally the expression for *terre vaine*, for we are distinctly told in the *Summa de legibus* that in the *terra vacua* cattle could pasture only from September until March, that is, on the stubble or rowen.[1] Hence *terre vaine* refers to the late pastures only, while *terre vuide* is any abandoned, rough pasture. But in time the latter word loses its distinctive meaning, while *vaine pâturage* becomes the common expression for "pasture."

In the *Codex Theodosianus* the term *terrae vacantes, vagantes* signifies abandoned, uncultivated land,[2] in Italy *vacuus* and *vacans* referred to neglected land in private possession,[3] and as in France the *terre vuide* was opposed to *terre pleine*, so here was employed the combination *vacuum et plenum*.[4] In the Theodosian Code we have the expression *vacuus et inanis* for the complete abandonment of property, which then is confiscated by the curia,[5] and this term is used in hundreds of documents in the Middle Ages.[6] In place of the older *vacuus*

---

[1] "Terre vero *vacue*, que a medio marcio usque ad festum Sancte Crucis in septembri defenduntur, alio vero tempore sunt communes, nisi clause fuerint vel ex antiquitate defense, ut haie et hujusmodi," E. J. Tardif, *Coutumiers de Normandie*, Rouen, Paris 1896, vol. II, p. 30.

[2] VII. 20. 3 and 8.

[3] "*Terra vacuum* ividem qui vinea fuit" (939), *Mon. reg neap.*, vol. I, p. 119; "*terra bacua* ubi prius domum fuit" (963), *ibid.*, vol. II, p. 109; "*terra uacante* in circuitu eius ubi aptum fuerit vineas cum arboribus pomorum" (946), *Archivio della r. Società Romana di Storia Patria*, vol. XII, p. 74.

[4] "Assignastis nobis montem vestrum *vacuum et plenum*" (10. cent.), Camera, *Memorie ... di Amalfi*, vol. I, p. 164.

[5] "*Vacuas vero et inanes* sine naturali successione fortunas sibi Curia vindicabit," XII. 1. 123.

[6] "Si quis de novis quod ab se substragere voluerit, vel proprio defendere,

there soon spreads in Italy forms derived from Fr. *vuid, vuit*, even more completely than did the *gain* words. Philologists, who construct history on abstract laws, have derived such words from a Lat. *vocitus* for *vacatus*. But there is not a shadow of a trace of such a word anywhere. While we do have *vocitus* for *vocatus*, a derivation from *vacatus* is absurd. In Italy we find only the words derived from *vacuus* and *vacans*, and also *vacivus*.[1] The philologists base their assumption of such a derivation on the Logudorian form *bogidu* in Sardinia, which, they say, is derived from *vocitus*. But fortunately we here possess early dialectic documents in the *Condaghe di San Pietro di Silki*, from the fourteenth century, in which some documents run back to the eleventh century. Here *vacans* occurs several times, but of *vocitus* and *bogidu* there is not a trace.[2] Hence *vocitus* is an impossibility as a basis for *void, vuit*. It is true that *vuit* took the place of the old *vacuum*, since there is little difference between a *pecia de vites* and a *vacuum*. *Vuit* was popular in France in the eighth century, but did not assume the distinct meaning of "empty, abandoned" until later, possibly not before the tenth century.

The German *Weide* is derived from *widis*, even as *Ohmd* and *Grummet* are derived from Fr. *gain*. *Weide* appears only late in OHG., is not recorded in Gothic, and has entered the northern languages only from the German. The oldest quotation for *Weide* is in the Hrabanian glosses of the ninth century. But if one turns to the respective passage,[3] one finds there "pascua ostarun pascua *uueide*," where the first pascua is a mistake for pascha, while *eid* in *uueide* is written over an

---

*vacuus et enanis* exinde exeat" (713), Brunetti, *op. cit.*, vol. I, p. 423, and again, vol. II, pp. 350, 372, 382, 402.

[1] "Terra *vaciba*" (1022), G. B. Nitto de Rossi, *Codice diplomatico barese*, vol. I, p. 19 (940), *Codex cavensis*, vol. I, p. 215, and very often.

[2] "Sa parte sua dessa uinia de funtana, cun pumu e *bacante* cantu ui aueat," G. Bonazzi, *Il Condaghe di San Pietro di Silki, testo logudorese inedito dei secoli XI–XIII*, Sassari-Cagliari 1900, p. 78 (N° 325) and again N°s 40, 248, 347.

[3] Steinmeyer and Sievers, *Althochdeutsche Glossen*, vol. I, p. 225.

old erasure. It can be shown that this gloss was written by a later hand, for in the alphabetic Bible glossary we find "pastum *uuinne.*"[1] Obviously, then, *inn* was erased, to make place for *eid*. Consequently the Hrabanian gloss cannot be used for the determination of the age of this word. The usual word for pasture is *mesti*.[2] But *uuinne* and *mesti* are themselves borrowed words. *Uuinne* is related to *gain*, as *gewinnen* is related to *gagner*, and *mesti* is Lat. *mixta*, which has also produced Span. *mesta* "pasture," which since the thirteenth century has played an important part in Spanish economic history. OHG. *mast*,[3] AS. *maeste*[4] is "common forest," where the pigs are fattened, wherefore it is translated by *pasnagium*. In the Spanish documents *ambae mixtae*, *maestae*, or *mestae* means everything which is used in common by adjoining neighbors, whether pasture or fishing. Before the thirteenth century most of the recorded cases refer exclusively to fishing rights,[5] but that is mere accident, for from the thirteenth century on *mestae* refers to the pasture.

[1] Steinmeyer and Sievers, *Althochdeutsche Glossen*, vol. i, p. 286.

[2] *Ibid.*, vol. iv, p. 84.

[3] "Ad Fregistatt sortes duas et Walt-*masta* ad porcos saginandum" (826), "quidam fidelis ... dedit bannum villae cum omni jure ex integro et justitia, quae vulgo dicitur *mast*" (999). However, both documents are spurious.

[4] "Gif non on his *maestene* unaliefed swin gemete, si quis obuiet porco sine licentia in pasnagio suo" (688–95?), Liebermann, *Gesetze der Angelsachsen*, p. 110 *f.*; "donne he his heorde to *maestene* drife, quando gregem suam minabit in pastinagium" (1025–60), *ibid.*, p. 447.

[5] "Et per illa Brana de Ordial, et per illas *mestas* de Freznedo, et per conforquellos, et inde ad illo rio de Rivilla" (780), *España sagrada*, vol. xxxvii, p. 306; "a meridie partibus suo porto integro, et suas piscarias, et suos rannales, et suos andamios, et saltus, usque in *ambas mixtas*, ad illo Trotino ... duas eremitas, Sancto Cosme et Damiano, que iacent contra parte de Mineo sub illa vereda, quae descendit ad *ambas mixtas* ... cum omnes suas cuintiones, et deganias cunctas ... quas fuisse de praesura antiqua scripturas veteres" (997), A. de Yepes, *Coronica general de la Orden de San Benito*, vol. v, fol. 438 b.; "per penna aurata et per illos carriles ... usque ad illo cauto ... inde per medium albeum usque ad *ambas mixtas* exceptas illas piscarias de Fiscaces, ibi vero in *ambas mixtas* restauramus, sicut in nostris testamentis habetur, et inde in *ambas mixtas* per medias albas usque ad Castellano" (1139), *ibid.*, fol. 439; "descendit per *ambas maestas* ad Fontem Panal" (960), *ibid.*, fol. 448; "de

OHG. *weide* is not certain before the tenth century, but it must have existed much earlier, because *widis campis* is recorded on German soil in the eighth century. As the pasture was chiefly used for hunting, we have AS. *vaeð* "hunting, roaming about, waves."

We turn once more to the *Atlas linguistique de la France* (N° 1384), in order to study the distribution of the *vuid* group on French soil. If we draw the same line as in *regain*, we have in the whole northwest the pure *vide* group, which here, as in regain, chiefly depends on literary influence. In the northeast, in Somme, Pas-de-Calais, Nord, Arden, we meet with *wid*, which in Belgium leans strongly towards *vud*, *vut*. From here a *void*, *voed* group takes a sharp southerly direction, while in Switzerland *vud*, *voed*, *wid*, *weid* meet side by side. Through the Provence run *vud*, *vuid*, *weid* forms, as *buit*, *bueid*, etc., here and there interrupted by literary *vide*. It is clear that the original *vuid* has developed in the direction of *weid* and *vud*. Considering the popular *vut* forms in Switzerland and the *vit*, *voet*, *vueit* in Raeto-Roman, it is not strange that Italian has *vuoto*, which is certainly of French late origin, for it has only the meaning "empty."

The fate of *vitatum* on the Spanish peninsula is especially instructive, because the many aberrations of the word have spread with the economic development of the pasture throughout the rest of Europe. According to the Visigothic law the fields bordering the road had to be surrounded by a fence or ditch,[1] otherwise the traveler along the road could not be kept from pasturing his cattle in the open fields.[2] The

inter *ambas mestas* ubi cadit Pisorica in Dorio, de inde ad Egica donec perveniatur a la Gascagosa . . . inde al Fontanar, de inde a las *mestas* ubi cadit Adagga in Dorio; et concedo ut nullus audeat piscare, videlicet ad Agga in Dorio, usque ad illas *mestas* ubi cadit Pisorica in Dorio" (1135), M. Férotin, *Recueil des chartes de l'abbaye de Silos*, p. 67.

[1] *Lex Visig.*, VIII. 4. 25 and 26.

[2] "*De apertorum et vacantium camporum pascuis.* Ne iter agentibus pascua non conclusa vetentur," *ibid.*, 27.

*apertorum camporum pascua* mentioned in this law is the same as the French *vaine pâture*, that is, stubble fields, while *vacantium camporum pascua* corresponds to the *terre vuide*. This is made absolutely certain from the corresponding Langobard law, where *stupla* and *pascua* are distinguished.[1] The identity of the two laws has long been observed, and it has been suggested that the Langobards have borrowed theirs from the Visigothic Code. One will look in vain in the Roman laws for its prototype, but it is evident that we are dealing with the economic institution of the Roman *arbustum vitatum*, which had to be taken care of and fenced in, to escape the fate of the vacant fields. A *terra vitata* could be defended, in order that it might remain in private possession, as regards pasturing, while wasteland and fallow fields were common pasture and could even be confiscated by the government. The semasiological change from *terra vitata* to *terra vetata* was natural and imperative, hence we not only find in the Visigothic law "*pascua non vetentur*," but in Aragon, Navarre and Gascony *vetatum* was the usual word for the *arbustum vitatum* of the Italians.[2] The *vedado* in Navarre has already been mentioned in connection with *arbustum*. In the sixth book of the *Fuero general de Navarra* we have specific mention of the rights exercised by neighboring villages in such a pasture. We get here a clear idea why *vitatum* was popularly changed to *vetatum*, for in such an enclosure the cattle and horses could pasture the whole year

[1] "Nulli sit licentia iterantibus erba negare, excepto prata intacto tempore suo, aut messem. Post fenum autem aut fruges collectas tantum vindicit couis terra est, quantum cum clausura sua potest defendere. Nam si cavallus iter facientibus de *stupla* aut de ipsa *pascua*, ubi alia peculia pascent, movere presumpserit, in octogild ipsus cavallus conponat, pro eo quod ipsos de arvo campo, quod est fonsaccri, movere presumpserit," *Ed. Roth.* 358.

[2] To the many quotations given in Ducange (sub *bedatum* and *vetatum*) the following few may be added: "Totam terram cultam et incultam et nemus et *bedad*" (1159), L'abbé Clergeac, *Cartulaire de l'abbaye de Gimont*, Paris, Auch 1905, pp. 150, 151; "boscum qui appellatur *bedad*" (1158), *ibid.*, p. 147.

round, while other animals were admitted only from September or November until March.[1]

In Spain the oldest form recorded in the documents is not *vetatum* but *divisa*.[2] That we are having here an enclosed pasture is proved by a document of the year 869, where a monastery is given right to gather fuel in a *divisio* and share pasture with a neighboring town.[3] This *divisa* has not survived, except in the stereotyped expression *hereditates et divisae*, in order to express complete possession of an estate, including the pasturage. In the province of Burgos the *divisae* are mentioned as lying in the outskirts, no longer as common property, but in private possession, the difference between *hereditates* and *divisae* being the same as between alodial land and such as has been acquired by presura.[4]

The obligation of the Langobard to the Visigothic laws has

[1] "La *defesa* (de cavayllos) deve ser *vedado* de la sancta Maria Candelor entroa la sant Johan ata que gayllos canten: et de que gayllos cantaren al dia de sant Johan entroa sancta Maria Candelor, puede paszer todo ganado," *Fuero general de Navarra*, p. 125; "*vedado* de bueyes deve ser del primer dia de sancta Maria Candelor entroa la sanct Martin ata que gayllos canten; et de que gayllos cantaren al dia de sanct Martin entroal dia de sancta Maria Candelor, puede paszer todo ganado," *ibid.*, p. 124.

[2] "Cum suas hereditates et *divisa* in monte" (762), Berganza, *Antigüedades de España*, vol. II, p. 370.

[3] "Ego Comite Didaco dono ad Sancti Felicis *divisiones* in montes, et fontes, id est de Valde Avuelo quantum potest portare cotidie cum vno carro . . . Et pro ad illo ganato *divisione* pari pasce cum illa Civitate Aukense," *ibid.*, p. 371.

[4] "Concedo etiam ut ubicumque habueritis *divisas* in omni Aucensi Episcopatu" (1068), *España sagrada*, vol. XXVI, p. 453; "trado ibi divisas guas in circuitu possideo. In Caraveio *divisam* quam ex parte matris heredito: In Mazzoferario *divisam* quam ex parte matris habeo. Et in Quintana Levaniaga *divisa* quam ex parte matris heredito ab omni integritate. Et in Villamajore tres *divisas*, una de meo patre Gustio Didaz, altero de meo germano Didaco Gustioz: terrtia de mea tia Domna Onneca. Has *divisas* Tibi Munioni Episcopo perpetuo jure concedo, ut serviant in Ecclesia S. Mariae semper Virginis cum suis adjacentiis, cum terris et vineis, cum pratis et montibus, cum ingressu et regressu ab omni integritate concedo" (1071), *ibid.*, p. 455; "villas eremas et populatas, decanias, et omnes alias *divisas* seu etiam hereditates . . . totum concedo Burgensi sedi perpetuo serviturum" (1076), *ibid.*, p. 459; "cum suas domos et *divissas*" (1056), M. Férotin, *Recueil des chartes de l'abbaye de Silos*, p. 12; "*divisero* e heredero en la villa" (1239), *ibid.*, p. 175.

already been observed by historians. It can also be shown that the Langobard documents of certain regions stand in some relation to the Visigothic documents. This is, no doubt, the case with those that employ *divisa* in a vague sense of "pasture." The earliest recorded instance is in a Carolingian document of the year 783, where we have the term "pascuis *divisis* et indivisi." [1] To the sensible "pascuis *devisis*" has been added the impossible "*indevisi*," for either *divisa* is not a divided pasture, or, if it is, an undivided pasture cannot be given away. This stereotyped expression *divisa et indivisa* is given in a number of documents at Amiata and Lucca, where the meaning cannot be ascertained, because it is never enlarged upon.[2] But we can show from a large number of Milan documents that the expression there occurs in company with other exceptional terms for Italy, which are common in Spanish documents. In a document of the year 840, with a prolific and useless pertinence, *divisum et indivisum* follows the term *interconciliaricis*.[3] Two years later *interconciliaricis* is changed to *inter concilium*.[4] This word goes through the most extravagant changes, through *inconcilibus, concelibus, concelibas, incelibas, conclivis, concilibas, celibas, coelibas*.[5] It is evident that this

[1] "Undecumque ad me devolutum est tam casis vineis terris silvis pratis pascuis *devisis* et indevisi," Brunetti, *op. cit.*, vol. II, p. 254.

[2] "Cultum et incultum, *deviso vel indeviso*" (821), *Archivio della r. Società romana*, vol. XVI, p. 299.

[3] "Ipsa predictis rebus cum casis in ipsas quinque locas vel alias tectoras cum curtis, ortis, areis, clausuris, campis, pratis, pascuis, silvis, salectis, sadiciis, castanedis, cerredis, roboretis, hamenecolariis, frontzariis, pascuis, usum aque, *interconciliaricis, divisum et indivisum*, omnia in omnibus," *Cod. Langob.*, col. 240.

[4] "Et omnes relique singolas terretorium seo de *inter concilium*, eo no mine *divisum et indivisum*," *ibid.*, col. 256.

[5] "Vineis, silvis, vicanalibus, *inconcilibis* locis, omnia et omnibus" (847), *ibid.*, col. 273; "*concelibus* locis, *divisas et indivisas*, coltum et incoltum, tam in monte quamque etiam in planis" (851), *ibid.*, col. 292; "vicanalibus, *concelibas* locas" (856), *ibid.*, col. 329 and (911) col. 653; "montibus, alpibus seo *incelibas* logas" (864), *ibid.*, col. 385; "*conclivis* locis *divisis*, ripis, rupinis" (914), *ibid.*, col. 784; "coerit ei da una parte via, da alia Sancti Abundi, da

strange word had the meaning of "pasture," but it was foreign to Italy, and in the middle of the eleventh century it disappears entirely. In Roman times *concilium* was the council held by the *conciliabulum*,[1] which itself was an administrative division after the forum, "quae colonia hac lege deducta a quodve municipium praefectura, forum, *conciliabulum* constitutum est.*"* Festus explains *conciliabulum* "locum ubi *concilium* convenitur." Isidor knows it as "pagi sunt loca apta aedificiis inter agros habitantibus, haec est *conciliabula* dicta a conventu secietate multorum in unum."[2] In Italy no trace of *conciliabulum* is left, but in Spain *concilium* survived in the sense of "community,"[3] hence the strange group of the Milan words was in some way transplanted from Spain. This seems to be proved by the use of the words *vicinalis*, *divisa* and *montes*, which are found with this *concilium* in the Milan documents, which are all distinctive Spanish terms, while *montes*, considering the fact that there are no mountains in Milanese territory, has developed out of the Spanish *divisa in monte* "forest pasture." We have already seen that the *divisa in monte*, like the *vedado* in Navarre, forms in Burgos the subject of constant discussions between adjoining villages and towns, hence the *interconcilium* of the year 842 can be nothing but the *interconfinium*, which Joannes de Janua[4] glosses with "terminus vel locus inter duos fines existens." Without a comparison

tercia *concelibis*, da quarta si qui sunt alii finantes" (992), *ibid.*, col. 1521; "usque seu *inter concillibas* locas" (984), *ibid.*, col. 1441; "coltis, et incoltis, *divisis, et indivisis*, usibus aquarum, aquarumque ductibus, et una cum finibus seu *celibas* locas" (1036), G. Giulini, *Memorie spettanti alla storia . . . di Milano ne' secoli bassi*, Milano 1857, vol. VII, p. 58; "pascuis, gerbis, *divisis et indivisis*, tam in montibus, quam in planitiis, usibus aquarum, aquarumque ductibus seu piscationibus, atque in *coelibas* locas" (1042), *ibid.*, p. 59; "*divisis, et indivisis*, una cum finibus, terminibus, accesionibus, et usibus aquarumque ductibus . . . seu *concelibas* locas" (1051), *ibid.*, p. 64.

[1] *Thesaurus linguae latinae*, sub *concilium* technice 2.
[2] *Ibid.*, sub *conciliabulum*.
[3] Ducange, sub *concilium* 3.                    [4] Ducange.

of the Milan with the Spanish documents the existence of *concilium* is unique in Italy, and inexplicable.[1] If *vetatum* of the Spanish documents is a transformation of *vitatum*, the still older *divisa* can only be some transformation of (pezia) *de vitis*, as recorded in the oldest Langobard documents. The incomprehensible *vitatum* changed into the comprehensible *vetatum* "forbidden" and *divisa* "separated, set aside." But there were many other corruptions of the original word. In Catalonia they spoke of a *devesa*,[2] while in Spain they at an early time passed over to *defesa*, which was understood and written as *defensa* "protected." In a document of the year 804 both *divisa* and *defesa* occur, and it is obvious that *divisa* refers to the termini mentioned before.[3] I have my doubts about the genuineness of this document, at least of the spelling *defesa*, since the document exists only in late copies and *defesa* is otherwise not recorded before the tenth century.[4] In the Provence this word does

[1] P. S. Leicht, *Studi sulla proprietà fondiaria nel medio evo*, Verona-Padova 1903, p. 37 *ff*.

[2] J. Balari y Jovany, *Origenes historicas de Cataluña*, Barcelona 1899.

[3] "Tribuo etiam in in loco qui vocatur Potancar ecclesias ... cum suis hereditatibus et terminis de penna usque ad flumen de Orone, cum molendinis et ortis et pratis et cum exitibus et regressibus adque cum omnibus sibi pertinentibus... Precipio quoque ut abeatis plenariam libertatem ad incidenda ligna in montibus meis ad construendas ecclesias, siue ad edificandas domos, aut cremandum, uel ad quodcumque necesse fuerit in *defesis*, in pascuis, in fontibus, in riuis, in exitu et regressu, absque ullo montadgo adque portatico. Adicio autem huic prefate uille seu monasteria uel ecclesias siue *diuisas* que suprascripte sunt, uel que tu aut successores tui adquirere potueritis," *Chartes de l'église de Valpuesta*, in *Revue hispanique*, vol. VII, p. 291 *f*.

[4] "Pratis, pascuis, padulibus, *defessas* lignarum, vel pascentes omni ganato per suis terminis" (963), Borganza, *Antigüedades de España*, vol. II, p. 400; "illa *defessa*, vel illo monte, dabo, et confirmo ab omni integritate. Ego Ferdinando Gundisalviz, sic pono foro super ipsa *defessa*. Si aliquis homo venerit in illo monte sine iussione Abbati pascere, aut ligna taliare, sic pono tali foro, vel cauto per vno bobe prendar vno carnero ... nullus domo auseus non sedeat per ibi intrare in illo monte, nisi solus, qui iussionem Abbatum de regula de Sancti Iuliani, et illos montes per ligna taggare, aut pascere, aut matera ad laborandum, aut derompere illos montes" (964), *ibid.*, p. 402; "pratis, padules, pascuis, *defessis*" (968), *ibid.*, p. 403; "cum *defessas*, et cum montes" (968), *ibid.*, p. 404; "qui scinderit ligna in ipsa *defessa*" (972), *ibid.*, p. 408; "molinis;

not appear before the eleventh century. Here we find the forms *deves, devesum, devensum, defensum, defensorium*.[1] In the Provençal language are recorded *deves, defes, deveza,* and the latter form is also found in Portuguese, while the Spanish has *dehesa*.

We have already seen from the Milanese documents that *divisa* stood by the side of *inter concilium,* that is, that it lay in the common land of adjoining villages. This is clearly shown in the English laws, where *divisa* is the common land [2] in which neighbors' troubles are settled,[3] wherefore it also means "first instance."[4] In Ine's law the Anglo-Saxon text has *gafolland* for *divisa,* that is, "land subject to a tax," such as is the case with pasture land, while one text slavishly translates it by *gedálland*.[5] This latter term occurs also in two tenth century documents, and in one of these it is distinctly mentioned as being common pasture, meadow and

*defessis,* pratis, pascuis" (1056), *ibid.,* p. 430; "pratis et *defesis,* pascuis et paludibus" (979), Férotin, *op. cit.,* p. 6; "serra cum sua *defesa* lignea" (1041), *ibid.,* p. 10; "pratos et *defesas* vel pomiferis" (1056), *ibid.,* p. 12; "ortis et pomiferis, cum pratis et *defessis*" (1073), *ibid.,* pp. 19, 21; "ponte atque pelago ad piscandum et saltu *defensso*" (1125), *ibid.,* p. 54.

[1] "*Devesum* in aqua" (1033) M. Guérard, *Cartulaire de l'abbaye de Saint Victor de Marseille,* Paris 1857, vol. I, p. 129; "de *devensu,* de pisces, de arboribus" (1060), *ibid.,* p. 404; "vineas male invasas *et defensorium*" (1090), *ibid.,* p. 600; "accessis sive exivis, defensis" (1044), *ibid.,* p. 49 et passim; "prata *defensa* et plantata" (1027), J. A. Brutails, *Etude sur la condition des populations rurales du Roussillon au Moyen Age,* Paris 1891, p. 254.

[2] " Si murdrum in campis patentibus et passim accessilibus inveniatur, a toto hundreto communiter, non solum ab eo, cuius terra est, suppleatur; si in *diuisis* accidat, utrimque pertranseat; si in aula regia sit, inde componat cui terra adiacebit," *Hen.* 91. 4; "si ceorli habeant herbagium in communi uel aliam compascualem (uel *divisionis, divisam*) terram claudendam," *Ine* 42.

[3] "Si inter compares uicinos utrinque sint querele, conueniant ad *diuisas* terrarum suarum," *Hen.* 57; "in *diuisis* uel [m] erchimotis," *Hen.* 57. 8; "inter compares in curiis uel *diuisis* uel locis suis," *Hen.*,34. 1a; "curiis uel *diuisis* parium," *Hen.* 9. 4.

[4] "Cil ki prendra larrun nez siwte e senz cri, que cil enlest, a ki il avera le damage fait, e il vienge apres, si est resun, qu'il duinse X sol. le hengwite, e si face la justice a la primere *devise* (et ad primam *divisam* faciet de eo justitiam)," *Leis Willelme* 4, 4. 1.

[5] "Gif ceorlas gaerstun haebben gemaenne oððe oþer *gedálland* to tynanne."

field.[1] In France *divisa, devesa* still occur in the twelfth century,[2] but most of the derivatives, such as *defay, defois,* are from *defesa* and *defensa.*[3]

From the above discussion it is evident that the Latin agricultural term *arbustum vitatum,* to express the enclosed vineyard which could be turned into a pasture only after the crops were in, or when the vines were so high that they could not be reached by the cattle, became in Spain the expression for any enclosed pasture, whether there were any vines in it or not. From Spain the idea of enclosures spread to France and England, where they played such an important part in the thirteenth century.

[1] "Das nigon hida licggeaŏ on gemang oŏran *gedállande* feldlaes gemáne and maéda gemáne and yrŏlande gemaéne" (961), J. M. Kemble, *Codex diplomaticus aevi saxonici,* Londini 1848, vol. vi, p. 39; "healf hid *gedaéllandes*" (966), *ibid.,* vol. iii, p. 6.

[2] "Inde ascendit per lo *deves* sicut aqua pendet" (1169), C. U. F. Chevalier, *Cartulaire de l'abbaye de Saint-André le-Bas de Nienne,* Lyon 1869, p. 303; "in clauso, et in prato, et in *devisio,*" C. U. Chevalier, *Chartularium Ecclesiae Petri de Burgo Valentiae* 1869, p. 4.

[3] See Ducange, sub *defensa* 3.

# FREDUM, FAIDA

In Holder's *Altceltischer Sprachschatz* LL. *veredus* "post-horse" is marked down as of Celtic origin. But the Romans derived the institution of the posts from Central Asia, specifically referred to by Herodotus as of Persian origin.[1] Indeed, Persian *barīd* "veredus, courier, messenger, running footman, a measure of two parasangs of twelve miles," *barīdan* "to send a messenger" is unquestionably older than Lat. *veredus*, for it is based on Assyr. *paradu* "to hasten, impetuous," *purīdu* "messenger, posthaste," which are enormously older than Persian *barīd* or Lat. *veredus*.[2] Our interest lies in the vicissitudes of *veredus* in Europe.[3]

The provincials, hence also the German colonists in Roman territory, were heavily taxed for the maintenance of highways by being obliged to furnish certain numbers of *veredi*, swift horses, and *paraveredi*, heavy draught horses carrying military supplies and other fiscal property. References in the Theodosian Code show that in the fifth century and possibly earlier the obligation to furnish *veredi* was commuted in the provinces to a pecuniary contribution, while the heavier draught horses seem to have been supplied for a long period afterwards. In and about Rome, possibly through all of Italy, a similar exchange took place by substituting fodder for the older *veredi*, so that we get references in Cassiodorus

[1] Herod. vIII. 98.
[2] Already correctly stated in P. Horn, *Grundriss der neupersischen Etymologie*, Strassburg 1893, p. 29.
[3] For the history of the *cursus publicus* and references to the next paragraph see Paul-Wissowa, *Realencyclopaedie*, and Daremberg and Saglio, *Dictionnaire des antiquités*, sub *cursus publicus*.

to *paraveredi et annonae*,[1] and it seems from the context that certain emoluments of the judges, called *pulveratica*, possibly traveling expenses, were in Italy in the sixth century abolished in favor of a supply of fodder for the *paraveredi*.[2] Indeed, we have not only here, but also in another passage, the specific statement that according to an old law a three days' supply of provision is supplied to the judges and nothing more.[3] This *annonae* is included in the common technical term *apparatus*,[4] which in the Frankish immunities quoted farther below is referred to as *parata*. The *veredi* were still in use for rapid communication, but the ordinary Goths and Romans were not permitted to use them for private purposes,[5] and these horses were apparently supplied by the state, for the Spaniards, who furnished the fast horses to the Roman government, were provoked when they were asked also to supply the usual *paraveredi*.[6] It was, indeed, Spain where the

[1] "Amoenitate civitatis in *paraveredorum et annonarum* praebitione proprii cives fatigantur expensis. quapropter ne laedat urbem amoenitas sua aut res praeconii fiat causa dispendii, *paraveredorum et annonarum* praebitionem secundum evectiones concessas in assem publicum constituimus imputari" (533), Cassiodorus, *Variae*, XII. 15.

[2] "*Pulveratica* quoque iudices funditus amputantes trium tantum etiam dierum praesulibus annonas praeberi secundum vetera constituta decernimus, suis expensis facta tarditate vecturis. legis enim administrantes remedio, non oneri esse voluerunt," *ibid.*

[3] "Iudices quoque provinciae vel curiales atque defensores tam de cursu quam de aliis rebus illicita dicuntur possessoribus irrogare dispendia: quod te perquirere et sub ratione legum emendare censemus . . . Iudex vero Romanus propter expensas provincialium, quae gravare pauperes suggeruntur, per annum in unumquodque municipium semel accidat: cui non amplius quam triduanae praebeantur *annonae*, sicut legum cauta tribuerunt. maiores enim nostri discursus iudicum non oneri, sed compendio provincialibus esse voluerunt," v. 14.

[4] "Atque ideo de veteribus frugibus prudentia tua futuram vincat inopiam, quia tanti fuit anni praeteriti felix ubertas, ut et venturis mensibus provisa sufficiant. reponatur omne quod ad victum quaeritur. facile privatus necessaria reperit, cum se publicus *apparatus* expleverit," XII. 25, and see in the *Index*.

[5] IV. 47, v. 5.

[6] "Exactorum quoque licentia amplius fertur a provincialibus extorqueri, quam nostro cubiculo constat inferri. quod diligenti examinatione discussum ad hunc vos modum functiones publicas revocare decernimus, quem Alarici atque Eurici temporibus constat illatas. *Paraveredorum* itaque subvectiones

fast horses had been procured since the fourth century,[1] and
even as late as the ninth century the Spaniards were expected
to supply *veredi*.[2]  Hence the highways are in Spain called
*via de vereda*.[3]

Louis I of Germany, apparently influenced by the con-
temporaneous revival of the Spanish supply of horses to his
brother, uses the expression *veredi aut veredarii* in a German
formula of a document,[4] but this formula is not used in any
other document that has come down to us.  But the combination *"veredos* vel *paraveredos* exigere" occurs sufficiently often,
to show that the old Roman distinction between the swift

exigere eos, qui habent *veredos* adscriptos, provincialium querela comperimus.
quod nullum penitus sinatis praesumere, quando per turpissimos quaestus
et possessor atteritur et commeantium celeritas impeditur" (523–6), *ibid.*,
v. 39.

[1] "Favore tuo factum est, ut evectionum adminicula sumeremus, quibus
familiares mei empturi equos curules ad Hispaniam commearent" (399), Sym-
machi *Epistulae*, VII. 48 (in *MGH.*, *Scrip. antiq.*), similarly VII. 105, 106.

[2] "Sicut ceteri Franci homines cum Comite suo in exercitum pergant . . . et
missis nostris quos pro rerum oportunitate illas in partes miserimus, aut legatis
qui de partibus Hispaniae ad nostras missi fuerint *paratas* faciant et ad sub-
vectionem eorum *veredos* donent, ipsi videlicet et illi quorum progenitoribus,
temporibus avi nostri Karoli, ad ipsum facere institutum fuit.  Si autem hi, qui
*veredos* acceperint, reddere eos neglexerint, et eorum interveniente negligentia
perditi seu mortui fuerint, secundum legem Francorum eis, quorum fuerunt,
secundum leges Francorum restituantur vel restaurentur" (844), *España
sagrada*, vol. XXIX, p. 452 and Devic et Vaissete, *Histoire générale de Languedoc*,
vol. II, Preuves, p. 244.  This is based on the privilege granted to the Spanish
fugitives in 815, *ibid.*, p. 98.

[3] "Finit se in carraria de *vereda*, quae discurrit de Turio pro ad porta de
Condis" (after 916), *España sagrada*, vol. XXXIV, p. 481; "usque in *viride
medio*" (900), *Portugaliae monumenta historica, Dipl. et chart.*, p. 9; "estrata de
*uerede* et sepe," *ibid.*, "agro que disrupit *urueda* integrum," *ibid.*, "in via quam
dicunt de *vereda*," *ibid.*, p. 11; "in istrada qui discurrit via de *uereda*" (921),
*ibid.*, p. 15.

[4] "Nullus dux vel comes nec quilibet superioris aut inferioris ordinis iudex
sive missus in eodem loco nec in omnibus ad eum pertinentibus, vel mansiones
sibi parare, vel invadere, aut pastum iumentis suis aut suorum diripere aut
inde *veredos aut veredarios*, exigere . . . audeant," E. de Rozière, *Recueil général
des formules du Vᵉ au Xᵉ siècle*, Paris 1859, p. 189.  So, too, in a French document: "Nullus judex publicus . . . ad causas audiendas, aut mansionaticos exi-
gendos, vel *paratas* aut *veredos* requirendos, ullo unquam tempore ingredi
audeat" (835), Tardif, *Monuments historiques*, p. 90.

and draught horses was not entirely forgotten.[1] We find,
however, here *freda*, as well as *veredos*, and this form appears
as *freda*, *frida*, *fridda*, *fretus*, etc., in the formula "*freda*
exigere" in hundreds of Frankish immunities from the
seventh century on.[2] That the Frankish immunity is based
on the Roman immunities is proved not only by their identity in spirit, but also in phraseology, for where the Roman
law "De immunitate concessa" of 365 speaks of "*vectigalia*
vel caetera eiusmodi quae inferri fisco moris est, sibi adserant
esse *concessa*"[3] the Merovingian documents have the equivalent *fredi concessi*.[4] *Freda* is not derived from *inferre*, the
technical term for "paying the tax or revenue," because
both in Italy and in France *inferendum* had the meaning of

[1] "*Freda* vel *parafreda* exigere," *MGH.*, *Formulae*, p. 398; "*viridos* sive
*paraveridos* tantos," *ibid.*, p. 49; "nec *freda* exigenda sive *parafredos*" (750),
Marini, *I papiri diplomatici*, p. 103; "*viredus* sive *paraveridus* decem" (716),
*MGH.*, *Dipl.*, vol. I, p. 76.

[2] "Ut nullus iudex publicus . . . *freda* nec sthopha nec herebanno recipere
nec requirere non praesumat" (664), *MGH.*, *Dipl.*, vol. I, p. 27; "ut nullus
iudex publicus . . . nec ad causas audiendum, nec fideiussores tollendum, nec
*freda* exigendum, nec mansiones faciendum, nec rotaticum infra urbes vel in
mercatis extorquendum, nec ullas paratas aut quaslibet redibutiones exactare,
praesumatur" (673), *ibid.*, p. 30; "et nullus quilibet de iudicebus . . . nec ad
causas audiendum, nec *frida* exigendum, nec mansiones faciendum, nec paratas
requirendum, nec nullas redebutiones requirendum . . . ipsa iudiciaria potestas
non praesumat ingredere" (662), *ibid.*, p. 37; "ut nullus iudex publicus . . . nec
ad causas audiendum, nec fideiussores tollendum, nec *freda* exigendum, nec
mansiones faciendum, nec rotaticum infra urbes vel in mercatis extorquendum,
nec ullas paratas aut quaslibet redibutiones exactare praesumatur" (683),
*ibid.*, p. 50, and, similarly, p. 56; "ut nullus iudex poplicus ad causas audiendum
vel *fridda* exigendum ibidem introitum nec ingressum habire non deberit"
(696), *ibid.*, p. 61.

[3] "Hoc ideo dicimus, quia nonnulli priuatorum elicitas suffragio proferunt
sanctiones, quibus *vectigalia*, vel caetera eiusmodi, quae inferri fisco moris est,
sibi adserant esse *concessa*: hoc, si quando militibus nostris, hisve, qui in Palatio
nostro degunt praestamus, adprobantibus se sacramentis militaribus adtineri,
quod concessimus firmum sit atque robustum," *Cod. Theod.*, XI. 12. 3.

[4] "Sub omni emunitate hoc ipsum monasterium vel congregatio sua sibimet
omnes *fredos concessos* debeat possidere," *MGH.*, *Dipl.*, vol. I, p. 17; "nisi sub
emunitatis nomine omni tempore cum omnes *fretas concessas* pars ipsius monasterii perenniter deberet possidere" (718), *ibid.*, p. 79, and similarly p. 81; "sub
inmunitatis nomeni, cum omnis *fredus concessus*" (716), Lauer and Samaran,
*op. cit.*, p. 24; "cum omnis *fridus* ad integrum sybymed *concessus*" (716), *ibid.*

"a special tax not included in the immunity," [1] hence it may be found in the same document with *freda*.[2] This *inferendum* was distinctly a yearly tribute and as such might be abolished,[3] and yet the influence of *inferenda* on *vereda*, so as to change it to *freda* (which, however, is not a yearly tribute but a special tax) is not excluded, for it occurs already in a document of the year 562, where it has distinctly the meaning of any revenue that may be included in the immunity.[4]

In the *Lex romana raetica curiensis* the Lat. "mulcta" and "sumtus vel expensae litis" of the *Interpretatio* of the Theodosian Code are translated by *fretum*,[5] i. e., here *fretum* has the meaning of "judicial fee, fine." But there are two passages where *fretum* refers to the "principale negotium" of the

[1] "Praesenti admonitione praecipimus, ut omne, quod mutuum pro eadem causa ab extraneis accipere poterant, a tua experientia in publico detur et a rusticis ecclesiae paulatim ut habuerint accipiatur, ne dum in tempore coangustantur, quod eis postmodum sufficere in *inferendum* poterat, prius compulsi vilius vendant et horreis minime sufficiant" (591), Gregorii I *Registri*, I. 42.

[2] "Annis singulis *inferendum* solidos sex *inferendos* in alios sex de remissaria auir pagensis *inferendo* in fisci ditiones reddebant . . . ut nullus iudex publicus in ipsas curtes ad agendum, nec ad *freda* exigendum . . . intraret . . . nisi quod ipsam *inferendam* idem abbas per se ipsum aut per missos suos annis singulis in sacellum publicum reddere deberet" (705), *MGH.*, *Dipl.* I, p. 65.

[3] "Tributo Saxones, quem reddere consuaeverant, per preceptionem Dagoberti habent indultum. Quinnentas vaccas *inferendalis* annis singolis a Chlothario seniore censiti reddebant, quod a Dagoberto cassatum est" (632), Fredegarii Scholastici *libri IV*, in *MGH.*, *Scrip. rer. merov.*, vol. II, p. 158; "centum vaccas *inferendales*, quae ei de ducatu Cinomannico annis singulis solvebantur . . . visus est omni futuro tempore, annuatim concessisse," *ibid.*, p. 415; "Dagoberchthus quondam rex . . . vaccas cento soldaris, quod in *inferenda* de pago Cinomaneco in fisce dicionebus sperabatur, ad ipsa sancta basileca annis singolis concessissit" (716), *MGH.*, *Dipl.* I, p. 74.

[4] "Per has praesentes iubemus praeceptiones ut neque vos neque iuniores vestri aut successores vel missi de palatio nostro discurrentes ipsum Gallum abbatem monasterii sui, amicis, susceptis vel qui per eundem sperare videntur, vel unde legitimo redebet mitio, inquietare, nec *inferendas* sumere, nec de res eorum in lege minuere audeatis. Sed liceat eis sub sermone nostrae tuitionis vel sub emunitate nostra quietos vivere ac residere," *MGH.*, *Dipl.* I, p. 12.

[5] "Quod si illi liberti ipsa causa persequere noluerint, ad suos persecutores nullum *fretum* pro tale causa non requiratur (erant a *mulctae* condemnatione securi)," IV. 8. 1; "si postea, cum inter illos directum iudicium fuerit, et iudices *fretum* et res fuerint redditas (propter repetendos *sumtus vel expensas litis*)," IV. 15. 2.   .

Code,[1] and these demand a special investigation. We find
in one of these passages a reference to two kinds of judges,
one called "publicus," the other "privatus." As the public
judge is invariably mentioned in the Frankish immunities as
the one who is not to exact the *fredum*, nor demand other
contributions, it is evident that his usual function is that of
collecting or causing to collect such revenues for the state.
This is borne out by the specific statement in the Raetian
laws that the public judges are those who sit in fiscal cases
and exact the revenue,[2] where the corresponding *Interpretatio* speaks of "exactores." They also attend to criminal
cases,[3] even of churchmen.[4] In the beginning of the sixth
century this judge was still called by the old name *rector
provinciae*,[5] whose functions had previously been identical
with those of the *iudex publicus*. This latter name was
appropriate for him even at that time for he was called
"iudex" and also had the supervision of "opera publica."[6]

[1] "Si quicumque homo ad duos iudices, ad publicum et ad privatum — hoc
est privatus, qui actor ecclesiarum est —, si ille homo de una facultatem ad
ambos illos iudices causa habere voluerit, ut ad unum de illos iudices iunior sit
et *fretum* conponat, et ad illum alterum iudicem actum querit: ille homo, qui
istum fecerit, ipsam rem vel actum, quem querit, non accipiet et insuper quintam
partem facultatis sue de illas res, qui sub illum iudicem habet, ad illam civitatem det, in cuius finibus res, de quo agitur, fuerit constituta," II. 16. 2; "nullus
iudex alienas res nec per forcia nec per nullo malo ingenio, absente illo, cuius
res sunt, nullus homo eas invadere non presumat, nisi si eas si per iudicium
potuerit vindicare, salvum iudices *fretum*," IV. 19. 1.

[2] "*Judices publicos*, qui fescales causas iudicant vel exigunt," XII. 2. 3.

[3] "Omnes causas criminales ante *publicos iudices* finiantur," XVI. 4. 1.

[4] "Clericus si de criminalem causam ante *publicum iudicem* accusatus fuerit,
sine omnem dilationem ipsam causam respondeat," XVIII. 11.

[5] "Formulae rectoris provinciae. Omnino provide decrevit antiquitas iudices ad provinciam mitti, ne possit ad nos veniendo mediocritas ingravari. Quis
enim latronum ferret audaciam, si longe positam cognoscerent disciplinam?
absolute poterat vis permissa grassari, si conquerens tardius crederetur audiri,
sed quanto melius in ipsis cunabilis adhuc mollia reprimere quam indurata
crimina vindicare! in compendium mittimus mala, si praesentia faciamus esse
iudicia. quis enim audeat peccare, cum supra cervices suas districtionem cog-
noverit imminere? Et ideo te illi provinciae rectorem per illam indictionem
nostra mittit electio . . . tibi fiscalium tributorum credita monstratur exactio,"
Cassiodorus, *Variae*, VI. 21.

[6] *Cod. Theod.* XV. 1 (*De operibus publicis*), passim.

The various immunities from the *iudex publicus* are immunities against the competency of his court. Thus, in addition to those mentioned above by Cassiodorus, we may cite the immunity from maintaining the court house, from the *mansionaticum*, which was subject to his jurisdiction by a law of the year 369.[1] If we now turn to the first of the two passages in the Raetian laws, we find that it is not permissible to pay the *fretum* to the junior judge, because the iudex publicus, with whom the "principale negotium" lies, is alone entitled to collect the *fretum*. We have already observed that in Italy the *annonae* had taken the place of the older contribution of *veredi*, and that these were used for the judge's fees. This is distinctly implied in a law of 383, where the judges are not permitted to exact from the provincials anything more than food and fodder.[2] In spite of the prohibition to exact horses, the Merovingians, as the documents show, not only exacted them, but also the pecuniary commutation, the *fredum*, for the *veredi*, or the *annonae* of the Italians, nay, the Carolingians found it possible to tax the Spaniards, not only with the ancient *veredi*, but also with the *fredum*.[3]

In the *Lex ribuaria* it is the *judex fiscalis*, that is, again the *judex publicus*, who collects the *fretum*, of which one third is paid over to the fiscus, "in order that the peace may be last-

---

[1] "Unusquisque iudex in his locis sedem constituat, in quibus oportet omnibus presto esse rectorem, non deuerticula deliciosa sectetur. Addimus sane, vt quisque provinciae praesidentem propria possessione susceperit, ager, quem diuersorium habuerit praedictus in transitu, fisci viribus vindicetur: ita enim iudices *mansiones* instruere, et instaurare nitentur," i. 7. 4.

[2] "Det operam iudex vt praetorium suum ipse componat. Caeterum comiti neque rectori prouinciae plus aliquid praestabitur, quam nos concessimus in *annonis, seu cellariis*," i. 10. 3.

[3] "Ut nulles judex publicus . . . ingredi praesumat, nec *freda* aut tributa vel paratas aut *veredos* seu mansiones accipere . . . audeat" (844), Devic et Vaissete, *op. cit.*, vol. II, Preuves, col. 234; but the document is, probably, spurious, as the other two documents where *freda* and *parafredi* occur (*ibid.*, cols. 364 and 366) certainly are.

ing."[1]  The same reference to the maintenance of peace is found in the composition of the *fredum* in the *Lex Baiuwariorum*,[2] but here the *fredum* includes surety, fideiussor, and pay, so that it is obvious that *pro fredo* means "for the keeping of the peace," hence a surety alone may be a *fredum*.[3]  Wherever, therefore, the combination *pro fredo* occurs, nearly always to be paid "in fisco" or "in publico,"[4] we have a reference to the maintenance of peace, a duty which in the fifth and following centuries was left to the great body of judges, immediately below the rectores provinciae, who were known as *defensores* or *assertores pacis*[5] and who were by special regal authority invested among the Visigoths with the right of "making peace."[6]

---

[1] "Nec nullus *judex fiscalis* de quacumque libet causa *freta* non exigat, priusquam facinus conponatur . . . *Fretum* autem non illi iudici tribuat cui culpa commisit, sed illi, qui solucionem recipit, terciam partem coram testibus fisco tribuat, ut pax stabilis permaneat," LXXXIX.

[2] "Et quisquis de res ecclesiae furtivis probatus fuerit, ad partem fisci *pro fredo* praebeat fideiussorem, et donet wadium de 40 solidis, et tantum solvat, quantum iudex iusserit, et quantum durius solverit, *tantum firmior erit pax ecclesiae*," I. 1. 6.

[3] "Et donet wadium comiti illo *de fredo*," 1. 2. 14.

[4] "Et *pro fredo* in publico solvat solidos 40, ut exinde sit reverentia sacerdotum, et honor ecclesiasticus non condamnetur neque praesumptio crescat in plebe," I. 1. 9; "si autem vim abstraxerit et iniuriam ecclesiae fecerit, conponat 36 solidos ad ecclesiam et *fredo* (*frido*) solvat in fisco 40 solidos, quare contra legem fecit et ecclesiae honorem non inpendit et Dei reverentiam non habuit, ut et alii cognuscant, quod sit timor Dei in christianis, et honorem ecclesiis inpendat," *Leges Alamannorum*, III. 3.

[5] "Quoties de paruis criminibus, id est, vnius serui fuga, aut sublati iumenti, aut modicae terrae, seu domus inuasae, vel certi furti, id est, detenti aut peruenti, sub criminis nomine actio fortasse processerit, ad mediocres iudices qui publicam disciplinam obseruant, id est, aut *defensores* aut *assertores pacis*, vindictam eius rei decernimus pertinere. Ad rectorem vero prouinciae illud negotium criminale perueniat, vbi de personarum inscriptione agitur, vel maior est, quae non nisi ab ordinario iudice, recitata legis sententia debeat terminari," *Interpretatio* to *Cod. Theod.* II. 1. 8.

[6] "Omnium negotiorum causas ita iudices habeant deputatas, ut et criminalia et cetera negotia terminandi sit illis concessa licentia. *Pacis* vero *adsertores* non alias dirimant causas, nisi quas illis regia deputaverit ordinandi potestas. *Pacis* enim *adsertor* est, qui sola *faciende pacis* intentione regali sola distinatur autoritate," *Lex Visig.*, II. 1. 15.

The Visigothic laws, as codified, have undergone considerable modifications from their Roman origin in the fifth century, but even through all the changes it is possible to notice that the old *evectio veredorum*, the furnishing of horses for the judges and bailiffs, lay at the foundation of at least a part of their fees. In Theudis' law of 546 the bailiffs are supposed to furnish their own horses while executing orders, that is, summoning a party, but they reimburse themselves from the person in whose interest they travel, by charging a solidus for each horse, four being the maximum allowed.[1] The *Lex Visigothorum* seems to have here an older text, for while there is the same reference to the bailiff's horses, nothing whatsoever is said about the pecuniary commutation. The interesting part of this latter law is the one which says that these horses are "for the road and dignity," so that where in the east the reference is to the maintenance of the peace, we have here a similar provision for the maintenance of dignity.[2] If we now go back to the fifth century we come to an intermediate time when the Visigoths, whether in Spain or in southern France, must have considered the commutation of the older *veredus* as intended for the maintenance of peace or dignity. Indeed, the judges are specifically referred to by Cassiodorus as *dignitates*.[3] This designation is ap-

[1] "Conpulsores vel executores decreto perstringimus, ut non pro sua conmoda exigant volumtate, sed ab eis, quos propria evectione conpulerint, subvectum tantum super eum accipiant caballorum. Nec illi prius conmoda compulsionis exigant, quam suas in iudicio litigantes exercent actiones: conmoda quoque iuxta huius consulti seriem accepturi, id est, ut in milibus quinquaginta accipiant per caballo uno solido uno, ea videlicet ratione, ut in minoribus causis duo tantum, in maioribus vero quatuor caballi sufficiant, et si quis plures caballos ultra hunc numerum ducere voluerit, absque ullo deductorum damno suo tantantum reputabit ornatu," K. Zeumer, *Ueber zwei neuentdeckte westgothische Gesetze*, in *Neues Archiv*, vol. XXIII, p. 78 *f*.
[2] "Saiones, cum pro causis alienis vadunt, si minor causa est et persona, duos caballus tantum ab eo, cuius causa est, accipiat fatigandos; si vero maior persona fuerit et causa, non amplius quam sex caballos et pro itinere et *pro dignitate* debebit accipere," II. 1. 26.
[3] "Tributa quidem nobis annua devotione persolvitis: sed nos maiore vicis-

parently not older than the end of the fifth century, whereas the use of *annonae* or *apparatus* for the judge's fees dates at least from the end of the fourth century.

We have accordingly two groups of derivatives in the Gothic language, from *veredus* towards the end of the fifth century and from a popular *redus* at some time in the fourth century. The first, in accordance with the designations *assertor pacis* and *dignitas*, current at the time, produces Goth. *ga-wairthi* "peace," *wairths* "worthy, dignified, worth, price," and from these are derived ONorse *veror̃*, AS. *weor̃o*, OFrisian *werth* "worth," Welsh *gwerth* "price," Lithuanian *vertas*, OPrussian *werths* "worthy," OBulgarian *vrêd* "harm," originally, as still in Croatian, etc., "worth." The Roman *reda* was originally a light carriage, especially adapted for the use of couriers [1] and it is not at all improbable that as such it was really of Gallic origin, as surmised by Roman writers. But *veredus* was already known to Martial in the year 101 as a fast hunting horse, hence the use of *veredus*, though not recorded, must popularly be much older, to have lost its original meaning of "posthorse." Now Rostowzew and Preisigke have shown conclusively that the Persian post existed uninterruptedly in the east from the time of Herodotus and Xenophon, [2] and the document of the year 259 B.C., which gives an account of the post in Ptolemaic Egypt shows that the Persian terms for various parts of the service intro-

situdine decoras vobis reddimus *dignitates*, ut vos ab incursantium pravitate defendant qui nostris iussionibus obsecundant . . . quaerat iudex inter vos causas et non inveniat . . . improbis iudicem, testem bonis moribus destinamus . . . cui vos convenit prudenter oboedire, quia utrumque laudabile est, ut bonus populus iudicem benignum faciat et mansuetus iudex gravissimum populum aequabili ratione componat," Cassiodorus, *Variae*, VI., 24; "exeunt a nobis *dignitates* relucentes quasi a sole radii, ut in orbis nostri parti resplendeat custodita iustitia," *ibid.*, VI. 2. 3, et passim.

[1] Daremberg and Saglio, *Dictionnaire des antiquités*, sub *cursus publicus*, p. 1657.

[2] M. Rostowzew, *Angariae*, in *Klio*, vol. VI, p. 249 *ff.*; F. Preisigke, *Die ptolemäische Staatspost*, *ibid.*, vol. VII, p. 241 *ff.*

duced into Egypt during the Persian domination, have reached Rome and the West through a Greek transformation of the vocabulary. This explains at once why we meet in the cursus publicus of the fourth century A.D. with what otherwise would seem to be hybrid words, such as *paraveredus* and *parangaria*. If then *veredus* could have entered the Latin language only through the Greek, we at once get the Greek βερέδος or βεραιδος as a much older term, which through an intermediary βρέδος would produce the recorded ρέδη, ρέδιον hence Latin *reda* "chariot," and through a form ἐρέδος the other forms ἐριδία, ἐρωδία "chariot," actually recorded by Hesychius. That βρέδος, that is, Fρέδος actually existed is proved by the Coptic *vrehi, verehi* "chariot" which cannot, as is generally done, be referred to the Semito-Egyptian *mārka buthah*, but is a transformation of βρέδος to βρέος, βερέος, which again are not hypothetical forms, for βέρρης "runner," βερρεύει "he runs" are recorded by Hesychius. Therefore there is absolutely no reason for deriving *reda* from the Celtic, for which there is no other authority than Quintilian's, but we must consider it as directly derived from the Greek of Ptolemaic Egypt.

While all the languages have derivatives from this *red-* distinctly referring to the postroads, the Gothic has no other meaning for this group than that of the current substitute for the supply of posthorses by the *apparatus* or *parata*,[1] which, however, the other languages also record. While the Gothic has *raidjan, ga-raidjan* "to arrange, prepare," *ga-raideins* "arrangement," *ga-raiths* "arranged, determined," OHG. has *reita* "vereda,[2] reda, chariot," *rîtari, ritari* "horseman, rider," *rîtan* "ride," *reiti* "paratus," *gareiti* "biga, falera, quadriga," AS. *rád* "riding, journey, way," *rad* "cart,

---

[1] "Mansio *parata*," a distinct reference to the well-provided post-station, is already used by Ambrose.

[2] "Vereda *reita, reida, reide, reit*," Steinmeyer and Sievers, *Althochdeutsche Glossen*, vol. IV, p. 107, also vol. I, p. 488.

chariot," *rídan* "to ride," *ridda* "knight, rider," *raed, hraed, geraed* "swift, quick, ready," ONorse *ríða* "to ride," *greiða* "to make ready," etc., OIrish *riadaim* "I drive," *reid*, OWelsh *ruid*, OBreton *roed* "plain, smooth." From this group cannot be separated Goth. *ga-rēdan* "to have a mind to," for in the compounds *ur-rēdan, faura-ga-rēdan* this *rēdan* has the meaning "arrange, determine." This at once connects ONorse *ráða*, AS. *ráedan*, OHG. *rātan* "advise," etc., with it. In the German *gerät* "advice, tool, harness" we have the two meanings connected. In the Slavic languages we have two series, *rad-* and *rend-*, which belong here. The first, giving Russian *rad* "prepared, glad," Polish *rada* "advice," etc., is obviously derived from the German. The nasalised form, which, however, in Lithuanian and Lettish also occurs unnasalised, is unquestionably older. We have OBulgarian *rędŭ*, Bulg. *red*, Pol. *rząd* "order," Lith. *rinda* "row," *redas* "order," Let. *rēdīt, rinda, rist, ridu* "to arrange."

The positive proof of the relation of this group of words to *veredus* in the sense of "apparatus, parata" is given by its presence in the Romance languages exclusively in the sense of "apparatus, parata," that is, of "equipage, harness, supply of horses for work," etc. We find here the LLatin forms *corredum* and *arredum* and its many derivatives. We have *arredio* "apparatus bellicus" recorded by Ducange in the 14. century, but the Italian *arredare*, Spanish *arrear*, OFrench *arréer*, Provençal *arredar, arrezar* "to equip, adorn" prove the existence of the word before. *Arezamentum* "equipment" is recorded in the 13. cent.[1] It is this *arez-*, more properly *arrez-*, which has produced *arnes* "baggage, equipment, household goods," etc.,[2] more especially "equipment of a

[1] "Et vasculis tam panis quam vini et de omnibus aliis *arezamentis* et rebus," *Acta Sanctorum*, October XII, p. 75.
[2] "Quod animalia militum et *arnes* sui corporis nec apparamenta domus non pignorentur" (1283), *Cortes do los antigüos reinos de Aragon y de Valencia*, Madrid 1896, vol. I, p. 151; "De cariando *hernesio* regis ad eum. Mandatum

horse, harness."[1] Similarly *corredum* is a close translation of "apparatus" and more especially refers to the contribution in kind due to the sovereign when passing through the country, provender, fodder,[2] but the Spanish *correo* has best preserved the original meaning of "post." There is a very large number of variations of these words,[3] and the OFrench *conroi, corroi* has preserved the original meaning of "apparatus."

This series of words, while representing the old connotation, is comparatively new in the documents, no recorded instance being earlier than the 12. cent. In Italy the corresponding word in the Frankish documents, that is, from the end of the 8. cent. on, is *foderum*. Previous to Charlemagne there is found not the slightest reference to the exaction of provender, because neither the Justinian Code nor the Langobard law mentions it explicitly, but beginning with the year 792 "*fredum* exigere" of the Frankish documents is for Italy changed to "*foderum* exigere,"[4] and this *foderum*

est vicecomitibus Lond' quod habere faciant Willelmo Hordel clerico unam bonam carectam ad denarios ipsius regis, ad *herenesium* regis ad eum cariandum" (1228), *Close Rolls, Henry III*, vol. I, 75; "quod nemini civi Civitatis Catinae cuiuscumque conditionis, et gradus existat, sit licitum ultra quantitatem unciarum auri trigintaquinque in *arnesio* promittere neque dare, quod si seous fecerit, et pervenerit in casu restitutionis dotis, quod maritus ipsum *arnesium* ultra dictam quantitatem lucrifaciat ipso facto, nulla servata actione ei cui competere possit ratione restitutionis *arnesii* supradicti, cui consuetudini renuntiari non possit" (1345), *Constitutiones Regni Siciliae*, p. 117.

[1] For this and similar meanings see Ducange, sub *arnense, arnescum, arnese, arnesium, arnexium, arneysium, arnitus, harnascha, harnasium, harnesiatus.*

[2] "Ut nec nostro, nec aliorum tempore quandam convivia, quae vulgo *Coreede*, vel giste vocantur, in villis praenominatis exigere, vel quaerere liceat" (1157), in Ducange sub *conredium;* "Imperatori servitium a vassallis deberi pro *corredo* Imperiali, ut videlicet quando Imperator transierit per illum locum, contribuat in sumptibus ejus," *ibid.*

[3] Ducange records under *conredium* the following: *conredum, corrodium, conreus, correda, conragium, conregium, conreium, correium, coureium, corrogium.*

[4] "Ut super servientes iam fatae ecclesiae mansionaticos vel *foderum* nullus audeat prendere aut exactare ullo umquam tempore, excepto si evenerit, quod nos ipsi aut dilectus filius noter Pippinus vel regale presidium propter impedimenta inimicorum partibus Foroiulensibus aut in fine Tarvisiani advenerint"

is also recorded as *frodum* [1] and *forum*. [2] These forms are by no means mere misspellings, but were actually in use, as is proved, for the first, by the forms *froyre, froyrage, frourerius,* recorded in Ducange, apparently from an intermediary *frodrum,* [3] and, for the second, by the OHG. *vure, fuora* "pastum." [4] Fodrum is referred to as "annona militaris," [5] so that we have in the change of the Frankish immunity for Italy a compliance with the old Roman institution by which annonae were paid instead of the *veredi.* There is a strange confusion of forms in the Germanic languages for "food" or "fodder." OHG. has not only the above-mentioned *fuora,* but also *fôtar, fôtida,* and the verbs *fuottan, fôtjan, fotarjan* "to feed." The Goth. records only *fôdjan* "to feed," *fôdeins* "food, nourishment," while the ONorse has both *fôðra* and *fôða* "to feed." The other Germanic languages have similar double forms. The documents show conclusively that at the end of the 8. cent. the current form in Italy was approximately *foder,* with probable phonetic variations, while the Goth. records only forms without the *r.* The latter can only be a back formation from the first, even as both forms exist side by side in the other Germanic languages. But the substitution of the "annonae" for the *veredi,* so characteristic for Italy, coupled with the substitution of *foderum, frodrum,* etc., for *fredum* on Italian soil, makes it certain that *foderum*

(792), *MGH., Die Urkunden der Karolinger,* vol I, p. 234. For further quotations of *foderum, fodrum* in Italy see J. Ficker, *Urkunden zur Reichs- und Rechtsgeschichte Italiens,* Innsbruck, 1874, vol. IV, in the *Index,* E. Mayer, *Italienische Verfassungsgeschichte von der Gothenzeit bis zur Zunftherrschaft,* Leipzig 1909, in the *Index,* and G. Waitz, *Deutsche Verfassungsgeschichte,* 2nd ed., vol. IV, p. 15 *ff.*

[1] "Nec *froda* exigenda" (spurious document), Ughelli, *Italia sacra,* vol. II, col. 244.

[2] See Ducange, sub *forum* 2.

[3] Ughelli, *Italia sacra,* vol. I, col. 419 (1188).

[4] Steinmeyer and Sievers, *Althochdeutsche Glossen,* vol. I, p. 346, vol. IV, p. 416.

[5] "Inhibuit a plebeis ulterius annonas militares, quas vulgo *foderum* vocant," Waitz, *op. cit.,* p. 16.

is a transposed form for *foredum*, from *veredum*, while *forum*, which may have influenced this change, is due to a confusion with *forum* "price at which provisions are sold in the market."[1]

Thus it appears that the earliest forms in the Germanic languages are those derived from the current *reda* of the Romans, which is even older than the Christian era and may have entered the Gothic language before the age of migration. Another set is connected with the Visigothic rule in Spain, producing the root *wairth-* in Gothic and similar forms elsewhere. A third refers to the Ostrogothic and Lombard substitution of the "annonae," producing the stem *fod-*. In France, where the *veredi* gave way to the monetary commutation, the *fredum*, the Germans formed the word *fridu*, OSaxon *frithu*, AS. *friðu*, *freoðo*, *freoð*, ONorse *friðr* "peace." From this root the Goth. has formed *ga-frithôn* "to atone," *freidjan* "spare," from the OHG. *friten* "to enclose, protect," while the French has stopped in *frais* at the meaning "expense."

---

In the Salic law the fine *fredum* is now paid to the fiscus, now to the judge, but there is one compound fine, *fredo et faido*,[2] which needs a thorough investigation, since the usual meaning of *faida* "blood feud" is here entirely out of place. The assumption that the blood feud played any part in Ger-

[1] "Exercitui destinato ordinante illo annonas fecimus secundum *forum* rerum venalium comparari" (535), Cassiodorus, *Variae*, x. 18; "et per omnes civitatis legitimus *forus* et mensuras faciat secundum habundantia temporis" (744), *MGH., Capitularia*, vol. I, p. 30.

[2] "Si cuiuslibet de potentibus seruus qui per diuersa possedent de crimine habere suspectus, dominus secrecius cum testibus condicatur ut intra xx noctes ipsum ante iudicem debet praesentare. Quod si institutum tempus, intercedente conuidio, non fuerit praesentatus, ipse dominus statutum sui iusta modum culpe *inter fredo et fedo* (*fretum et feitum, fredo et faido, fredum et foedum*) compensetur," *Pact.* 12; "*inter freto et faido* sunt MDCCC. din. x," xxxv. 7, cod. 1; "si ei fuit judecatum ut in *ex faido et fredo* solidos quindece pro ac causa fidem facere debirit" (693), *MGH., Dipl.*, vol. I, p. 59.

manic law as a Germanic institution is incorrect, for, although Tacitus distinctly refers to such a custom among the Germans, the practice of it in law is amply accounted for by the Roman decrees, which countenanced it in certain cases. It has arisen from the legality of killing in self-defence, as laid down in the *Lex Cornelia de sicariis*, which has been of great importance in shaping certain later enactments, of which I shall speak at another time. What makes the derivation of the German feud from the Roman precedent a certainty is not merely the resemblance of the two, but certain verbal identities, which exclude every chance of accidental resemblance. In the year 323 it was enacted that one who led the barbarians treacherously, "*scelerata factione*," against the Romans, should be burned,[1] and in 391 it was specifically ordered to lynch the attacking highwayman without legal procedure,[2] and a few years later (397) a man joining a rebellion, "*quisque sceleratam inierit factionem aut factionis ipsius susceperit sacramenta*," was beheaded as a "*majestatis reus*," while his possessions were confiscated.[3] *Factio* is frequently mentioned in the *Codex Justinianus*[4] and in the glosses in the sense of "sedition," while *factiosus* is "seditious."[5] Hence the *Lex Alamannorum*, which has a caption

---

[1] *Cod. Theod.*, VII. 1.

[2] "*Liberis resistendi cunctis tribuimus facultatem: ut quicumque militum, vel priuatorum, ad agros nocturnos populator intrauerit, aut itinere frequentata, insidiis adgressionis obsederit, permissa cuicumque licentia, dignus illico supplicio subiugetur, ac mortem quam minabatur, excipiat, et id quod intendebat, incurrat: melius est enim incurrere in tempore, quam post exitum vindicari; vestram igitur vobis permittimus ultionem, et quos sermo est punire iudicio, subiugamus edicto. Nullus parcat militi, cui obuiari leto oporteat ut latroni*," IX. 14. 2.

[3] IX. 14. 3.

[4] "*Seditionum concitatores vel duces factionum*," 1. 6. 9. D. 28. 3, 1. 16. D. 49. 1; "*sceleratam inire factionem* cum aliquo," 1. 5. pr. C. 9. s; "*latrones qui factionem* habent," 1. 11. 2. D. 48. 19.

[5] "*Eruptio factiosa*," 1. 2. 3. C. 11; "*familia factiosa*," 1. 13. 2. D. 39. 4; "*factiosus δημοκόπος, νεωριστής, στασιαστής, πολυμήχανος*, rixas et scandala gerens, fallax, deceptor, falsus," *Corpus glossariorum latinorum*.

"de eo qui mortem ducis consiliatus fuerit," exactly corresponding to the *Lex Cornelia,* quite correctly renders this
in one redaction by "De *factiosis.*"[1]

The Anglo-Saxons know the feud under the Latin name of
*factio,* and here, too, *factiosus* is the king's enemy, the outlaw, the "majestatis reus." King Eadmund tried to abate
the illegal feuds by determining that the murderer alone was
subject to blood feud; that if a relative gave him protection,
all the relative's property was forfeited to the king, and he
himself became subject to the blood feud; that if a relative
of the murdered person avenged himself upon any one else
than the actual murderer, he became an outlaw before the
king and lost all his possessions.[2] Thus we have here a mere
extension and combination of the Roman laws. The murderer and he who privately starts a *factio,* to avenge a person's death, are equally outlaws, "majestatis rei, inimici
regis," who lose all their property. It is obvious that AS.
*faehðe,* which renders the Lat. *factio, faidia,* is identical with
it, the first being derived from the second, and *fah, gefah,
fáh (mon),* a back formation from this *faehðe,* which appears
here as a translation of "inimicus regis,"[3] is used by Aelfred
for *factiosus.*[4]

In the Langobard laws the exclusion of the blood feud is
introduced by the formula "cessante *faida* id est inimicitia,"
a proof that *faida* is a strange word which needs glossing, but
"inimicitia" is identical with "inimicitiae *factio*" of the

---

[1] xxiv, cod. B.

[2] "Si quis posthac hominem occidat, ipse sibi portet inimicitiae *factionem,*"
ii, *Ead.* 1; "ut omnis tribus illo sit extra *factionem,* preter solum malefactorem,"
*ibid.,* 1:1; "si quisquam cognationis sue firmet eum postea, reus sit omnium que
habebit erga regem et portet *faidiam* (*factionem*) erga contribuales mortui,"
*ibid.,* 1. 2; "si ex mortui cognatione quis vindictam perpetret in alium aliquem
preter ipsum malefactorem, sit inimicus regis et omnium amicorum eius et perdat omne quicquid habet," *ibid.,* 1. 3.

[3] Also *Aelf.* 42; 42. 1, 4; 5. 3; ii *Aethelst.* 20. 7.

[4] "Si quis *factiosus* (*fahmon, fagmon, gefahmon*) incurrat uel ad ecclesiam
confugiat," *Aelf.* 5.

Anglo-Saxon laws, hence *faida* and *factio* are identical.[1]
Again, the Langobard law reads "De *faidosis* et armis infra
patriam non portandis," [2] where *faidosus* is the previously
mentioned *factiosus*, and the chapter "De rusticanorum
seditionem" (Roth. 280) is a close rendering of the *Lex
Cornelia*,[3] but here the formula "concilios et seditionis
facere" is identical with the "in concilio et in *facto*" [4] of the
Genoese formula, as preserved in the 12. cent., where *factum*
stands for *factio*. This *factum* is not an accidental change
from *factio*, but a confusion with *ex facto*, *in factum* of the
Roman laws, which Ulpian uses for "ex maleficio, ex delicto,"
while Modestin writes "ex peccato" for it.[5] This significance has not maintained itself in the later Roman law, but
the Germanic laws use *ex facto*, *inter facto*, *in facto* to con-
note the fine for a misdeed, chiefly such as is connected with
murder. The Langobard laws cited above have no need for
the *fredum* of the Franks, because the composition for the

[1] "De feritas et conpositionis plagarum ... sicut subter adnexum est conponatur, cessante *faida* hoc est inimicitia," *Roth.* 45; "ideo maiorem conposi-
tionem posuimus quam antiqui nostri, ut *faida*, quod est inimicitia, post ac-
cepta suprascripta conpositione postponatur," *Roth.* 74; "nam si mortua
fuerit, conponat eam secundum generositatem suam ... cessante *faida*, eo quod
nolendo fecit," *Roth.* 75; "reddant simul summa praetii, cessante *faida*, ideo
quod nolendo fecerunt," *Roth.* 138; "ita previdimus propter *faida* posponenda,
id est inimicitia pacificanda," *Roth.* 162; "cessante in hoc capitulo *faida* quod
est inimicitia," *Roth.* 326; "nolumus ut inimicidias cessent et *faida* non habeant," *Liutp.* 119; "et sit causim finita absque *faida* vel dolus," *Liutp.* 136.

[2] *MGH., Leges*, vol. IV, p. 628 (lib. I, tit. 37).

[3] "Si per quacumque causa homines rusticani se colligerint, id est *concilios
et seditionis* facere presumpserit," etc.

[4] "*In concilio* insuper neque *in facto* sis ut commune ianue uultabium uel
flaconem aut medietatem montis alti amittat" (1130), *Monumenta Historiae
Patriae*, vol. VII, col. 35; "nos iuramus quod ab hoc die in antea non erimus *in
consilio vel in facto* quod commune ianue uel perdat castrum portuueneris"
(1139), *ibid.*, col. 64; "*factu neque in assensu* ... et non ero *in consilio neque
in facto*" (1144), *ibid*, col. 98 *f.*; "et non erimus *in consilio neque in facto*, ut
imperator suas duas partes amittat" (1146), *ibid.*, col. 122.

[5] H. Erman, *Conceptio formularum actio in factum*, etc., in *Zeitschrift für
Savignystiftung*, vol. XIX, *Romanistische Abtheilung*, p. 301 *ff.* For quotations
see C. G. Bruns, *Fontes iuris romani antiqui*, 7th ed., pp. 218, 219, 220, 229, 235,
242.

*faida* includes the amount paid over to the fiscus "for the keeping of the peace." There is but one reference to *fredum* in Rothar's law, where it has the meaning of "refuge, asylum," which at once throws a light on the Gothic words from *fredum*, which refer to similar ideas. This special use in Italy is due to the importance of the churches and asylums "for the keeping of the peace." Within their walls the prisoner was free from the civil authorities. Hence *fredum* means "the enclosure of the peace asylum, refuge," and in this connotation it occurs among the Langobards as *fraida*.[1] In the Salic laws we find the combination as *ex faido et fredo*, to express the whole composition due to the court for a misdeed, but there is one text which still reads correctly *in facto et freto*,[2] hence the OHG. *faida* "feud" has arisen from *factum* "misdeed, feud." In the Bavarian and Frisian laws the identity of *faidosus* and *factiosus* is well preserved, the two texts keeping close to the context of the *Lex Cornelia*.[3]

The *ex facto* of the Romans has given rise to two extremely important groups of concepts in the Romance and Germanic languages, represented by the nouns *misfactum* and *forisfactum*. *Missus* was the technical term for a discharged soldier in the Roman Empire,[4] hence *missum facio* very early acquired the meaning "I discharge, dismiss."[5]

---

[1] "Si mancipium alienum refugium post alium fecerit, id est in *fraida*," *Roth.* 275.

[2] "*In facto et freto*, sol. xv," xxxv. 6. cod. 3.

[3] "Si quis hominem per iussionem regis vel duci suo, qui illam provinciam in potestatem habet, occiderit, non requiratur ei nec *feidosus* (*feutosus, feitosus, fehitus, faidosus, feitus*, idest *gifeh*) sit, quia iussio de domino suo fuit, et non potuit contradicere iussionem; sed dux dependat eum et filios eius pro eo; et si dux ille mortuus fuerit, alius dux qui in loco eius accedit, defendat eum," *Lex Baiuw.*, I. 28; "si vero homicida infra patriam est, nec iuret, nec aliquid solvat, sed tantum ut superius *faidosus* permaneat, donec in gratiam cum propinquis occisi revertatur," *Lex Fris.*, II. 7; "homo *faidosus* pacem habeat in ecclesia, in domo sua, ad ecclesiam eundo," *ibid.*, Add. I.

[4] Daremberg and Saglio, *Dictionnaire des antiquités*, sub *missus* 7.

[5] "Obsecundatoribus sacrorum scriniorum equorum, ad militare subsidium, ab honoratis proxime venire iussorum, *missam faciamus*. nullus igitur vel aetati

It is thus that *missa* "mass" developed from the original custom of giving the Eucharist at the dismissal of the church service, even as it was the usual expression in the Frankish courts for "discharge from observation of a duty."[1] Thus *mis-* came to be identical with ex "out,"[2] the legal term *ex facto* was by the ninth century rendered as *misfactum*,[3] the prefix *mis-* thus acquired the meaning of "wrong, miss-" and was soon attached to prendere,[4] loqui and other words to give to them a contrary or disagreeable significance. This *mis-* was very popular in the Frankish Empire, and not

praesenti, vel in relicum, tale si quicquam emerserit, aut equorum oblationibus, aut quibuscunque praeterea, de collatiuo omnium, postulatis, parere cogantur" (382), *Cod. Theod.* VI. 26. 3; "quid in Timaeo etiam arce quadam et quodam philosophiae uertice de anima pronuntiauerit, placitae breuitatis gratia *missum facio*," A. Engelbrecht, *Claudiani Mamerti Opera*, Vindobonae 1885, p. 128.

[1] "Sic ergo ait lectio evangelica cujus in subdito mentionem fecistis. Vos autem dicitis, si dixerit homo patri suo aut matri, corban, id est Haebraica lingua munus illud specialiter quod obsequio devotae oblationis offertur, tibi profuerit, hoc est patri aut matri, et jam *non missum facitis* eum quidquam facere patri aut matri (Marc. VIII. 11). Puto vos autem hoc sermone ordiri, qui revera ipsum specialius in epistola memorastis, quod vel unde dictum sit, non *missum facitis*. Quod omnino nihil est aliud quam non dimittitis. *A cujus proprietate sermonis, in ecclesia palatiisque sive praetoriis missa fieri pronuntiatur, cum populus ab observatione dimittitur*. Nam genus hoc nominis etiam in saecularis auctoribus, nisi memoriam vestram per occupationes lectio desueta subterfugit, invenietis. Ergo non *missum facitis*, id est, non dimittitis quidquam facere patri vel matri, a quo honorari senio parentali, non verbis tantum, sed rebus obsequiisque praeceptum est," (6. cent.) *Alcimi Ecdicii Aviti Epistolae*, in Migne, vol. LIX, col. 199 *f*.

[2] "Moris itaque est, hoc post matutinum diluculum mox omnibus patere; post tertiam vero diei horam, emissis omnibus, dato signo, quod est *mis*, usque in horam nonam cunctis aditum prohibere," *Liuthp.* v. 9, in Ducange, sub *missus*.

[3] "Illis hominibus, qui contra me sic fecerunt sicut scitis, et ad meum fratrem venerunt, propter Deum et propter illius amorem et pro illius gratia totum perdono, quod contra me *misfecerunt*, et illorum alodes de hereditate ed de conquisitu et quod de donatione nostri senioris habuerunt excepto illo, quod de mea donatione venit, illis concedo" (860) *MGH.*, *Capitularia*, vol. II, p. 158, also p. 298.

[4] "Et illi homines, qui in isto regno contra seniorem nostrum dominum Karolum *misprisserunt*, si se recognoverint, propter Deum et propter fratris sui deprecationem, quicquid contra eum *misfecerunt*, eis vult indulgere," *ibid.*, p. 299.

only are the French *méfaire*, *méprendre* the direct descendants of this *misfactum*, but *mis-* having been adopted also by the German population of France, the Goths, in their Bible translation, which was made in France about the year 800, adopted the legal term *misfactum* and literally translated it by *missadeps*, while *misfactor* was similarly rendered by *missataujands*, and similar terms are found in all the Germanic languages.

Before *mis-* took the place of "ex," *foris* had played that rôle among the Merovingians. In a Ribuarian law, which is an extension of the *Lex Cornelia*, it is provided that the highwayman or traducer may be killed, provided the slayer swears at court on the forty-second day that he killed the guilty man for an *ex facto*, that is, for a crime which makes a person an outlaw.[1] Here the *ex facto* has been changed to *forfactum*. If *forfactum* is the crime which outlaws, *forfactotus* would be the criminal who commits that crime, hence the title of that Ribuarian law, apparently of a later origin, has the corrupted form *forbattutus*,[2] which is universally used in certain Merovingian documents which deal with the killing of an outlaw.[3] As *for-* had the specific mean-

---

[1] "Si quis hominem super res suas conprehenderit, et eum ligare voluerit, aut super uxorem, aut super filiam, vel his similibus, et non praevaluerit legare, sed colebus ei excesserit, et eum interficerit, coram testibus in quadruvio in clita eum levare debet, et 40 seu 41 noctes custodire, et tunc ante iudice in harao coniurit, quod eum de vita *forfactum* interfecisset. Sin autem ista non adimpleverit, homicidii culpabilis iudicetur. Aut si negaverit cum legitimo numero iuret, quod hoc non fecisset," LXXVII.

[2] "De homine *furbattudo*."

[3] "Qui vero edictum nostrum ausus fuerit contempnere, in cuiuslibet iudicis pago primitus admissum fuerit, ille iudex collectum solatium ipsum raptorem occidat, et iaceat *forbatutus*," Childeberti II. *Decretum* (596), *MGH., Capitularia*, vol. I, p. 16; "ideo etenim, dum sic veritas conprobaretur,veniens iam dictus ille adprehensam manum vel arma predicti iudicis, sicut mos est, apud homines 12, manu sua tertia decima, dextratus vel coniuratus dixit, quod, dum ipse sollemniter sibi ambulabat, iam dictus ille quondam eum malo ordine adsallivit et evaginato gladio super eum venit et super ipsum livores vel capulationes misit et res suas illas ei diripere voluit; et postquam istas presentes livores recepit, necessitate conpulsus ipsum placavit, per quem mortuus iacet; et in sua orta contentione vel in sua movita atque per suas culpas ibidem inter-

ing "ex, out," the exlex, outlaw, was also known as the *for-bannitus*, and outlawing, banishment was similarly designated as *forbannum*,[1] where *for-* corresponds to "ex" and bannum to "lex." If we now turn to the *Carta Senonica* in which *ferbatudo* occurs, we find that it is coupled with *frodanno*, namely "*frodanno et forbatudo*." We immediately perceive that this is a corruption of "*in fredo et ex faido*" of the Salic law, which there was given as the whole composition for a misdeed, while here it is a mere legal formula, apparently not accompanied by the actual composition, for murder in self-defence. We have already seen that the Genoese formula of the 12. cent. for "being in sedition" was "*in consilio et facto*," where "*in facto*" grew out of "*ex facto*" of the Roman law. We have evidence that this formula is much older[2] and that "in consilio" was confused with "ex facto" producing the verb *forsconsiliare* "to plot against one."[3] This *for-*, which in French has survived in *forfait*, has ultimately produced the German prefix *ver-*, as in *verwirken*, AS. *forwŷrcan*, etc., which are used as translations of *forisfacere*, even as *misfactum* has produced Goth. *missadeps*.[4]

fectus fuit; et sic est veritas absque ulla fraude vel coludio, et in sua culpa secundum legem ipsum *ferrobaltudo* fecit," *Formula Turonensis* 30, in *MGH.*, *Formulae*, p. 153; "homo alicus nomen ille, ira factus, apud arma sua super me venit et colappus super me misit; et sic mihi Deus directum dedit, ego ipso de arma mea percussi, talis colappus ei dedi, per quid ipse mortuus est; et quod feci super me feci. Et ego hodie ipso facio frodanno et *ferbatudo* infra noctis 42, sicut lex et nostra consuetudo est, apud tris aloarius et 12 conlaudantes," *Carta Senonica* 17, *ibid.*, p. 192.

[1] "*Ferrebannitus*" (561–584), *Edictum Childerici*, in *MGH.*, *Capitularia*, vol. I, 9; "de teloneis qui iam antea *forbanniti* fuerunt" (779), *ibid.*, p. 51; "comes qui latronem in *forbanno* miserit" (819), *ibid.*, p. 148.

[2] Cf. the caption in the *Lex Alamannorum* "de eo qui mortem ducis consiliatus fuerit" and "*concilios* et seditionis facere" of *Roth.* 280.

[3] "Ut nemo suo pari suum regnum, aut suos fideles, vel quod ad salutem et prosperitatem ac honorem regium pertinet, discupiat aut *forsconsiliet*" (851), *MGH.*, *Capitularia*, vol. II, p. 72; "nec in vita, nec in membris, neque in regno illorum eos *forconsiliabo*" (860), *ibid.*, p. 155; "nec eum in ipsa portione . . . decipiet aut *forconciliabit*" (870), *ibid.*, p. 192.

[4] I leave for another time the investigation, how much the Goth. prefixes *fair* and *fra* represent this Lat. *foris*.

I have already pointed out that AS. *fáh* is a back formation from *faehðe*, but this shorter form is also recorded in Goth. *faih*, which has even better preserved the original meaning of *faida* "dolus,"[1] that is of *ex facto*, hence *bi-faihōn* "to take advantage of." This cannot be separated from ONorse *feikn* "misdeed," AS. *fácen*, OS. *fêkn*, OHG. *feihhan* "trickery," ONorse *feigr*, AS. *faége*, OHG. *feigi* "outlawed." All these words arise from the enormous importance which the *Lex Cornelia* has played among the Germans in France, in making them abhor the *factio*, which even in Rome led to the blood feud.

[1] "In lege Cornelia *dolus* pro *facto* accipitur," *Codex Justinianus*, 1. 7. D. 48. 8.

# TESTIBUS IDONEIS

In the *Lex salica* we several times find *sunnis*, in connection with tricare, tenere, detenere, in order to express a legitimate delay which would excuse a person's non-appearance in court.[1] If we compare these passages with the corresponding ones in the Visigothic [2] and other Germanic laws, it appears that *sunnis*, *sonia*, etc., is morphologically and semantically derived from Latin *idoneum*, as shall be shown further on.

In the Visigothic laws *idoneus* is the reliable, better situated servant, as opposed to the servus vilior, inferior, rusticanus.[3] But we also get here the combination *"testis idoneus,"* as in the Roman laws, for the reliable witness, that is, one who is of better birth and well-to-do and, therefore, would not be inclined to perjure himself.[4] *Idoneum* could also be

[1] "Ille uero qui alium mannit et ipse non uenerit, si eum *sunnis* (*sumis*) non tricauerit (detenuerit) . . . ," I. 1. 2 (in J. H. Hessels, *Lex Salica*, London 1880); "si ipse, cui testatum est, noluerit inde exire et eum aliqua *sunnis* (*sonies*, *sumis*) non tenuerit (detenuerit)," XLV. 2 b; "et si quis commonitus fuerit et eum *sunnis* (*sumnis*, *sumis*) non tenuerit (detenuerit)," XLVII. 2; "et eos *sunnis* (*sonnis*, *sumis*) non tricauerunt (tenuerint, detenuerint"), XLIX. 2; "et *sunnis* (*sumis*) eum non tenuerit (detenuerit)," L. 4; "nec *sunnia* adnuntiauerit . . . ad XL et II noctes *sunnia* adnuntiauerit . . . et eos certa *sonia* detrigauerit. et toti uenire non possint . . . pares suos *sunia* nuntiant," LXXVIII. 7; "quod si ei placitum *sunnis* detricat (detenuerit)," *Pact*. 5 and 17.

[2] On the relation of the *Lex salica* to the Visigothic laws read M. Krammer, *Kritische Untersuchungen zur Lex Salica*, in *Neues Archiv*, vol. XXX.

[3] "Ingenuus quidem pro *idonea* ancilla absque infamia C verbera ferat, pro inferiori vero . . .," *Leg. Visig.* (ed. Zeumer), XII. 15; "si quemlibet libertum *idoneum* . . . pulsaverit addicendum . . . nam si inferior fuerit atque rusticanus . . .," VI. 1. 5; "si certe ingenuus servum alterius decalvaverit . . . det eius domino solidos x, si vero *idoneum*, c flagella suscipiat," VI. 4. 3; "quamvis *idoneus* servus . . . nullatenus indebite contumeliosus aut sediciosus presumat existere," VI. 4. 7.

[4] "In duobus autem *idoneis testibus*, quos prisca legum recipiendos sancsit auctoritas, non solum considerandum est, quam sint *idonei* genere, hoc est

employed in regard to a reliable document or a sufficient proof.[1] If we turn to the corresponding Visigothic law about summoning to court, we at once see that the Salic *sunnis* is nothing but the legal proof, by means of reliable witnesses or by oath, that sickness, floods, or a snowstorm have prevented the defendant's appearance before the judge.[2] This law is identical with the one given in Digest II. 11, and the manner in which it was applied may be seen from an interesting case at the Synod of Donatists in Carthage in the year 411. A bishop was prevented by sickness from attending, so he sent a proxy to excuse his absence and sign for him, when the tribune and notary Marcellinus, who carried on the proceedings in a strictly legal fashion, pronounced his "probabilis et rationabilis excusatio est." [3]

Precisely the same conception of *idoneus* is found in the *Lex romana raetica curiensis*, where the "clericus *idoneus*," the well-to-do, "reliable" clerical is opposed to the "in-

indubitanter ingenui, sed etiam si sint honestate mentis perspicui adque rerum plenitudine opulenti," *ibid.*, II. 4. 3; "seu per scripturam sive per *idoneum testem*," II. 5. 11; "sacerdos ipse vel iudex sivi alii *testes idonei* eandem olografam scripturam ... confirment," II. 5. 16; "*idoneis testibus* quibus merito fides possit adhiberi, aput iudicem ... adprobare," VI. 5. 19.

[1] "Post hoc querenda ab utrisque partibus in scriniis domesticis instrumenta cartarum, ut contropatis aliarum scripturarum suncriptionibus adque signis possit agnosci, utrum habeatur idonea, an roprobetur indigni ... tunc ipse, qui scripturam profert, exibitis testibus esse *idoneam* et inlesam scripturam adfirmet," II. 5. 17; "sed et res omnes, tempore nuptiarum acceptas seu promissas, mulier vel puella sibimet vindicabit, si per *idoneam* probationem convicerit maritum, de quo agitur, sub ingenuitatis spe sibi sociatum esse," III. 2. 7.

[2] "Si tamen admonitum aut aegritudo ad veniendum nulla suspenderit, aut inundatio fluminum non retinuerit, vel aditum non obstruxerit, in quo montes transituri sunt, conspersio superflua nivium; que necessitas utrum evidenter evenerit, an per excusationem videatur opponi aut *idoneis testibus* aut suo iuramento firmabit," *ibid.*, II. 1. 19.

[3] "Aleodatus episcopus dixit: Julianus aegritudine praepeditur; sed ne videretur aliquo pacto defuisse, Presbyterum misit, per quem suam absentiam excusaret, et ipse pro illo subscripsit. Et alia manu: Recognovi. Marcellinus v. c. Tribunus et Notarius dixit: *Probabilis et rationabilis excusatio est*," Mansi, vol. IV, p. 143.

ferior," while the credible witness is known as "*idonia* persona," [1] even as is explicitly stated in the Burgundian laws. [2]
This conception of the reliable witness has arisen from the
current connotation in the sixth century of *idoneus* as "well-
to-do, mighty," wherefore, for example, Cassiodorus constantly opposes the *idoneus* to the *tenuis*. [3]

If we now turn to the Germanic laws which are further
removed from the Roman prototype, we find a large number
of corruptions of the original *idoneus*. The Langobards made
of it a verb *idoneare, edoniare, aduniare* "to purge oneself
legally by means of reliable witnesses," [4] that is, it is identical with the above-mentioned "*idoneam* probationem,
*idoneis* testibus firmare, probare.*" In the *Lex ribuaria* we

[1] "Si ipse clericus de bona gente est vel suas res habuerit, aut *idoneus* ap-
paruerit, inter ipsos curiales officium publicum faciat. Si autem ipse clericus
inferior persona est, inter collegiatos officium faciat," xvi. 1. 4; "omnis homo
in iudicio pro causam suam tales testes presentare debet, cui fide reprovata non
est; sed *idonias* personas in sua causam quilibet homo presentare debet," xi.
15. 4.

[2] "*Idoneis*, quibus credi possit, *testibus* fuerit conprobatum," ii. 2; "certe si
quinque testes ad praesens inventi non fuerint, tres *idoneos testes* loci illius
consistentes, quorum fama nunquam maculata est, praecipimus subscriben-
dos," xcix. 2., also xliii. 3, lxxxiii. 1, *Lex romana* xi. 3; "a iudice fide integra
et moribus *idoneus* deputetur," *Lex romana* xliv. 2.

[3] "Ne tenuis de proprio cogatur exsolvere, quod constat *idoneos* indebite
detinere," *Variae*, i. 19; "provincialium it aque nostrorum̹ saepius querela
comperimus possessores *idoneos* Saviae non solum casarum suarum tributariam
functionem in tenuem resilisse fortunam, verum etiam scelerato commercio
aliquid exinde suis applicare compendiis, ut functio publica commoditas sit
privata," *ibid.*, v. 14, and often.

[4] "*Edoniare* mundare, purificare," *Glossa cod. eporediani* (ed. G. H. Pertz),
"*edoniare* id est absoluere," *glossa matrit.*, "*edoniare* liberare seu defendere ul
firmare inberare," *gloss. caven.* "Si quis qualecunque hominem ad regem in-
cusaverit quod animae perteneat periculum, liceat ei, qui accusatus fuerit, cum
sacramentum satisfacere et se *eduniare* (*edoniare, idoniare, idoneare, ei donai e,
aduniare*)," *Ed. Roth.* 9; "non est possibile ut homo possit *eduniare* (*ae-, a-,
edoniare, i-*)" *ibid.*, 2; "aut se *edoniet* (*sedoniit, se idoneare* studeat, *se aedoniet,
se idone et, se ipsum donet*)," *ibid.*, 272; "si quis porcus aut pecora asto animo
in donum alterius miserit, et se non ausaverit *eduniare* (*e-, i-, a-doniare*)," *ibid.*,
345; "si pro quacumque culpa homo p̓ulsatus fuerit ab alio, et negaverit, liceat
eum se *eduniare* (*idoneare, ae-, e-doniare, aduniare*)," *ibid.*, 364; "si eos quicumque p̓ulsaverit, liceat illis cum sacramentalibus suis legitimis se *idoniare*," *lib.
pap. Grim.* 2.

get both the older "cartam *idoneam* confirmare" and *idone-are*,[1] but the latter occurs in the form *etuniare* and *exuniare*, of which the first has led to English *atone*, as though derived from "at one." That *atone* is derived from France is proved beyond any shadow of a doubt by the survival of a corruption of *etunis* in Bayonne in the twelfth century. The respective document fortunately has survived in two additional variants, one from Rouen, the other from Oleron.[2] Where Rouen uses *idoneus* or *exonium*, Oleron speaks of *essoyne*, while Bayonne uses *tenis*, so that there cannot be the slightest doubt as to their identity.

| Rouen | Oleron | Bayonne |
|---|---|---|
| 4. Nisi *idoneam* excusacionem die precedenti majori notam fecerit. (p. 10.) | Ne a dit au maior *raizonable* excusacion por quei il ne puchet estre. | Si combien excusacion no affeite conneisser lo davant die au maire. |
| 24. nisi ipse justam habuerit *excusacionem*. | se il n'a ogu dreite *des-accusame*. | si ed non a dreiture *tenis*. |
| 25. nisi qui tenet curiam habeat *exonium* justum. (*ibid.*) | si cil qui tent la cort ne ha *essoyne*. | si aquel qui tin sa cort no a dreiture *tenis*. |
| 28. sine licentia majoris vel sui corporis *exonio*. (p. 36.) | sans congé dou maior et dous esquevins. | seis lezer dou maire o seins *tenis* de son cors. |
| 29. major debet eum punire secundum *exonium* per quod debeat remanere (*ibid.*) | | si no a arresonable *tenis*. |

The expression "*idonea* excusacio" at Rouen shows how *idoneum* came to mean "legal excuse, essoin," while the forms *idoniare, adoniare, exadoniare, exsoniare, exoniare,*

---

[1] "Et si quis in posterum hoc refragari vel falsare voluerit, a testibus convincatur, aut cancellarius cum sacramenti interpositione cum simili numero, quorum roborata est *idoneam* confirmet (*idoniare* studeat, *et unia* restituat, *et hunia* restituat, etc.)," LIX. 2; "quod si carta in iudicio perforata *idonea* (*idoniata, etuniata*) fuerit . . .," LIX. 3; "absque pugna cartam suam super altario positam *idoniare* (*etuniare, exuniare*)," LIX. 5; "omne factum eius *idoniare* (*adhuna, adunare*) studeat," LXVII. 1; "cum sacramento se *idoniare* (*edoniare*)," LXXI.

[2] A. Giry, *Les établissements de Rouen*, Paris 1885, vol. II.

which are found in the Alemanian[1] and Frankish[2] laws and in later documents show how *sonia, sunnis* was formed. *Idoniare* has been understood as *ad-oniare*, and, from analogy with "excusare," this has been changed to *exadoniare* and *exoniare, exsoniare*, producing *soniare*, while the ablative *idoneis* has given the form *soniis, sonnis, sunnis*.[3] This *sonia* was already known in the seventh century,[4] and, if certain works are correctly dated in the sixth century, it must have

---

[1] "Si autem tres annos induraverit opus ancillae, et parentes eius non *ex-adoniaverunt (exionaverunt)* eam, ut libera fuisset," XVII. 2; "liceat illum alium cui crimen imposuit, cum tracta spata *exidoniare (id-, ex-, exs-, ad-, exad-oniare)* se contra illum alium," XLIII; "cum sacramentalis se *edoniet (id-, exed-oniet)*," LXXXVIII. 2; "ipsam cum 12 medicus electus aut cum spata tracta quilibet de parentes *adunaverit," Pactus* 33.

[2] "Per sacramentum aut cum ferro se *exoniet," MGH., Formulae, Collectiones iudiciorum Dei*, I. 6; "de hac causa non redebio nisi isto *edonio* sacramento," *ibid., Form. Andec.* 11b; also 15, 50b; "quicquid iam dictus ille de hac causa iuraverit, verum et *idoneum* sacramentum dedit," *Form. Turon.* 31; also 40; "in nullo non redibio nisi isto *etunio* sacramento," *Form. Senon.* 21 (*idonio*, 22); "sed uno alteri de causa reputata esset obnoxia, iusiurandum constituit, ut se ad sepulcrum sancti Eparchii consignaret *ydoneam," Vita et virtutes Eparchii*, in *MGH., Scrip. rer. merov.*, vol. III, p. 562; "cum hoc dixisset, illico confracta catena ex collo cecidit et manibus eandem super feretro proiecit et apparuit *idonea*, qui fuerat absque noxa poena punita," *Passio Leudegarii, ibid.*, vol. V, p. 350; "me *idoneum* hoc in opere a mendacio ideo defendere puto," *Vita Boniti, ibid.*, vol. VI, p. 119; "*testis* debet collegi *idoneus," Lex salica* XXXIX. 3 (cod. 2); "septem rachinburgius *idoneos," ibid.*, L. 3; "*idoneum* sacramentum," *ibid.*, CII. 2 (cod. 11); "se *idoneum* esse cognoscere," *ibid.*, CVI. 3, 6; "cum duodecim uiros *idoneos* iurare," *ibid.*, XLVII. 2; "*idoneare* se," *ibid., Ex-trav.* B. 2; "*idoniare* se per sacramentum," *ibid.*, LXXIV. 3; "non aliter sed cum *idoneis testibus* pergant" (796), *MGH., Leg.* sec. III. 2, p. 194, and similarly pp. 262, 829, and *MGH., Capitularia*, vol. I, pp. 75, 122, 124, 160, 180, 190, 220, 269, 282, 297, 328, 332.

[3] "Ad hanc sinodum Philippus rex Galliarum legationem suam direxit, seque ad illam itiner incepisse, sed legitimis *soniis* se impeditum fuisse mandavit," *Bernoldi Chronicon*, in *MGH., Scriptores*, vol. V, p. 462; "legati Domini mei Henrici Regis ad vos venient infra terminum Ascensionis Domini, exceptis legitimis *sonnis*, id est morte vel gravi infirmitate, vel captione absque dolo," *Vita S. Gregorii Papae*, in *Acta Sanctorum*, May VI, p. 137; "ne infirmitas aut legitima *sonnis* eum detinuerit," *Vetus placitum in Vita Aldrici*, in Ducange.

[4] "Ipsi nec vinisset ad placitum, nec misso in vice sua derixisset, nec nulla *sonia* nunciassit adfirmat" (692), J. Tardif, *Monuments historiques*, Paris 1866, p. 24; "nec ipso mundeborone suo inlustri viro Ermechario, quem per ipsas praecepcionis habuit achramitum, nullatinus praesentassit, nec nulla *sonnia* nonciasse adfirmat" (693), *ibid.*, p. 26.

been popular much earlier. The expression *"sonia nuntiare"* of that period shows that *sonia* has either the legal meaning "excuse," or "that which furnishes a basis for that excuse, affliction, trouble, worry caused by delay, delay." In a sixth century Bible text it is the translation of cura *"care,"* [1] and in the Graeco-Latin glosses [2] it is rendered by μέριμνα, φροντίς, while *soniari* is μεριμνᾶν. The same meaning is given to it in the *Sortes sangallenses* [3] and in the writings of the eighth century.[4] The French language has not only *soin* "care," but also "excuse, essoin," [5] while the Germanic languages have evolved a number of important words out of the original "testibus *soniis.*"

Gothic *sunjōn* "to verify, excuse, justify," *sunjōns* "apology, defence, answer," *sunja* "truth," OHG. *sôna, suona* "judgment, reconciliation, peace," MDutch *soene, swoene,* Dutch *zoen* "atonement," *soenen* "to kiss," OFrisian *sôna* "reconcile," Norwegian *sone* "to atone" are identical in form and meaning with LLatin *sonia.* In ONorse, *syn,* in the compound *nauðsyn,* means "necessity, impediment," which con-

---

[1] "Curis huius vitae, *soniis* saecularibus," *Rheinisches Museum,* vol. XXXII, p. 586.

[2] *Corpus glossariorum latinorum.*

[3] H. Winnefeld, *Sortes sangallenses,* Bonnae 1887: "noli dimittere persona de qua *soniaris* in dubio erit condemnatio," p. 21; "non es fugiturus; noli *soniari,*" p. 36 and 37; "noli *soniari,* quia non est obligata domus tua," p. 42; "de *sonio* liberaris ut deo adiuvante ad filios tuos reuerteris saluus," p. 44. The author wants to put the origin of these Sortes back into the second century, chiefly because the office of the *aediles* is mentioned in them, but it is evident from the quotations (amicus tuus *aedilem* te facit, per aliqua persona poteris esse *aedilis,* aeris *aedilis* et amicos multos habebis) that the reference is to an honorable title and social position, and not to a magistracy, even as the " *aedilis* ecclesiae" (see Ducange) was in Merovingian times the name for a curator in the church, an honorable distinction. From this *aedilis* comes OHG. *edili* "noble."

[4] "Si comis in suo ministerio iustitias non fecerit, misso nostro de sua casa *soniare* faciat usque dum iustitiae ibidem factae fuerint" (779), *MGH., Capitularia,* vol. I, p. 48; "illi qui antiquitus consueti fuerunt missos aut legationes *soniare,* ita et modo inantea et de parveridis et omnia eis necessaria solito more *soniare* faciant" (800), *ibid.,* p. 85.

[5] "S'il n'avoient leial *sone*" (1214), in Godefroy, where more quotations may be found.

notation in OHG. has been left to the common alternative of the documents, *sumnis* "legal necessity, delay," from which has been formed the verb *sûmen* "to tarry, delay." This meaning has not entered into any other Germanic languages but Dutch *zuimen*, which is merely a borrowing from the German. Now, the usual formula in which *sonia* occurs in the Merovingian and Carolingian laws and documents is "*sonia* nuntiare," that is, "to show a legal excuse." This "*sonia* nuntiare" is recorded in Gothic in "*sunja* gateihan," "to tell the truth," and I shall now show that *teihan* is derived from "testibus."

In Gothic *teihan* is identical with "nuntiare" in meaning, but in the other Germanic languages the corresponding verb means "to accuse, charge with," so in AS. *têon*, OHG. *zîhen*. These verbs are distinct from Goth. *taiknjan*, OHG. *zeih-hanen*, etc., which alone are related to Lat. *dico*, Greek δείκνυμι. It is merest accident that the two forms somewhat coincide, for the meanings of Goth. *teihan*, etc., are distinctly derived from the rubric "*testibus soniis*," which was used in every case where the seriousness of the charge demanded reliable witnesses. This "*testibus soniis*" was popularly pronounced *testibusonis*, *tehtibusonis*, and as such it has survived in the AS. *tiht-bysig* "infamatus et accusationibus ingravatus," a back formation from *tiht-bysignis*, *testibusonis*. This appears clearly from the first recorded case in 959, when the phrase is used for "one under heavy accusation and not to be believed by the people,"[1] for precisely then the accused person would have to purge himself by three credible witnesses. Now, the long rubric *testibusonis* has survived in Old French in the abbreviated form *busun*, *busuigne* "legal necessity, important affair,"[2] which has ultimately pro-

---

[1] "Et si quis fuerit accusationibus infamatus et populo incredibilis," III *Ead.* 7. For other quotations see Bothworth's Dictionary.

[2] "E si alcun jethed les chatels fors de la nef senz *busun*, sil rendet," *Leis Willelme* 37. 3 (1090–1135), in Liebermann, *Die angelsächsischen Gesetze*, p. 515;

duced *besoin,* but which in the oldest AS. case, of about 950, still means "necessitas, solicitudo."[1] Thus French *besoin* and English *business* go back to *testibusonis,* but, while the whole has produced the AS. *tihtbysig,* the first part *tiht,* OHG. *zicht,* means "accusation, crime," and from this has come by a back formation Goth. *teihan,* and so forth.

"a mei affert ceste *busunie,*" *Lib. Psalm.,* p. 366, in Godefroy; "e si parfei-sums la *busuine,* de ses *buesuignes* fist le rei mult avancer," *ibid.*

[1] "Ne *bisignisse* mettes and woedes haebende, nec solicitudinem escae et vestis habendam."

# QUOVIS GENIO

THE earliest documents of the Middle Ages frequently use *ingenium*, in connection with *malum, inicum*, in the sense of "deception." [1] *Ingenium* is generally abbreviated to *genium*, in Italian documents also to *ienio, zenio, senio*, and the phrase "per *quovis genio* substraere" or one like it is employed to express that which in Roman law is known as *malus dolus*.[2] In France, especially in the south, *ingenium* is, since the tenth century, recorded

[1] "Nisi, malo ordine per forcia et *inico ingenium* ipsi agentis predicto Drogone, de potestate sua abstraxsissent" (697), J. Tardif, *Monuments historiques*, Paris 1866, p. 31; "volumus etiam . . . vt nulla praepotens persona predictam Ecclesiam proprietario iure per *nullum ingenium*, per nullam censuram, aut beneficiali ordine, et praeceptali auctoritate nitatur inuadere" (724), Troya, *op. cit.*, vol. III, p. 380; "nec per cartulam concambiationis neque per convenientiam libelli neque per *ullum inienium*" (724), *ibid.*, p. 384; "si quis per *malum ingenium* in curtem alterius miserit aliquid . . . quod furatum est," *Lex salica* XXXVI. 4; "et si per odium aut *malo ingenio*, nisi per iustitiam faciendam, hominem diffecerit" (779), *MGH., Capitularia*, vol. I, p. 49; "ut iuntitias ecclesiarum, viduarum, orfanorum et reliquorum omnium sine ullo *malo ingenio* . . . faciatis; nam si tale aliquod *ingenium* inter vos factum fuerit" (806), *Fontes rerum bernensium*, Bern 1833, vol. I, p. 220 f.; "in omnibus ero, absque fraude et *malo ingenio* et absque ulla dolositate seu deceptione," Rozière, *Recueil général des formules dans l'empire des Francs du Vᵉ au Xᵉ siècle*, Paris 1859, vol. I, p. 7.

[2] "Nec possit ei pater per *quolevit genium* aliquid dare aut hereditatem relinquere" (gloss. cporcd. *genio* conludio) (731), *Ediltum Luitprandt Regis*, Ann. XIX. 3; "*quocumque genio* aliquid abstractum" (862), *Cod. Langob.*, col. 369; "per *covis zenium* subtraere" (919), *HPM., Chartae*, vol. I, col. 123; "per *couis ienium* infrangere" (973), *ibid.*, col. 242; "per *couis ienium* subtrahere" (1035), *ibid.*, col. 509; "*qualis genium*" (801), *Codex cavensis*, vol. I, p. 5; "*quodlibet genium*" (803), *ibid.*, p. 6; "per *quodvis genium*" (858), *HPM., Chartae*, vol. I, col. 337, *Cod. Langob.*, cols. 244, 274, 346, 448, 1617, etc.; "per *cotvis sienium*" (1045), *Codice diplomatico padovano dal secolo sesto a tutto l'undecimo*, p. 180; "per *covix genium*" (1008), *ibid.*, pp. 135, 249, 278, 297.

as *engan, enganno,*[1] but in Italy *ingannatio* is given as early as 843.[2]

*Ingenium, genium* is extremely common in another formula, "*quovis genio* conquirere," to acquire in anyway not definitely established by ancient law, i. e., in war, by natural increase, interest, etc.[3] In Spain and Portugal *ganare* is used

[1] "De ista hora in antea . . . non *enganera* sua persona, suo domno, suo sciente . . . ni per suo *ingenio* ni per sua conscientia suo sciente" (985), Devic and Vaissete, *op. cit.*, cols. 301, 312 *f.*; "neque per nostrum *ingenium* . . . sine nullo illorum *enganno* et sine lucro" (1020), *ibid.*, col. 373; " et pleu Bernardus jamdictus per suam fidem et per suum dictum plivid, ut non *ingannat* Rainardum jamdictum de isto placito" (1056), *ibid.*, col. 489 and similarly cols. 938, 942, 949, 968, 982; "erimus adjutorio domino Deo, et Sancto Petro sine *enganno*" (1028), *Gallia christiana*, vol. I, p. 49; "sine *inganno*" (1083), Teulet, *Layettes du Tresor des chartes*, vol. I, p. 29; "sine *enganno*," *ibid.*, pp. 82, 84, 90, 107, 124, etc., C. Douais, *Cartulaire de l'abbaye de Saint-Sernin de Toulouse*, Paris 1887, pp. 74, 91, 497, etc., Guérard, *Cartulaire de l'abbaye de Saint-Victor de Marseille*, Paris 1857, vol. I, p. 172; "sine *inganno*" (1147), *España sagrada* vol. XXXV, p. 416.

[2] "Lunfrit de cives Placentia, qui cum ipso infantulum fuisset et super rebus eius ambulasset et extimasset, ne ad ipsum infantulum aliqua *ingannatio* facta non fuisset . . . et paruit eorum, quod nulla *ingannatio* ei facta non erat," J. Ficker, *Forschungen zur Reichs- und Rechtsgeschichte Italiens*, Innsbruck 1874, vol. IV, p. 18.

[3] "*Quoque genio* alienatum aut traditum" (716), Troya, *op. cit.*, vol. II, p. 254; "omnem conquistionem, quod genitori tuo, quas de ribus Sancto Ecclesie per Anticessoris meis cumquiset per *qualibet ingenio*, et possidet usque in diebus vite sue, qui in hanc domo Sancte Ecclesie ante nos fuerunt: tam per nos, et jamdixi, per *qualivet ingenio* quem cumquirere potuet de ribus Sancte Ecclesie" (737), *ibid.*, vol. III, p. 635; "quicquid . . . aut nobis traditum vel commutatum fuit, vel in antea ibidem comparatum aut de *quolibet ingenio*, legibus ad nos pervenit," Pardessus, *op. cit.*, vol. II, p. 398; "per *qualicumque genio* vel titulo . . . advenerat" (766), *Cod. Langob.*, col. 59; "*quocumque genio* conquirere," *ibid.*, col. 60; "quod mihi usquemodo conquisistes aut in antea conquerere potueritis per *quodlibet ingenium*" (766), *ibid.*, col. 61; "quicquid per ipsam cartulam concessisti, aut postea *quoque ingenio* adquisisti" (784), *ibid.*, col. 112; "que ipsa sibi *quocumque ingenio* juste et legaliter undecumque vel a quibuscumque acquisivit, aut in antea acquirere potuerit" (852), *ibid.*, col. 524; "dono cultilem seu et masseritias quantascumque in iamdicto uico cistè mihi per cartulam et comparantionem aut per *quale vis ingenium* ibidem adquisiuero" (848), *HPM., Chartae*, vol. I, col. 46; "quantumcumque ibi visi sumus abere, aut porcio nostra ibi obvenit aut obvenire debet, tam de paterno quam de materno, uel de *quacumque libet ingenio* legitime ordine ad nos obvenire debet usque in exquisitum" (888), Bruel, *Recueil de Cluny*, vol. I, p. 38 *f.*; "quicquid de genitore meo, vel genitrice mea, vel de *calecumque ingenio* mihi atvenit" (893), *ibid.*, p. 60; "tan de alaudo, tan de conquisto, aut de *qualecumque ingenio* ad nos advenire potuerit" (904), *ibid.*, p. 95, and often.

where elsewhere this formula is written,[1] hence *ganatum* refers to everything not owned alodially, especially to cattle.[2] This *ganare* is obviously derived from *genium*, but *quo genio*, *quo zenio*, *quovis genio*, etc., have also left behind them a large variety of forms, which are recorded from the tenth century on. We find in Venice *guadagno*,[3] in Aragon *guataniagare*, *guadanare*,[4] in Provence *gadaignare*, *guadanare*, *gazain*.[5]

[1] "Quicquid potui *ganare* vel applicare atque apprendere" (747), *España sagrada*, vol. xl, p. 357; "nostras hereditates quantas habuerimus et *ganare* potuerimus usque ad obitum nostrum" (874), *PMH., Dipl. et char.*, vol. i, p. 5; "et partibi cum ipsos filios meos iam superius nominatos meo *ganato* et meas uillas et mea criazon" (875), *ibid.*, p. 8; "et omnem mea rem quanta ego uisa sum auere quantaque aueo de auolenga et de parentela quam etiam et de mea *ganatura*" (908), *ibid.*, p. 11; "sive de parentum meorum, vel comodo etiam de *ganantia*" (972), *ibid.*, p. 65 f.; "et habuimus illa hereditate de nostra *ganancia* quam comparauimus" (1002), *ibid.*, p. 114; "damus ipsas hereditates . . . siue et alias que de hodie in die *ganare* et augmentare potuerimus in qualibet *ganantia*" (1039), *ibid.*, p. 187 and often; "et alium quodcumque *ganare* potuerimus, ut traditum pro remedio animarum nostrarum" (940), Berganza, *Antigüedades de España*, vol. ii, p. 381; "ortos, domos, armenta, vestimenta, tam mobile quam et immobile, quod *ganavimus*, vel *ganare* potuerimus in hoc seculo" (947), *ibid.*, pp. 391, 395; "cum omnibus prestationibus suis, quantum nos ibidem *ganavimus*" (998), *España sagrada*, vol. xl, p. 407.

[2] "Omni *ganato*, tam mobile, quam etiam immobile" (945), Berganza, *op. cit.*, p. 389; "illo *ganato* de Caradigna pascendi" (972), *ibid.*, p. 409; "impleverunt illud monasterium de omni *ganato*" (934), *España sagrada*, vol. xl, p. 400; "a paucis namque annis *ganavi* alfagara" (1029), *ibid.*, vol. xxxvi, p. xxxiii; "adhuc etiam concedo, ut nullus sit ausus . . . proprium *ganatum* pignurare alicujus canonici, qui homines cum *ganato* vivo habuerit" (1105), *ibid.*, vol. xxxviii, p. 344; "pannos et alium *ganatum*" (1032), *ibid.*, vol. xix, p. 395.

[3] "Nullus Venetus audeat ultra Pollam mancipia transportare, neque in terra Graecorum, neque nullis locis ea donare, excepto si acciderit, ut de sua captivitate se redimere debeat, aut pro tali causa unde *guadagnum* accrescat in patria" (960), S. Romanin, *Storia documentata di Venezia*, Venezia 1853, vol. i, p. 371.

[4] "Cum quantum ibi abeo *ganatu* et adhuc potero *guataniagare*" (1025), E. Ibarra y Rodriguez, *Coleccion de documentos para el estudio de la historia de Aragon*, Zaragoza 1904, vol. i, p. 126; "et omnia quae hodie in antea poteritis adquirere vel *guadanare* in tota mea terra" (1069), Muñoz y Romero, *op. cit.*, p. 248; "quod ubi habueritis hereditates in tota mea terra vel *guadanare* poteritis" (1075), *ibid.*, p. 251.

[5] "Dimitto ambobus filiis meis totum quod lucratus sum, hoc est quod *guadanavi* in castello de Buciagas" (1118), Baluze, vol. ii, p. 488; "totum quantum de te ibi adquisitum et *gadaignatum* habemus" (1127), Devic and Vaissete, *op. cit.*, vol. v, col. 941; "quod suus lignages *gadanet* per ben et per fe" (1141), *ibid.*, col. 1049; "le sobredit deutor devo he convengo pagar he redire le cabal el *gazain* a so moniment" (1205), Tardif, *Layettes*, vol. v, p. 55.

Before discussing the fate of this group in the European languages, I shall ascertain the causes that led to the popularity of *ingenium* and *genius* in the formulae.

At the end of the second century and later *ingenium* has the meaning of "machination, shrewdness, trickery,"[1] and in the sixth century Gregory already knew the technical term *quolibet ingenio*,[2] even as it was used in a Merovingian document of the year 587 [3] and regularly in the Visigothic laws.[4] By the side of *ingenium* Gregory the Great used *genius* in the sense of "good intention,"[5] while Cassiodorus employed it earlier for "honor, truth, splendor" and

---

[1] "O nouum inreligiosae mentis *ingenium*," Salvianus, *Ad ecclesiam* III. 30 (*Corp. scrip. eccl.* vol. VIII, p. 278); "ubi valere non potuisti ingenio detestandae subtilitatis tuae," Lucifer Calaritanus,*De sancto Athanasio I.* XXVI (*ibid.*, vol. XIV, p. 111); "sed stipem ut tollant *ingenia* talia quaerunt," Commodianus, *Instructionum* I. XVII (*ibid.*, vol. XV, p. 22); "cuius symboli iter custodientes omnes hereses doctrinas instituta uel dogmata, quae sibi altercationem non *ingenia*, sed studia fuerunt," Prisciallianus 45 (*ibid.*, vol. XXIII, p. 37); "quod autem ex nouo *ingeniis* et calumniis repperitur," *ibid.*, 56, (p. 44); "proclamant e uero episcopo ac dicente, quod saepius hic *ingenia* quaereret, qualiter eum ab episcopatu deiceret," Gregorius Turonensis, VI. 22 (*MGH.*, *Scrip. rer. merov.*, p. 262); "facto *ingenio* cum satellite allegatur," *ibid.*, VIII. 26 (p. 340); "iurant partes per Dei omnipotentes nomen et inseparabilem Trinitatem vel divina omnia ac tremendum diem iudicii, se omnia quae superius scripta sunt absque ullo dolo malo vel fraudis *ingenio* inviolabiliter servaturus," *ibid.*, IX. 20 p. 377); "callida machinamenta commeantium, ac simulatae obseruationis *ingenia* et fraudes" (381), *Cod. Theod.*, VI. 29. 6.

[2] "Nec hunc sub *quolibet ingenio* vel argumento cuipiam Judaeorum venundandi facultas sit" (596), Gregorii I *Registri*, VI. 29 (*MGH.*, *Epistolae*, vol. I, p. 407); "ut eum stricte debeas commonere ne filios suos *quolibet ingenio* vel excusatione foris alicubi in coniugio sociare praesumat" (599), *ibid.*, IX. 128 (vol. II, p. 128).

[3] "Neque a domna Brunichilde neque a filio suo Childeberto rege filiisque suis *quolibet ingenio* uel tempore repetantur," *MGH.*, *Capitularia*, vol. I p. 14.

[4] "Si quecumque mulier siue principis opem aut quocumque *ingenio* seu cuiuslibet auxilio intenderit inter se et virum divortium fieri," III. 6. 2; "si . . . quocumque tempore de eorum patrocinio quacumque subtilitate aut *ingenio* vel argumento fraudis vel leviter de eorum patrocinio se auferre voluerint," V. 7. 20.

[5] "Honorem et *genium* ex humilitate vendicetis"(593), Gregorii I *Registri*, IV. 1 in *MGH.*, *Epistolae*, vol. I, p. 233; "quatenus adeptae dignitatis meliori *genio* resistendi Donatistis possibilitas disponatur" (591), *ibid.*, p. 92; "vigoris ecclesiastici *genium* congrua" (599), *ibid.*, vol. II, p. 173, and often.

*geniatus* for "honorable, pleasant, joyous," [1] and Ennodius likewise reveled in the use of *genius* in the same sense, employing it more than one hundred times in his writings. It follows from this that previous to the sixth century *ingenium* meant "evil intention," while *genius* was identical with "good intention," hence derivations from the first generally have a connotation of badness, while words derived from *genius*, like Span. Port. Cat. Ital. *gana* "desire, intention," Span. *ganar* "to earn" are free from this connotation. In order to determine the cause for the vowel change from *gen-* to *gan-* I have to discuss the root *QVR* "fire," which is found in all the Eurasiatic languages, but only so much of it in the sub-form *QVN* as concerns the matter in hand.

The semantic primary meaning "fire, shine" has been preserved in all languages. We get Chinese *kwang* "light, splendor, clear, honor, éclat, naked, smooth." In Sumerian we have *kun* "illumination, break of day, shine," by the side of the *QVR* forms *gibil, gibir* "fire, burn," *par* "shine, white," *bir* "shine, light, éclat," *bil* "fire, burn." In the Dravidian languages some have *bel-*, others *ven-* for "to shine." Similarly we have Egyptian *uben, uban, wan*, Coptic *uain, uein* "to shine," Sanskrit *vani* "Agni, God of fire," and, as in Sumerian *kibir, gibil* means "wood for making fire by friction," so here *vana* means "wood, forest, bush, forest home," and from *van-* "to burn" one proceeds to *van-* "to wish, obtain, surpass, possess," in Old Iranian *van-* "tree, to wish, obtain, surpass." In the Slavic languages *gor-* "to burn" and *bêl-* "white" represent the *QVR* forms, while in Celtic *vind-*, Welsh *gwyn*, Cornish *guyn*, Breton *gwenn*, Old Irish *find* "white" the *QVN* forms are represented, even as

---

[1] "Ad *genium* dignitatis tuae credimus pertinere," *MGH.*, Cassiodori *Variae*, p. 214; "qui amplissimum genium pretiosae libertatis acceperat" (511), *ibid.*, p. 175; "ex quibus habebunt *genium* mores, si parentes publicos minores contigerit inveniri" (535), *ibid.*, p. 306; "regalem quin etiam mensam conviva *geniatus* ornavit" (510), *ibid.*, p. 38, and often.

Gothic *wēns* "hope," ONorse *ván* "expectation, hope," AS. *wén* "expectation, hope, suspicion," OHG. *wān* "expectation, hope, illusion," *wunnia* "joy, lust," although removed from the original meaning "to burn," seem to belong here. Lat. *venus, veneror, venustus* show how the semasiological change may have taken place, while *venor* "to hunt," no doubt, is a development of "to desire strongly, conquer, obtain." The corresponding group in Greek is γανάω "to shine, glitter," γάνος "splendor, beauty," γάννυμαι "to rejoice." The gloss for γάνος in Hesychius is most instructive. He writes γάνος παράδεισος, χάρμα, φῶς, αὐγή, λευκότης, λαμπηδών, ἡδονή, thus combining all the meanings which have resulted from original "to shine," and the meaning παράδεισος at once shows that Semitic *gan* "garden" is not to be separated from this group.

Whatever the origin of *genius* may have been, it has in the fifth and sixth centuries received all the connotations of Greek γάνος, and, since the earliest *gan-* forms in the Romance languages occur in the south of France and in Spain, one is led to the conclusion that the Greek language, which was still spoken there in the sixth century, had with its popular γάνος affected the Latin *genius*, creating the popular *gano*. This *gano* is preserved in Basque *gano* "agreeable, secret, smartness in work," *ganoraz* "elegant, smart," *ganu* "smartness, inclination." The LLat. *ganire, gannire, gannare* "to make fun" are certainly not to be separated from Greek γάννυμι "to rejoice" and may have aided in the change of *ingenium* to *ingannum*.

In the Provence *quovis genio, quovis zenio*, or a similar form, has produced *guazanh*, which has spread over all Europe in the sense of "gain, garner, autumn." Everything that is not inherited but is obtained by personal labor, grace of nature, fortune of war was in OProvençal *gazanh, gassan, gazan* "gain, success, labor," *gazanha* "gain, interest," especially "profit from the cultivated field, crops," hence *guasandor, gazanhador, gaanador, gaaniador* "plowman, farmer," *guasanhar, gazanhar, gadanhar, cazanhar, gasanhar, gaanhar* "cultivate the ground, attend to farming, maintain, earn a living," *gazanhatge* "tillable land."[1] In the eleventh century one hears frequently of the cultivation of such lands as remained heretofore unworked, *terra plana*,[2] which then becomes known as *terra arabilis*,[3] but especially as *terra ganabilis*.[4] Such cultivable lands, reclaimed from the pastures, or, rather, the returns from such lands, *guagneria, garneria*, were bequeathed or donated in the same way as other lands.[5] It is clear from the quotations that the forms *gaaign-, gaign-*, etc., in the north are of later origin and evolved from the original Provençal *gazanh*. *Ingenium* has in the north produced *engigne, enjinne, engin* "habilité, adresse, ruse, fraude," *malum ingenium* has led to OFr. *malengien* and, as is proved by Engl. *malinger*, to French *malingre* "sickly." From the south have proceeded OFr. *engan, enjan, engaing* "ruse, tromperie, fourberie, peine, travail," *enganay* "adresse, habilité, ruse," *enganner, enguenner, enjanner* "tromper." Even so the Prov. *gazanh* has spread in the north as *gahaigne*,

[1] Spanish *guadaña* "sickle," i. e., "tool for cutting the crop," is no doubt, not to be separated from this group.
[2] "Praeterea dono eis intra *terram planam* si invenitur, aut de silva ad complanandum tantum quantum exarare possit in elaborando par boum in anno, totidem etiam ad elaborandum vel complanandum pratum unde boves vivere possint" (1067), G. Ragut, *Cartulaire de Saint-Vincent de Mâcon*, p. 10.
[3] "De *terris arabilibus et planis*, quia divise non erant, judicatum est ut si alii illas laborarent per laudationem et preceptum obedencialis vel ministri ojus ... illas haverent et redditus eorum ipsi inter se dividerent usquequo terre, per consensum utriusque partis, ad equalem divisionem pervenirent," *ibid.*, p. 9.
[4] "Terra *cultibilis*, que vulgariter *waignale* dicitur" (1200), *Recueil belgique, Comté de Hainaut*, vol. I, p. 4. In Ducange still more quotations may be found.
[5] "Augmentavi etiam ipsum domum propriis rebus et reditibus, id est, molendinos ... et omnia prata mea que in ipsa villa habebam, et totam *guagneriam* meam de villa ipsa" (1088), *Cartulaire de Saint-Jean d'Angély*, vol. I., p. 84; "dereliquit totam ipsius terrae *gaharnariam (gagneriam)*" (1091), *ibid.*, vol. II, p. 135; "*garneriam*" (1092), *ibid.*, p. 92.

*gaaigne* "grain, profit, butin, terre labourable, récolte, fruit, froment qu' on sème en automne," and the *Coutumier de Normandie* has preserved the original meaning of *gagnable* "les terres non cultivees enciennement nommes *gagnables*, sauvages ou sauvees de la mer."[1]

It is interesting to observe the development of the group in Breton. The insular Celtic has no common expression for "profit, work, produce." Irish has *gean* "pleasure" (Gaelic "mood"), which goes back directly to Lat. *genius*, and *gen* "laughter," *gno* "scorn," which are derived from Lat. *gannire*, Gr. γάνος, and possibly *gangaid* "deception" may be related to *genius, ingenium*, but it knows nothing of the special evolution in France. Welsh *gen* "understanding, soul" is similarly from the Latin, and *gwyn* "bliss, excitement" is not to be separated from Celtic *gwyn, gwen* "white, pleasant, blissful," but *gweini* "to serve," Cornish "*goon, gun, gwon, gwen* "work, cultivation, planting," *gones, gonys* "cultivate, work," *gunithiat* "laborer," *gwon, gon* "field, common meadow" cannot be separated from MBreton *gounit* "gain, to earn." These are certainly not to be separated from French *gaain*, etc., even as Breton *gwenaat, ijinaat* "rendre ou devenir fin, ruse, adroit," *gwended, gwender* "flexibilité, souplesse, adresse, industrie, intrigue, ruse," *ganaz* "fourbe, traître, perfide, double" are derived from *ingenium, genium*.

If we now turn to the Germanic languages, we find that by the side of the *win-* group, which is directly related with that of all the other Indo-European languages, there has grown up another *win-* group, not represented in Gothic, but found in the other related languages, with the semantic meaning "gain, profit, fruit of labor, strife." It is found in OHG. *cawin*, AS. *gewin*, MLG. *gewin*, for which only the AS. has developed a verb *winnan* "to labor, toil, strive, win, get, attain." It is not likely that this has evolved from the

[1] In Ducange, sub *gaaignable*.

original *win-* group, but it must be assumed, in the light of the universal evolution in the West from *genius*, that in German territory *genius* has given *gwin-*, *win-*. The very absence of this from the Gothic and the comparatively late appearance of *ganar* in Spanish and French show that the same cause has operated in the Germanic and in the Romance languages. But the Prov. *guazanh*, *gasanh*, which goes back to *quovis genio*, has in the Germanic languages been considered as a derivative in *ga-*, producing Gothic *asans* "time of harvest, harvest field," *asneis* "day laborer, hireling," OLG. *asna* "tax, revenue," AS. *esne* "servant, youth," MLG. *asnen*, *hasnen* "wage, reward," *menasle*, *manasle*, *meinasme* "earnest money," OHG. *asni*, *asnari* "hireling," ONorse *anna*, *ǫnna* "to work, provide a living," and, as French *garneria* stands by the side of Prov. *gasanh*, so we also find the rotacised forms OHG. *arnôn*, MHG. *arnen*, AS. *earnian*, Engl. *earn*, MLG. *ernen*, MD. *arnen*, *arenen*, *aernen* "earn," MHG. *erne* "harvest." Although these simpler forms are frequently recorded, yet OHG. *gawinnôn*, *gaarnôn*, AS. *geearnian* are far more popular and are the forms from which the shorter words have developed. Gothic *asans* has produced OBulg. *yesen'*, Prussian *assanis* "autumn," and even the form *gen-* seems to be retained in OBulg. *žen-* "to harvest."

# FEUDUM

In Carolingian times *fiscus* was frequently employed as an abbreviation for *villa fiscalis*,[1] but this was not a new development of the word, for it had been employed in that sense in a document of the year 717 [2] and is, no doubt, genuine in the interpolated one of 566.[3] *Fiscus* had popularly a vacillating meaning, for it implied anything from which the state derived an income. In the fifth century *fiscalia* was the legal expression for the taxes from a praedium,[4] while in the beginning of the sixth century *fiscus* became the current term for "tribute, anything from which a revenue is derived," more especially "Gothic revenue."[5] It also meant "the fixed

[1] "Actionarius ad *fiscum* nostrum, qui vocatur Romaricus mons," *MGH.*, *Formulae*, p. 293; "ex quibusdam *fiscis* nostris, id est Duria, Clodoua," *ibid.*, p. 317; "ad ius *fisci* regalis qui dicitur Andernacus," *ibid.*, p. 324.

[2] "Una cum illo forestario nomene Lobicino, qui commanit in *fisco* nostro Vetus Clippiaco," Sauer and Samaran, *op. cit.*, p. 27.

[3] "In *fiscis*, villis, agris," *Cartulaire général de Paris*, p. 6.

[4] "Parati sumus pro singulis annis pro eadem praedia *fiscalia* conpetentia solvere" (489), Marini, *I pap. dipl.*, p. 130.

[5] "Quicumque Gotorum *fiscum* detrectat implere, eum ad aequitatem redibitionis artetis, ne tenuis de proprio cogatur exsolvere" (507–511), Cassiodorus *Variae*, I, 19, in *MGH.*, p. 24; "ut stagnis Decemnovii paludibusque secretis sine *fisco* possideas" (507–511), *ibid.*, p. 65; "species quae ad *fiscum* pertinet" (511), *ibid.*, p. 94; "antiqui barbari ... *fiscum* possessi cespitis persolvere ac superindicticiis oneribus parare cogantur" (520), *ibid.*, p. 151; "quapropter ille casarum suarum *fiscum* ... desiderans sine aliqua imminutione publicae utilitatis inferre" (537), *ibid.*, p. 366. It is regularly used in this sense in the *Lex romana curialis* (*MGH.*, *Leg.*, vol. v); "Quicumque homo de res puplicas, unde *fiscus* exit, aut villam aut qualecumque terra comparare voluerit, non potest ipsam facultatem emere sine tributum aut sine censum, quod de ipsa terra exit," III, 1; "si quis homo qualecumque rem fescalem per annos V inter presentes sine omne censu reddito sine omne inquietudine possederit, liceat ei si ipsas res sine *fisco* possidere," IV, 12; "illi, qui *fiscum* regis exigunt, tales esse debent, ut per sua negligencia de ipso fisco minus non exigant, nisi quod iustum est, nec plus exigere non presumant, nisi quod iustum est," X, 61; "si quis homo de facultatem suam, quam habet, si forsitan exinde aut *fiscum* aut alium

yearly rent,"[1] and, because it was a specific sum paid by the emphyteute, it was understood as *fixum*[2] and popularised in Italy as *fictum*. This confusion is based on the technical expression "*ad fixum* canonem," which in the fourth century was used of the yearly dues to the fiscus.[3] What formerly was paid *ad fiscum* soon was rendered *ad fictum*, "according to a settled agreement." But there is still another word which has entered into this group and has aided in further changing *fictum* to *fioto*. What was annually paid to the fiscus is in itself a kind of emphyteusis, hence we hear in the seventh century of possession "*enfeteuticario* modo,"[4] and in the ninth century the emphyteutic contract is known simply as *emphitecarius*, *fiotecarius*,[5] and the formula "*enfiteuticario*

publicum aut laboratum a parente reddere debet," xi, 1; "curiales, qui *fiscum* aut publicum actum exigent, non occulto eos eligantur, sed ad eleccionem multorum bonorum hominum," xii, 2, 1; "si aliquis homo in causa publica occupatus fuerit et non fuerit ad presente, quando *fiscus* exigitur," xii, 2, 2; "nec *fiscus*, nec tributus exinde non exeat," xvii, 10; "si quis homo ad alterum hominem aut de *fisco* aut alico alium debitum debet," x, 8; "quicumque homo terra habuerit, unde *fiscum* solvere debeat, si ipsum censum dare non potuerit, ille exactor, qui ipsum *fiscum* tollere debet, ipsa terra unde ipse census exire debet, vindat," xi, 3, 1.

[1] "Et de vico Varonaces exigitur *fiscum* in mense septembrio, sol. iii et denar. iiii" (650), Troya, *op. cit.*, vol. ii, p. 493; "*fisco* vel censo" (814), *HPM.*, *Cod. Langob.*, col. 170.

[2] "*Affixam* pensionem reputantes prestande" (844), Fantuzzi, *op. cit.*, vol. i, p. 86.

[3] "Ut habeat ipse Johannes *ad fictum* sub censu reddendo libellario nomine usque ad annos viginti," *MGH.*, *Leges*, vol. iv, p. 596; "persolvat exinde singulis annis censum . . . *afictuo* per tempus quadragesime" (848), *Cod. Langob.*, col. 284; "reddunt *ad fictum* in argento" (905), *ibid.*, col. 706.

[4] "*Enfeteuticario* modo postulastis largiri si minime cuiquam a vobis per *enfetus* sunt largita vobis," Marini, *I pap. dipl.*, p. 199.

[5] "Ad scribendos libellos et *fidecarios*" (891), L. Schiaparelli, *I diplomi di Guido e di Lamberto*, p. 30; "ad scribendos libellos et *fiothecarios*" (898), *ibid.*, p. 98; "libellorum et quarumcumque legalium cartarum conscriptionibus seu *fiothecariis* vel emphiteosi" (900), L. Schiaparelli, *I diplomi italiani di Lodovico III e di Rodolfo II*, Roma 1910, p. 13; "per libellum aut emphiteosin vel *fiothecaria*," *ibid.*, p. 14; "conscriptiones et *emphitecarios*" (898), L. Schiaparelli, *I diplomi di Berengario I*, p. 73; libellos et *fiotecarios*" *ibid.*, p. 74; "libellorum et quarumcumque legalium cartarum conscriptionibus et *phiotecariis* vel emphiteosi" (894), *ibid.*, p. 43; "per *emphiteoticariam*," *ibid.*, p. 44.

modo largiri," which was still in use in Ravenna in the tenth century,[1] shows that in it lay the germ of the feudal system. But that this *ad fictum* is identical with *ad fiscum* is shown by the use of *fictus* in the sense of "treasury," where the Carolingian formula uses the stereotyped "quod *fiscus* noster recipere aut sperare potuit."[2]

In France we get, from the ninth century on, *feus, fevus* for "fiscus, fiscal property, emphyteutic land," that is, for the current meanings of *fictus* in Italy. That these words are semantically the same as *fiscus* is proved, not only by the stipulatio duplae "componat . . . una cum *feudo*,"[3] where generally stands "componat una cum *fisco*,"[4] and the use of *a feo*[5] where the Italian documents have *ad fictum*, but also by the specific equation "*fisco*, id est *fiodo*,"[6] and the arbitrary interchange of *fevus* and *fiscus* in the same region.[7] It can be easily shown that this *feus* has arisen directly from *fiscus*, but to do so we must first investigate a formula which was employed in payments to express the legal value of money.

[1] "*Emfiteuticario* modo postulamus largiri" (943), Fantuzzi, *op. cit.*, vol. IV, p. 174.
[2] "Quod *fictus* eorum reciperet aut sperare potuerit tam de carris quam de sagmatibus siue de nauali remigio" (845), *HPM.*, *Chartae*, vol. I, col. 42.
[3] H. Doniol, *Cartulaire de Brioude*, Clermont Fd., Paris 1863, p. 32 (944?).
[4] "Inferat vobis una cum *fisco*," *ibid.*, p. 107.
[5] "Cujus erat *feuz*" (956), Devic and Vaissete, *op. cit.*, vol. V, col. 225; "illo alode de Limanico, quod Grimaldus habet *a feo*" (961), *ibid.*, col. 241 f.; "ipsas vineas, quod Pontius de Tezano tenet *a feo*" (990), *ibid.*, col. 317; "non possint vindere, nec alienare, nec bescamiare, nec *ad fevum* dare" (1025), *ibid.*, col. 380.
[6] "Locis illis tantum exceptis quae in *fisco, id est in fiodo* noscuntur haberi" (1097), H. Goffinet, *Cartulaire de l'abbaye d'Orval*, Bruxelles 1879, p. 4.
[7] Thus, e. g., in Vendôme (Ch. Métais, *Cartulaire de l'abbaye cardinale de la Trinité de Vendôme*, Paris 1893, vol. 1): "Est quidem *fiscus* iste, sicut supradictus miles tenebat eo tempore" (1037), p. 29; "de cujus tenebat *fisco*" (1040), p. 49; "juxta legem *fisci* comitis Gausfredi" (1049), p. 146; "ea ratione in *fiscum* dedit" (1049), p. 150; "qui illas in *fiscum* tenebant" (1062), p. 367; "donatum in *fevum*" (1040), p. 97; "Salomon *fevum* suum . . . ab illo accepit sibi" (1046), p. 117; "tulit ei Salomon suum *fevum*, quod ab eo tenebat" (1046), p. 119; "alodium quod tenebat ab eo in *fevum*" (1057), p. 206; "de *fevo* Archembaldi prepositi" (1062), p. 265; "tenendam in *fevum*" (1070), p. 358; "qui de ipso *fevum* tenebant" (1080), p. 446.

In the first century before Christ we hear in Rome of *ex obrussa* as an expression for gold proved pure by assaying.[1] Ingots of gold and coins were stamped with *OB* or *OBR* for *aurum obrussum, obryzum, obraetium,*[2] as a guarantee of their purity, and not only the Merovingians thus stamped their coins, but the Arabs also used *obriz* for such purposes. The origin of the word seems shrouded in darkness, but can easily be explained. In Assyrian *çarapu* is "to purify," *çarpu* "silver, money," *çurrupu* "assayed, pure," but the origin of this group is in itself not clear. We find the group in all the Semitic languages, Heb. *çaraf* "to purify metals," Aram. *çârâfa* "melting pot," Syr. *çrîfâ* "assayed, pure," *çrâfâ* "melting oven," Arab. *çarf* "full valued," *çirf* "pure," and in Sanskrit we have a popularly transformed word from it, *jātarupa* "shining, gold," as though it were *jāta* + *rupa* "born form." The Coptic *črōp*, *žlōf* "incense pot, oven," which seems to go back to a late Egyptian *t'aroba* "a kind of a vessel," is apparently not to be separated from the Assyrian words. It is to be assumed that the Assyrian *çarpu* "silver" has reached the West through the Syrian or Hebrew and has produced Slavic *srebro*, Gothic *silubr*, Lithuanian *sidabras* "silver." Even as the Babylonian mina bore the Aramaic inscription *mna melk* "the King's mina" for the benefit of the Western trade, so the ingots must also have contained an Aramaic *çurpu, çurrupu* "pure," which, being written backwards by the Romans, because of their reading it from left to right produced *obrus, obrussa*. One is led to this assumption, because some coins bear the inscription *BO* for *OB*, showing that the writing was either from left to right or from right to left,[3] and because the forms *isibro, sebro, idibro*

[1] Ch. Daremberg and E. Saglio, *Dictionnaire des antiquités grecques et romaines*, sub *obryzum*.

[2] *Sylloge epigraphica orbis romani*, vol. II, N° 1574.

[3] "BO ist sicherlich nur die Umkehrung von CONOB," Luschin von Ebengreuth, *Der Denar der Lex Salica*, in *Sitzungsberichte der k. Akademie der Wissenschaften in Wien* 1911, p. 35 ff.

at Nonantola in the eighth century,[1] although unquestionably developed from *ex obrussa, ex sobrussa*, as already recorded in Petronius, point to a possible contamination with the inverted form. The Germanic and Slavic words for silver, instead of being derived from Syrian or Hebrew, as assumed by me before, may not be older than the Nonantola forms, hence may have entered into those languages at a comparatively late date.

However this may be, only the fate of *obrussa* is of importance for our present purpose. Matthew xxvii, 9, is based on Zechariah xi, 12, 13, where there is reference to thirty pieces of silver thrown into the melting pot to test their purity,[2] but the text has been changed to "καὶ ἔλαβον τὰ τριάκοντα ἀργύρια, τὴν τιμὴν τοῦ τετιμημένου," in Latin to "et acceperunt triginta argenteos *pretium appretiati.*" The commentators have wasted much paper on this *pretium appretiati*, without even distantly comprehending its meaning. The passage in Zechariah was written, say, in the third century B.C., when the purity was still assayed, while the author who quoted it in the Gospel wrote about the year 100 A.D., when the stamp guaranteed such purity. At that time the Roman formulae of sale and fine not only mentioned the price (pretium, τιμή), but specifically referred to the legal purity of the coin (probi, dominici, augusti, χρυσίου καθαροῦ, ἀργυρίου ἐπισήμου) tendered in payment.[3] But

---

[1] "Auri optimi del *sebro*" (752), G. Tiraboschi, *Storia dell' augusta badia di S. Silvestro di Nonantola*, Modena, 1785, vol. ii, p. 17; "auri optimi *isibro*" (752), *ibid.*, p. 19; " auri *idibre*" (800), *ibid.*, p. 33.

[2] I follow the Septuagint for Zechariah, because, in spite of the New Testament and its commentators, the Hebrew text is hopelessly corrupt. The very questionable יוֹצֵר has been rendered by "ager figuli, potter's field" (or "aerarium," if it is read אוֹצָר) in the New Testament. But the Septuagint has a sensible text, which shows that its Hebrew original did not have יוֹצֵר but מִצְרָף. In the Aramaic script it is very easy to mistake ם for יו, and apparently the final ף has disappeared. The "ager figuli," then, rests on a blunder.

[3] "Pretium ejus denarios DC accepisse et habere se dixit" (142), P. F. Girard, *Textes de droit romain*, 4e éd., Paris 1913, pp. 844, 846, 847; "eosque

the use of *obryzum* at Rome, just like the formula of sale of
the sixth century *"pretium* placitum et definitum . . . auri
solidos dominicos *obriziatos,"* [1] shows that an abbreviated
form *pretium appretiati* must have existed from the start,
even as we find *"ad pretium* placitum et deffinitum auri solidos *appretiatos"* in a document at Farfa in 716. In this latter
document *appretiati* has the general meaning of "full value"
and refers also to olive trees.[2] In τιμὴν τετιμημένου of the
New Testament we have merely a translation of the popular
Latin *pretium appretiati,* and the clause "reticulum aureum
*ex obrussa"* used by Petronius shows that *obryziatum,* hence
also *appretiatum,* must have been popular at an early time,
and the popular etymology which changed *obryziatum* to
*appretiatum* produced the verb *appretiare* "to appraise."

denarios ducentos, probos, recte numeratos accepisse" (166), *ibid.,* p. 848;
"accepit pro libertate ejus . . . drachmas augustas (δράχμας σεβαστάς) dua
millia ducentas" (221), *ibid.,* p. 849; "τιμῆς τῆς συμπεφωνημένης . . . . δρα-
χμῶν . . . ἥνπερ τιμὴν ἀπέσχεν ὁ πεπρακὼς παρὰ τοῦ πριαμένου" (298), J.
Bry, *Essai sur`la vente dans les papyrus gréco-egyptiens,* Paris, 1909, p. 196 *ff.*
"Le mot συμπεφωνεμένης (convenu) accompagne presque toujour le mot
τιμῆς (prix), mais il est rarement seul et le participe ἐσταμένης (fixe) ou
συναροσάσης (agréé de part et d'autre, employé surtout dans les actes de basse
époque) lui sont ordinairement joints," p. 202. One also finds the expressions
σεβασμίου ἀργυρίου (144), νομισμάτια δεσποτικά, p. 207, ἀργυρίου Σεβαστῶν
νομίσματος, etc., p. 208. See also A. Berger, *Die Strafklauseln in den Papyrusurkunden,* Leipzig and Berlin 1911, p. 31 *ff.* and P. Jouguet, *Papyrus de Théa-
delphie,* Paris 1911, p. 174 (χρυσίου καθαροῦ, 312 A.D.), p. 175 (ἀσήμου καθαροῦ, 312 A.D.).

    [1] "Venditores ad eundem emptorem Peregrino vestrñ juxta placitum suum
*praetii* nomine id est auri solid. dominicos probitos *obriziacos* optimos pensantes" (539), Marini, *I pap. dipl.,* p. 173; "omnes *pretium* inter eos placitum
et definitum aureos solidos dominicos probitos *obriziatos* integri ponderis" (572),
*ibid.,* p. 184; *"pretium* inter eos placitum et definitum pro sstas sex uncias
idest auri solidos dominicos *obriziacos* optimos pensantes" (591), *ibid.,* p. 187.

    [2] "Uendidimus eibi uiro in monasterio sanctae Mariae genitricis Dei et
domini nostri ihesu christi, oliuetum nouellum quod est iuxta fines scappligiami
ad *pretium* placitum et deffinitum auri solidos *appretiatos* numero VIII. Similiter et ego barbatus uendidi uobis et suprascripto monasterio de alio oliueto
oliuas tallias numero XIJ *appretiatos,* et accepistis auri solidis XIJ. Similiter et
ego ualerianus cum fratre meo baronicone uendidi ad iam dictum monasterium
oliuas tallias IIII *appretiatos* et acceptis solidis IIIJor," *Regesto di Farfa,* vol. II,
p. 25.

In the ninth and tenth century documents at Cluny we find sensible stipulationes venditionis which do not materially differ from those of the second century,[1] but when we get, in place of the usual valuation "ad argentum valens," the other "in re preciata valens,"[2] we learn that other objects besides gold and silver could be given in a sale, as we, indeed, learn specifically from a document of the year 680.[3] This pretiatium has arisen from the *pretium appretiati* of the earliest times and means "full value, legal tender," even as *appretiatum* has that meaning in the Visigothic and Bavarian laws.[4] By the side of this res pretiata we find in the Cluny documents a formula *feus cumpreciatus*,[5] where obviously *feus* means "property, object of value," while *cumpreciatus* does not occur anywhere else but here. *Feos cumpreciatus* can have arisen only from *fescum* or *fiscum preciatum* "property of full value," even as in the Farfa document of the year 716 we found "tallias *appretiatos*." We have already seen

[1] "Tibi a die presente vendimus, et accepimus de vos precium sicut inter nos complacuit adque convenit ad arbitrium et voluntate nostra solidos v et medio" (845), A. Bruel, *Recueil des chartes de l'abbaye de Cluny*, vol. I, p. 10 *f.*; "vendimus, tradimus adque transfundimus, et accipimus de vobis precium in presente sicut inter nos convenit, valentes solidos II et denarios VI" (870), p. 15 *f.*; "accepimus nos de te precium forte sicut inter nos placuit atque convenit, et est et argente valente solidos v" (870), p. 17; "et inde accepimus de vos precium invalentem solidos VI" (874), p. 24; "accepimus de te precium valentes solidos c" (874), p. 25.

[2] "In *re preciata* valente dinarios VI" (839), p. 45; "in *rem preciato* valente solidos II" (909), p. 114.

[3] "Et accepimus a vobis precio in quo nobis bene conplacuit, hoc est solidos auri purissimi septingentos, et pallios quatuor valentes solidos CC," Devic and Vaissete, *op. cit.*, vol. II, Preuves, col. 44.

[4] "Quamquod *adpreciatum* rationabiliter mille solidorum valere summam constiterit," *Lex Visig.* III. 1. 5; "et cum celeriter et cum 12 solidos conponat auro *adpreciato*," *Leg. Baiuw.* I. 4, 6, 9.

[5] "In argento, vel in *feos compreciatus*" (881), p. 29; "in argento vel in *feos compreciatos*" (881), p. 30; "in *rem cumpreciatus*" (885), p. 33; "in argento et *feos valentes*" (889), p. 46; "in *feus conpreciato* valentes" (893), p. 58; "in *feos conpreatus*" (895), p. 64; "*feus conpreciatus* valente" (900), p. 77; "in *feo conpreciato*" (904), p. 94; "in *feos cumpreciatus*, valentem" (909), p. 115; "cc est in argento vel in *res conperciatas*" (919), p. 204; "in *rem compreciatu*" (920), p. 211; "in *feos preciatos*" (923), p. 227, etc.

that *fiscus*, through *fictus* and *emphyteusis*, had the tendency
to become *feodus*, *feus*. This is further proved by the use of
*fisce* for *fisci* in Merovingian documents,[1] which was pronounced *fise*, even as it is recorded in a genuine document of
the year 716,[2] while *fesco* for *fisco* is constantly met with.[3]
Obviously, then, a form *fis* or *fius*, or, more likely, *feus*, leading to a popular *feu* "property," was common in the eighth
century in the neighborhood of Cluny, that is, in the region
where the Gothic was spoken, and this *feu* is quite correctly
rendered in Gothic by *faihu*.

It is generally assumed that Gothic *faihu* is derived from
Lat. *pecu*, but this is contrary to every probability. When-
ever a word means "property" and "cattle," the latter is
derived from the first and never vice versa. Slovak *statek*
"property" produces Bohemian *statek* "cattle," while Bohemian *dobytek* has successively produced the meanings "property, money, cattle, animal"; similarly Bulgarian *blago*
"property" precedes Croatian *blago* "treasure, cattle." [4]
English *cattle* follows LLat. *catallum* "property" and French
*avoir* "sheep" has developed from LLat. *avere* "property."
Similarly Gothic *skatts*, OHG. *skatt* "treasure, money"
precedes OSlav. *skotŭ* "cattle." This Gothic *skatts* has
arisen from LLat. *excoctum*, used by Ennodius in the fifth
century as an equivalent for *obryzum* [5] and frequently re-

[1] "Inter parte *fisce* nostri" (710), Tardif, *op. cit.*, p. 37; "de parte *fisce*"
(766), *ibid.*, p. 40; "in *fisce* dicionibus" (716), *ibid.*, p. 41; "partibus *fische*"
(745), H. Wartmann, *Urkundenbuch der Abtei Sanct Gallen*, vol. I, pp. 15, 31,
41, 46, etc.
[2] "De parte *fise* nostri," Lauer and Samaran, *op. cit.*, p. 25.
[3] *Urkundenbuch der Abtei Sanct Gallen*, p. 6, and frequently in *Lex romana
raetia.*
[4] N. Jokl, *Studien zur albanesischen Etymologie und Wortbildung*, in *Sitzb.
d. k. Akad. d. Wiss. in Wien* 1911, p. 6.
[5] "Caminis *excocta* fabrilibus verba," F. Vogel, *Magni Felicis Ennodii
Opera*, in *MGH.*, *Auct. antiq.*, vol. VII, p. 47; "homines omni artis lima con-
positos et caminibus fabrilibus *excoctos*," *ibid.*, p. 50; "*excocta* fornacibus urbani-
tas," *ibid.*, p. 152; "mundior *excocti* fulgescat luce metalli," *ibid.*, p. 157.

corded later in the same sense.[1] That this Germanic *skatt*
originally meant *excoctum* is proved conclusively by the
*scazwurf*, or the freeing of the widow by a coin, because the
formula of the Germanic law "solidi aeque pensantes et
*scat*"[2] can only mean "solidi of full weight and purity."
So, too, Lat. *peculium* "property" precedes *pecunia* "money"
and *pecu* "cattle," for the stem *pek, pak* means "to tie" in
all the Eurasiatic languages, and the cattle were called
*pecu*, not, as somebody has foolishly stated, because the cattle
were tied in the stalls, but because, like German *pack*, the
root means "to tie up a bundle," and the original meaning
was "bundle, fahrendes Gut." Hence a derivation of Gothic
*faihu* from Lat. *pecu* is an absurdity, especially since Gothic
*faihu* does not mean "cattle." So, too, in Anglo-Saxon *feo*,
*feoh* means "money, property" and only incidentally
"cattle," for which generally *nieta* is used. Only in Germany, where money was scarce, did cattle take the place of
money, but the Germanic laws invariably reduced the value
of such cattle to solidi, because the fine was originally com-
puted in solidi and not in cattle.[3]

The forms *feo, feoh, faihu* are identical with the French
*feu*, and it is obvious from my investigation that French *feu*
goes back uninterruptedly to *fiscus*, through a contamination with *fixum, fictum, feoticarius*, from *emphyteucarius*, and
that to the same contaminations are due the LLat. *feudum,
fedum, fevum*, etc.

---

[1] "Aurum *coctum*" (749), *Regesto di Farfa*, vol. II, p. 36; "solidos auri ad
purum *excocti*" (887), *Gallia christiana*, vol. II, p. 5; "sexcentorum solidorum
auri ad purum *excocti*" (816), *MGH., Formulae*, p. 308.
[2] "Ille qui viduam accipere debet, tres solidos aeque pensantes et *scat* habere
debet," *Zeitschrift für Savigny Stiftung*, vol. XXIX, p. 59.
[3] *Lex ribuaria* XXXVI, 11, and *Lex saxonum* LXVI.

# ALLEGATUM

THE word *alode* occurs for the first time in a Frankish document of the year 629–639,[1] and in a confirmation of the year 709 we find *alote* distinguished from "comparatum" and "adtractum," from what is bought and otherwise acquired.[2] In the *Formulae* and elsewhere this *alote* occurs generally in the combination "de *alote* parentum, paterna, materna"[3] or, especially in the Salic formulae, as in the document of the year 709.[4] The first expression is, no doubt, the original one, even as it is the older, for the clause "heredis meos in *alote* derelinquere," "to leave the heirs in the paternal estate,"[5] like "de *alote* parentum" precisely corresponds with "ex successione, ex jure parentum" of the Italian and German documents,[6] while the Germanic laws which bear the title

[1] "De *alode* ma [terna . . . ]," Ph. Lauer and Ch. Samaran, *Les diplômes originaux des mérovingiens*, p. 6.

[2] "Quicquid in suprascriptis mansis, tam de *alote* quam et de conparatho, seó de qualibet adtractho ibidem tua fuit possessio vel domenacio," *ibid.*, p. 21.

[3] "Illas porciones meas, quem ex *alote* parentum meorum aei legibus obvenit vel obvenire debit," *MGH.*, *Formulae*, p. 4, et passim; "tam de *alote* parentum quam de conparato vel de qualibet adtractum" (691), Lauer and Samaran, *op. cit.*, p. 14; "tam de *alode* parentum quam etiam de quolibet adtracto" (798), *Wirtembergisches Urkundenbuch*, Stuttgart 1849, vol. I, p. 54.

[4] "Quem de parte parentum tam de *alote* quam et de conparato, vel qualibet atracto ad me legibus obvenit," *MGH.*, *Formulae*, p. 229; "quicquid in praedictis locis nostra est possessio, tam de *alote* quam de conparato, vel qualibet adtracto ad nos noscitur pervenisse," *ibid.*, p. 245, and pp. 143, 160, 164, 204, 207, 208, 267, 268, 283, 475.

[5] "Dum advivo, per vestro beneficio tenere et usufructuare faciam; in ea vero ratione, ut aliubi ipsa res nec vindere nec donare nec alienare nec ad alias casas Dei delagare nec in naufragium ponere nec ad proprium sacire nec heredis meos in *alote* derelinquere pontifitium non habeam ad faciendum," *ibid.*, p. 236.

[6] "Obvenire ex successionem" (539), Marini, *I pap. dipl.*, p. 172; "ex jure et successionem matris suae" (540), *ibid.*, p. 175; "aut de jure parentum aut de concessione regum," Troya, *op. cit.*, vol. II, p. 537; "que ex successione parenti

"De *alodibus*" speak in the text, not of *alod,* but of "here-ditas."[1] Not a trace is to be found of *alod* before the seventh century anywhere, because it is a corruption of *allegatum* only in Merovingian France, as I shall soon show.

To avoid the possibility of deception in donations, these had to be written in a conventional and solemn manner and had to be deposited with a judge or in the Curia. Constantine expressed this with the words "actis etiam adnectendis, quae apud judicem vel magistratus conficienda sunt,"[2] to which the *Interpretatio* says "gesta vero donationum aut apud judicem, aut apud curiam *alleganda* sunt." In that same year it was determined that this *allegatio* could not take place outside the province of the donor,[3] and a hundred years later a donation without a proper *allegatio* was declared void,[4] while still later the *Lex Burgundionum romana* begins with the irrevocability of a gift to children by the father, if it has been "gestis *allegata.*"[5] When Odoacer offered certain possessions in Sicily to Pierius, the latter had them recorded in Ravenna,[6] and two years later the flaw in an un-

advinet" (740), Brunetti, *Cod. dip. toscano,* vol. II, p. 499; "de hereditate de pater" (773), *PMH., Dipl. et chartae,* vol. I, p. 1; "ereditate que auemus de parte de pater" (908), *ibid.,* p. 11; "quantum parentes mei in hereditate dimiserunt" (735), *Wirtemb. Urkb.,* vol. I, p. 3; "omnes res proprietatis meae, quicquid de successione parentum meorum mihi obvenit, vel de dotationibus regum, seu de comparatum, vel commutationes" (731), *ibid.,* p. 20; "cedente paternica hereditate" (799), *ibid.,* p. 55.

[1] "De *alodibus.* Si quis absque liberi defunctus fuerit, si pater materqui subrectis fuerint, in hereditate succidant, etc.," *Lex rib.* LVI, and similarly *Lex sal.* LIX.

[2] *Cod. Theod.* VIII. 12. 1.

[3] "Ut nulli liceat extra prouinciam laremque suum donationum instrumenta apud acta *adlegare,* sed in quo domicilium habuerint, adquae possessiones constitutae sunt aput suum ordinarium judicem" (316), VIII. 12. 3.

[4] "Sed iam *allegatas* apud curatores donationes, et gesta confecta valere necesse est" (415), VIII. 12. 7.

[5] "Donationem, quam pater de rebus propriis in filium filiamve conscripserit et gestis fuerit *allegata* . . . firmissimam permanere," I. 1 (*MGH., Leg.* sec. I, vol. II, p. 1).

[6] "Si jussum sit gestis *adlegari* his actis aedicere non gravetur" (489), Marini, *I pap. dipl.,* p. 128.

recorded piece of property, caused by the premature death of the conveyor, is remedied by the *allegatio* of the surviving wife.[1] The clause of allegation occurs in all the Ravenna donations of the sixth century,[2] and the French formulae of allegation of the sixth and seventh centuries which are based on the Roman law also use *"gestis alligare, adlegare, ligare, obligare."* [3] while it is specifically mentioned in an immunity that it took the place of the *allegatio.*[4]

The *Codex Theodosianus* speaks of a *"hereditas approbata allegationibus,"* [5] and it becomes clear from a Visigothic formula that a will, being in its nature a donation, was recorded as an *allegatio,*[6] even as this had been specifically

---

[1] "Quoniam antea vivo marito meo de ac ipsa casa scribturam feceramus sed quia morte praeventus ut eam minime potuimus *allegare* nunc necesse mihi fuit ut epistolam nomini meo facerem ubi ei dono casam juris mei" (491), *ibid.*, p. 131.

[2] "Rogatorum a me nobilissimorum testium vel propriae manus meae subscribtione firmavi quam cum cum gestis nos Actoresque vestros quibuslibet duxeritis *allegandam"* (523), *ibid.*, p. 132; "simul et testes pariter ut subscriberent conrogavimus *alligandi* quoque archivalibus gestis" (551), *ibid.*, p. 182; "gestis etiam quibus volueritis *allegandi* liberum ex nostra permissionae nostrum ulterius minime requirentes consensu sumatis arbitrium" (553), *ibid.*, p. 133; "quam et si gestis municipalibus *allegare* maluerint . . . liberam tribuo et concedo ex more licentiam *allegandi"* (6. or 7. cent.), *ibid.*, p. 139; "subscripsi testibus a me rogitis optuli subscribendam *allegandi* etiam gestibus quibus vobis placuerit et tempore quo volueritis" (6. or 7. cent.), *ibid.*, p. 142; "testibus a me rogitis optuli subscribendam quam si gestis municipalibus *allegare* voluerint Actores Ecclesiae liberam tribui ex more licentiam *allegandi"* (6. cent.), *ibid.*, p. 145; "gestis etiam municipalibus *allegandi"* (619), *ibid.*, p. 190.

[3] "Et ut hec donatio a nobis pro divina retributione plenius fac . . . robur manus nostre subterfirmavimus, et fratrum nostrorum venerabilium vel magnificorum civium Pictavensium supscriptionibus firmare curavimus, atque gestis municipalibus inserendum juxta consuetudinem Romane legis . . . *ligare* decrevimus" (657), *Bibliothèque de l'Ecole des chartes*, vol. LIX, p. 243; "apud laudabilitatem vestram gestis municipalibus *inligarem"* (657), *ibid.*, p. 244; see also *MGH., Formulae*, in the *Vocabulary.*

[4] "Decrevi etiam per hanc cartulam immunitatis et cessionis meam, basilicam superius nuncupatam, sine gestorum *obligatione* manere" (566), R. de Lasteyrie, *Cartulaire général de Paris*, p. 6.

[5] II. 9. 3.

[6] "Post transitum meum die legitimo hanc voluntatis meae epistolam apud curiae ordinem gestis publicis facias adcorporare," *MGH., Formulae*, p. 585.

provided for by Theodoric for the Ostrogoths.[1] There cannot
be the slightest doubt about the derivation of *alod* from this
*allegatum*, but it is also possible to ascertain how the phonetic change has taken place. In a donation of the year 615
which, in spite of some interpolations, is based on a genuine
document, occurs the clause "saepius *laudatus* tam de fisco
quam de comparato," [2] which is identical with the previously
mentioned "tam de *alote* quam de comparato" and means,
"the property, consisting of fiscal and purchased land, has
been frequently recorded." Here *laudare*, a much used word
for "to confirm," has taken the place of *allegare* "to record,"
which is quite natural, since the officers of the curia who confirmed the record bore the title of *laudabilitas*,[3] *laudabilis* vir,[4]
and the legal record was known as "*laudabiliter* adlegatum."[5]

[1] "Testamenta, sicut leges praecipiunt, *allegentur*: hoc modo fides voluntatis
alienae titubare non poterit," *Edictum Theoderici* 72 (*MGH., Leg.*, vol. v).

[2] "Mihi placuit delegare ut villa Minione, sita in territorio Parisiaco, cum
vineis quae fundi ratione aptae ad plastarias et vinitores esse noscuntur, quas
mihi domnus Clotarius rex dedit, dum laicus fui, fundumque quem dedit saepius *laudatus* tam de fisco quam de comparato possidendum, sanctae ecclesiae
Parisiacae, sub cujus gratia nutritus sum, ad integrum volo esse donatum,"
*Cartulaire général de Paris*, p. 8.

[3] "*Laudabilitas* vestra . . . ut publica momenta suscipiat et, patefactis codicibus, gesta, cum a vobis fuerit subscripta, mihi nobilitas vestra, ut mos est,
tradi precipiat," *MGH., Formulae*, p. 137; "ut ipsam donationem apud *laudabilitatem* gestis monecepalibus debiam adlegari," *ibid.*, p. 170; "epistolam illam,
quem in dilecta sponsam tuam de rebus propriis tui conscribere vel adfirmare
rogasti, sicut mos et lex est, gestis municipalibus apud *laudabilitatem* honorati
ipsius civitatis alegarae adque adfirmare decrevi," *ibid.*, p. 176; "ad *laudabilitatem* vestra adcrescere deberem et haec epistola . . . ut ipsos secundum
lege Romana in ipsa civitate ante curia publica debeat in legitima totius hereditatis sue instituere hereditate . . . ut predicta epistola iuxta morem et consuetudinem gestis monicipalibus alegare atque firmare debeant," *ibid.*, p. 209.

[4] "Unde ego te vir *laudabilis* illum defensore necnon et vos honerati, que
curas puplicas agite adsidue . . . ut, quando volueritis et malueritis, vel mihi
necessarium fuerit, ut mos est, gestis municipalibus eam faciatis ablegare cum
petitiones nostras," *ibid.*, p. 28; "Arvernis aput vir *laudabile* ipso defensore . . .
abeo, que gestarum alegatio cupio roborare," *ibid.*, p. 29; "peto obtime defensor,
vosque, *laudabiles* curialis atque municepis, ut mihi codices publicus patere
iubeatis, quia habeo aliquid, que gestis prosequere debeam," *ibid.*, p. 97, and
pp. 98, 170, 176, 202, 209.

[5] "Hoc consultum est, ut, quicumque liberta persona de rebus propriis

From a confusion of *allegatum* and *laudatum* have arisen, *alaudum, alod, alot,* etc.

The Anglo-Saxons who frequently made their borrowings unnoticeable by translations into their language, have quite correctly rendered "*hereditas allegata*" by *bocland,* i. e., property recorded in a book. Where Alfred wrote *bocland,* the Quadripartitus used "terra testamentalis,"[1] while others employed "libera terra, terra hereditatis"[2] for it, and later Cnut wrote quite correctly "*alodium,* id est *bocland,*" where the Quadripartitus has "in hereditate sua terram" 'and the *Consiliatio Cnuti* circumscribes by "libera terra."[3] As in England the *folcland* is opposed to the *bocland,* so, on the continent the fiscal land with personal liberties and stated obligations is opposed to free land, with personal burdens, and the feudal system evolved from the former because circumstances were more favorable for its development.

It now remains to be shown why the Franks, who were not strict in the matter of recording, adopted the word *allegatum* as an expression for land enjoying immunities. In the law of 316 we find the clause "actis adnectendis," which seems to imply that, although another law of the same year uses the expression "apud acta *adlegare,*" the original form was "apud acta *alligare.*" The change to *allegare* is, no doubt, due to the fact that the free land of the veterans was held by them lawfully, "*a lege* habeant," as it says in the law of 364,[4]

---

facultatis suae aliquid conferrae voluerit, hoc per seriem scripturarum *laudabiliter* debeat esse *adlegatum* adque subter firmatum, qui hac condicione et iurae postulat praeturium et gestis requirit municipalibus," *ibid.,* p. 175.

[1] "Se mon se ðe *bocland* haebbe, & him his maegas laefden, de eo qui terram testamentalem habet, quam ei parentes sui demiserunt," F. Liebermann, *Die Gesetze der Angelsachsen,* p. 74 f.

[2] *Ibid.,* vol. II, p. 26.

[3] *Ibid.,* vol. I, pp. 294, 317, 365.

[4] "Habeant ex vagantibus, sive ex diversis, ubi elegerint agros, et *a lege* habeant, ut sibi soli eorundem fructos cessuros esse cognoscant: nullum ex his agris stipendium, nullam annuam praestationem postulavimus," *Cod. Theod.,* VII. 20. 8.

or "ut *legibus* convenit," as we have found in the formulae. The immunity of the German soldiers took the place of the *allegatio*, which was obligatory on the Roman citizens, hence the immunity of 566 correctly states "cartulam immunitatis sine gestorum *obligatione* manere." It is this *a lege* which gave way to *a laude*, because the donation of an immunity was in itself a confirmation of the right to the free land. Nothing but the Roman immunity could have created the Frankish *alod*.

INDEXES

# WORD INDEX

| | | | |
|---|---|---|---|
| LLat. | *forbannum*, 163. | Ger. | *frisch*, 107. |
| LLat. | *forbattutus*, 162. | LLat. | *friscum*, 107. |
| LLat. | *forbatudum*, 163. | OHG. | *frisking, etc.*, 107, 108. |
| LLat. | *forestarius*, 104. | LLat. | *friskinga*, 107. |
| LLat. | *forestis*, 104, 107, 108. | OHG. | *frîten*, 156. |
| LLat. | *forfactum*, 162. | OS. | *frithu*, 156. |
| Fr. | *forfait*, 163. | OFr. | *fro, etc.*, 105. |
| LLat. | *foris-*, 162. | LLat. | *frodannum*, 163. |
| LLat. | *forisfacere*, 17, 163. | LLat. | *frodrum*, 155. |
| LLat. | *forisfactum*, 160. | LLat. | *frodum*, 155. |
| LLat. | *forsconsiliare*, 163. | Lat. | *frons*, 122. |
| Celt. | *forst, frost*, 104. | Bret. | *frost*, 104, 105. |
| OHG. | *forst*, 104. | Celt. | *frost*, 104, 105. |
| LLat. | *forum*, 155, 156. | LLat. | *frostum*, 105. |
| AS. | *forwŷrcan*, 163. | LLat. | *frourerius*, 155. |
| OHG. | *fôtar*, 155. | LLat. | *froyre, etc.*, 155. |
| OHG. | *fotarjan*, 155. | LLat. | *frusca*, 124. |
| OHG. | *fôtida*, 155. | LLat. | *fruscella*, 124. |
| OHG. | *fôtjan*, 155. | Ital. | *fruscio*, 124. |
| Fr. | *fracas*, 106. | LLat. | *frussatum*, 105. |
| Fr. (d) | *frachous*, 106. | OHG. | *fuora*, 155. |
| LLat. | *fraidia*, 160. | Ital. | *fuscello*, 124. |
| Fr. | *frais* (fresh), 108. | | |
| Fr. | *frais* (expense), 156. | OFr. | *Gaaign-, gaain-*, 179. |
| Bret. | *fraost*, 104, 105. | Fr. | *gaain*, 180. |
| Fr. | *frapper*, 106. | Prov. | *gaanhador, etc.*, 179. |
| LLat. | *frasca*, 105, 107, 124. | OHG. | *gaarnôn*, 181. |
| Ital. | *frascare*, 106. | LLat. | *gadaignare*, 175. |
| LLat. | *frascata*, 105. | LGer. | *gadem, etc.*, 97. |
| LLat. | *frascerium*, 105. | LLat. | *gades, etc.*, 90, 91. |
| Bulg. | *fraste*, 104. | LLat. | *gadi, gai*, 90. |
| Ital. | *fratta*, 106. | Prov. | *gadi, etc.*, 91. |
| LLat. | *frecum, etc.*, 105. | OHG. | *gadingi, etc.*, 37. |
| LLat. | *freda, etc.*, 145, 146. | OHG. | *gadum*, 97. |
| LLat. | *fredum*, 146, 147, 148, 149, 154, 156, 158, 160, 163. | AS. | *gafolland*, 140. |
| | | Goth. | *gafrithôn*, 156. |
| Goth. | *freidjan*, 156. | LLat. | *gagiolum*, 87. |
| AS. | *freoðo, freoð*, 156. | Fr. (d) | *gagnable*, 180. |
| LLat. | *fresca, etc.*, 105, 107. | Fr. | *gagner*, 133. |
| OFr. | *frestiz, fraitiz*, 105. | LLat. | *gahagium, etc.*, 87, 97, 99, 100. |
| LLat. | *fretum*, 145, 146, 147, 148, 160. | Fr. (d) | *gahaigne*, 179, 180. |
| | | LLat. | *gahamalus*, 74. |
| Fr. (d) | *freucher*, 106. | Pol. | *gaič*, 90. |
| ON. | *friðr*, 156. | Prov. | *gaim*, 129, 130. |
| AS. | *friðu*, 156. | OFr. | *gain*, 128, 129, 130, 132, 133. |
| OHG. | *fridu*, 156. | Pol. | *gaiowe*, 90. |
| OHG. | *frinskinga, etc.*, 108. | Russ. | *gait'*, 90. |
| OHG. | *frisc*, 107. | LLat. | *gaium*, 87, 89, 90, 98, 99, 100, 102, 104. |
| LLat. | *frisca, frusca*, 108. | | |

MLG. *geiwin*, 180.
Sum. *gibil, gibir*, 177.
LLat. *giregar*, 61.
Prov. *giregare*, 64.
Bret. *gloat*, 99.
Ir. *gno*, 180.
Lith. *gojus*, 90.
Corn. *gologhas*, 40.
Corn. *golyas, etc.*, 40.
Ital. *gomereccio*, 130.
Croat. *gomila*, 74.
Russ. *gomola*, 74.
Slav. *gomolya*, 74.
Corn. *gones, etc.*, 180.
Corn. *goon, etc.*, 180.
Slav. *gor-*, 177.
Wel. *gorest, etc.*, 104.
Prov. *gouibre*, 129.
MBret. *gounit*, 180.
LLat. *grafio*, 21, 22, 24.
Lat. *gravitas*, 21.
AS. *grefe, greve*, 21.
ON. *greiða*, 152.
Croat. *gromila*, 74.
Ital. *grumereccio*, 131.
Ger. *grummet*, 131, 133.
LLat. *grumulus*, 74.
Prov. *grupir*, 66.
LLat. *guadaignare, etc.*, 175.
LLat. *guagneria*, 179.
LLat. *gualdator, etc.*, 88, 104.
LLat. *gualdeman*, 88.
LLat. *gualdus*, 28, 84, 85, 86, 87, 89, 98, 99, 100, 102, 104.
LLat. *guallarus, etc.*, 88.
LLat. *guardator*, 88.
LLat. *guardatorius*, 88.
LLat. *guardia*, 64, 65, 88.
LLat. *guardianus*, 88.
LLat. *guarens, etc.*, 61.
LLat. *guartho*, 59.
Prov. *guasanh*, 181.
Prov. *guasanhar, etc.*, 179.
LLat. *guastum*, 106.
LLat. *guataniagare*, 175.
Corn. *guel*, 99.
OBret. *guelenes*, 99.
Corn. *guelfôs*, 99.

OFr. *guepir*, 66.
Prov. *guepir*, 66.
LLat. *guerire*, 61.
OFr. *guerpir*, 66.
Prov. *guerpir*, 66.
LLat. *guerra*, 63.
Prov. *guerregare*, 64.
Prov. *guerrigiare*, 64.
Corn. *guiliat*, 51.
OBret. *guiliat*, 51.
Corn. *guillua*, 40.
Fr. *guimeau*, 130, 131.
LLat. *guirens*, 61.
Corn. *gulat*, 99.
Corn. *gunithiat*, 180.
LLat. *gurpire*, 65, 66.
Corn. *guyn*, 177.
Bret. *gwenaat*, 180.
Bret. *gwended, etc.*, 180.
Bret. *gwenn*, 177.
Wel. *gwerth*, 151.
Wel. *gwlad*, 99.
Corn. *gwon, etc.*, 180.
Wel. *gwyliad, etc.*, 40, 50.
Wel. *gwyliadur*, 40.
Corn. *gwylls*, 99.
Wel. *gwyllt*, 99.
Celt. *gwyn, etc.*, 180.
Wel. *gwyn*, 179, 180.
AS. *gylt*, 50.

OHG. *Hac*, 99.
OBoh. *hag., etc.*, 90.
AS. *haga*, 100.
Ger. *hagestolz*, 119.
ON. *hagi*, 99.
OHG. *hagjan*, 99.
OHG. *hagustalt*, 119.
AS. *hagusteald*, 119.
Fr. *haie*, 100.
Goth. *haitja*, 45.
Boh. *hájiti*, 90.
Arab. *hamal*, 74.
LLat. *hamallatus*, 69, 75.
LLat. *hamallus*, 69, 70, 74, 75.
Copt. *hamalogi*, 56.
OHG. *hamalôn*, 74.
LLat. *hamedius*, 69, 70, 71, 75.
Arab. *harab, etc.*, 66.

# SUBJECT INDEX

*Adoptionist heresy* of Spanish Goths combatted by Agobard, Alcuin, Hincmar and Skeireins, xlix–lix.

*Agens,* — "surety, legal representative," among the Teutons *homologus*, 67, 68, 71, — later replaced by *gerens, garens*, 67.

*Agentes in rebus*, in Roman law, executive officers, 10, — titled *devoti*, 30, — in Germanic states important officers of courts, due to former employment of Germans in this function, 35.

*Ager occupatorius*, state land, under Roman law subject to seizure by veterans for cultivation, 81, 82. See *rudis ager, caduca mortuorum bona, squalidus*.

*Agobard*, — see *Adoptionist heresy, Skeireins*.

*Alcuin*, called by Charlemagne to fight Adoptionist heresy, l, — commentary on St. John basis of many medieval commentaries, liv. See *Skeireins*.

*Alfonso I* colonises Galicia devastated by Arabs, 78, 79.

*Allegare, etc.*, Roman formula in donation, 192, 193, 195, — original form probably *alligare*, 195, — interpreted correctly by Anglo-Saxons, 195, — adopted by Franks to denote land enjoying immunity, 195. See *etymology*.

*Alode*, first used in document of 629–39, 191,— of inherited land, 191–2, corrupted from *allegatum* only in Merovingian France, 192, 194, explanation of the corruption, 194–6.

*Alsaccia*, Ribuarian formula of distress, 42, etymology, 43.

*Anglo-Saxon laws*, 14, 140, 158–60, 195.

*Antrustio*, see *trustis*.

*Appretiatum*, see *Matt., xxvii*, 9.

*Aprision*, see *presura*.

*Arabic* influence in Germanic, 62, 65–7, in Slavic, 74.

*Arbustaria*, (Italian document of 904–5) tax for pasturing in the forest, 113, 116.

*Arbustata* (terra, etc.) about Naples, (1) *arbustum vitatum* (X cent.) 111, — (2) woodland, (XI cent.) 112.

*Arbustum* (often with *vitis*) a grove for supporting vines, used as a pasture, 110, — *arbustum vitatum* (S. Italian documents to XII cent.) the same, 111, — in Spain (*arbusta* in VIII cent., but generally *bustum*, 115, 119) any enclosed pasture, 115, 119, 141, — whence institution spreads via France through Europe, 119, 141, — bringing a large linguistic family, 119. See *buscus, etymology, vitata*.

*Arian*, see *Skeireins*.

*Arius*, see *Skeireins*.

*Atone*, etymology, 168.

*Baccalarius*, a peasant (poor or unmarried) in charge of a corral (*bustum, boalaria, baccalaria*), 119, — in sense of "bachelor," spreads from S. France, 119, — relation to *Hagestolz*, etc., 119.

*Bavarian laws*, 72, 149, 160, 188.

*Biological evolution* not physically operative in field of human actions, xxiii.

*Blends*, — *allegatum: laudatum*, (alod)

laws and medieval documents, (*socio fisco*) 2–4, 10, 12, — (2) *inferre*, 4–10, — estates of condemned criminals, 82, 157, — abandoned land (*vacuus et inanis*) 131, — in medieval times executed by *imminens*, 25, — *sacibaro*, 14–15, — *sagio*, 11, 12, 27, 45, — *sculdais*, 44–5, — *thiufadus*, 29, 30, — *trustis*, 27–8, — *tunginus*, 22, 26, 45, — *wittiscalcus*, 33–4.

*Corvée* (*warcinium*) due from free serfs, 58.

*Criminal procedure* in Germanic law derived from edicts of Theodosian Code, 49.

*Cyril*, see *Skeireins*.

*Debt* (legal sense), in Celtic, Germanic and Slavic, due to contact with Roman law, 47–9, — all words in European languages "debt, guilt, pledge," derived from Latin, 49. See *dulg-*, *pleg-*, *skuld-*.

*Decanus*, synonym of *tunginus* in Pithoean glosses, 23, — confused with *ducena*, 38. See *etymology*.

*Devotus*, in Theodosian Code, of a soldier who paid his taxes promptly, 11, — in Roman law, honorific title of executive officers, 11, 30–1, 34–5. See *etymology*, *thiufadus*.

*Distrain*, from legal formula, *distringente fisco*, 27.

*Distress*, in Roman law, 42–3, — in Frankish law, 23–4, 26, 41–3, — Frankish formulas, 27, 40–2, — these corrupted from Roman, 23, — in Irish law borrowed from Frankish, 42. See *alsaccia*, *solem collocare*.

*Divisa* (*divisa in monte*) = "pasture," in common land between villages, 138, 140, — older than *vetatum* in Spain, 136, 139, — passes from Spain to N. Italy, 137–8, — first in Italy in a Carolingian document of 783, 137, — word corrupted from (*pezia*) *de vitis*, 139, — subsequent

corruptions, (*devesa*, *defensa*, *dehesa*, *defay*), 139–41.

*Donations*, record prescribed by Roman law, 192, — Roman formula, 192–3, 195, — wills recorded as such in Gothic law, 193–4. See *alode*.

*Ducena*, office of *ducenarius*, 22.

*Ducenarius* (Roman) judge in minor cases, introduced by Augustus, 22, — could not summon debtor without warrant, 23. See *tunginus*.

*Dulg* - (LLat. dulgere) (1) = "debt," in Celtic, 45, — in Slavic, 45, 51, — in Gothic, 45, 47, — not elsewhere in Germanic, 47, — (2) = "festival," in Germanic, Baltic, Slavic, 47, — (3) = "assault, wound, strike," in Germanic, and Slavic from OHG., 47. See *skuld-*.

*Dulgere*, synonym of *indulgere* in eighth century, 45. See *etymology*, *indulgere*.

*Edictum Theoderici*, 47, 68–9, 71, 194.

*Emphyteutic contract*, in Italy (IX cent.) *emphitecarius*, *fiotecarius*, 183, — contains germs of feudal system, 184, — requires holders of vineyards to keep up and improve estate, 111, — mention of swine tithe, 107.

*Etymology* of derivatives of *allegatum*, 192, — *arbustum*, 118–124, — *çarapu*, 185–6, 189, — *cohortis*, 65, — *decanus*, 38–9, — *devotus*, 31, 35, 37–9, — *dulgere*, 45, 47, 51, — *excoctum*, 189, — *extrudere*, 28–9, 37, — *factio*, 158, 164, — *fiscus*, — 188–90, — *foris*, 160, 162–3, — *gaium*, 90–1, 97, 99, 100, — *genius*, 128–33, 174–5, 177–81, — *gerere*, 61–4, — *gravitas*, 21, — *hariba*, 65–7, — *homologus*, 69–72, 74–5, — *hostis*, 20, — *idoneus*, 165, 168–72, — *ingenium*, 179–80, — *missus*, 160–62, — *mixta*, 133, — ὁμολογητής, 75, — περίβολος, 92, 93–7, — *plagiare*, 48, — *pug-*, πυκ-,

57, — *QVR-*, *QVN-*, 177–8, — *reda*, 151–4, — *scala*, 100–1, — *schola*, 33–5, — *sculca*, 43, 45, 47, 50–1, — *scutum*, 43–5, 49–50, — *squalidus* (*gualdus*) 88, 98–9, — *socio*, 3, 12–15, 20, 27, — *tunginus*, 26–7, 36–7, — *vasaria*, 57–60, — *vasta*, 103–8, 126, — *veredus*, 145, 151–3, 155–6, — *vigilia*, 40, 50–1, — *vitatum*, 116, — *vitis*, 125–8, 131–4, 136, 139–41.
*Exculeator* (*exculcator, excultator*) British scouts in Notitia Dignitatum, 40, — shorter form *culeator* shown by Wel. *gwyliadur*, derived from Lat. *vigilia*, 40.

*Factio*, in Roman law "treason" 157, — in AS. law, 158, — identity of *factio* and *faida* (AS. faehðe) 158–60. See *etymology*.
*Fagia*, etc., derivation from *gafagium*, 89.
*Faida* (1) OHG. *faida*, from Lat. *factum*, 160, (cf. Salic *faido*, 156, 160) (2) LLat. *faida*, from *factio*, 159.
*Faihu* (Goth.) from OFr. *feu* = fiscus, property, 189–90, — not from Lat. *pecu* "cattle," since "property" is an older significance than "cattle," 189–90.
*Ferquidum*, irregular spelling, 7, — no definite meaning and misunderstood, 5, 6, — first used in document of 739 (*in ferquide loco*), 5, — probable origin, 10, — reference to a special fine in Langobard laws, 4, — in Langobard documents always in connection with stipulatio duplae, 7, — originally meant a double fine, 5, 7.
*Fiscus*, in sixth century, "tribute," anything from which revenue is derived, 182, — a fixed yearly rent paid by the emphyteute, 183, — word corrupted successively in Italy to *fixum, fictum, fiotum* (under influence of enfeteuticarius) 183, — in France to *fescus, fis, feus, feo*, etc., 184, 188–90, — by misinterpretation

of legal formula *fiscum pretiatum*, 188. See *etymology*.
*Folk-etymology*, — *appretiatum*, 187, — *atone*, 168, — *buccellarius*, 53, — *defensa*, 139, — *divisa*, 139, — *fictum*, 183, — *fixum*, 183, — *grummet*, 131, — *homolegius*, 76, — *roughings*, 129, *vetatum*, 139.
*Forest*, idea develops comparatively late, 98, — not in Gothic, 98, — swine-pasture, 107–8, 133, — pasture-tax, 107–8, 113, 116, — right of cutting timber and firewood, 120. See *gaium, gualdus, wald*.
*Forestis*, (Frankish) first recorded in 556, of fisheries, 104, — derivation from *vasta*, 104, 126, — sense of "forest" acquired, 104, — word passes from OHG. to Slavic, Magyar and Roumanian, 104, — developments in Romance, 105–6, — replaced after 776 by *gualdus* in German documents, 104.
*Foris-*, in Merovingian documents replaces *ex-*, 16, 162, — shortened to *for-*, 163, — ultimately Ger. *ver-*, 163. See *etymology*.
*Frast- > frasc-*, discussed, 105–6.
*Friskinga*, in St. Gall documents corresponds to swine tithe of Lucca, 107–8, — in OHG. = victima, hostia, 108, — yearling pig, paid as tithe, 108, — name derived from *frisca* = "waste land," 108, — sense of "fresh" secondary in Romance and German, 108.

*Ga-* initial, understood as prefix *ga-*, 60, 89, 99, 181.
*Gain* (rowen, 128) in sixteenth century altered to *regain*, 129, — study of dialectic forms, 129–31, — (1) *gaim, waim*, in Provence, 129, — passes to Italian (*gomereccio*) 130, — German (*Emde*, etc.) 131, — (2) *regain*, in dialects north of Bordeaux-Chalons line, 130, — (3) *rewain*, in dialects south of Belgium, 130, — passing into Provençal

www.ingramcontent.com/pod-product-compliance
Lightning Source LLC
Chambersburg PA
CBHW020404100426

42812CB00001B/190